P9-AGA-022

NAVY LEAGUE
OF THE UNITED STATES

Civilians Supporting the Sea Services
For More Than a Century

by

Richard L. Wright

Dedication

To the men and women
of the
United States
Navy,
Marine Corps,
Coast Guard,
and
Merchant Marine

Who have kept America free

"It seems to me that all good Americans, interested in the growth of their country and sensitive to its honor, should give hearty support to the policies which the Navy League is founded to further. For the building and maintaining in proper shape of the American Navy, we must rely upon nothing but broad and far sighted patriotism of our people as a whole and it is of great importance that there should be some means by which this patriotism can find an effective utterance. Your society offers just the means needed."

Theodore Roosevelt
Navy League Journal (1905)

Navy League of the United States

Civilians Supporting the Sea Services
For More Than a Century

First published in the United States by the Navy League of the United States, 2300 Wilson Boulevard, Arlington, Virginia 22201. Please direct inquiries to: Navy League of the United States (703) 528-1775.

© 2006 by the Navy League of the United States, Arlington, Virginia
All rights reserved. No part of this book may be reproduced or utilized in any form or by any means, electronic or mechanical, including photocopying and recording, or by any information storage and retrieval system, without prior permission in writing from the publisher.

ISBN 0-9762370-2-4

Book Design: John W. Alexander
Dust Jacket Design and Graphic Design Assistance:
Risa K. Emmling, Multimedia Specialist, Empire Video, Inc.

Printed and bound by Elegance Printing and Book Binding, Inc. in Hong Kong, PRC

"I want to say to all of you in the Navy League of the United States that our Sailors, Marines, Soldiers and Airmen are watching America very closely. They are watching the way America and Americans are responding to their labors in the far corners of this earth.

And I want to thank you for the message you are sending. It is clear. It is unequivocal. Your message sends them a clear indication that you support ... you believe ... in the sons and daughters of America."

Admiral Vern Clark, USN
Chief of Naval Operations
Sea-Air-Space Exposition
March 2005

© 2005 Boris Feldblyum

In the fall of 2005 Navy League staff moved into a the new corporate headquarters at 2300 Wilson Blvd., Arlington, Va.

Morgan L. Fitch, left, National President of the Navy League, presents color photographs of the nuclear task force and a model of USS *Long Beach* (CGN-9), to Senator George Murphy (R-California), on January 19, 1966.

INTRODUCTION

If every journey is said to have a first step, then the one that is culminating with the publication of this book had its origins almost 40 years ago. In the mid-1960s, former Navy League of the United States National President Robert Crown, desirous of getting an updated history of the organization, asked Professor Armin Rappaport if he would be willing to update his book, *The Navy League of the United States*. Rappaport's seminal work ended its telling of the League's story as the nation entered the Korean War. The professor declined, and so began a long journey through the end of the 20th century and into the next.

Several others were offered the job. Some, like Captain William Thompson, USN, had to decline when promotion took him to flag rank with its attendant responsibilities, in Bill's case becoming the Navy's Chief of Information.

Subsequently, Navy Leaguers like Rosalind Ellis, as the League's Historian, undertook interviews of past national presidents. National President Jack Kennedy appointed John Stegman League Historian subsequent to Ellis; a few oral interviews of League leadership were conducted, but little progress was made on actually getting an updated text.

Several additional attempts were made at getting an acceptable draft, particularly as the Navy League approached its 2002 Centennial, but all fell short of desires. Finally, we found Captain Richard Wright, USN (Ret), a United States Naval Academy graduate, and former U.S. Naval Sea Cadet, to edit previous efforts, conduct additional research, and bring the League's story up to the present. In his efforts he was particularly aided by Paul Dickson, himself an accomplished writer, who did important research in the Library of Congress shortly before Wright joined the effort. John Alexander, who has worked with the League on other book projects, was enlisted to select photographs, liaison with the publisher, and provide the book's layout and dust jacket.

As a guide to using this book, either to read through or as a reference, Chapter I is an overview of the current Navy League of the United States, what we do, and how we operate. Chapters II through VI build off Rappaport's book, from the Great White Fleet to the outbreak of the Korean War, with additional material from sources not available to him at the time. The retelling of the League's first fifty years also benefits from four decades of additional perspective on the story of the Navy League and the sea services, particularly in the period between the end of World War II and the outbreak of fighting in Korea five years later. Chapter VII addresses the 1950s, when the League's orientation and focus fundamentally changed, particularly through the advent of the Sea-Air-Space Exposition and the United States Naval Sea Cadet Corps. Chapters VIII through XI cover the tumultuous 1960s, the last two decades of the Cold War, and on into the 21st century, ending in the autumn of 2005. Appendices and a detailed set of Notes offer supplemental material further developing some points or events in the narrative. A listing of all references consulted in preparing the book is also included.

We feel some vital elements of the Navy League's story are still not fully developed, particularly the transformation of the organization beginning in the late 1950s, from a limited autocracy to that of a full-fledged democracy. And while the Navy League perhaps now has made visible more public disputes and disagreements in the process of running the organization, the end results are proceedings made known to every Navy Leaguer, and policies that truly represent the feelings and desires of the organization's membership, not just senior leadership.

To get "the rest of the story," the Navy League will have to build a quality archival data base, including the proceedings of local councils, the heart and soul of the organization, and make available to future researchers and writers the extensive documentation of meetings of directors and leadership now largely inaccessible.

Fortunately for the author, *Seapower* magazine and its predecessors, available at League national headquarters, provided much material. We also relied, to a considerable extent, on recollections of living past national presidents and other Navy League leaders who were in senior positions of leadership at key moments over the past four decades.

We recognize our limitations but are proud of the result. The Committee has recommended an undertaking of formalized archiving at both the national and council levels.

We want to emphasize that this book is not intended as a history of the Navy, Marine Corps, Coast Guard, and U.S.-flag Merchant Marine. It is offered as a tribute to the Navy League of the United States as civilians in support of the sea services for more than 100 years.

Why this book? Over the years, particularly in seeking new members, we are asked: "What is the Navy League?" and "What does the Navy League do?" We hope that this book answers these questions.

Finally, from the vantage point of more than fifty years as a Navy Leaguer serving at all levels, with some ten years of sabbatical to serve on the National Exploring Committee of the Boy Scouts of America, first as Commodore of Sea Exploring and later as Vice Chairman for Specialty Exploring, the Chairman accepts full responsibility for any errors and/or omissions in this work.

Morgan L. Fitch Jr.
Chairman, Book Committee
Navy League of the United States

PREFACE

Founded in 1902 with the support of President Theodore Roosevelt, the Navy League of the United States has been a powerful voice advocating a strong maritime component to our national defense. Its goal, for more than a century, has been the development of a Navy, Marine Corps, Coast Guard and U.S.-flag Merchant Marine second to none. Thousands of men and women have proudly worn the Navy League membership pin, keeping the public informed about the importance of seapower to America's political and economic prosperity.

The League's local councils provide direct support to active duty sea service personnel and their families while helping build America's future through successful youth programs like the Naval Sea Cadet Corps and the Navy League Foundation Scholarship Program.

Navy Leaguers have sought to make certain that the United States attends to the ever-changing needs of its sea services. As citizens in support of the sea services, they have never wavered from this responsibility. From its earliest days to the present, the Navy League's primary mission has remained support of a strong national defense posture through maritime preparedness.

This illustrated history of the Navy League of the United States is told within the context of the development of the sea services: the United States Navy, Marine Corps, Coast Guard and U.S.-flag Merchant Marine. It indicates the inextricable link between Americans who "go down to the sea in ships" and their "civilian arm," which the Navy League of the United States has sought to be since its founding 103 years ago.

One journey of a century's duration is done. This book sets the stage for the next.

FOREWORD

by
Senator John W. Warner, R-Va.
Chairman, U.S. Senate Armed Services Committee

Sea power. That's the heart and soul of the Navy League of the United States, and an enduring, critical component of America's national security and economic prosperity. For more than 100 years, the Navy League has never, never failed to keep Americans focused on the need to maintain strong, modern and ready maritime forces to defend the nation and defeat our enemies overseas.

I am humbled to have been asked to say a few words about an organization that it has been my privilege to interact with for much of my adult life. As one who volunteered for service as a 17-year-old Sailor in the closing period of World War II, and, later, as a Marine officer during the Korean War, I was privileged to render modest service to my country. During my time in uniform, I was able to appreciate first-hand how the Navy League made a difference in the lives of our servicemen and women, and their families. Later, as Secretary of the Navy, I recognized the power and potential of the Navy League as an advocate for military preparedness, constantly urging the Congress to meet its Constitutional mandate to "maintain a Navy."

Now, as Chairman of the Armed Services Committee, I can attest that the League's support for the Sea Services is both effective and appreciated. Building the ships and systems that will keep the Navy and Marine Corps on the cutting edge in the 21st Century requires focus and effort each year in the Congress. The Navy League provides important and valuable advice to lawmakers as they make decisions affecting our sea services, and the organization also helps focus attention on our shipbuilding industrial base and civilian maritime infrastructure.

For each of the Sea Services, there are tough times and not-so-tough times; but the contributions of the Navy League have remained consistent through the peaks and troughs, no matter the sea state. The League is unique among military support organizations in that it is completely open both to veterans and to those who have not served in uniform. This membership policy eliminates any perception that Navy League advocacy for particular programs or weapon systems grows out of the services' own self-interest. The civilian volunteers of the Navy League have nothing to gain from their work beyond the satisfaction of helping America remain strong, and contributing to the well-being of our Marines, Sailors, Merchant Mariners, Coastguardsmen and their families.

I can think of no finer legacy than that. And I am humbled to be able to contribute a very small part to this wonderful book that celebrates the history and accomplishments of the Navy League. May the organization and its superb volunteers enjoy another hundred years of achievement and service!

John Warner

The Knapp Company, Inc., New York

This 1909 Navy recruiting poster is by artist Rolf Armstrong and was first published in 1909.

TABLE OF CONTENTS

October 1904 cover of The Navy League Journal * The Official Organ of the Navy League of the United States

Chapter I
The Navy League: What It Is, What It Does

Congratulations to the members of the Navy League of the United States as you celebrate your 100th birthday. The Navy League's proud mission of serving the U.S. sea services at home and throughout the world is as important today as it was 100 years ago. During these extraordinary times, I commend your support of the men and women of the U.S. Navy, Marine Corps, Coast Guard, and the Merchant Marine. I also applaud you for informing American citizens and elected officials about the vital role our sea services play in protecting our national security and economic interests. Best wishes for a memorable anniversary celebration and for continued success in supporting the sea services of the United States of America.

This letter from President George W. Bush was one of hundreds of congratulatory messages received during the centennial year of the Navy League of the United States. The letter expressed his personal appreciation, as commander in chief, for the Navy League's continuing support of the nation's sea services and recognized that the League's support of the sea services must continue.

From the organization's 1902 beginning, it has sought to serve and support all of the nation's sea services, the Navy, Marine Corps, Coast Guard, and U.S.-flag Merchant Marine, as well as a strong national defense program. The Navy League is not a military organization. No active duty members of the armed services of the United States may be members.

As an Internal Revenue Code Section 501(c)(3) tax exempt, non-profit corporation, the Navy League has carried out its mission of keeping the American people and their elected leaders, and the nation's print and broadcast media, informed about the importance of sea power, both naval and commercial, for America's economic and national security.[1] Over a tumultuous century it has bordered on bankruptcy on several occasions and challenged Presidents, Secretaries of the Navy, and Secretaries of Defense in their understanding and support of the sea services. But while its tactics have varied, and success not always marked its path through the corridors of government and power, the end result after a century of endeavor has been consistent with the League's goal since its founding: From an inconsequential, fourth-ranked Navy at the time of its founding, the Navy League of the United States has witnessed the fleet's growth into the most powerful the world has ever known.

The League's intent and goals are succinctly contained in the eleven elements of its Statement of Policy:

* We of the Navy League of the United States stand for a strong America—a nation morally, economically, and internally strong.
* We believe that the security of our nation and of the people of the world demands a well-balanced, integrated, mobile American defense team, of which a strong Navy, Marine Corps, Coast Guard, and Merchant Marine are indispensable parts.
* We support all Armed Services to the end that each may make its appropriate contribution to the national security.
* We know that in a free nation an informed public is indispensable to national security and, therefore, we will strive to keep the nation alert to dangers which threaten—both from without and within.
* We favor appropriations for each of the Armed Services, adequate for national security, economically administered.
* We oppose any usurpation of the Congress's constitutional authority over the Armed Services.
* We urge that our country maintain world leadership in scientific research and development.
* We support industrial preparedness, planning and production.
* We support efforts of our government to achieve worldwide peace through international cooperation.
* We advocate a foreign policy which will avoid wars—if possible; if not, win them!
* We pledge our loyalty and allegiance to the government and to the flag of the United States, and will work toward the furtherance of the principles stated herein.

For all its lineage and heritage, as from its humble beginnings in New York City, the Navy League has remained a remarkably transparent organization. Virtually all of its operations and activities are carried out in full view of both its own members and the general public. And while it takes strong positions on major maritime and national defense issues representing the well-informed consensus of League membership at large, it is also small enough and sufficiently engaged at the local level to take on issues such as base encroachment, support of local sea service related activities in colleges and high schools, and to have more than one dance, dinner, or golf tournament on the year's social calendar.

Similarly, its more than 66,000 members are very broad-based. Some League members are Navy, Marine Corps, Coast Guard, or U.S.-flag Merchant Marine retirees, but most are not. Others have served in the Army or Air Force, or in one of America's guard or reserve components. Presidents of the United States and a number of senators and representatives have been members of the Navy League before, during, or after their time in public office. Included on the League's membership roster during the organization's first century of service have been an array of movie stars, professional athletes, captains of industry, and nationally known writers, editors, and other media professionals. However, the majority of League members are simply everyday American citizens.

But while broadly based, to accomplish its education mission and have an impact on national issues affecting the sea services, the League's national headquarters is located in Arlington, Virginia, just south of the nation's capital. Serving as its principal liaison with Capitol Hill is the League's Office of Legislative Affairs, which conducts legislative and issue research focusing on sea service needs and concerns, specifically tracking and monitoring legislation. The office routinely communicates with the Military Coalition, the Navy/Marine Corps Council, and the Navy/Marine Corps and Coast Guard Caucuses in the House of Representatives.

A particular focus is placed on Congressional staff members, where there are literally hundreds of new professionals from all over the nation serving for the first time in the nation's capital. Many of these staff members are assigned to committees with jurisdiction over national defense programs and funding. With only a small number having ever served in the military and/or worked in the national defense field, the League stands ready to help them in every way it can.

In addition to coordinating all League functions on Capitol Hill, the League's Office of Legislative Affairs also serves as the principal League conduit to the Departments of Defense, Homeland Security, Transportation, and the five military services, Veterans' Administration, Maritime Administration, and the National Oceanic & Atmospheric Administration.

Beyond the boundaries of the nation's capital, the organization's principal means of communications with both its membership and the general public are through the internet and League website (www.navyleague.org), publications, press releases, national and local speakers programs, sponsorship of symposia and seminars, issuance of white papers, and special reports on major national defense issues. Each member of the Navy League receives a monthly copy of *Seapower* magazine, a copy of the annual *Seapower Almanac*, and a quarterly *The Navy Leaguer* newsletter. Many League councils have their own newsletters, and annual competitions are held among large, medium, and small councils for the best in the League. The Honolulu, Hawaii, Council is known for the consistent long-term general excellence of its publication *Fore 'n Aft*. League newsletters are particularly important for their focus on the organization's programs and activities at the grassroots level, and serve as an invaluable communication tool between councils and the local communities and sea service organizations and commands they support.

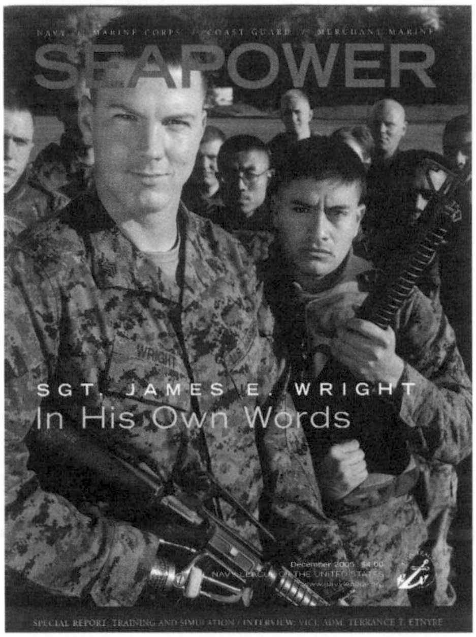

The League and its nearly 300 councils throughout the United States and overseas also communicate through actions, by working with local and national youth groups, and by sponsoring and participating in the League's annual Sea-Air-Space Exposition in Washington, D.C., the largest maritime exposition in the world. The League encourages and supports parades and other patriotic activities on national holidays, and supports events such as Fleet Week and birthdays for the Navy, Marine Corps, and Coast Guard.

Particularly important, and made deliberately visible to the public, is the Navy League's role in ship commissionings. The League's involvement, while largely as a spectator for the first seven decades of the 20th century, was enhanced in the 1980s as state-of-the-art Aegis guided-missile cruisers began rolling out of the builders' ways in Maine and Mississippi. Rather than traditional commissionings in the shipyard, to herald the arrival of a truly revolutionary warship, Rear Admiral Wayne Meyer, principal architect of the Aegis system, approached the Navy League regarding the feasibility of organizing, and funding, highly visible ships' commissionings in ports and locations with discernible ties to the ship in terms of name or purpose. The League agreed to take on this responsibility, one which has continued for more than two decades, and for all new ships being added to the fleet.

More visibility, non-traditional locales, and a public venue means increased costs, and with strict government regulations regarding commissioning ceremony expenditures, only an organization like the Navy League can approach both the

USS *Bunker Hill* (CG-52)

defense industry and local government and business associations seeking financial assistance. For example, when the Aegis cruiser USS *Bunker Hill* was commissioned in 1986, with Senator Edward Kennedy as the commissioning speaker, the Massachusetts Bay Council talked with the Boston Chamber of Commerce to arrange, and in several cases fund, the location, transportation, and security aspects of the ceremony. The council also approached the defense industry for support in bringing the entire event off, including receptions before, and after, the actual event. The upshot was that almost 12,000 Bostonians witnessed the commissioning of USS *Bunker Hill* on September 20, 1986, within sight of the monument commemorating the historic battle for which she was named.

The Navy League's role in numerous ship commissionings is vitally important to each sailor, for it is his or her ship that will be the "best" in the fleet, and one deserving of special consideration on a day that each "plank-owner," (member of the ship's first crew) will never forget. The degree of commitment of each League council, to raise the monies and run all activities connected with a ship commissioning, is considerable, and for many councils, a recurring one. For example, the Massachusetts Bay Council (formerly Eastern Massachusetts Council), in addition to the 1986 commissioning of USS *Bunker Hill* (CG-52), has sponsored the commissionings of the Oliver Hazard Perry-class frigate USS *Samuel Eliot Morison* (FFG-13) in 1980, and two Arleigh Burke-class guided-missile destroyers, USS *Ramage* (DDG-61) in 1995, and USS *Preble* (DDG-88) in 2002.

On such events as ship commissionings, the Navy League's role is unique. Yet in other aspects it differs little from other civic and patriotic organizations such as the Association of the United States Army, Air Force Association, Reserve Officers Association, and Naval Reserve Association. On many issues the Navy League works closely with these associations and others to ensure that men and women serving on active duty are adequately compensated and enjoy the same quality-of-life benefits available to other American citizens.

But the Navy League's role on the national scene is unique because of several defining characteristics that distinguish it from other defense-oriented associations:

* It is nonpartisan, with no ties to any political party.
* It is independent, both ideologically and financially.
* It is a "civilians only" organization; League bylaws stipulate that "Commissioned and Warrant officers or enlisted personnel of any branch of the armed services are not eligible for membership while on active duty. Reservists are eligible for membership but, while on active duty, are not eligible to vote or to hold office." The Navy League is the only U.S. defense oriented national organization to adopt this exclusionary rule, which provides it with a freedom to speak out on any matter with total independence from the sea services it supports. League leadership's testimony and editorials can never be construed as being in the self interest of its members.
* Its operations and policies are arrived at through democratic processes rather than the desires and beliefs of individual directors. The nature of League governance has moved substantively in this direction since the early 1960s and while not necessarily leading to concise, "gentlemanly" deliberations and quiet acquiescence, the town meeting-style construct of deriving League positions and governing procedures has served the institution well, particularly over the last half-century.

Essential to understanding the manner in which the Navy League operates is the fact that the organization functions on two levels: national and council. Throughout its history, the relationship between these components has proven a constant subject of discussion, reform, and action by League leadership at all levels. In fact, other than the fiscal condition of the League, which has oftentimes been tenuous at best, and membership levels, the near continual shaping and refining of the relationship between the national and council levels has consumed considerable leadership effort internal to the League.

As a result, 103 years after the League's founding, councils at the local level are not to take positions on national issues of importance to the sea services. Rather, League nationally-elected leadership crafts and establishes policy, and all levels of the organization then publicize and support it locally. This "top-down" management philosophy permits councils to execute their mission and meet League goals through a sound understanding of the League's position.

Thus, determination of this policy is not an ad hoc procedure. Rather, positions on issues of salient importance are carefully crafted by the Maritime Policy and Resolutions Committee, normally headed by the national president, and presented for ratification at the annual meeting of members during the League's national convention. Only after resolutions have been fully considered, in a sometimes rancorous, lengthy fashion, and approved by the membership at large do they become part of the League's *Maritime Policy* statement for the coming year.

This iterative process requires numerous committee and subcommittee meetings over a period of several months, accompanied by sea service program briefings and reading of policy papers, congressional testimony, and other professional literature. It is completely democratic in its workings; more than half of the League's current 253 national directors serve on these committees. The probable topics of each year's resolutions are publicized well in advance and usually include, in addition to omnibus resolutions on the Navy, Marine Corps, Coast Guard, and U.S.-flag Merchant Marine, a limited number of resolutions on other defense topics of major national importance.

The League's *Maritime Policy 2005* is illustrative. Much more than an assemblage of declarative statements of advocacy, the statement is divided into sections: Preface, The Sea Services, Marine Transportation, Shipbuilding and Infrastructure, and Personnel Policies. The Sea Services section deals with programmatic specifics of various Navy, Marine Corps, Coast Guard, and U.S.-flag Merchant Marine issues, largely as they are affected by the continued funding demands of the war on terror. A particular note of concern is expressed over the funding requirements of the Coast Guard to replace its aging fleet of cutters and aircraft; referring to the Coast Guard Commandant's statement that it will take twenty years, the League opines, literally underlining its concern: "In reality, *America can't wait that long.*"[2]

Section III of the *Maritime Policy 2005* statement addresses the issue of America's marine transportation system, specifically citing the needs of the nation's inland waterways, ports, and their intermodal connections. Also included in this section is a detailed discussion of the condition and woes of the domestic U.S. shipbuilding industry and related issues affecting the nation's industrial base.

Operations and governance of the entire Navy League are currently specified in the *Operations Manual, 5th Edition with Change 1, Navy League of the United States, 2004.* Duties and responsibilities of the Board of Directors, Executive Committee, national directors, national president, vice presidents, other elected and appointed officials, as well as several committees are contained within this document.

Day-to-day operations of the League are largely the responsibility of the Steering Committee, which exercises all powers of the Executive Committee, except when the Board of Directors or Executive Committee is in session. Created in the early 1960s to establish League goals and priorities and comprised of the national president, chairperson of the National Advisory Council, all vice presidents, the treasurer, corporate secretary, and judge advocate, it is responsible for League operations, as determined and assigned by the national president, in the following specific areas:

* Community Education and Information Technology
* Corporate Affairs
* International Relations
* Legislative Affairs
* Membership and Marketing
* Public Relations
* Region Presidents' Liaison
* Sea Services Liaison
* Strategic Planning
* Youth Programs

"Support of the councils is essential. These are the people who make it happen; they are the driving force of everything we do."

The recommendations and work of the Steering Committee in order to achieve the League's organizational goals are subject to approval of the Executive Committee and the Board of Directors.[3]

Calvin H. Cobb Jr., longtime League Judge Advocate and National President 1989-1991, has noted that in the 21st century the real responsibility for the functioning of the League rests with the Board of Directors; the National President exists to "implement the policies of the Board of Directors." When some presidents have "strayed from that path" and sought to establish an "imperial presidency" it has caused problems within the organization. Cobb notes, "Volunteer organizations like the Navy League require collegiality at their uppermost levels for them to work."[4]

John J. Spittler, national president 1979-1981, agreed with Cobb, maintaining that his successes as leader of the League were due to the "great people who worked with me" ... "I could not have had a better crew." Spittler maintained, "I simply was the guy up front for a lot of people who were willing to sacrifice their time and money to make the organization work."[5]

To make it work at the national level, the Navy League is administered by 24 national committees, led by a chairman and composed of anywhere from a half dozen to two dozen directors. A single national officer is assigned responsibility for each committee, reporting to the national president.[6]

Although broad policy addressing national and international maritime issues as well as the establishment of goals and priorities for the organization are set at the national level, in reality most of the League's day-to-day work, particularly on programs supporting the men and women of the sea services on active duty and their families, is carried out, not from "on high" at national headquarters, but rather at the community level, by members of local League councils. John A. Panneton, elected national president in June 2005, is the first to admit: "Support of the councils is essential. These are the people who make it happen; they are the driving force of everything we do."[7]

Panneton is stating what all League leaders, particularly since the early 1950s, readily admit. Perhaps Calvin Cobb, national president from 1989-1991, said it best in his final "President's Message" to the League in June 1991: "Our officers give devotedly and unstintingly of their time and talents, and we have a dedicated and highly professional headquarters staff. But the real strength of the Navy League is in our councils and individual members. They provide the direct support to our sea services personnel, and they interface with our fellow citizens whose support for a strong U.S. defense program is indispensable."[8]

But to many Navy Leaguers, the organization is a "local," and not a "national" activity; as much a social institution as one to discuss and resolve issues of national importance. Various councils have independent funding separate from the national coffers. Because each council is chartered, the national organization cannot take monies from them; the only disciplinary action available to national headquarters is to withdraw a council's charter. Several councils have special endowments, awards programs, and scholarships administered and awarded at a local community level.

For example, distinct from the League's national awards program, the New York Council, since the mid-1980s, in association with the Theodore Roosevelt Association Foundation, has awarded an annual Theodore and Franklin D. Roosevelt Naval History Prize for a book examining various aspects of the history of the sea services. Selected by a panel of distinguished academics in addition to members of both organizations, award winning subjects have ranged from War Plan Orange (the strategy to defeat Japan) and Admiral Hyman Rickover, father of the nuclear Navy, to consideration of the Navy's role in the Persian Gulf and a narrative of the largest single ship rescue ever (14,000 Koreans at the close of the Chosin Reservoir campaign in 1950) by the SS *Meredith Victory*.

As befits the council from which sprung the entire Navy League organization, the New York Council also has a host of other awards including the "Admiral Bergen Industry Eagle," named after former League National President John Bergen, the "Knox Owl Media Award," named after Franklin Roosevelt's wartime Secretary of the Navy, Frank Knox, and the "Roosevelts Science Gold Medal," named after both former presidents, who also served as assistant secretaries of the Navy.

The activities in which councils are involved vary substantially, and are highly dependent on their size and geographic location. What follows is not an all-inclusive listing of councils or delineation of all activities, but a representative sampling of what has, and is, happening at the local level throughout the United States and in several overseas councils.

While some councils largely exist as a social venue for meeting with local business community and political leaders to gain their support for the sea services, others elect to promote the importance of seapower through community education seminars involving active duty and retired individuals as well as academics from local universities and colleges. Others observe the anniversaries of significant events in America's naval history that occurred within their locales, such as the 1813 Battle of Lake Erie that wrested control of the Great Lakes from Britain, honored annually in September by Ohio councils from Akron-Canton, Youngstown, Columbus, Cincinnati, and Toledo-Erie Islands.

Other councils sponsor special events to honor America's past naval heroes. In late 1992 the Greater Cincinnati, Ohio, Council gave its members an opportunity to experience living history by bringing together 16 former World War II submarine commanding officers, including two Medal of Honor winners, to recognize and honor their achievements in winning the two-ocean war. Coordinating the gathering was John J. Schiff, a past council president and longtime supporter and major donor to the Navy League. Then-Council President David Nelson termed the event "one of the most moving experiences of my life. These men are true American heroes."[9]

Some councils host visiting foreign dignitaries and foreign naval personnel such as the Newport County, Rhode Island's "Welcome Aboard" luncheon for international students at the Naval War College's Naval Command College. Such hosting can also include that of crews of foreign ships making port calls; one such event that occurred in Boston in the mid-1970s and involved the Eastern Massachusetts Council, as will be seen, was particularly important within the context of the Cold War.

Many councils "adopt" ships and submarines of the sea services (many more than one), sponsor Sea Cadet divisions or Naval or Marine Corps Junior Reserve Officer Training Corps units at local secondary schools. For example, the Baltimore, Maryland, Council is a principal supporter of the Training Ship Constellation-Fort McHenry Division of the Naval Sea Cadet Corps and contributes to youth programs at Baltimore-area high schools with junior Navy and Marine Corps Reserve Officer Training Corps programs. The council provides funds for a scholarship program of the Baltimore Maritime Museum conducted aboard the Coast Guard cutter *Taney* (WPG-37), the museum's flagship, and the only survivor of the 1941 attack on Pearl Harbor still afloat. *Taney* also serves as the site for Baltimore's annual Pearl Harbor Day ceremony, an event in which the council is always involved.

During the 21st century, one of the most aggressive local councils has been the Santa Barbara, California, Council. Between 2000 and 2005, membership soared from 35 to nearly 1,500, making it one of the top League councils in terms of both individual recruiters and overall council membership gains. As will be discussed in detail in Chapter XI, the Santa Barbara Council's "adoption" of the aircraft carrier USS *Ronald Reagan*, and its co-sponsoring, along with the Hampton Roads Council, of the 2003 commissioning ceremony, established new precedents in terms of fund-raising innovation, activities, and amounts of money garnered for the event. More recently, its August 2005 hosting of the 1,092-foot-long aircraft carrier, for its first visit to Santa Barbara, was an overwhelming success largely due to the round-the-clock work of 20 council members and its partnering with more than 20 business and community groups in the local area. One particular challenge, getting the Santa Barbara City Council to waive its $35,000 harbor fee which could have placed the visit at risk, was met only at the last minute by a concerted public relations campaign in the local media and engagement of several local celebrities for their help.

But in the end, the three-day ship visit went off without any significant problems. From western-style barbecues to sports events, wine-tasting to escorted tours to the nearby Reagan Library and Western White House Ranch, the event was an unqualified success, and netted the Navy League and Santa Barbara Council 300 new members in the process.

Santa Barbara Council President Connie O'Shaughnessy-Los, who was also president during the events leading up to the commissioning of the *Reagan*, has continued her earlier strategy of partnering with local businesses and other community organizations to accomplish many of the council's activities. Los believes that outreaching to other organizations is one of the best ways to educate the public about the League and its mission, because when they work with local councils and people they know, and they see what the League is doing, who it is supporting, and why, it gives them real insight into the Navy League.[10]

USS *Pittsburgh* (SSN-720)

The Pittsburgh, Pennsylvania, Council has adopted the nuclear attack submarine USS *Pittsburgh* (SSN-720), sponsoring numerous social activities for the crew, hosting crew members who visit the ship's namesake city, and promoting trips to visit the Groton, Connecticut, homeported boat. The council also sponsors the Pittsburgh Battalion of the Naval Sea Cadet Corps and the Sea Cadet training ship *Captain Neil Judd*. The Pittsburgh organization also has an annual tradition, common among many League councils, of presenting a

Navy sword to the top graduating midshipman at the Naval Reserve Officer Training Corps unit at Carnegie-Mellon University.

The San Diego County, California, Women's Council, as expected, given the very large number of sea service personnel assigned to the area, cooks monthly dinners for upward of 80 families at the local United Services Organization facility. Council members sponsor bake sales to benefit the Armed Forces Young Men's Christian Association, serve as volunteers at the United Service Organization Airport Center, host receptions and tours for numerous allied and coalition armed services personnel assigned to a number of San Diego-based schools and training facilities, and support two adopted ships: the guided-missile frigate USS *Rentz* (FFG-46) and the Coast Guard patrol boat *Edisto* (WPB-1313).

Close involvement with the Coast Guard is a tradition shared by the Navy League's Saint Louis, Missouri, Council. With an inland location, albeit one on America's greatest waterway with a major Coast Guard headquarters nearby, the Saint Louis Council has a unique perspective on both the challenges and requirements of the Coast Guard and problems facing the U.S.-flag merchant fleet. Council members played a key role in obtaining and transporting a nine-ton anchor, 13-feet tall, from the World War II era aircraft carrier USS *Langley* (CV-1) to downtown Saint Louis, where it now serves as a memorial to the U.S.-flag Merchant Marine. Council members also work closely with the Saint Louis Cardinals baseball organization to support Navy recruiting in the area, sponsor a youth and charity golf tournament, and support a number of Sea Cadet and Reserve Officer Training Corps units in the local area.

The Stockton, California, Council, founded in the 1960s by George Ernest, executive director of the Stockton Chamber of Commerce, has scored a number of "firsts" as a Navy League council. Among these are the first husband and wife team—T. Cole Hackley and Dr. Carol Ann Hackley—to serve individually as national directors, national committee chairs, and national vice presidents, and the first council in the region to host a U.S. Coast Guard ball.

USCGC *Kiska* (WPB-1336)

During the 1970s, the Stockton Council responded to Chief of Naval

Operations Admiral Elmo Zumwalt's call for local base commanders to implement local youth services encampments to aid the nation's youth in moving off city streets during the hot summer. When the commanding officer of the naval communications station asked for help the Stockton Council took over the whole effort and established their own program. The commanding officer agreed that he would provide whatever resources they needed. Employing an empty firehouse on the communication station's grounds, the week-long program, with youth from local cities staying aboard base, attending classes, and touring different naval facilities and ships, was led and administered by Navy Leaguers from the Stockton Council.

Another unique Navy League council is found in Hilo, Hawaii, located on the

OpSail 2000

photo by CW03 Edwin Bailey, USNR (Ret.)

Members of USS *America* (CV-66) crew form a Big Apple as the ship steams into New York Harbor.

east side of the island of Hawaii. Although a seaport, there are no Navy ships or units based there. The Hilo Council, formed in October 1964, likes to point out that it is "the largest naval unit on the Big Island." But its solitary position has not dampened the enthusiasm of Hilo Council members for traditional activities. They have adopted the Coast Guard Cutter *Kiska*, provided Sailor-of-the-Quarter and -Year awards to deserving crew members, and sponsored an annual *Kiska* Appreciation Day. The Hilo Council works with the sponsors of the International Festival of the Pacific to coordinate visits and participation of sea service units in the event. It also acts as the official liaison between the Navy and the annual Merrie Monarch Hula Festival, the premier hula and Hawaiian cultural event in the world with competitors coming from many nations.

Like the Hilo Council and its support of two festivals on the island of Hawaii, other councils are actively involved in the planning and execution of well known international events such as the traditional July 4th International Naval Review and Tall Ships Parade held in the harbor of New York City. The Baltimore Council was a co-sponsor of the millennial *Op Sail 2000*, the largest sailing ship event since Liberty Weekend in 1986 in New York Harbor. Both San Francisco and New York

City host Fleet Weeks, the largest annual port visit by the Navy on each respective coast; both events are hosted by local Navy League councils; the New York Council is on the Steering Committee for the event and responsible for much of the entertainment arranged for thousands of sea service personnel visiting the city.

And then there are the unique, one-time events. For example, in October 1999 the Hampton Roads, Virginia, council sponsored a model home as part of a "Homearama" in Tidewater, Virginia. The Manor-style home was designated "The Admiral's Quarters," taking its inspiration from the stately homes along Admirals' Row at the Norfolk Naval Base originally built for the 1903 Jamestown Exposition. The Hampton Roads Council assisted in the procurement of artwork and naval memorabilia to display throughout the home, and the guest suite featured historic relics from Norfolk and the Naval Museum, including a bell from the first USS *Virginia* (BB-16). Naturally, the home sold during the event. Hampton Roads Council President (and former Congressman) Owen Pickett noted that an event like Homearama "drew interest and created awareness for the Navy League." Council Executive Director Maryellen Baldwin added that "the challenge for us was to think outside the box and do something different ... The Navy League has a more well known name and clearly made a statement in this area by participating."[11]

While most councils are located within the borders of the United States, several of the League's most important groups, especially to forward-deployed sailors and Marines, are found throughout the world, particularly in East Asia and Mediterranean regions. Overseas councils face challenges largely unseen by the rest of the League: great distances from U.S. military installations, infrastructure, and sea service populations; shifting political and social climes not always friendly to either U.S. international policy or military presence; the need to develop strong relationships with local nationals and government; and a necessarily proscribed population base from which to draw its membership.

Some overseas councils reflect long-term American interests and presence in the region dating from the middle of the 20th century. For example, the Korea Council, based out of Seoul, Korea, in addition to greeting and hosting each Navy ship when it makes a port call, is also extensively involved in supporting sea service personnel permanently stationed ashore in Korea. Such support includes Sailor-of-the-Quarter and-Year recognition, awards, banquets and annual golf tournaments and picnics. The annual Maritime Night Party recognizes the Christmas holiday season for personnel stationed far from home, and numerous prizes are provided by the council for award by lottery drawing.

The Korea Council also sponsors a program that keeps alive memories of the sacrifices made by American and allied forces, as well as South Koreans, during the four-year-long conflict that tore the peninsula apart in the early 1950s. War veterans recall their experiences for younger people born after the conflict, and

American and allied veterans returning to Korea are escorted to the Demilitarized Zone, offered dinner in the General Mess of the United States Forces Korea, and oftentimes participate in the annual dinner hosted by Commander of Naval Forces Korea. More than 15,000 Korean War veterans have visited Korea since inauguration of the program, and many have sent letters of thanks for the hospitality offered by the Korea Council. The Korea Council also sponsored a monument to the 1950 Inchon Landing in McArthur Park in Inchon, Korea, and, at the dedication ceremony hosted 60 Korean War veterans for a luncheon at a nearby restaurant.

USS *Safeguard* (ARS-50)

The Navy League also has a significant overseas presence in Japan and very active councils in both Tokyo and Sasebo. When the salvage ship USS *Safeguard* (ARS-50) returned from a six-month deployment in October 2005, the Sasebo Council arranged for the Yosakoi Dance Team to perform on the pier. After the ship had tied up, to the shouts, whistles, and applause of Navy Leaguers and other Sasebo community members, Japanese and American, the council hosted a family picnic of hot dogs, hamburgers, and barbecue for the *Safeguard*'s crew and their dependents. Jerry Havens, president of the Sasebo Council, in an e-mail to his members several days later noted:

> Speaking with the captain and many of the crew members, they were in awe of the magnitude of Sasebo's return celebration. ... In my 30 years of Navy life, I never once experienced such a rousing homecoming. ... I cannot express the pride I felt-being a part of an organization that treats our junior-most Sailors as VIPs (Very Important Persons) upon their return from sea.[12]

The commanding officer of USS *Safeguard* sent his own message of appreciation to the Sasebo Council:

> The incredible outpouring of support yesterday was one of the

> most moving and rewarding events I've experienced in my naval career. Your efforts in welcoming our sailors back ensured that every one of them felt special and knew that they were returning to a close-knit community. ... We are extremely grateful. It's great to be home.[13]

South of Sasebo, Japan, the Singapore Council of the Navy League supports the Logistics Command, Western Pacific, the United States Air Force's 497th Training Squadron and Coast Guard, Department of Homeland Security, and Marine Corps security and support units. Chartered in 1994, its activities include supporting the Navy Ball, Navy Supply Corps dinner, the Marine Corps Ball and, most importantly, home hospitality and in-home entertaining for visiting sailors and Marines passing through this vital port on one of the world's busiest and most strategic waterways, the Malacca Strait. In that context, tours arranged for Singapore Armed Forces units of visiting Navy ships and sponsorship of speeches by visiting U.S. military and Department of Defense officials take on considerable importance in terms of national security.

The Singapore Council has a very broad membership, from Americans living abroad for business purposes, to those just wanting to express their appreciation for military men and women. And it is particularly "well connected" to both the local government and Washington, as the United States Ambassador to Singapore, Frank Lavin, is both a Navy Reservist and a Navy Leaguer. League National President Sheila M. McNeill, 2003-2005, recalled that when she first met Ambassador Lavin, she was somewhat taken aback when he asked her, "What can we do to improve our Navy League?"[14]

Visiting Navy League officials are frequently surprised at the genuine feeling of appreciation for the United States they encounter when visiting foreign councils. For example, in the summer of 2004, with the United States engaged in a war unpopular with European societies in general, National President McNeill and her husband Arlie visited France, Italy, and Spain. She was curious as to how she would be received as she arrived at the first overseas council meeting in Cannes, France; she was greeted by a council membership made up more than 80 percent by foreign nationals. The tone of her reception was established by the first guest that presented himself. He was a Frenchman wearing a cowboy hat in honor of the United States and he wept as he described the liberation of his country more than a half century earlier.

The following day, as the League National President laid an American flag wreath in a ceremony at the memorial commemorating the liberation of France during World War II, numerous citizens of Cannes told her of the enormous gratitude they felt toward the Untied States. As McNeill would later relate, "they hugged both Arlie and me, kissed us, and asked us to thank the U.S. Sixth Fleet for protecting them and for their part in preserving freedom in their part of the world."[15]

This perhaps surprising reality is fortunate for the men and women of the sea services. For the decades-long reduction in American bases and naval stations overseas, concomitant with sea service operations centered in Central and Southwest Asia over the past 15 years, have put a premium on the infrequent port visits transiting to or from the Arabian Gulf and its surrounding environs. Thus, there is no better sight to that Navy or Coast Guard sailor or Marine enroute to fight the global war on terror than a "Welcome" sign and beach party sponsored by the Navy League Council in Palma de Mallorca or Barcelona, Spain, or a reception hosted by the French Riviera-Monaco and Provence Councils for returning forward deployed units after six months or more in the sand, heat, and humidity of the Arabian Gulf.

For example, in July 1999 the USS *Ross* (DDG-71), an Arleigh Burke-class guided-missile destroyer with an embarked destroyer squadron staff, pulled into Marseilles, France, following four months of extended combat operations off the Balkan Coast during the North Atlantic Treaty Organization's *Operation Allied Force.* The officers and crew were met pierside by Ms. Deborah J. Cozzone, State President of the France Overseas Councils and head of the Provence, France, Council. Ms. Cozzone had been the initial president of the Marseille, France, Council, when it had been formed in 1990 on the advice of the U.S. Consul General to provide support to the men and women of the many 6th Fleet ships that were visiting the ports of Marseille and Toulon. Previously, ships' companies had been bused from Toulon to Cannes, France, to attend events of the League council there. With the creation of the Provence Council, that trip was no longer necessary.

In the first three months after its creation, the Provence Council hosted more than 30 ships. Each one was presented with a package of social and community relations packages. Aided by the support and advice of Colonel James L. Jones, (later Marine Corps Commandant and Supreme Allied Commander, Europe, and Commander, United States European Command), the Provence Council coordinated football games between American and European teams, "Days of Hope" events for children with cancer at local McDonalds franchises, and American sailors assisted French citizens in repairing and painting facilities for the poor of southern France. Especially popular were events featuring wine tasting, olive picking, race car driving on local Formula 1 racetracks, and attendance at local opera dress rehearsals.[16]

Nine years later, having hosted countless port visits, by the time *Ross* had tied up at a Marseille commercial pier in July 1999, Ms. Cozzone had already coordinated with the U.S. charge de affairs and Consul General to host two receptions for the men and women of the ship. She had also discussed with the husbanding agent issues such as transportation for the ship's crew to and from the Marseille city center because of the ship's distant location (for security reasons) within the extensive commercial shipping infrastructure of France's largest port.

U.S. Navy Photo Danny Ewing, Jr

Sailors from USS *Harry S. Truman* (CVN-75) enjoy visiting Marseille, France.

In addition to hosting a dinner at her own home for a dozen naval officers and chiefs, Ms. Cozzone, to meet the particular desires of *Ross* officers and the embarked staff, arranged an official visit to the Museum of the French Foreign Legion and a daylong driving tour through the extensive ruins of the Roman Empire still extant in southern France, including the internationally renowned Pont du Gard aqueduct and the amphitheater and temple at Nimes.[17]

Overseas League councils can also serve to facilitate relations between Washington and their respective host nations. For example, the Madrid, Spain, Council has assumed the role of interfacing between American defense industry contractors and Spanish military commands. The Council hosts a monthly dinner meeting whose attendees include the Spanish Minister of Defense, Chief of Naval Operations, ambassadors from several nations, and officers from all branches of the United States armed forces.

More traditional activities of the Madrid Council include an October gala ball celebrating the Navy's birthday; recognition of a Sailor-of-the-Year from the nearby naval installation in Rota, Spain; a U.S. Memorial Day wreath-laying at the statue of Admiral Farragut in the town of Ciudadela, (where the American naval hero's father was born), another wreath-laying at the early 1800s graves of several American sailors buried in nearby Mahon, and annual sponsorship of the top cadet from the Spanish Naval Academy to travel to the United States to see Washington D.C., the Naval Academy, and naval facilities in Norfolk and Newport News, Virginia.

Though far from all-inclusive, the events cited aptly depict the nature of the work the Navy League does throughout the world for the men and women of the sea services. Perhaps unknown outside of the lifelines of the ships affected, it is an indispensable rendering of support for those who wear the uniform, support not proffered or funded at the national level, but rather through the time, fiscal commitment, leadership, and initiative of individual councils and their memberships. Thus, members who have served at the highest levels of League leadership are the first to assert that the heart and soul of the Navy League of the United States is found, not at national headquarters, but in its councils, both in America and overseas.

And this assertion is true on Washington's Capitol Hill as well. Regardless of the skill and acumen of the national staff and members of the League's Office of Legislative Affairs, political reality is that the real power of the Navy League to influence legislative decisions affecting the sea services resides at the council level and their individual members. It is those Navy Leaguers who know their representatives and senators best, have the easiest access to front offices, and can most readily, honestly, and frankly affect policy.

That is not to say that all members of the Navy League adapt easily to the role of politico or lobbyist for the sea services on Capitol Hill. Indeed, nothing could be further from the truth, and most League members are reluctant to, and consequently do not, get involved in the political process. There is no "standard" Navy Leaguer. Council members represent an unusually broad spectrum of personages, with varying levels of knowledge of any of the sea services. Some may have served in one of the nation's armed services; some are affluent, most are not. Some possess special professional expertise, working experience, or political influence at the local or state level, while others are simply interested, concerned citizens willing to give themselves to a purpose they feel is worth their time and consideration.

Members of the Navy League have certain things in common: They all believe in, and support, a strong U.S. national defense program. They also believe that seapower, both naval and commercial, has played, and will continue to play, an important military and economic role into the 21st century and will be essential to America's continued economic prosperity.

Individually and through their council officers, all members of the Navy League are able to contribute to the development, ratification, and support of League national policies on a broad spectrum of national defense and sea service issues. They are encouraged to support these policies through letters to the editor, speaking out at public forums, and communicating views to those who represent them in Congress.

They also are asked to personally participate, as Navy Leaguers, in local and national programs created specifically to help sea service men and women and their families. They do this in numerous ways: working on local and national awards programs, sponsorship of christenings and commissionings of Navy and Coast Guard ships, "adoption"

U.S. Navy Photo

USS *Ronald Reagan* (CVN-76) arrives at Rio de Janeiro for a port visit.

Members of the Naval Sea Cadet Corps are often called upon to serve as color guards.

of ships, air and ground units, and bases and stations throughout the United States and overseas, serving as community liaisons between service recruiting offices and local school systems, supporting and participating in Armed Forces Day celebrations, and by raising funds for building and improvement of family service centers, nurseries, daycare centers, and other on- and off-base facilities designed to support those in uniform and their families.

Council members work without compensation and receive little public recognition. However, each year a committee appointed by the League's president meets at national headquarters in early spring to select 15-20 councils whose activities during the previous year have been particularly meritorious and deserving of recognition. These councils are honored during special ceremonies at that year's national convention by being designated "Outstanding" or "Meritorious" Councils.

The Navy League has created and financially supported two of the nation's finest youth programs: the Naval Sea Cadet Corps and the Navy League Cadet Corps. An earlier consideration of the formation of the Sea Cadets in the 1960s considered it "the most ambitious and viable program undertaken by the Navy League in the post-World War II era."[18] And the organization has done nothing but grow in importance and size in the ensuing four decades.

The United States Naval Sea Cadet Corps is a federally chartered, non-profit, civilian, youth training organization for young people, ages 13-17. With a 2004 registered enrollment of 10,625 Cadets in 287 Sea Cadet and 87 League Cadet units operating in 47 states, Puerto Rico, Guam, and Iceland, the Corps is sponsored by the Navy League and supported by the United States Navy, Marine Corps, and Coast Guard as well as corporate, memorial, individual, and special friends.[19]

Summer training programs for both Sea Cadet and League Cadet units are funded primarily through a Congressional grant included in the annual Defense Appropriations Bill; for 2005, the grant totaled $1.7 million.[20]

The Naval Sea Cadet Corps is an organization dedicated to helping American youth achieve personal success. As stated in the *2004 Annual Report*, its goals are:

* To develop an interest and ability in basic seamanship and seagoing skills.
* To instill the virtues of good citizenship and strong moral principles in each Cadet.
* To demonstrate the value of an alcohol-free and gang-free lifestyle.
* To make each Cadet aware of the prestige of a military career and increase the advancement potential of those who serve.

The organization allows teenagers to experience military life and develop skills in basic seamanship and its naval adaptations. Sea Cadets are exposed to a broad range of subjects designed to develop the "whole person" concept. They have numerous opportunities to participate in hands-on training in active duty and reserve Navy and Coast Guard ships, shore activities, and training commands. Although most Sea Cadet training and activity is conducted in a naval environment, absolutely no future sea service or any armed service obligation is required because of participation in the program. The United States Naval Sea Cadet Corps is an educational, not a recruiting, program.

From the perspective of a near half-century, the success of the Naval Sea Cadet Corps has been an enduring "bright and shining moment" for the Navy League. James Ward, Sea Cadet Corps national chairman in 2003, has observed, "Thanks to the assistance provided by all branches of the U.S. military, including the reserve components, and to the hard work and dedication of hundreds of highly motivated and supremely qualified adult leaders, the Naval Sea Cadet Corps training today is the most sophisticated youth-development program in the nation."[21]

In a letter to the Navy League in 1991, Master Chief Petty Officer of the Navy Duane Bushey, the senior enlisted person in the service, noted the value of the Naval Sea Cadet Corps to the nation:

> Knowledge gained in the Sea Cadets prepares these young adults for a possible naval career but, more importantly, it prepares them for success in any profession. Their training instills values, integrity, responsibility, and accountability ... I can think of no better program to prepare American youth to be future leaders of our country. Young people with the core of values which this organization instills are our biggest asset and our country's brightest promise of continued success.[22]

The Marine Corps Confidence Course helps Sea Cadets build strong bodies and learn the value of teamwork.

And not only has it helped thousands of young Americans become more patriotic and responsible citizens, it has also sparked many a Sea Cadet's interest in pursuing a lifelong career in the sea services; in 2005 7.5 percent of the midshipmen at the Naval Academy were former members of the Naval Sea Cadet Corps.[23] In their adult lives, many former Sea Cadets have assumed positions of leadership in their local communities and on the national level. Flag and general officers, businessmen, astronauts, national officers of the Navy League and other organizations, and numerous public officials at all levels of government have credited their Sea Cadet training as the foundation for much of the success they have achieved in their careers.

One of the most celebrated Sea Cadets was Navy Captain David Leestma, who served as both an astronaut and, following retirement, the National Aeronautics and Space Administration's Director of Flight Crew Operations. Interviewed in 1996, Leestma noted, "My time spent in the Naval Sea Cadet Corps was the beginning of this journey with the Navy that has been a lifetime experience."[24]

The training curriculum followed at local Cadet drill sites during the school year, oftentimes at naval and military bases, including National Guard and Reserve Training Centers, adheres faithfully to the organization's founding principles and operational philosophy. Sea Cadets and League Cadets wear uniforms similar to those worn by active-duty Navy men and women. At local drill sites they participate in a carefully selected variety of activities under the close supervision of Sea Cadet officers and instructors, and oftentimes by active-duty and Reserve naval and military personnel.

The local training includes both classroom and hands-on practical instruction in basic military requirements, water and small-boat safety, naval history and traditions, and various nautical skills. The Navy's *Bluejacket's Manual* serves as the basic instructive text throughout much of the training regimen. Through Sea Cadet leadership, the values of patriotism, courage, self-reliance, team work, and accountability are emphasized.

Not unlike the active duty armed services, promotions within the Sea Cadets are based on merit. Recruits enter as E-1s and upon successful completion of boot camp and other academic requirements may be advanced to the Seaman Apprentice rate (E-2). As cadets receive additional training, they may advance through the rate structure, eventually attaining the rate of Chief Petty Officer (E-7). Indicative of the effort required to achieve the Corps' highest rate, the 78 Naval Sea Cadets who were promoted to Chief Petty Officer in 2004 averaged 59 days of fundamental and advanced training with Navy and Coast Guard units nationwide. Each also passed the same Non-Resident Career Course required of their active duty counterparts.[25] In addition, all Corps Chief Petty Officers graduated from the Corps' own

USS *Ronald Reagan* (CVN 76) under construction at Newport News Shipbuilding.

Leadership Academy.

Summer training, required of all Sea Cadets after their initial enrollment, starts with two weeks of recruit training that, like all other Cadet training, is closely supervised by both Sea Cadet and active-duty Navy and Marine Corps personnel at bases, stations, and regional recruit training sites. In 2004 there were 19 Recruit Training Classes at 18 locations; these locations were required to accommodate the increased demand for quotas and to keep travel costs to a minimum. Over 2,500 Sea Cadets attended recruit training in 2004.[26]

After cadets have successfully completed their basic training, they are eligible to participate in more advanced training opportunities directly related to current Navy, Marine Corps, and Coast Guard active-duty assignments and responsibilities. These opportunities include Airman School, Sea-Air-Land (SEAL) Team

Training, Federal Aviation Administration Ground School and Flight Training, Amphibious Training, Seabee Indoctrination, Medical Training, Leadership Academy, and Submarine Orientation.

A total of 9,170 training opportunities were available to Sea Cadets in 2004. Although challenged by the large number of naval units forward deployed in the global war on terror, the Corps took repeated advantage of offers from other military hosts to provide resources and billets to facilitate Cadet training. Even with a large percentage of the Navy committed overseas, Cadet training spanned the spectrum from recruit training at traditional Navy "boot camps" to embarking in the newly commissioned aircraft carrier USS *Ronald Reagan* (CVN-76) and going from Norfolk, Virginia, to the ship's new homeport of San Diego, California, via the Straits of Magellan.[27]

As a member of the 18-nation International Sea Cadet Association, the United States Naval Sea Cadet Corps also participates in a highly competitive, merit-based exchange program. Cadets in 2004 were placed in Sea Cadet units in Australia, the United Kingdom, Sweden, the Netherlands, Hong Kong, Korea, and Bermuda.[28] A special program is maintained between American and Canadian Sea Cadets, with traditional exchanges conducted in Nova Scotia and British Columbia and, in the United States, in Norfolk, Virginia, and Fort Lewis, Washington.

In the mid-1950s, Navy League formation and sponsorship of the Sea Cadets helped to fill a void in programs available to America's youth. Similarly, when there were no effective Department of Defense programs to help career military people transition to civilian life after retiring from active duty, the San Diego Council initially created, and the League on a national basis subsequently implemented, *Operation Highline*, filling an important gap in the personnel area.

The League's local and national awards programs and annual Sea-Air-Space Exposition are renowned in their respective fields. League publications addressed to the general public, *Sea Power* and *Seapower Almanac*, formerly *(The Almanac of Sea Power)* are both internationally known and highly respected.

From the time of its founding, League membership has been proactive, public-spirited, and vigorously independent. One need only read the "Letters to the Editor" sections of the monthly publication *Seapower* to sense the bold, outspoken nature of members concerned with the well-being of the sea services. League members are not at all reluctant to criticize either an article's author, statements of an interviewee, or the "disappointing acquiescence" of positions taken by the League's senior leadership or editorial staff. Reviewing a selection of letters written over the last decade would reveal members' unequivocal concerns about shipbuilding, the size of the fleet, bringing back battleships to provide fire support for Marines, the demise of a dedicated mine warfare force, naval aviation, or the always tenuous state of the U.S.-flag Merchant Marine. The passing of Admiral Arleigh Burke in

1996 resulted in numerous sea stories and tributes to the man, as a warrior, diplomat, and bastion of the Navy League for his many years, from those who knew him personally as a friend or worked for him as a subordinate.

British military historian John Keegan believes two decisive factors determined the outcomes of both 20th century World Wars: America's industrial strength and the key role played by its naval strength in controlling the seas.[29] The Navy and the Navy League, together, shared in both those triumphs.

But in a new century, it remains to be determined if seapower will play as important a role as it did in the old. In 2005 new challenges confront the Navy League: increasingly fewer members of Congress have military experience in any armed service, the presence of the sea services throughout the nation is being reduced as bases, reserve centers, shipyards, naval stations, and supply depots are closed, and competition for the federal budget dollar, particularly in procurement and research and development accounts, is as keen as ever.

Not surprisingly, the nature of many of these challenges, in the broadest sense, is not unlike those confronted by the sea services themselves: How to carry out previous missions and responsibilities while at the same time transforming the organization to better meet uncertainties and challenges of a new era.

But challenges have been present since the League's founding. How and why the Navy League of the United States started, and how it evolved into the effective, fiscally sound and stridently independent organization it is today is a fascinating story that begins with men of vision and purpose at the turn of the last century.

Theodore Roosevelt Collection, Harvard College Library

Departure of Great White Fleet from Hampton Roads, Virginia, on December 16, 1907. Photo shows Edith Roosevelt to the immediate left of Theodore Roosevelt, daughter Ethel third from right.

Chapter II
Building American Seapower 1902-1911

It was an age of optimism: America at the turn of the century. Progress was inevitable; technology in business and the home was on the march, making life better for all. In the 35 years since the Civil War, a predominantly agrarian country had vaulted from fourth to first place among the world's industrial powers. A loose collection of different regions had been woven into a united nation by expanding railroads, newspaper chains, mass production, and nationwide marketing.

Of this period, author Henry James would note, "The will to grow was everywhere written large, and to grow at no matter what or whose expense."[1] And that indomitable will to grow had seen the United States, at the close of the 19th century, engage, fight, and win a short war against Spain, a former European power.

The ability of the United States to so quickly and decisively defeat the Spanish on both land and sea, on battlefields more than 10,000 miles apart, shocked the world's great powers. Henry Luce's proclamation in the 1940s that the 20th century was America's came two generations late. In fact, the "American Century" began at Manila Bay when Commodore George Dewey leaned over the rail of USS *Olympia*'s pilothouse and called to her commanding officer, "You may fire when you are ready, Gridley." The battle of Manila Bay was the United States Navy's first fleet action involving iron and steel warships, and the paradigm for a new century, and the emergence of a new global military, as well as economic power, was set.

The horizons for a boundless America were now limitless. For more than 100 years, a regional focus had seen Americans conquer a continent. Now, at the turn of a new century, this focus had widened to a global perspective, with the idea that North America was but an island whose shores were washed by two oceans. From the American Revolution to the period following the Civil War, the United States Navy had largely existed to protect the homeland, albeit at times (in the well-known fighting traditions of John Paul Jones and Stephen Decatur) off far-distant shores.

John Paul Jones

Stephen Decatur

But now all had changed. The American frontier was "closed," and in its place had been forged an empire beyond the contiguous North American land mass. It was an empire created by politicians, businessmen ... and naval officers. Breaking free of its Civil War era mentality and technologies, and separate and distinct from the Army, the United States Navy had transformed itself at the turn of the 20th century into an instrument of diplomatic and military prowess extending and defining American interests throughout the Western Hemisphere to the farthest reaches of the Pacific.

From this new perspective the United States was particularly well suited for the exercise of naval power. With the energy of Manifest Destiny still present, farseeing eyes still looked to the west, far beyond the Pacific shore. In recognition of this fact, between 1883 and 1905 the U.S. government spent over $1 billion revitalizing the Navy. By the turn of the century, excluding the war years with Spain, naval expenditures were averaging $118 million per annum.[2]

With the 1901 death of William McKinley from an assassin's bullet, Theodore Roosevelt became President. As a former Assistant Secretary of the Navy, he had been responsible for ordering George Dewey to coal his ships in Hong Kong and be prepared, on short notice, to seek out and destroy the Spanish Fleet in the

"Control of the sea by maritime commerce and naval supremacy means predominant influence in the world."

Philippines in 1898. As biographer Edmund Morris has observed, Roosevelt "had acquired a fund of naval expertise unmatched by any politician in any country. It would prove a priceless asset when he began to deal with 'ships, ships, ships' again, as President of the United States."[3]

Thus, the impetus for accelerating development of the Navy gained an indefatigable champion in the Rough Rider. The new occupant in the White House was a fervent disciple of the principles and teachings of United States Navy Captain Alfred Thayer Mahan, whose seminal work *The Influence of Sea Power Upon History*, published in 1890, was required reading by heads of state of all the world's powerful nations, or those aspiring to power at the turn of the century.

Mahan's work was particularly popular in Germany, where it was fervently admired by Kaiser Wilhelm, his State Secretary Alfred von Tirpitz, and numerous German Navy League clubs; by the end of the first decade of the new century, Germany's Navy was second only to Great Britain's.[4]

The conclusion of Mahan's work unequivocally led its avid readers, including navalists worldwide, to the conclusion that an aspiring nation's future in the new 20th century lay in the sea:

> Control of the sea by maritime commerce and naval supremacy means predominant influence in the world ... [and] is the chief among the merely material elements in the power and prosperity of nations.[5]

Like Mahan, President Roosevelt believed in the offensive nature of naval forces, their flexibility in employment, and their particular utility as a tool of national power wherever and whenever the commander in chief decided to act in America's interest. For President Roosevelt, the United States Navy was, in essence, his oft-mentioned "Big Stick."

Within months of becoming President, echoing Mahan, Roosevelt spoke of the need for America to "build and maintain an adequate Navy" or "accept a secondary position in international affairs, not only in political but in commercial matters."[6] Serving, in effect, as his own Secretary of the Navy (as another Roosevelt would do three decades later), he wrote that since becoming President he had been "straining every nerve to keep on with the upbuilding of the Navy."[7]

In 1903 construction began on seven battleships, with more in the offing. Though ranked fourth in the world behind Great Britain, France, and Russia in ships built or being built (and notably ahead of Germany, though the Kaiser's Navy possessed more dreadnoughts of heavier armor and armament), the United States

Navy had more tonnage being built in shipyards than any nation but Britain. The precedent set by Europe's leading seafaring nations, particularly Great Britain and Germany caused considerable interest in the state of American seapower. Public support grew in favor of the formation of a civilian organization that would advocate the need for a strong, modern Navy.

Most of the preliminary work required for the formation of a civilians-only educational organization dedicated to the promotion of America's naval and commercial sea power was initially carried out by members of the Naval Order of the United States[8] meeting at the New York Yacht Club, the New York State Naval Militia convening in the wardroom of the *New Hampshire*, an old wooden ship moored at the foot of 26th Street in New York City's East River, and several U.S. Naval Academy alumni groups concentrated in the New York area. Not surprisingly, the idea that a group of citizens should join forces to form an organization that would lay before the American public and national leadership the rationale for a naval force adequate to defend the United States and protect the nation's interests overseas was encouraged by shipbuilders, munitions makers, steel manufacturers, and others.

A Companion of the Naval Order of the United States, lawyer, and Spanish-American War veteran Herbert Satterlee returned from Great Britain in 1902, where he had observed a civilian organization in support of the Royal Navy which called itself the "Navy League." Impressed by what he had observed, he urged the Executive Committee of the Naval Order's New York Commandery to undertake the formation of a similar organization.

In November 1902, Rear Admiral Albert Smith Barker, commandant of the New York Navy Yard, took up the subject in his address to the members of the Naval Order, who had gathered at the Yard for their annual meeting. Barker urged the Naval Order to help form an organization that would "enlighten the people and tell them what a Navy means to the country and what it ought to mean to them."[9]

There was no disagreement from members of the Naval Order, which appointed Jarvis B. Edson to work with representatives of other Navy-oriented patriotic societies and associations on a committee to explore the creation of a new organization, patterned after the British Navy League, that would promote the interests of the U.S. Navy and U.S.-flag Merchant Marine and educate the American people about the importance of sea power. After obtaining the support of the Naval Academy Alumni Association and the Navy Department itself, a committee met at the New York Yacht Club to draft a constitution for the new organization to be named the "Navy League of the United States."

The draft constitution of the League was both clear and precise. The League's membership would be organized into local "sections." Any five U.S. citizens living in any area of the country could form a section, and there would be no restrictions on race, gender, or political persuasion. To encourage the recruiting of members, each section would be permitted, in order to meet its own expenses, to retain 25 percent of the "national" League dues paid by the members of that section. Representatives from each section, one for every 100 members, who had to be elected by the members of that section, would meet annually to elect the League's Board of Directors and to determine League policy on major naval issues.

Any American could join the Navy League, except for naval or military personnel on active duty and members of Congress. Members of those two groups were barred from the organization for their own protection and to preclude a conflict of interest in League policy decisions. The Board of Directors, having jurisdiction over execution of policy, was empowered to appoint the League's officers and employees as well as an Executive Committee which would act for the Board when it was not in session. The Board could also create other committees considered necessary for fulfillment of its mission.

The League's Certificate of Incorporation and bylaws, largely drafted by Satterlee, were presented in late December 1902 to the Secretary of State of the State of New York. But with the year-ending holiday, state business was not being conducted, so the Certificate of Incorporation and bylaws were not signed, filed, and recorded by New York's Deputy Secretary of State until January 2, 1903.[10]

On January 15, 1903, the League's incorporators formally adopted the League's constitution and appointed the organization's initial Board of Directors, which would serve until the League's first national convention. A week later the Board elected Benjamin F. Tracy, former Secretary of the Navy, as President, and William G. McAdoo, a former Assistant Secretary of the Navy, as Vice President.

Tracy, a U.S. attorney in Brooklyn and a brigadier general in the Union Army during the Civil War, was no novice at naval affairs. He had displayed a quick grasp of the principles of seapower as enunciated by Alfred Mahan while serving as Secretary of the Navy in the administration of President Benjamin Harrison. Tracy had little need to be taught the efficacy of seapower. He had long been a strong advocate of an "armored battleship Navy" and the Navy adopting a Mahanian "fighting" rather than defensive position on sea control. His first annual report as Secretary of the Navy, in November 1890, had called for the construction of 20 armored battleships to "beat off the enemy's fleet on its approach." Writing at the same time as Mahan, but before the latter had been published to world acclaim, Tracy decided that the American way of war at sea, "though defensive in princi-

USS *Kearsarge* (BB-5)

ple, may be conducted most effectively by being offensive in its operations."[11]

Navalists were heartened by the creation of a new patriotic organization headed by one of the nation's top navalists. But despite a well-known and nationally respected "big-Navy man" heading an organization whose principal purpose would be to educate the American people about the continuing need for naval and mercantile sea power, the birth of the Navy League went virtually unnoticed by the press.

Armin Rappaport, in his study of the organization's first 50 years, *The Navy League of the United States*, noted that the organization's arrival on the national scene could not have been timelier:

> Complacency had already set in. The spirit of Manifest Destiny ... [that] had been responsible for prewar congressional interest and popular support of the new Navy had subsided. Sentiment had again to be aroused, and the public made aware of the continued need for maintaining the Navy's strength ... [and] here was the League to do the job.[12]

Assuming that their own pro-Navy views coincided with those of the White House, League leadership focused on Congress as its first educational target. In addition to dealing directly with individual members of Congress, the League's founders believed that an equally effective way to influence members of Congress would be through the American people.

Moving quickly, the new national officers, by then operating from the League's first national headquarters at 32 Broadway in New York City, began issuing pamphlets articulating the need for a strong Navy. In July 1903, the inaugural issue of *The Navy League Journal* was published. Its first page contained a photograph of Theodore Roosevelt and its second page was a copy of the congratulatory letter from President Roosevelt to the Navy League's first National President.

Writing nine decades later, Navy League National President William C. Kelley would note the vision and intent Roosevelt had for the nascent organization:

> As President, Roosevelt recognized the need, particularly in a democratic nation where civilian control of the military is a key political tenet, for a civilian educational organization to serve as the link between the military and civilian communities, and he envisioned the Navy League as the ideal organization to provide that needed bridge of understanding and communication.[13]

Within the first six months of the League's founding, 13 League councils had been formed, from New York City to Seattle, Washington, validating the League's goal to serve as a national organization. By October 1903, 10 new councils had been added and it appeared that the organization was on firm footing.

However, the League's national officers grossly overestimated their own salesmanship abilities and the spontaneous generosity of shipbuilders and suppliers as well as other companies that stood to profit financially from the building of a bigger and more powerful Navy. Mistakenly, League founders "confidently looked," Rappaport notes, "to a membership of 20,000 by the year's end" and even "dreamed of two million [members] in five years."[14]

The reality fell significantly short of expectations. By the end of its first year of operations the League had only 166 members and a cash balance of $537.71.[15] In sharp contrast, the German Navy League in 1900 had a membership of 566,000, more than 1,000 branches, and an operating budget of $200,000.[16]

Navy League of the United States membership increased slowly over the next several years. The cost of publishing and distributing the *Journal* consumed most of the League's operating revenues, leaving little for pamphlets, broadsides, and the other educational materials planned.

Meanwhile, pacifists, anti-imperialists, and "small-Navy" advocates opposed to the Navy League's aims and goals grew stronger and more politically influential. League leaders and other navalists sought to counter arguments in favor of a constrained naval building program by pointing out that almost every President since George Washington had advocated the building and maintaining of a naval force strong enough to defend the United States against foreign invasion or other aggressive sea-based actions.

Theodore Roosevelt, naturally, continued to point out that a nation's naval/military strength was not necessarily an indication of aggressive intentions. "A good Navy," he summarized, "is not a provocative of war. It is the surest guaranty of peace."[17] Aware of the importance of the Japanese victory over the Russian Baltic Fleet in May 1905 in the Tsushima Strait, Roosevelt's interest in the state of the American Navy was accentuated. Upon learning the extent of the victory, the President wrote a congratulatory letter to a Japanese diplomat, asserting that "neither Trafalgar nor the defeat of the Spanish Armada was as complete."[18] Then, in a subsequent missive to Secretary of War William Howard Taft written the same day, Roosevelt voiced a longer range concern:

> It seems to me this country must decide definitely whether it does or does not intend to hold its possessions in the Orient ... If we are not prepared to build and maintain a good sized Navy ... and ... establish a strong and suitable base ... in the Philippines, then we had better give up the Philippines entirely.[19]

Roosevelt's continued advocacy of the Navy remained undiminished,particularly given the evident rise in the maritime power of Japan. By 1906, three out of every four capital ships in the Navy had been built since the Spanish-American War. Congress had authorized construction of 31 new ships, including 10 battleships. The United States Navy now ranked third in the world in terms of tonnage. Reviewing a naval formation three miles long from his yacht *Sanguis* in September 1906 in Long Island Sound, the President turned to a companion and exclaimed, "By George! Doesn't the sight of those big warships make one's blood tingle?"[20]

The Great White Fleet in Long Island Sound

But Roosevelt's unrestrained enthusiasm for naval affairs was failing to transmit into power, influence, and most importantly, funding, for the new organization. Except for publishing in *The Navy League Journal* Roosevelt's statements on the need for a strong Navy, the League did little to distinguish itself during its early years. Finances remained a major problem. League income in 1905, its third full year of operation, was a meager $6,155.57, almost all of which was used for administrative expenses, publication of the *Journal*, and the salary of a secretary.

The League also suffered from structural and leadership problems. Although a national organization, most of the League's sections were concentrated on the Atlantic and Pacific coasts. There were very few members in the heartland. Moreover, by late 1905 exertions on behalf of the League had taken their toll on Benjamin Tracy. Recognizing the need for new and more vigorous leadership, the Board of Directors met in November and elected Horace E. Porter National President.[21]

Porter, extremely energetic, made a number of moves to put the League back on course, the most important of which was scheduling the League's first national convention in Washington, D.C., in December 1905. Attendance was light, but 11

Navy League President Horace E. Porter

councils did send representatives who took several actions to improve League fortunes. The first was the appointment of three new committees: ways and means, press and banquet, and legislation. The second was the appointment of a salaried "organizer" to travel throughout the country to recruit new members. The third was to endorse two bills that had been drafted by the Navy Department and were under consideration on Capitol Hill. One would organize a Naval Reserve; the other would increase the size of the naval militias that already had been formed in many states.

The principal speaker at the first Navy League National Convention was Secretary of the Navy Charles J. Bonaparte. Delegates were invited to the White House, where they were warmly greeted by President Roosevelt. It appeared to be a new beginning for the organization.

But appearances were deceiving. The League's financial misfortunes continued. Recruiting of new members continued to fall below expectations. So did advertising revenues from the *Journal*, which was discontinued after the December 1906 issue. Complementing these organizational challenges, the League failed to garner public and congressional support for both a larger shipbuilding program and passage of personnel legislation of particular importance to the Navy.

The test came at the League's second Annual Convention in February 1907, again in Washington. The attendees, 150 delegates representing 79 councils, again approved the personnel and shipbuilding resolutions, and one supporting a subsidized merchant marine. To establish a sounder financial footing, a levy of annual assessments on League councils was approved to help meet the organization's overhead expenses. To ensure that the Board of Directors remained aware of the concerns and sentiments of the organization's membership at large, an advisory council was created composed of representatives of councils throughout the country. President Roosevelt delivered the closing address, in which he both congratulated the League for its patriotism and urged them to return home and "put pressure on their congressmen" to pass the administration's program.

The President's vote of confidence was much appreciated by the convention attendees, but they could do almost nothing to carry out the mandate given them. With no magazine, and only $200 remaining in the treasury, the League was in no position to start the national campaign needed to influence Congress. In the end, on Capitol Hill the personnel bill was not even considered and no funding was provided to build the one battleship that had been authorized.

Additional setbacks followed. Despite Roosevelt's December 1907 dispatch of the Great White Fleet, (16 first-class battleships, "348,000 tons of white-painted armor and gunmetal ready to sail at his command"[22]), to circumnavigate the globe as a showcase for the United States and its Navy, his naval personnel and ship construction programs continued to languish on Capitol Hill. The Navy League, nearly broke and dispirited, held no national convention and issued no press releases. An unofficial substitute for the recently deceased *The Navy League Journal, The Navy,* an independent monthly, proved so embarrassing in its news coverage and editorial positions on issues affecting the Navy Department that League leadership felt compelled to sever its connection with the magazine. The *Army and Navy Journal,* a leading publication of the era, noted "the melancholy breakdown of the ambitious project to form a United States Navy League."[23]

Organizational and fiscal adjustments continued into 1908. The League was plagued by a near continual lack of sufficient fiscal resources; there was neither an annual convention nor any press releases. Rappaport, reviewing the League's first six years, rendered a caustic verdict: "The record of achievement was negative; the confidence and expectations of well-wishers had been betrayed."[24]

But throughout 1908 the League's treasury began to be slowly replenished by voluntary contributions from several wealthy members. A "Founders' Fund" was established to purchase a headquarters building which would both eliminate the rental burden and significantly raise the organization's prestige with the general public.

By 1909 the League's reputation was largely restored. President Porter, representing the United States at the Second Hague Conference, became convinced that the European powers were drifting toward war. Returning to the United States and desirous that the Navy League play a role in alerting the nation to the need for naval and military preparedness, Porter initiated a series of actions recommitting the League to its original goals.

In February 1909 the League sent hundreds of copies of a letter to newspaper and magazine editors throughout the country explaining the need for congressional approval of the Navy Department's personnel bill, which President Roosevelt had again submitted. The letter was complemented by a circular, sent to every League council, which explained the purpose of the bill and asked for signatures on a resolution of approval that would be presented to Congress.

A new field director was hired to direct a more effective membership recruiting program, funds were provided to send retired Rear Admiral Robley Evans, who had commanded the Great White Fleet on the first leg of its around-the-world cruise, on a cross-country lecture tour, and the dates and venue for that year's League convention were changed to February in Fort Monroe, Virginia, to coincide with the fleet's return to Hampton Roads.

Theodore Roosevelt Collection, Harvard College Library

President Theodore Roosevelt addresses the crew on board USS *Connecticut*, (BB-18) the flagship of the Great White Fleet, on February 22, 1909, in Hampton Roads, Virginia.

Navy League members were present February 22, 1909, when 28 ships of the Great White Fleet returned from their around-the-world voyage. Exclaiming to onlookers from his Presidential yacht *Mayflower* that "I could not ask a finer concluding scene for my administrations," President Roosevelt went aboard the fleet's flagship USS *Connecticut* (BB-18) and told the assembled sailors, "You, the officers and men of this formidable fighting force, have shown yourselves the best of all possible ambassadors and heralds of peace."[25]

And, like the sea service they were supporting, thanks largely to the changes instituted by Porter, the Navy League was beginning to have an impact of its own. Rear Admiral Charles Sperry, having turned over command of the Great White Fleet, was now commander of the Navy's Atlantic Fleet and told the convention attendees that, "Unless we have a Navy League which will create and formulate and consolidate ... public sentiment, you may be sure that the Navy will not live long."[26]

The best evidence of the League's growing power to influence national issues was that it became a convenient target for pacifist and anti-imperialist groups. The New York Peace Society branded the Navy League as being filled with "the most dangerous set of men since the oligarchy of slaveholders in the fifties."[27] But the League pushed on, expanding the scope of its own promotional activities, mailing a summary report of that year's convention to the nation's major newspapers, and following up with a short booklet entitled *Patriotic Reasons for the Navy League of the United States*.

The widely distributed booklet was the League's first major promotional effort on its own behalf. It spelled out, concisely and persuasively, the principal goals of the Navy League: The building and maintaining of "an adequate Navy, economically administered, with a strong merchant marine and militia in reserve"; a "continuing and consistent" naval shipbuilding program; and an improved system for the promotion of officers and the living and working conditions of enlisted personnel. It also issued a call for "all citizens, those living in the interior of the

Theodore Roosevelt Collection, Harvard College Library

Review of North Atlantic Squadron from Presidential yacht *Mayflower*, from left: Admirals Brownson, Davis, Evans, Theodore Roosevelt's secretary Wm. Loeb, Theodore Rooselvelt, Secretary of the Navy Bonaparte. September 3, 1906, Oyster Bay.

country as well as on the seacoasts," to join the Navy League.

The League was equally vigorous and imaginative in its efforts to recruit new members, retain current ones, and reinvigorate the organization. Councils were encouraged to meet more frequently and to host dinners to which citizens representing a broad section of the local community would be invited. Circulars were sent to a select list of local and nationally prominent civilians inviting them to join the Navy League. Reproductions of an endorsement from Roosevelt's successor, William Howard Taft, were attached to all circulars.

Additionally, League leadership consolidated some of the smaller councils, and established a new council attached to the national headquarters; distributed copies of *Patriotic Reasons* to a carefully compiled list of 5,000 citizens throughout the United States; and prepared and distributed approximately 40,000 copies of three educational pamphlets, *Why a Strong Navy, Naval Program for 1909*, and *President Roosevelt's Message on the Four Battleships*, along with a chart showing the comparative naval strength of the United States and the world's other naval powers.

By the end of the year the League had gained an additional 1,318 members, the "Founders' Fund" showed a net increase of almost $13,000, and the *New York Herald* commented editorially that, "after a long period of inaction," the League "seems to be infused with a new life and its latest efforts to create a sympathetic practical interest in our Navy are at last meeting with encouraging success."[28]

In 1910, the League distributed a new pamphlet, *Is a Strong Navy a Guarantee of Peace?* League members sent hundreds of letters to congressmen and senators urging increased funding for the Navy's shipbuilding program.

But despite such efforts, victories accomplished as a result of the League's efforts in the final two years of Roosevelt's second term, and Taft's four-year presidency, were modest at best. True, by 1907 the Navy had 20 battleships, but so few smaller combatants that many navalists viewed it as "top-heavy." But opposition even to this number of ships and attendant naval expenditure was considerable. Some insisted that the very fact that the United States was building up the size and capabilities of its Navy would compel other nations to follow suit.[29] Others argued that expenditures as large as those requested by the Navy would bankrupt the nation and were not needed because the United States was unlikely to go to war at any time in the foreseeable future.

There was no clear-cut victor in the pamphlet battle and war of words, but the greatest obstacle proponents of a "big Navy" faced was the traditional isolationism of the American people and the belief that the Atlantic and Pacific Oceans were a sure guarantee against foreign entanglements. Despite concerns expressed by many of the inevitability of a European conflict, most Americans believed that if war were to break out, it would be confined to that continent and its colonial empires and, except for a few minor inconveniences, certainly not involve the United States.

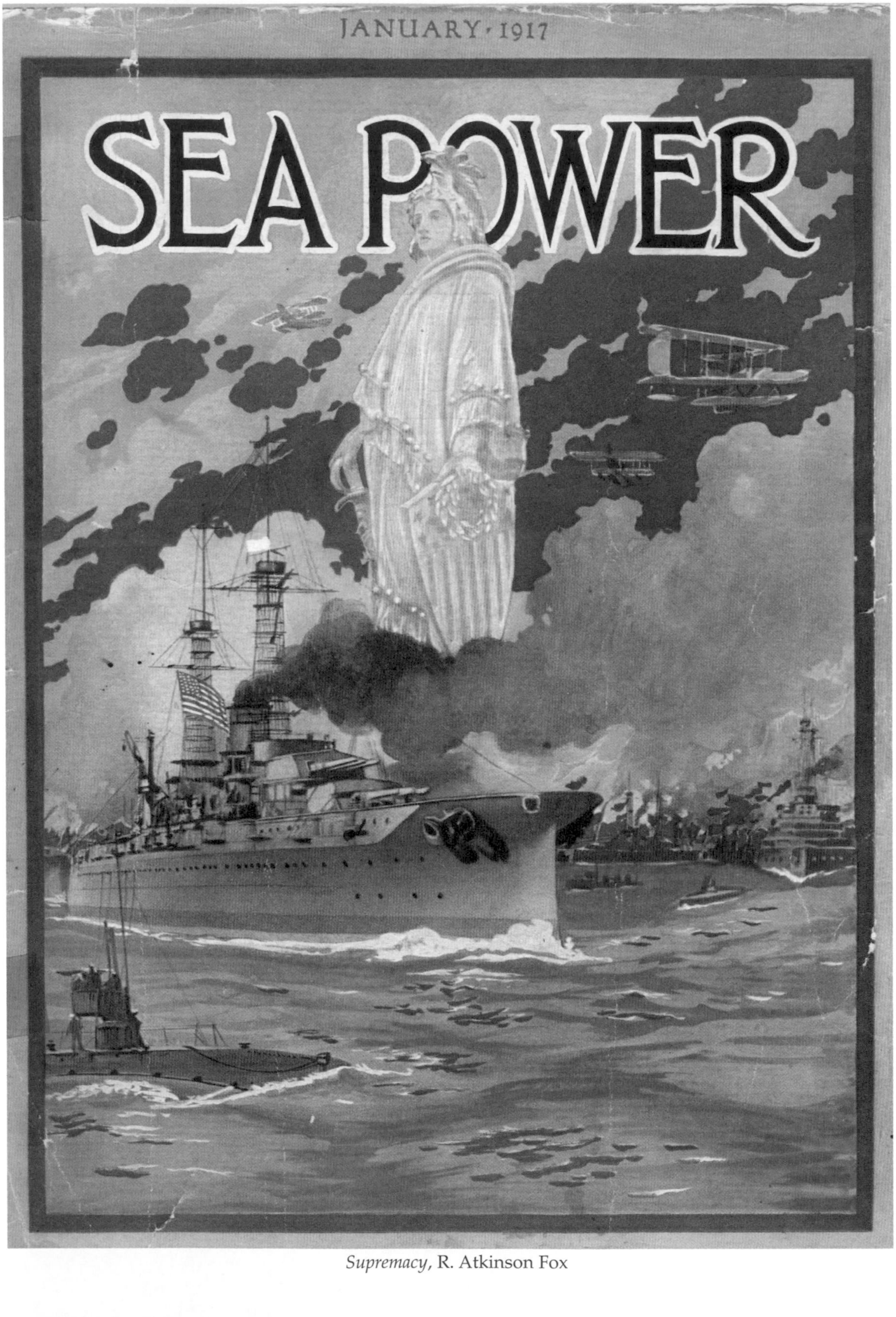

Supremacy, R. Atkinson Fox

Chapter III
American Seapower and World War, 1912-1918

The years 1912-15 marked the turning of the tide of political and public opinion in favor of those who advocated a more robust U.S. national-defense program in general and the building of a bigger and stronger U.S. Navy in particular. Such sentiments were clearly evident at the Navy League's 1912 Convention held in Washington and attended by both President Taft and former President Roosevelt; 33 states and the Territory of Hawaii were represented. The largest delegation was from the Pacific Coast "whose people clamor for an adequate Navy."[1]

The Presidential election of 1912 provided the first evidence that the long-running League educational program to convince Americans of the need for a strong Navy had been effective. As it did under Presidents Roosevelt and Taft, the Republican Party supported higher appropriations for national defense. The Progressive Party, despite protests from Jane Adams and other members, heeded Roosevelt's call for preparedness and endorsed the building of two major capital ships annually, plus an unspecified number of smaller surface combatants, submarines, and auxiliary ships. The Democratic Party's platform also advocated building a Navy adequate to meet the nation's needs. The party's defense plank had been drafted by a committee headed by Perry Belmont, a League member and former chairman of the House Foreign Affairs Committee.

Reassured by the fact that all three major national parties had endorsed a strong Navy, the League continued its traditional policy of nonpartisanship during the election year of 1912. It rejected a request from Roosevelt's campaign managers that the organization support the former President in his bid to return to the White House.[2]

President Woodrow Wilson

Woodrow Wilson, who emerged triumphant in the election, recognized the need for national preparedness and in the first term of his presidency things went reasonably well from the Navy League's point of view. Among the principal speakers at the League's eighth annual convention in April 1913 was the new Assistant Secretary of the Navy, Franklin Delano Roosevelt, who urged the attendees to continue their efforts to build a stronger and more effective fleet. It was the beginning of more than a three-decade relationship between the League and one of America's foremost politicians ... and navalists.

The League continued its educational program into 1913. To rally support for, among other legislative items on its "highest-priority" list, a four-battleship naval construction program and a new personnel law, the League sent several pro-Navy pamphlets to a select mailing list of about 5,000 editors, members of Congress, other prominent citizens, and various libraries throughout the United States.

The League pamphlets pointed out that the recent effort, at The Hague in 1899 and 1907, to limit armaments through voluntary international agreements had accomplished nothing. Thus, a strong Navy was needed not only to protect the U.S. homeland but also to help maintain peace in general. The League substantiated the latter assertion by attaching to one of the pamphlets a list of the numerous occasions in which U.S. Marines and/or naval landing parties had restored order or prevented the outbreak of conflict in Central America and the Caribbean.

The League also launched a new lecture series, sending retired flag officers into dozens of major cities throughout the country to advocate a stronger Navy. One of the speakers, Admiral Richard Wainwright, added a ringing endorsement of the Navy League itself. "The only antitoxin for war," he told the Cleveland Chamber of Commerce, "is the Fleet, to be taken in doses of four battleships annually. And the most effective peace society is the Navy League."[3]

The relationship between the League and the introspective President was off to an excellent start. The organization's leaders took additional encouragement when, shortly after taking office, Wilson promised, in a meeting with a League delegation, to propose to Congress not only the new personnel law but also the formation of a national defense council which the League had long advocated.

While Wilson did not commit himself to a larger shipbuilding program, because of his previous statements he was already considered to be a "big-Navy" man. In addition, Wilson's new Secretary of the Navy, Josephus Daniels, had been an editor and publisher of *The Raleigh News and Observer* and had consistently supported Taft's naval policies.

Disenchantment set in, slowly but incrementally, when Wilson remarked only generally on naval affairs in his first annual message to Congress. Shortly thereafter, Daniels proposed, in his own annual report, the funding of only two battleships, eight destroyers, and three submarines. The Navy's General Board had recommended four battleships and a larger number of smaller vessels.

The Navy League swallowed its disappointment. Despite a feeling among some League members that the Secretary was in sympathy with the international peace movement, officially the League maintained that Daniels had limited his request to the maximum number of ships he thought Congress would approve. But the League did revive its speakers program and began serving as a clearing house for other groups and organizations seeking information about the Navy and why it was needed.

The wait-and-see approach the League took toward the new administration was reflected at a League dinner gala in April 1914 at the Waldorf Astoria Hotel in New York City. Present were guests of honor Secretary of the Treasury William McAdoo, retired Rear Admiral Alfred Mahan and Secretary of the Navy Daniels, who used the occasion to call on the League to continue its fight for a fleet adequate to carry out the missions it had been assigned.

The League continued soliciting support for the naval bill that eventually passed both houses of Congress. Providing funding for two battleships, six destroyers, and eight submarines, it was signed into law by the President on the last day of June 1914.

The tranquility of the summer of 1914 was shattered that same month, first by two pistol shots in Sarajevo, Bosnia, followed by a general mobilization of the major European powers and resultant invasion and war in August. The world would never be the same again.

Initially, as the war degenerated into a bloody slugfest and stalemate between similarly armed, equipped, and trained men, advocates of continued U.S. neutrality and non-involvement took heart in a conflict that seemed to be largely confined to the continent and remote outposts in Africa and Asia. President Wilson continually sought an end to the carnage enveloping Europe from the North Sea to the Mediterranean, hoping to serve as an interlocutor for peace negotiations between the Allied and Central powers. This was official United States policy and Secretary Daniels was ordered by the President to ensure all naval officers refrained "from public comment of any kind upon the military or political situation on the other side of the water."[4]

But such directives to officers in uniform apparently did not apply to the

Assistant Secretary of the Navy. Roosevelt publicly sided with those who advocated further preparedness, including the Navy League, and passed information to representatives on Capitol Hill indicating, contrary to administration claims, that the Navy was not ready for war. The majority of its second-line battleships were out of commission and 18,000 more men were needed in the fleet. When this information became part of a congressional investigation on the true state of national defense, with anti-Wilson overtones, Roosevelt feared he would be fired. Still, his beliefs were clearly in agreement with preparedness advocates, and in self-justification of his actions he wrote his wife Eleanor, "The country needs the truth about the Army and the Navy instead of a lot of soft mush about everlasting peace which so many statesmen are handing out to a gullible public."[5]

But that "soft mush" was swept away in May 1915 when the R.M.S. *Lusitania*, considered one of the greatest ocean liners afloat, was sunk off the southern coast

R.M.S *Lusitania*

of Ireland by a torpedo fired from a German submarine. The sinking of the *Lusitania* shocked the world and nowhere more so than in the United States, where 128 Americans were among the dead.

Within the Wilson cabinet, matters reached a fever pitch with the resignation of Secretary of State William Jennings Bryan. Almost immediately, the President asked Congress for defense preparations on a scale not seen since the Civil War, and the Navy was the first beneficiary.

With the pendulum of national consciousness clearly swinging toward "preparedness," the Navy League took the lead. It announced an ambitious educational program to rally the American people to the cause. Speakers were sent into all congressional districts considered to be weak on national defense or the need for a strong sea service. The League's four field secretaries were charged with organizing League state committees, supervising their operation, and meeting with civic and fraternal groups as well as with other defense-oriented organizations and associations.

League recruiting was helped significantly by these and other efforts. By the autumn of 1915, 21 state committees had been established, 3,000 new members had joined, and the presidents of 10 national women's organizations had volunteered to serve on the national board of the Women's Section of the Navy League.

Robert Thompson was elected as the League's third National President in August 1915, succeeding the aging Horace Porter. Signifying the increased importance of the League in national proceedings, Thompson purchased a Beaux-Arts mansion being built on the corner of Sheridan Circle and 23rd Street in Washington, D.C., ensconced in the diplomatic community of the nation's capital. With his move to the nation's capital, the center of League activity also shifted south with him.[6]

The new National President started a new round of vigorous activity with the formation of additional state committees and scheduling, in the last two weeks of November, 10 preparedness rallies in major cities stretching from Washington, D.C., to New Orleans. A campaign in Chicago in the first week of November featured luncheons, dinners, speeches, the showing of patriotic films, and a chartered train trip to the Great Lakes Naval Training Station, with a resultant gain of 1,000 new members.

In speeches, press releases, magazine articles, and films, League representatives hammered home the message that, in a world at war, the United States itself was in grave danger and had little choice but to build up its naval and military strength. The League's peace platform focused on the Navy as the principal guarantor of America's national security. That premise mandated the building of an oceangoing fleet second to none.

To achieve the second-to-none goal, the League said, would require a major sustained shipbuilding program spread over five years to give the nation a combat-capable fleet large enough to defeat the Navy of any potential adversary, legislation to give younger officers more command opportunities, creation of a Naval Reserve large and capable enough to augment the active-duty Navy in time of war or other national emergency, and the building and maintenance of a merchant fleet adequate to provide overseas support for the Navy's combat vessels.

The League's call for preparedness was echoed in numerous editorials in major newspapers and magazines, and in speeches by members of Congress and other citizens. It was repeated in policy statements issued by other organizations such as the new National Security League.

But success had its price and, as the most active and persistent of the preparedness groups, the League was accused of promoting militarism and supporting increased naval appropriations to serve the financial interests of its national officers. Automobile magnate Henry Ford underwrote a pamphlet called *The Navy League Unmasked*, and Representative Clyde H. Tavenner accused the League, during House debate on naval appropriations, of being "a general sales bureau for ...

[the defense industries]" and "a branch office of J.P. Morgan."[7]

At a much-publicized "great peace meeting" in Philadelphia, William Jennings Bryan, determined to keep America from drifting into war, accused the League's national officers of being "the paid agents of shipbuilders and munitions makers." In response, the League threatened Bryan with a libel suit if he could not substantiate his allegations; he subsequently retracted the charges. Wisconsin Senator Robert La Follette derisively referred to J.P. Morgan and other munitions makers as "dollar-scarred heroes who organized the Navy League of the United States."[8]

While Bryan and La Follette appeared to be genuine peace advocates, Representative Tavenner's credibility suffered severely when the League revealed that the Illinois congressman not only had expressed a willingness to call off his attack if the League would support a bill (which Tavenner had proposed) requiring the government manufacture of arms and ammunition, but also that Tavenner had been trying during that same time frame to have a government armor-plate factory built in his district.

Efforts against preparedness were addressed by the League's response that it was not a militarist organization and that its efforts were not a result of recommendations or support from the nation's shipbuilders and munitions makers. The League maintained that the principal difference between it and peace advocacy groups was that it was realistic enough to recognize that the simple desire for peace was not enough. That desire had to be matched with the willingness to maintain the naval and military strength needed to deter the outbreak of war.

In December 1915, President Wilson sent to Congress the largest appropriations bill ever devoted to naval expansion by any nation. Under the bill, which had the full support of the Navy League, by 1925 a "great Navy second to none" of 10 battleships, six battle cruisers, 10 light cruisers, 50 destroyers, 100 submarines, and 80 other ships of various types and sizes would be built at a cost of approximately $100 million per year.

Wilson campaigned vigorously for the bill, asking for support to build "incomparably the most adequate Navy in the world."[9] With no end in sight to the global conflict, the President's advocacy of preparedness measures was largely shaped by his desire that America's security be guaranteed in the future, regardless of who won the war. His support of the naval bill was not intended to propel America into immediate intervention in the war raging on the continent an ocean away.

Not sharing the President's sentiments, the League felt no similar restraint and created more state committees, arranged more speeches to diverse groups throughout the nation, and increased its fervent advocacy of the bill through press releases and articles in the League's publications.

The League did not limit itself to a war of words. It also organized a new Naval Reserve Committee, which helped create a pool of speedy yachts, motor boats, and trained personnel that could help the Navy in such tasks as submarine hunting, scouting, and convoy duty. It staged rallies, meetings, and parades in support of naval preparedness. It served as a clearinghouse for the background papers and other materials needed to refute pacifists' arguments. Its Women's Section planned and conducted National Service School courses to prepare women to help the American Red Cross in the event of a national disaster or other emergency, including war.

The results were significant, and statistically impressive. With an operating budget of only $50,000 the League distributed more than half a million pamphlets in 1915, held 349 national-defense meetings, and provided preparedness literature for an estimated 1,650 colleges, debating societies, and civic and fraternal groups.

The most important event in the League's naval-appropriations campaign was the 1916 National Convention, again held in Washington in April. An estimated 500 delegates attended, hearing professors, influential political leaders, and admirals speak for three and a half days on every aspect of naval preparedness. The 1916 Naval Appropriations Bill submitted by President Wilson was discussed, dissected, and debated.

At its conclusion, the convention endorsed a series of interrelated resolutions urging Congress to approve the bill as submitted by the President, authorize a special bond issue to help finance the shipbuilding program, abolish the volunteer system in favor of conscription, and legislatively create both a Navy general staff and a Council of National Defense.

The Washington venue guaranteed that, no matter what their own positions on the bill, most members of Congress would be fully aware of what the League was advocating. But the League was taking no chances. Every speech delivered during the convention was reprinted and circulated to members who had not attended the convention. The speeches were distributed throughout the nation to newspaper and magazine editors for use as background for news stories and editorials.

But opposing peace groups were also energized and the net effect of the League's efforts was less than expected. In May 1916, the House Committee on Naval Affairs released its version of the bill, recommending only a one-year, 42-ship construction program that included five battle cruisers but no battleships. The full House kept the battle cruisers but cut seven more ships, of lesser tonnage, before passing the measure.

Preparedness advocates planned a protest demonstration but dropped the idea because the League would not participate. The decisive voice was that of League President Thompson, who pointed out that the bill, no matter what its defects, was at least "a step in the right direction," and provided $125 million more for the Navy than had previously been appropriated for any one fiscal year.[10] Moreover, the House would not have the final say. The Senate had to weigh in with its version of the bill, and if there were any differences between the two houses, a conference committee version also would be needed. Meanwhile, the League and like-minded organizations would continue both their public and behind-the-scenes advocacy for a more adequate shipbuilding program.

The real tipping point in favor of the bill, for many members of Congress, and many editorial writers, was the May 1916 Battle of Jutland. Admiral John Jellicoe, commander of the Royal Navy's Grand Fleet, using his 37 dreadnoughts to good advantage against the 21 dreadnoughts in the German High Seas Fleet, fought 50 miles west of the coast of Denmark in what would be seen, with the benefit of hindsight, to be the decisive naval engagement of the Great War. While the battle itself was not fought to a decision, the German High Seas Fleet never again emerged to contest Britain's control of the seas.

www.firstworldwar.com

British Grand Fleet, 1914

The most important of the lessons learned from Jutland, in the view of the preparedness advocates, was that the battleship was still the most powerful weapons platform in any fleet. Thus, if the United States were to become a true world power it would need a world-class Navy, with world-class battleships.

What happened next in Washington was a victory beyond the most ambitious dreams of the preparedness groups: the Senate version of the naval bill, made public at the end of June, completely restored the Wilson Administration's naval program and reduced the original five-year timetable to three years. The House reluctantly gave in and the President signed the naval appropriations bill, the largest and most far-reaching in the nation's history up to that time, in August 1916. The three-year building program called for construction of 156 ships, at a cost of $600 million; construction of the first 66 ships was to start as soon as possible. Ten battleships and six battle cruisers were included in the program, with four of each scheduled for construction in the first year.

The Navy League received considerable credit for the Naval Act of 1916, which included, in addition to the shipbuilding program, congressional approval of several other initiatives the organization had been fighting for: establishment of a Naval Reserve, an increase in the Navy's personnel strength, promotion of officers by selection rather than seniority, and creation of a Navy general staff.

Although its major objectives had been accomplished, the League's leadership realized there still was much work to be done, starting with the rebuilding of the merchant marine. They also recognized that, despite the League's success in educating the press and much of the American public about the need for a strong Navy, like the shipbuilding program, the League's educational efforts had to be continuing, consistent, and indefinitely carried on.

Despite its tradition of neutrality in politics, the League printed, in *Sea Power*, a list of the members of Congress who had voted against the Naval Act of 1916. Several members so identified were defeated in that year's congressional elections. With Germany's announcement of the resumption of unrestricted submarine warfare in January 1917, President Wilson could no longer ignore Berlin's conduct. Calling Congress into joint session February 3, 1917, he announced that the United States was severing diplomatic relations with Germany. He did not ask for a declaration of war.

There was another tense month of waiting, during which several American merchant ships were sunk by German U-boats. Those advocating the United States remain clear of the global conflict stepped up their own efforts. But the Navy League and other navalists and preparedness groups, most of Congress, and scores of newspaper editors and other prominent citizens believed that war could no longer be avoided.

Wilson met with his Cabinet on March 20, and asked for their advice and recommendations. The feeling was unanimous. The following day, the President announced that he was calling Congress into special session on April 2 to discuss "grave matters of national policy."

On that day, with great reluctance but firm purpose, Wilson called for a declaration of war against Germany. Senate debate on the President's request ended April 5. Wilson signed the War Resolution that same day. While not apparent at the moment, America had reached a point of no return in its shift, first evident in the Great White Fleet circumnavigating the world almost a decade earlier, from isolation to international involvement.

On May 4, the six destroyers of Commander Joseph K. Taussig's Destroyer Squadron 8 arrived at the Royal Navy's base at Queenstown, Ireland. When asked by the British commander when his ships would be ready for duty, Taussig's reply, "We are ready now, sir!" became famous on both sides of the Atlantic. On May 24 the first American convoy sailed from Hampton Roads, Virginia, for Europe. On

December 7, 1917, five American coal-burning battleships (no tankers could be spared to carry additional fuel oil to the British Isles) under the command of Rear Admiral Hugh Rodman joined the British Grand Fleet in the North Sea. Three additional battleships were subsequently sent to Ireland to release Royal Navy forces for Britain's anti-submarine warfare effort.

Largely because of Navy League National President Robert Thompson's foresight, the organization had started its own preparations well before President Wilson had met with Congress to ask for a war declaration. After enactment of the War Resolution, the League signaled its readiness to sign on "for the duration." After meeting with senior Navy Department officials, the League agreed to take on two important assignments: help with recruiting, and provide comforts for sailors and relief for their families.[11] To carry out these tasks, a Navy League War Relief Committee was created to serve as administrative headquarters and provide continuity in planning and publicity.

Most of the work was carried out by the League's councils, each of which was responsible, in its home community, for recruiting for the sea services, caring for sea-service dependents, and providing comforts to young men serving in the Navy or Marine Corps. To assist in recruiting, foster local pride, and increase overall community awareness of the Navy and its needs, the councils also were urged to adopt Navy ships named for hometown heroes, or for the cities and states in which they grew up. This was the beginning of the League's ship-adoption program.

The League's World War I Navy recruiting program, announced on March 27, 10 days before the declaration of war, actually started with behind-the-scene preparations more than a month earlier. The League set 100,000 recruits for the Naval Reserve and active-duty Navy as the program's initial goal. League headquarters printed and distributed more than a million small stickers featuring a red, white, and blue banner bearing the words "Your Country Calls, Join the Navy" (a second version ended with the appeal to "Join the Marines"). The stickers were sent to

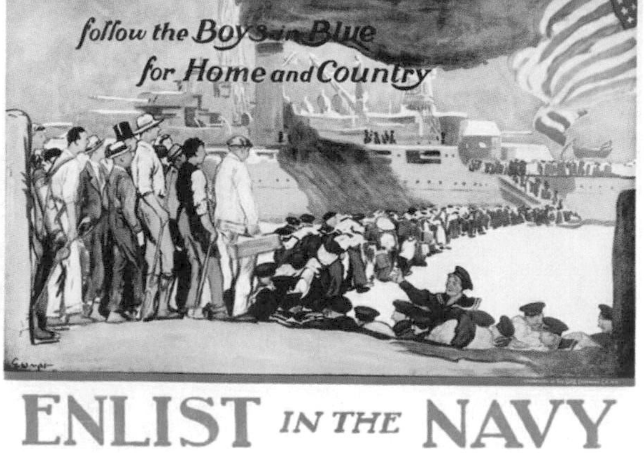

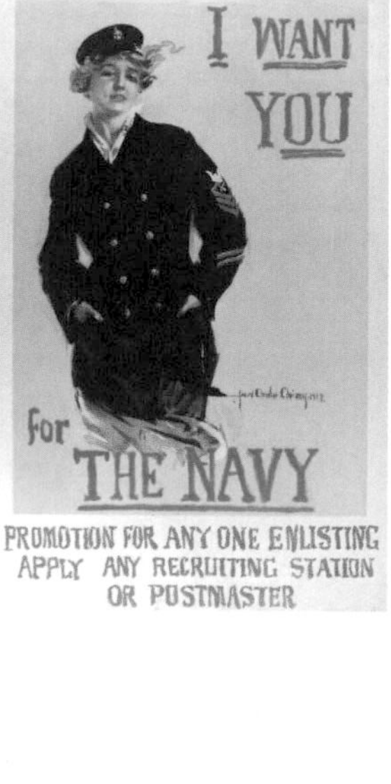

automobile manufacturers, along with a request that a sticker be put on each automobile leaving their factories. Insurance companies were asked to put a sticker on each of their policies. All League councils were given supplies of stickers for additional local distribution.

In addition, articles in *Sea Power* promoted recruiting, and extolled the accomplishments, not only of the Naval Reserve, but of the "corps of able women" serving at the Bureau of Supplies and Accounts and in other Navy shore commands.

The results of these and other efforts were impressive. As noted in the January 1918 issue of *Sea Power*, Navy officers assigned to recruiting duty in the Midwest told headquarters that the Navy League was responsible for 50 percent of the enlistments in that section of the country. Lieutenant Commander L.B. Porterfield of the Navy's Bureau of Navigation wrote that the service not only had "obtained and is obtaining recruits in sufficient numbers to meet its requirements" but even had to "suspend enlistments in certain ratings which are in excess." The assistance provided by the Navy League, he said, had been "particularly valuable" in the Navy's recruiting effort.

In the December 1918 *Sea Power*, another officer said that he had "almost despaired" of meeting his recruiting goal 11,000 men "from the Central Division [13 middle-western states]" so he asked the Navy League to help by "putting on a big publicity campaign." His request "was met most enthusiastically," he said, "with the result that ... the Central Division was the first ... to furnish its quota, although it is the only division without a seacoast."

Meanwhile, the work of the Navy League's Comforts Committee also was proceeding due to the hard work and organizational efforts of the national committee chaired by Mrs. James Carroll Frazer, who in June 1919 was elected the League's first woman Vice President. Members of the committee included Mildred Dewey, widow of Spanish American War hero Admiral George Dewey, and Eleanor Roosevelt, wife of Assistant Secretary of the Navy Franklin Roosevelt.

"If you can't join the Navy, help the men who can—join the Navy League."

The principal mission of the Comforts Committee was to provide cold-weather clothing to the crews of Navy ships on station in the North Atlantic and to Marines on the fighting front in Europe. Mrs. Dewey initially headed up the knitting program, and it was one of the major donation successes of the war. The comfort items provided by the Navy League and other patriotic organizations during World War I gave the men on the fighting front, on the high seas as well as in the trenches, a much appreciated extra margin of warmth, health, and safety. Sweaters, scarves, gloves, and watch caps, none of which were routinely provided by the government, at no cost to the individual soldier, sailor, or Marine, were among the principal articles of clothing needed by the

The principal mission of the Comforts Committee was to provide cold weather clothing to the crews of Navy ships on station in the North Atlantic and to Marines on the fighting front in Europe.

troops.

What made the work of the League's Comforts Committee even more important was that the mountains of clothing provided by, or through, the League to crews of Navy ships and to Marine units in France were not and could not be purchased on the open market. They simply were not available, except in limited quantities and at a very high cost. Instead, they had to be personally knitted, item by item, by Comforts Committee volunteers throughout the United States and overseas.

During the 19 months that the United States was an active participant in the war, more than 300,000 women (and a few men) were engaged in the massive coast-to-coast effort, to alleviate the Navy Department's own clothing deficiency. Working through its local councils, many of which had been formed specifically to carry out the Comforts Committee's mission, League headquarters distributed the standard knitting instructions needed, and provided free yarn to women who could not afford to buy it. The women involved represented a broad cross-section of American society and ranged in age from pre-teenagers to great-grandmothers.

Thanks to the League's advance planning, and the fact that a similar program had been started six months earlier by the women of England, an estimated 70,000 items of knitted clothing either had been made or were in the making only four months after America's entry into the war. By war's end, approximately 2,000,000 woolen garments of various types had been knitted by the League's women volunteers and distributed to young Americans fighting overseas as well as to French, Russian, and other Allied sailors.

In addition to the knitted garments, Navy League headquarters and individual

League councils purchased and distributed rubber boots, pea jackets, sewing kits, and recreational items such as books, phonographs, playing cards, and games of various types, as well as cigarettes, pipes, and tobacco. Tooth brushes, pen knives, pens, pencils, stamped envelopes, and stationery helped fill out the "Comfort Bags" that were prepared at the League's national headquarters in Washington and shipped overseas.

The work carried out by the Comforts Committee provided the League a national level of awareness and appreciation not previously enjoyed by an organization concentrated on both coasts and in the nation's capital. Thousands of letters of appreciation, generously supplemented by local and national news coverage, poured into League headquarters from ship and unit commanding officers, and individual sailors and Marines all over the world.

As reported in *Sea Power*, the Navy League Council in Paris, France, was asked to work in "close cooperation" with the French Navy League and to "send information regarding methods of affording relief to French sailors' families." In early 1918, French President Raymond Poincare presented France's Legion of Honor to the President of the Paris Council in recognition of "services in behalf of Franco-American relations ... since the beginning of the Great War." The League's London Council worked closely with the Navy League of Great Britain throughout the war, and was publicly commended by the victor of the Battle of Jutland, Admiral Sir John Jellicoe.

The League's patriotic work was not limited to the Allied capitals. It extended north to Canada, across the Pacific to Asia, and to the Southwest Pacific as well. As related in *Sea Power*, a League council was formed in Manila at the urging of the wife of the Navy's senior flag officer in the Philippines. The ladies of the League's Montreal Council solicited donations, from "every householder in the city," for sailors and dependents, and received "a considerable amount of money donated for this purpose." The Navy League was working "in perfect harmony with the Red Cross," according to a report received from Vancouver, British Columbia, and was shipping a large number of knitted articles to Montreal, "and from there to some naval base on the other side of the Atlantic." The Auckland, New Zealand, Council was praised by the American consul general for its work in creating and improving the "very cordial feeling existing" between the two countries. A letter received from Shanghai reported that "some of the sailors on board American destroyers in the war zone" were wearing woolen socks "knitted for them by 10 little slave girls of China." The girls had "found a home with the Slave Refuge in Shanghai," the letter continued, where the American woman who headed the Refuge had taught them to knit. The girls "were exceedingly anxious to have their work given to the American boys who are fighting freedom's battle," the letter said, "and these 10 pairs of socks represent their first contribution."

The League's other programs of support for the sea services continued as America's commitment in men and material to the war effort increased. To assist with the Navy's recruiting effort, League members drove young men to local recruiting stations. The League also established an "emergency driving corps" to chauffeur Navy officials around Washington, D.C., and other major cities. Women members frequently volunteered to drive trucks loaded with knitted garments and other comfort items being shipped overseas. They also sent clippings from local newspapers to ships at sea to show Navy men what was being written about them, and to keep them abreast of what was going on at home.

Navy Leaguers wrote thousands of letters to the young Americans serving overseas to keep their spirits up. When those who were wounded returned home for convalescence, League volunteers visited them in hospitals, took them home for special holidays, and hosted them on picnics, river cruises, and other recreational events. For sailors on shore duty and those on ships in port, League councils along the Eastern seaboard made arrangements for local baseball fields, golf courses, and other sports facilities to be available for use during off-duty hours.

The League effort was not limited to fun and games. The League established a Bureau of Legal Aid to provide counsel for sailors involved in civilian or military litigation and worked with the Metropolitan Life Insurance Company to establish an insurance program by which the dependents of sailors and Marines would receive $1,000 in the event of the death of the person insured. The League also supported Liberty Loan drives, featuring personal appearances of celebrities such as movie star Mary Pickford, throughout the country to help fund the Navy's ship-construction program.

Families of those in uniform were given special attention in several other ways. Local councils were encouraged to visit the families of personnel deployed overseas, to help family members of working age find employment, and to find nurseries for children of working mothers. Many councils provided cars and drivers to help in family emergencies, secured price reductions in local stores for naval and military families, and helped locate servicemen for worried parents and loved ones.

www.nhptv.org

Actress Mary Pickford made personal appearances to promote Liberty Loans designed to help fund the Navy's ship construction program.

The League also created its first formal youth program during the war years by establishing what was called "The Bainbridge Squad." The members of the squad, 27 teenage men from the Washington, D.C., area, drilled regularly, with wooden rifles, in front of the League's headquarters offices. Many of them helped out with various office chores. They wore homemade white uniforms similar to those worn by active-duty sailors and regular Navy insignia. The unit was disbanded after the war but several decades later served as a prototype for the League's "Buddy Program" and Naval Sea Cadet Corps of the 1950s.

Support activities directly related to the commencement of hostilities did not deflect the League from its ongoing responsibility to educate the American people, the nation's press, and the legislative and executive branches of government about the needs of the sea services. Press releases, situation reports, and updates on the state of the Navy and Marine Corps, pending legislation, and various national defense issues of special importance were regularly sent to all League members, educators, members of the press, captains of industry, members of Congress, and senior uniformed and civilian Navy Department officials.

League leadership also addressed several major national defense issues of considerable importance, mailing 20,000 letters to members and the national press in February 1917 to urge support for that year's naval appropriations bill, and following up with a nationwide campaign that resulted in the dispatch to Congress of more than 165,000 telegrams urging an increase in the Navy's manning level. The League took a bold stand on other legislation of both short- and long-term consequence. With a number of East Coast states lobbying Congress to station battleships in the approaches to their ports to forestall any German Navy attack on American soil, the League accepted the less-than-popular task of explaining the futility of a coastal defense strategy.[12]

The World War I work of the Navy League continued with hardly a break. "If you can't join the Navy, help the man who can — Join the Navy League!" became the slogan of the moment. In state after state, the League not only contributed significantly to the sea-service recruiting campaign but also helped maintain public, media, and political support for the overall war effort. The clothing and morale items provided by and through the League's Comforts Committee served as a tangible link between the American people and the sailors and Marines fighting the war "over there." Alberta Johnston Denis, later author of several books in the 1920s and 1930s, composed a march entitled *The U.S. Navy League* that included lyrics appropriate for the time such as "With your pocketbook o'erflowing, and your larder good and full, Just do without a dainty, and buy a hank o' wool ... "[14]

In Washington, mass mailings of the League's publications and pamphlets continued to spell out the need for a strong U.S. Navy, U.S. Marine Corps, and U.S.-flag Merchant Marine after the Great War was over. But these efforts required the mustering of all of the League's human and financial resources. And despite significant monetary contributions by J.P. Morgan, Charles Schwab, Henry Cabot Lodge, and several of the League's national officers, the League was deeply in debt even before the end of the war. By April 30, 1918, the shortfall was just over $39,000.[15]

But more than just fiscal problems were confronting the League. In August 1917, in direct contrast to its laudable efforts and achievements in the war effort, an increasingly acrid dispute between the organization and Secretary of the Navy Daniels threatened not only the League's World War I legacy, but prospects for its continued existence beyond the conflict.

Josephus Daniels

The dispute's principal cause was an explosion at the Mare Island Naval Shipyard July 9, 1917, in which five people were killed. The League was anxious, as were many others, to determine the cause. The United States had been at war with the Central Powers since April, and fears and concerns were rampant throughout the nation about the possibility of sabotage of America's nascent war effort.

It was well known that the German government was financing such disruptive acts as placing a bomb on a steamship, starting fires, creating incidents at munitions plants, and stirring up strikes at steel plants. It was in this context that the League issued an unofficial report based on "a communication from an official source" which treated the Mare Island explosion as a conspiracy and stated that "a dangerous softness was evident in the handling of labor questions by the Navy Department."[16] From the League's perspective, Secretary Daniels had bowed to labor union pressure to keep the Navy's investigation of the incident from public disclosure.

Daniels was furious, branding the League's report "false and slanderous." Incensed that the League would insert itself into what he believed was solely an issue for the Department of the Navy to investigate and resolve, in a statement released to the press, the Secretary maintained that the League's letter "shows a malicious intent to discredit the Navy Department and the capable officers who are doing everything possible to ferret out the cause of the accident and obtain evidence that would fix the responsibility."[17]

But Secretary Daniels's response to the League's report went far beyond an acerbic response for the nation's newspapers. He banned all League staff and volunteers from any Navy or Marine Corps installation, and in public speeches asserted that the League was in truth the "anti-Navy League" and its leadership irresponsible. In a letter to the National President, Daniels asserted that "the chief service which you and the other officials of the Navy League can render to the Navy is to resign at once."[18] In a particularly embarrassing move for the League, Mrs. Dewey resigned her position in the Comforts Committee. The situation did not improve when, in turn, League National President Thompson demanded Daniels's resignation.

At the same time, growing competition between the American Red Cross and

the League about how best to serve the families of U.S. fighting men left senior League leadership with the distinct impression that Secretary Daniels was favoring the Red Cross as the vehicle to distribute donations and relief, as opposed to the League. It was not a situation that augured well for the continued existence of the organization.

In late 1917 it was reported that the current leaders of the League would refuse reelection so that the rupture with the Department of the Navy could be repaired. Thompson's replacement as National President was rumored to be "Colonel" Theodore Roosevelt, providing, according to *The New York Times*, "that the organization no longer hide its light under a bushel, but continue openly to do the constructive and charitable work it planned to do at the outset of the war."[19] But at the National Convention in early January in New York City, National President Thompson resigned, to be replaced, not by the ex-President of the United States, but by W. Cameron Forbes. In his letter of resignation, Thompson stated his reason for resigning—"advancing years and physical infirmities"—and pointedly expressed regret that the Secretary of the Navy was continuing "his hostile attitude toward the League."[20]

This was a low point for the League, but it did not prevent or slow down any efforts on the part of the men and women of the League to serve the sea services. Despite its problems with the Navy Secretary, the League received thousands of letters and cablegrams expressing appreciation for knitted goods, books, money, candy, and hundreds of other items to make the terrible war a little more bearable.

As the war entered its final exhaustive stages with another German offensive in 1918, an emergency call from French hospitals for linens, bandages, and sleeping garments was received by the League. The Comforts Committee immediately responded with thousands of garments provided at no charge, prompting a surprising public compliment from Secretary Daniels praising the League's response. For its part, the Committee heeded counseling by Assistant Secretary Roosevelt to "sit tight, keep on knitting, and not rock the boat." Displaying the political flair that would eventually carry him to the White House, FDR made the point that the Navy Secretary's ire with the League was with its senior leadership, not the Comforts Committee or rank-and-file membership.

Regardless of its relationship with Secretary Daniels, in November 1918, at the time of the armistice, the Navy League of the United States was the most visible of the nation's preparedness groups. But appearances were deceiving, and with the war over, the League began losing members faster than it could replace them. The organization was to have difficult years ahead, threatening on several occasions to make the League itself one of the last casualties of World War I.

NAVY DAY
OCTOBER 27TH
In the air, on the surface, and under the sea, the Navy maintains the traditions on which it was founded. It will ever be Our First Line of Defense.

Chapter IV
The Time Between the Wars 1919-1940

The end of World War I found the Navy with a huge and balanced fleet, having expanded from 67,000 men when war was declared to nearly 500,000 men and women on Armistice Day. Support from President Wilson and Congress was evident with major expansion plans to resume active deployments in the Pacific and create a powerful West Coast fleet to offset newly-won Japanese possessions, former German colonies seized during the war. Many senior naval officers openly discussed prospects of a war with Japan; the service's first chief of naval operations, Anglophobic Admiral William Benson, argued that regardless of the war's outcome Britain was equally likely to be the major rival for naval domination after the war. From the admiral's perspective, the post-World War I British Empire was intent on dominating the world's seas and trade routes.

Benson clashed repeatedly with senior British political and naval leaders at the 1919 Versailles Peace Conference, so much so that it would later be called "the naval battle of Paris." President Wilson was sufficiently concerned that he summoned Secretary Daniels to Paris to attempt to defuse the acrimonious relationship between the heretofore "allied" naval leadership. He failed; Benson was adamant, in negotiating naval terms of the treaty, that the United States would not stop building its Navy until it was truly "second to none." He was hardly diplomatic in his characterization of Great Britain's designs: "In the future her sole naval rival will be the United States, and every ship built or acquired by Great Britain can have in mind only the American fleet."[1]

The League's national officers were encouraged by the administration's first postwar funding request for the Navy, which, when unveiled by Secretary Daniels in November 1918 continued the theme of "a Navy second to none" and called for the appropriation of $1.8 billion for the construction of additional warships of all types during the following three years.

It was not long, though, before the League's hopes that Wilson and Daniels shared its view of naval/military preparedness were disabused. In December 1918, with the war over, Daniels, bowing to fiscal and political realities, cut the shipbuilding plan almost in half, to $976 million.

The Wilson Administration was not solely to blame for the political/budgetary debacle that later evolved, and eventually resulted in the dissipation of much of the Navy's wartime strength, including many of its new-construction ships and most of its manpower. Navy leadership's ambitious plans for the fleet after the armistice, which saw it particularly useful in terms of long-term diplomacy and defense against future conflicts, failed to take into account the war weariness of the Allies and resurgent isolationism that again became a dominant political factor in the United States. In reality, regardless of the Wilson Administration's desires, the election of Republican majorities to both houses of Congress, combined with the end of the war and public demands to cease "unnecessary" spending, would have doomed any major new shipbuilding program offered by either party, even before the 1918 request had gone to Capitol Hill.

League leadership and other preparedness advocates had hoped that, because of the war, the nation's citizenry would be better informed in the fields of foreign affairs and national defense than it had been prior to 1917. It also had been hoped that America's elected leaders and the general public would realize that the United States could no longer view world events aloof and uninvolved.

Instead, pacifist and isolationist sentiments surged throughout the country. The once-promised millennium of world peace and a "world made safe for democracy" had not arrived. After the slaughter and privations of war half a world away, Americans felt their efforts and sacrifices had not really been worth it. And with President Wilson insisting on no modifications to his hard-fought peace agreement finally achieved in Paris in June 1919, in 1920 the U.S.

1919 Versailles Peace Conference

Senate twice voted against ratifying the Treaty of Versailles.

Notwithstanding its avowed non-political stance the Navy League provided considerable support to opponents of the treaty. Naturally the League itself did not publicly politicize the ratification process, but it did have an editorial observer in Paris for much of the time the treaty was being negotiated. Of particular concern was England's desire to maintain its position of having the world's most powerful Navy.

The latter condition was particularly difficult for the U.S. delegation to the Paris Peace Conference to accept. But the British had a trump card. If the United States continued to insist on carrying out its stated objective of building a Navy "second to none," England would not join the League of Nations.

In the end this argument was persuasive enough that Wilson agreed, as a compromise, both to "suspend work on the battleships laid down in late 1916" and "withdraw his request to Congress to complete the rest of the ... shipbuilding program" that had been previously planned.

The President's willingness to abandon the shipbuilding program resulted in a renewal of the previous Navy League antagonism directed toward his administration. The abrupt reversal on shipbuilding was too much to accept and was used by League leadership to remind members that they still had work to do. "A political policy that one day advocates 'the greatest Navy in the world' and the next day the abandonment of a matured building plan," editorialized the October 1919 issue of *Sea Power*, "exhibits the need for a body of public opinion intelligent enough to define and militant enough to require an adequate Navy and merchant marine. ... That is the duty of the Navy League, and it is as commanding now as it was a decade ago." Little more than a year later, in the November 1920 issue of *Sea Power*, the League continued the argument, noting that, "As to dollars and dreadnoughts, a Navy cannot be improvised overnight, nor in a month or a year."

Despite its unhappiness with the Wilson Administration's revised naval policy, the League did not, either as a national organization or through councils, campaign specifically against the Treaty of Versailles. However, it did report regularly, both in *Sea Power* and through letters to editors, and to members of Congress, what it perceived to be major flaws in the treaty.

One of the earliest and most influential in the series of *Sea Power* articles was one authored by Elihu Root. The former Secretary of the Departments of War and State discussed the pros and cons of the treaty in the form of an open letter, printed by the Navy League, to Senator Henry Cabot Lodge, chairman of the Senate Foreign Relations Committee. Root, while believing the treaty should be ratified for the sake of cooperation with America's allies in Europe, nevertheless expressed misgivings about certain provisions of the treaty that conflicted with U.S. constitutional law.

In the end, the United States did not ratify the Treaty of Versailles, nor did it join the League of Nations. But the Senate's rejection of the Treaty of Versailles was one of only a few significant victories in the 1920s for the League. In most other matters the League lost prestige and influence, many of its members, and several times came close to bankruptcy.

Within a year after the end of the Great War, the still-unresolved dispute with Secretary of the Navy Daniels had clearly taken its toll on the Navy League. When queried by Congress as to how long the Department of the Navy's ban on League activity would persist, Daniels replied, "until it is dead and damned and reconverted and we need it."[2] Membership plummeted, leadership grew increasingly disheartened, and by late spring 1919 the League's debt had grown to more than $138,000.

Former National President Thompson once more came to the aid of the organization. In exchange for a one-time $100 League good-faith payment to him, he assumed responsibility for the entire debt. Along with another major contributor, and future National President, Robert Kelley, he also pledged to contribute $20,000 for the following year's operations.[3]

But an even more ominous portent was the fact that one-quarter of the League's membership failed to renew their membership for 1920. Attendance at the organization's February 1920 National Convention was poor; with Secretary Daniels's sentiments toward the League well known, few senior officers and navalists were willing to invite the ire of the Secretary and attend events sponsored by, or in support of, the Navy League. The nation's attention was shifting away from armies and navies, and toward peaceful pursuits; the continued existence of the Navy League was in doubt.

With the election of Warren Harding and a "return to normalcy," naval disarmament soon became an overwhelming political force in both domestic and international politics. But by 1921 such was the dislike of Secretary of the Navy Daniels that the departure of the Wilson Administration was perceived to be good news, not only for the League's national officers and membership in general, but also for the senior leadership of the Navy and Marine Corps. The incoming Navy Secretary, Edwin Denby, had served on active duty in both services: in the Spanish American War as a member of the Detroit Naval Militia, and in World War I as a member of the Marine Corps.

The Navy Department and Navy League leadership settled their differences as soon as Josephus Daniels left office. The day after Warren Harding was sworn in as President, Denby was the guest of honor and principal speaker at the League's annual dinner. Two days later, he officially lifted the ban on Navy League access to naval installations that Daniels had ordered almost three years earlier.

Denby's actions did not represent a complete capitulation on the part of civilian leadership. The Navy League would "cooperate, not interfere," with the Navy Department, Denby commented, and although free to offer advice and suggestions, would "recognize the Department's complete supremacy in the carrying out of the country's naval policy." Denby was also increasingly of the opinion that the Navy League should be disbanded, believing that it had already accomplished the mission for which it was created in 1902.[4]

The change in political leadership in the White House and new civilian leadership in the Department of the Navy did little to reverse the course of affairs on matters of national defense. Denby played only a minor role at the 1921 Washington Conference on the Limitation of Armaments that President Harding convened during his first year in office. Portrayed as a Republican alternative to the League of Nations, the U.S. delegation to the conference was led by Secretary of State Charles Evan Hughes. The few uniformed and civilian Navy leaders permitted to attend were seldom consulted, and had little influence on the content and wording of seven treaties and 13 resolutions that were signed during or immediately following the conference. Writing more than three decades after the fact, World War I Army veteran and fifth cousin of Franklin Roosevelt, Nicholas Roosevelt, accurately captured the public sentiments of the moment:

Secretary of State
Charles Evan Hughes

> The Washington Conference was hailed by most Americans as inaugurating permanent peace in the Pacific. The Navy League and those few individuals who campaigned for a strong Navy were branded as warmongers, while the Harding, Coolidge, and Hoover Administrations allowed the Navy to stagnate. My own friends alternated between ridicule and indignation when I insisted that neglect of our naval strength exposed us to the danger of a Japanese attack.[5]

Of greatest importance, the agreement termed the *Five-Power Naval Limitation Treaty*, after specifying some exceptions, limited the total capital ship (battleship and aircraft carrier) tonnage of each of the signatories: the U.S. Navy and the Royal Navy could not exceed 525,000 tons, the Japanese Navy 320,000 tons, and the French and Italian Navies 175,000 tons; no single ship could exceed 35,000 tons and no ship could carry a gun in excess of 16 inches. The treaty required the United States to scrap four battleships already built. Significantly, the treaty also marked

Congressman Carl Vinson

the first time that Great Britain had conceded parity to any other naval power since the Napoleonic Wars.

To a nation tired of war and anxious to slow the naval arms race that many believed had led to the global conflict recently concluded, Congress agreed to the Five-Power Treaty and the destruction of 787,740 tons of Navy ships under construction or already in the active fleet. There were "numerous inequities in the agreement," an upcoming young Democratic Congressman from Georgia, Carl Vinson, pointed out to his House colleagues. Eleven of the ships that the United States agreed to scrap were from 30 to 45 percent complete, and already had cost the American taxpayers $350 million. "We destroyed ships which a prudent nation would have retained," he said. "We kept some ships that should have been eliminated." Vinson's views did not convince enough other members of Congress to make a difference, and the Navy lost the ships.[6]

The decline in fleet numbers was mirrored in the decline of the fortunes of the Navy League. In the final year of the Great War there were 9,350 members on its rolls. By 1922 the total had declined by more than two-thirds, to an estimated 3,100 members. With membership dropping precipitously and advertising revenues shrinking, the League was perilously close to bankruptcy and would have been in worse fiscal shape had it not been living rent-free at its new headquarters office in a building owned by former National President Thompson. Other leaders contributed, but not enough to reverse the League's perilous financial condition. An ambitious plan, conceived early in 1921, to raise an emergency fund of $10,000 by asking one hundred of the League's most loyal and affluent members to contribute $100 each netted an embarrassing total of $1,000; by mid-1921 the deficit had grown to almost $15,000.[7]

At a June meeting of the League's Board of Directors, National President Henry Breckinridge voiced his opinion that, having carried out its mission, the Navy League should disband. Signaling the seriousness of the situation, he submitted his own resignation.

The Board did not act on Breckenridge's dissolution recommendation, but did accept his resignation and elected financial contributor Robert Kelley as the League's new National President. But, reflecting its precarious financial state, League leadership also voted to cut the headquarters staff to three personnel and suspend publication of *Sea Power*, the principal drain on the organization's treasury.

Thus, the League lost its most powerful national voice, a situation not rectified for 14 years.

In lieu of *Sea Power*, and at admittedly less cost, Kelley and the League's other national officers closed the communications gap by writing and distributing—to editors, members of Congress, and League councils throughout the country and overseas—circulars, pamphlets, and press releases on important naval issues of the day. And, just as important as his large and frequent monetary donations, National President Kelley made another significant and long-lasting contribution by working with the Navy Department to establish, publicize, and support an annual day "on which the people of the country would be reminded through the concerted efforts of numerous patriotic organizations, of the Navy and its value to them."[8]

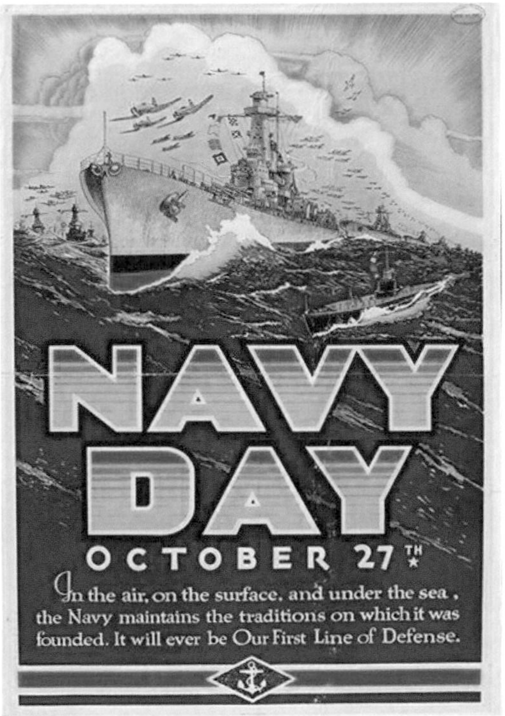

The first national Navy Day celebration, on October 27, 1922, a date selected because it was the birthday of former President Theodore Roosevelt, was chaired by former League National President Breckenridge and was a spectacular success.[9] Tens of thousands of Americans flocked to see the Navy on display. Navy ships hosted open houses in most of America's major port cities, as did Navy shore stations, both coastal and inland. Hundreds of newspapers and magazines contributed to the favorable publicity by using fact sheets provided by the Navy League to write Navy Day articles and editorials reaching millions of readers.

Although it was not a national holiday, Navy Day did receive special recognition from the President of the United States. In a letter to Secretary of the Navy Denby, and reflecting the painful cuts in fleet numbers being enacted by his administration under the terms of the Five Power Treaty, President Harding wrote:

> From our earliest national beginnings the Navy has always been, and deserved to be, an object of special pride to the American people. ... It is well for us to have in mind that under a program of lessening naval armaments there is a greater reason for maintaining the highest efficiency, fitness and morale in this branch of the national defensive service. I know how earnest the Navy personnel are devoted to this idea and want you to be assured of my hearty concurrence.[10]

The decision to cease publication of *Sea Power*, along with additional contributions from some of the society's wealthiest members, helped the League to weather the acute financial problems it faced in the 1920s. Nonetheless, the loss of thousands of members, and the revenue they provided, in the time between the wars caused serious damage, not only to the League's educational programs, but also to its efforts to help those serving their country in uniform. The extent of these losses is evident in the League's year-end membership numbers (see Appendix E). The organization's membership stood at what was then an all-time high, 10,700 members, at the end of 1921, but the next year plummeted to only 3,100 members. The year-end totals varied in a narrow range over the next 22 years, and did not again reach the five-figure level until 1944, when membership rose to 14,515 members.

In retrospect, the situation in the sparse decades of the 1920s and 1930s might have been far worse. The Navy League might actually have had to close its doors permanently, but for three mitigating factors: the annual Navy Day celebrations, which kept both the League and its educational message in the national spotlight at least once a year; the expansion of the organization's mission to include a broader focus on personnel matters and the nation's defense industrial base; and continuing League influence in Washington.

Navy Day celebrations lasted at least several days, and in some of the nation's larger coastal cities a week or more, usually when there were a number of major ships in port at the same time. The second Navy Day, October 27, 1923, was an even bigger success than the first. Fully supported by President Coolidge, who penned a letter citing the Navy as "the first line of defense," League National President Robert Kelley complemented this statement by issuing one of his own, noting that in contrast to then-current pacifist organizations, the League believed that the "way to maintain peace" was "to have sufficient strength to ensure respect of our voice in the councils of nations."[11]

Navy Day proclamations were issued that year by 31 governors and more than 100 mayors. Dozens of cities scheduled and carried out special commemorative exercises and activities ranging from parades and open houses to receptions and wreath-laying ceremonies.

In New York City, which also proclaimed Navy Day "Roosevelt Day" in honor of the man who was "always fertile in ideas for the improvement of the fleet and indefatigable in carrying them out," a *New York Times* editorial noted that the value of the Navy would not impress Americans unless, in the context of the Washington Naval Treaty, "the fleet shall be equal in armament, auxiliaries, guns, and personnel to the fleet of Great Britain. Nothing must be left undone to maintain this parity."[12]

In addition, an estimated 450 newspapers with a combined circulation of 20,000,000 carried major news stories and/or editorials, almost all of them favorable, about the U.S. Navy and its people. Using materials provided by the Navy

League, many articles and editorials focused on the need to maintain an adequate defense.

The consecutive success of two Navy Day celebrations persuaded League leadership that the organization had a future, and a membership drive in the western states was initiated as well as a fundraising effort to purchase a headquarters building in Washington. It would also house a research library for editors, reporters, and academics writing about naval history or contemporary naval issues. In July 1924 a building was purchased on Seventeenth and E streets in the northwestern district of the nation's capital.

The third annual commemoration of Navy Day, October 27, 1924, saw an estimated 1,000,000 Americans board U.S. Navy ships in Atlantic, Pacific, and Gulf Coast ports. From early morning to late evening the Navy occupied center stage in the national consciousness and was featured not only in newspapers and magazines but also on the radio, in theaters, and in high school and college classrooms. More than 500 newspapers featured editorials on the state of the fleet. All but six of them stressed the need for the United States to build the Navy up to the ship numbers and tonnages permitted in the arms-limitation treaties.

President Calvin Coolidge

When Congress reconvened in December 1924, the Navy League initiated publicity that sought to leverage the good feeling generated by Navy Day celebrations less than two months earlier. In a circular distributed to all members of the House and Senate, and to approximately 5,000 editors, the League commented on the annual report on the state of the Navy submitted by new Secretary of the Navy Curtis Wilbur. After noting the secretary's recommendations for building up the fleet's strength not only in ships, but also in personnel, the circular also illustrated, through the use of charts and tables, the superiority British and Japanese Navies possessed in almost every type of ship, particularly cruisers and long-range submarines.

The League release, timed to coincide with the congressional voting on that year's naval appropriations bill, was widely reproduced and commented on. It also was reprinted in the *Congressional Record* and discussed on the House floor. Newspapers throughout the country helped significantly by reiterating, in their own words, the League's rationale for parity with the British and Japanese fleets, America's two leading naval competitors at that time. The bill passed Congress before the end of the year and was signed into law by President Coolidge.

Similar campaigns, somewhat more sophisticated and with a slightly different focus, followed in each of the next two years. Recalling the price paid for disagreeing publicly with Secretary Daniels eight years earlier, in January 1925 the League was quick to distance itself from severe critics of the Coolidge Administration's efforts in defense. Refuting any League connection with one critic featured prominently in a *Washington Post* article, League Executive Secretary William Galvin wrote a letter to the editor noting that the League "prefers to rely upon a campaign of education which, if it err, shall err on the side of conservative statement."[13] After establishing there was no relation between the prominent critic and the League, Galvin stated the League's position on current fleet numbers:

> The Navy League is convinced that the United States Navy is far below the 5-5-3 ratio established at the Washington conference, but that situation does not call for alarm but merely for sane correction. The League stands by the Washington conference, in spite of the sacrifice involved. And it believes in carrying out the positive as well as the negative implications of the naval limitation treaty, namely, that the United States Navy be maintained on a basis of equality with Great Britain and five-thirds as strong as the Japanese Navy in every essential respect."[14]

In March 1925, the League distributed 50,000 copies of a thought-provoking new circular, *Insular America*, to state and national legislators, members of the cabinet, magazines and newspapers, Navy and merchant marine officers, leaders of civic and patriotic organizations, and 1,600 prominent businessmen. Authored by future National President William Gardiner, it asserted that, despite land boundaries with Canada and Mexico, the United States was an "island nation" dependent for its very existence on international commerce. Thus America needed both a U.S.-flag Merchant Marine, large and economically healthy enough to transport a reasonable share of America's exports and imports, and a combat-capable U.S. Navy ready at all times to defend the nation and protect America's overseas commerce.

During the summer of 1925 an event occurred internal to the Navy League that was to have repercussions for the next 43 years. Answering a position for a stenographer at a monthly salary of $75 at League headquarters was a nearly 17-year-old Washington native, Evelyn Collins, recently graduated from the Saint Dominics Business School. At this time there were but three permanent staff; with her hire, Evelyn became the fourth.

Although initially uncertain of working in an office filled with older men, she began a 43 year career, and her final job description listed 27 different responsibilities she had, "ranging from production of the steering committee agenda to advising the National President." Throughout good times and not, peace and war, Evelyn Collins was to earn the undying admiration, respect, and support of a legion of co-workers, as well as League and Navy leaders. (Her life's work in support of the Navy League is detailed in Appendix A.)

Navy Day celebrations for 1925 expanded further on the "island nation" theme. At luncheons, dinners, wreath layings, and other public ceremonies, Navy Department officials, members of Congress, and state and city officials expounded on the importance of America's foreign trade and the need for a strong Navy to defend it. Editorials and articles in daily and weekly newspapers and magazines carried the same message to millions of other citizens. In addition, a special one-reel film, *Don't Give Up the Ship*, highlighting the importance of merchant ships to the U.S. economy, was prepared by Eastman Kodak and shown to movie audiences throughout the country.

Those and other achievements notwithstanding, the lack of a monthly magazine continued to reduce the organization's overall effectiveness. So did the League's precarious financial situation. But League leaders found that pamphlets and other circulars, widely distributed and targeted to the most influential readers, could carry the same message as the magazine, at lower cost, and with almost equal effectiveness. Acting on that conviction, they wrote and distributed to members of Congress, the press, the cabinet, educators, and others, nine more press releases in the first six months of 1926 alone.

Each release focused on a different but important naval subject: *Tables of Comparative Naval Power*, for example, and the *Reduction of Armaments*. But they all stressed two major points. The first was that the United States should immediately build the additional ships needed, in all classes, to bring the fleet up to the levels set in the arms-limitation treaties. The second was that American security demanded the building and maintaining of a fleet equal in all respects to Great Britain's Royal Navy (and, it was implied, to the Imperial Japanese Navy as well). The League asserted that U.S. delegates to future arms-limitation conferences "should be governed by the fundamental principle of retaining adequate means for protecting the United States and its policy."[15]

The fate of naval aviation was also a subject of continual concern to the Navy League in the 1920s. When U.S. Army Air Service Brigadier General Billy Mitchell sank the German battleship *Ostfriesland* off the Virginia Capes in 1921, he asserted that airpower, not seapower, would become the supreme offensive weapon of the future. According to Mitchell, control of the seas rested in the air, not on the water's surface. Many naval aviators agreed with the broad outlines of Mitchell's argument. But his brash, headline-grabbing tactics and penchant for outspoken statements made enemies of many in the naval service, as well as his own Army chain of command.[16]

Ironically, in many respects Mitchell ended up being the unwitting godfather of naval aviation. Naval aviators used the results off the Virginia Capes to press for aircraft carriers and better planes, asserting that if the Navy did not develop this capability, Mitchell's air service would steal it from them in a land-only service orientation. Reacting to these concerns, the Navy established the Bureau of Aeronautics in 1921, the first new bureau created since the Civil War! Rear Admiral William Moffett was placed in charge, a position he would hold for 12 years.

Throughout this period the Navy League remained firm supporters of the development of naval aviation, aligning itself with Representative Vinson on the House Naval Affairs Committee, who was also working closely with Rear Admiral Moffett. Even with Billy Mitchell's personal self-destruction and court-martial for insubordination in 1925, the fate of naval aviation remained of concern to naval leadership. Aware that the Royal Air Force had subsumed the Royal Navy's aviation arm after World War I, much to its detriment in the eyes of Navy and League leadership, the service continually sought, in public statements and Congressional testimony, supporters to keep naval aviation "sea based." Finally, by 1928, the struggle appeared won, and Rear Admiral B. Domvile, Director of Naval Intelligence, maintained that "Moffett has tackled the subject with almost fanatical zeal, supported by the whole nation from the President downwards."[17]

Courtesy of Navy-Marine Corps Relief Society

Recruits form "Human Flag" at Naval Training Center Great Lakes.

The League also began paying greater attention to Navy and Marine Corps personnel needs. Technological advances in propulsion, communications, and gunnery required a better trained, more highly educated, and more technologically proficient pool of manpower. While the men the Navy needed were available in the early postwar years, the money to pay them was not, with the executive and legislative branches of government more interested in reducing government spending than maintaining a strong Navy.

League concerns over the status of the fleet and Marine forces were not shared by the public at large. In the social climate of the 1920s, the tenets of pacifism and isolationism were attractive to a majority of Americans who hoped that the United States could avoid further international entanglements such as those that had dragged a reluctant nation into the Great War.

A second Naval Arms Limitation Conference convened in Geneva, Switzerland, in June 1927, but ended in failure seven weeks later. Its failure convinced some "small-Navy" proponents that the United States would be naive to depend on other nations to provide for the common defense of the United States. Erstwhile allies Britain and France were understandably more concerned with protecting their own colonial empires than they were about safeguarding similar American political and economic interests overseas.

The Navy League took, and deserved, a large share of the credit for the firm stand taken by the U.S. delegation against what even the British press criticized as the "blunders" and "bluffs" of their own delegation. This time, instead of waiting to do battle in Washington against the inequities in a treaty that American diplomats had already agreed to in principle, William H. Gardiner, a retired public utilities executive and member of the League's Executive Committee wrote and distributed precautionary press releases and pamphlets in advance of the Geneva conference. Many of these appeared in one form or another in the daily press, and several were reprinted in national magazines.

In terms of U.S. national interests, the Geneva Conference was far from the failure it was alleged to be. In fact, it served as a much-needed reminder that the U.S. Army, Navy, and Marine Corps were and would continue to be not only the most reliable but also, sometimes, the *only* naval and military forces the nation could count on in times of international crisis.

President Coolidge was among those newly converted to this view. In his first annual message to Congress after Geneva he pointed out that "Where there is no treaty limitation, the size of the Navy which America is to have will be solely for America to determine."[18] Although by reputation one of the most frugal of all U.S. presidents, Coolidge followed up those words with approval of the Navy Department's request for 71 new-construction ships, all to be laid down within the following five years and completed by 1937.

The Navy League's interaction with Congress and the public in working to get the shipbuilding bill into law consumed over a year of hard work and showed the League at its best in the time between the wars. From the beginning, the League seized the initiative and sought to build congressional support for the request through a well-executed public relations/legislative action plan.

On December 27, 1927, it issued *Naval Parity: The Outlook After Geneva*, the first of eight League press releases on the shipbuilding bill. In January 1928 the League's Executive Committee met to authorize expenditure of the funds needed to continue the campaign, and that same evening had a dinner meeting with members of the Naval Affairs Committees of both the House and Senate, to plan the strategy needed to move the bill as quickly as possible through both houses of Congress.

Continuing the campaign in support of the Coolidge shipbuilding plan, in February the League issued a statement, distributed to almost 3,500 newspapers, refuting peace-group claims that enactment of the shipbuilding bill not only would impose "a crushing tax burden" on the American people but was not needed in any case because other Navies of the world were relatively weak compared to the U.S. Navy. The League statement used easily accessible data, already on the public record and therefore available to all citizens, to show that almost all of the alleged tax burden would be borne by a very small fraction of the American people—specifically, the 3,000,000 who paid income taxes. Moreover, the statement continued, the Navies of France, Great Britain, Italy, and Japan all were larger and more combat-capable in various respects—age, speed, tonnage, and armament—than the U.S. Navy was at that time.

In late February 1928 the House Naval Affairs Committee approved an abridged version of the bill authorizing only one aircraft carrier and 15 heavy cruisers. Recognizing that this was probably as good as could be expected from Congress, on March 2 the Navy League issued two press releases strengthening the arguments for passage of the bill: *The Present Cruiser Situation*, and reprints of a Senate document on the Geneva Conference proceedings. On March 17, 1928, the revised shipbuilding bill passed the House by an overwhelming margin, 287-58, despite the vociferous opposition of peace organizations.

The next move was up to the Chairman of the Senate Naval Affairs Committee, who, seeking to expedite the process, reported the bill from his committee in early May and simultaneously moved that it be considered. When the full Senate rejected his motion, he asked the Navy League to help by providing some representative "expressions of public opinion." On May 5 the League rushed an appeal to 250 newspapers urging that they come out in favor of the bill's rapid passage by the Senate, rapid meaning before the 70th Congress.

USS *Portland* (CA-33)

Within one week, more than 125 editorials,

70 of them supporting the League's position, were received at national headquarters. But it was too late. The Senate adjourned May 29 without considering the measure, and did not meet again for more than six months.

Though disappointed, the League, rather than criticizing the Senate for its failure to act, issued a "state of the fleet" press release on June 11 that praised Congress for the "generous appropriations" provided to the Navy. The release also praised the House for passing the shipbuilding bill and implied that the Senate would take similar action in the second session.

Ironically, additional though unintended support for the bill came from the leaders of Great Britain and France when both nations reached the Anglo-French Naval Accord that resolved their own differences on naval issues but completely ignored the United States, Italy, and Japan. President Coolidge, who already had told the British and French governments that the U.S. government had some serious objections to the agreement, displayed his ire in a nationwide Armistice Day address in which he used many of the same "big-Navy" arguments the League had been using for the past year.

The President pointed out that the United States had the longest coastline of any nation in the world and was dependent on the seas for raw material imports and the export of its agricultural products and manufactured goods. It had distant possessions and protectorates throughout the world, but no overseas land bases. Moreover, without seeking dominion over any other nation, it had become one of the world's great powers in both political and military terms, and had a moral requirement to use that power both to protect its own interests and to promote global peace and stability. For all of those reasons, Coolidge maintained, the United States needed a powerful two-ocean Navy and that Navy must include a fleet of heavy long-range cruisers.[19]

Workers in the New Deal Program

Taking no chances, the League started a new publicity campaign specifically aimed at the Senate. It issued another press release January 7, 1929, showing that, according to a large number of newspapers, public opinion in favor of the bill had climbed to an almost 8:1 ratio.

When the bill was introduced in the Senate in late January all its members had in their possession copies of the League's latest release on newspaper public opinion polls. The bill passed the Senate without change and was signed into law by President Coolidge.

While the cruiser bill might have passed on its own merits, particularly given Presidential and congressional displeasure over the Anglo-French Naval Accord, the League deserved credit for its innovative and well-planned educational campaign over a year's duration, a plan executed in close cooperation with both the Navy Department and the House and Senate Naval Affairs Committees.

It was one of the Navy League's finest hours in the time between the wars, and it came not a moment too soon. Three weeks after the cruiser bill became law, Herbert Hoover took the oath of office. Seven months later, the Great Depression, together with fleet reductions agreed to in the 1930 naval talks in London, would guarantee there would be no major additions to the Navy's shipbuilding program for several years.

As difficult as the 1920s had been for the U.S. armed services, the 1930s were worse. The stock market crash of October 1929 initiated a worldwide economic unraveling that culminated in the Great Depression of the 1930s and forced severe reductions in the naval appropriations bills submitted to Congress by President Hoover.

President Herbert Hoover

The Navy League vigorously fought additional cutbacks in fleet strength, but to no avail. A third arms-limitation conference, eagerly supported by a depression-ridden Hoover Administration, convened in London from January through April 1930, and imposed additional limitations on ships not covered under the Five Power Naval Limitation Treaty of 1922.

The United States was the only nation that fully adhered to the provisions of the London Naval Treaty, but that was not recognized at the time. Navy League Presidents Walter Howe and his successor, William Gardiner, led the League counterattack against the inequitable treaty provisions to which the U.S. delegation had agreed, but to little effect. In a May 28, 1930, coast-to-coast radio address, Gardiner spoke to numerous deficiencies in the treaty and explained how it would weaken the U.S. Navy, but not the navies of any of America's potential adversaries. But the American people, the press, and the Congress, focused on the moribund state of the nation's economy, had little interest in naval affairs when faced with breadlines, soup kitchens, and record unemployment.

Armin Rappaport, in his half-century history of the League, summarized its dilemma for the forthcoming decade: "After 1930, League officials should have known their limitations. The entire history of the society should have taught that a prevailing current of opinion could not be diverted. The most that could be achieved was to channel, direct, and strengthen an existing stream."[20]

Hoover, especially when compared to his successor in the White House, would be characterized as "anti-Navy" in most naval histories. However, in reality he was a strong supporter of certain aspects of the Navy, particularly naval aviation. He had followed developments in aviation throughout the 1920s, failed to support Billy Mitchell's desire to assume control of naval aviation, and shortly after becoming President twice overrode recommendations from the chiefs of naval operations that Rear Admiral William Moffett, considered the "Father of Naval Aviation," be retired.

But as the economic situation deteriorated throughout 1930, and continued calls for reductions in federal spending were heard in Congress, President Hoover agreed in January 1931 to additional cuts in that year's shipbuilding program and the complete elimination of the 1932-1933 program. This was too much for William Gardiner, now the League's National President. A talented writer capable of wielding a vitriolic pen, he decided to go on the attack. With his predecessor Walter Howe collaborating, Gardiner wrote a 16-page brochure, *The President and the Navy*, caustically listing all the mistakes the President had made, in their opinion, in decisions affecting the Navy.

The mistakes delineated were many, but the two League leaders made some grievous errors of their own, the most ill-advised being the personal attack on the President. They accused Hoover of displaying "abysmal ignorance of why navies are maintained and of how they are used to accomplish their major mission."[21] A later and more temperate version of the Gardiner-Howe broadside downsized the "abysmal ignorance" accusation to a less pejorative charge of having an "unconstructive record." But it was too late; the damage had been done.

Wisely, Hoover did not reply in kind but calmly ordered a formal investigation, to be carried out by a "committee of inquiry" to "examine the accuracy" of the allegations of incompetence that were included in the Gardiner-Howe pamphlet. Four of the five members of the committee were personal friends of the President, and two of them were members of the Navy League as well. Retired Admiral Hugh Rodman, former commander in chief of the Navy's Pacific Fleet as well as the battleships that had operated with the Royal Navy toward the end of World War I, was the only naval officer on the committee.

The committee deliberated in closed session for four days, but called no witnesses. It also did not, as many League adversaries hoped, investigate the organization further in terms of both its sources of operating funds or connections with industries that would benefit from a robust shipbuilding program. The committee's report, released in November 1931, neither denied nor affirmed the charge of "abysmal ignorance." The report did say that the Gardiner-Howe pamphlet "contained many inaccuracies, false assertions, and erroneous conclusions," but the committee provided few specifics to substantiate the allegation.[22]

Public opinion was mixed. Some editorials rebuked the Navy League for openly criticizing the President. Particularly strident was the *Washington Post*, declaring that "the Navy League can not afford to assume responsibility for any document which even by implication constitutes an insult to the President."[23] The *Post* continued:

> No summing up of the condition and prospects of the Navy, whether the statements are true or false, can be justified if it contains reflections upon the good faith of the President of the United States. The public resents such attacks, from whatever quarter they may come.
>
> The President of the Navy League is author of the pamphlet in question ... he has been utterly reckless in his expressions of opinion, and has taken an unwarranted liberty with the League by making it responsible for his outburst.
>
> Differing deductions would be drawn even from the agreed statement of facts. The Navy League pamphlet, whether its statements concerning the Navy are facts or mixtures of fact and error, would not have been objectionable if its author had confined himself to a discussion of the Navy.
>
> The President of the United States should not be compelled to take any action whatever when he is subjected to insult.[24]

Of opposing view, the American Legion, *Chicago Tribune*, and *New York Herald Tribune* sided with the Navy League, the latter scathingly calling the report "a shocking revelation of haste, carelessness, and misquotation, to say nothing of avoidance of the main issue."[25]

In the end, though, the American people, and most of the nation's newspapers and magazines, were more dismayed by the performance of the League's leadership in carrying out what many regarded as a personal attack against the President than they were about Hoover's alleged lack of naval expertise.

The national media took one final look at the controversy in their annual Gridiron Dinner, held in the nation's capital in December 1931. With the intent of the traditional celebration being "to set the world aright with song and satire and jest," before 400 guests at the Willard Hotel—including President Hoover and Navy League President Gardiner—the controversy was satirized in a parody of the Gilbert and Sullivan operetta "H.M.S. Pinafore." Gardiner saw himself characterized as "Little Ignorance" who, though "up on statistics of characteristics of cruisers and aircraft and guns," was tried and convicted by the Navy's admirals of false charges of "Abysmal Ignorance" leveled at certain unnamed individuals. The *New York Times* summarized the results of the skit as "Hoover Sees Himself Defeat the Navy League in Skit Built on 'Pinafore,'" incorrectly noting in its summary of the parody that "the sentence was that he [Gardiner] should apologize, something his real-life counterpart refused to do when President Hoover demanded it."[26]

www.gilbertandsullivan.org

A parody of H.M.S. Pinafore pitted Navy League President William Gardiner against U.S. President Herbert Hoover.

The debacle with President Hoover encouraged the League's adversaries to again criticize the organization. In early 1932, the historian, political scientist, and anti-navalist Charles A. Beard unleashed a sharp attack in his *The Navy: Defense or Portent*. Focused largely on the Navy League and "all the interests of cupidity arrayed behind it," Beard charged that the League was largely a front for industrial interests benefiting financially from building a big Navy, and alleged that "every armor maker in the United States was represented when the League was founded." Using the League's dispute with President Hoover to encourage "a nationwide discussion of these questions," Beard asked "Are measures of armament to be determined in fact by the civil branches of the Federal Government? Or are they to be dictated by the naval bureaucracy ... supported by a power array of active cupidity ... armor plate manufacturers, munitions-makers, merchant marine promoters ... [and] the jingo press."[27]

Beard concluded his book with a direct attack on the League in the context of its "ignorance" attack on President Hoover:

> The business of directing the enterprise of adult education in the sphere of proper armament for defense belongs to disinterested citizens, not to Navy Leagues, Navy bureaucrats, armament profiteers, and facile journalists paid by concerns with dividends at stake.[28]

Thus, the end result of the successive Harding, Coolidge, and Hoover Administrations in the 1920s and early 1930s largely reflected the sentiment of the American public, now deeply troubled by the Great Depression, that the Navy was large enough to do what tasks its government demanded of it. Despite League protests, there was little sentiment on Capitol Hill, ravaged by the nation's increasingly prostrate economy, to remove Hoover Administration strictures against hav-

President Franklin Roosevelt

ing the Navy built to prescribed treaty limits. Armin Rappaport noted, as far as President Hoover was concerned, "it was not a matter of disarmament or naval race but was, primarily, a question of economy."[29]

But to League leadership the question of fleet size and capability involved more than just economic issues. American participation, and in some cases even leadership, of the naval disarmament conferences throughout the 1920s and 1930s, along with the sentiments expressed by Charles Beard and others, signaled a return to isolationism and apathy combined with outright rejection of navalism.

Fortunately for the League, with a national membership of only 3,607 in 1931 and recurring fiscal problems that inhibited all but the most necessary expenses, a significant change for the better began in 1933 when an old friend, Franklin Roosevelt, succeeded Hoover as the nation's President. By that time, another League and Navy supporter, a junior congressman from Georgia, Carl Vinson, had become chairman of the House Committee on Naval Affairs. Between them, the President and the congressman slowly reversed the course of the previous decade, and, when they were done, had built the largest and most powerful Navy in the history of the world. And there to assist in that task was the Navy League of the United States.

It is difficult to overestimate the impact Franklin Roosevelt had on both the U.S. Navy and the Navy League. From the days of his youth he had been fascinated by ships at sea, an inclination no doubt fostered and encouraged by his uncle, the first Roosevelt to occupy the White House. By the time of his election to the presidency Franklin Roosevelt had collected one of the finest personal collections of seafaring art and model ships in the country. In no time, the new President made clear his inclination toward the Navy, oftentimes referring in cabinet meetings to the sea service as "we" and the Army as "you."

Though a keen student of Alfred Thayer Mahan and his vision of massive battleships and large fleets in tight formations, Roosevelt was also fascinated by nascent air power, the building of new ships, such as aircraft carriers, and the effect these developments would have on fleet operations. Oftentimes, to the frustration of chiefs of naval operations and naval architects, the President would be found at night in the White House or "relaxing" at his home in Hyde Park, New York, closely examining shipbuilding blueprints and the latest aircraft designs. As President, he was inclined to make "helpful" suggestions, and not at all reluctant to assert his Presidential authority over generals and admirals, particularly in the realms of politics, economics, and strategy.

Roosevelt's powerful command of geography often left his cabinet members and aides amazed, as he pinpointed obscure locations of maritime events on the globe in the Oval Office or on charts provided by the Navy or War Departments, and frequently cited mileages and sailing times between ports which, when subsequently checked by naval officers, were found to be remarkably accurate in terms of time and distance.[30] In his memoirs, Supreme Court Associate Justice Robert H. Jackson wrote that, when he was Attorney General in the mid-1930s, "President Roosevelt had an interest in this Department [Justice] second only to that perhaps of the Navy, to which we often jokingly referred to as 'the President's branch of the service.'"[31]

While the ascendancy of Roosevelt to the White House brought happier times for both the fleet and the League (veteran members recalled his having stood by the organization when Josephus Daniels barred it from access to naval installations and sought its dissolution), immediate relief for the Navy, in the context of the desperate circumstances under which the former Assistant Secretary entered the Oval Office, was not forthcoming. But, as a signal of intent, Roosevelt appointed Virginia Senator Claude A. Swanson, a "big-Navy" advocate, as Secretary of the service. As chairman of the Senate Naval Affairs Committee in 1916, Swanson had played a key role in shaping the naval appropriations bill that had built the fleet to the strength needed for its Great War missions.

But the ravages of inadequate spending in the 1920s, exacerbated by a nation deep in the throes of the Great Depression, made achievement of a larger Navy, treaty-constrained or not, a difficult proposition. By 1933, more than a decade of minimal expenditures had resulted in a fleet at only 65 percent of the force structure, and more than 158,000 tons below the limits established by the Five-Power Treaty. Morale was low, ships were poorly maintained, promotion abysmally slow (future League National President Calvin Cobb's father spent 16 years, 1917-1933, as a lieutenant commander!), and training was little more than an afterthought.

Congressman Carl Vinson

At the start of the Roosevelt Administration the Navy had 79,700 enlisted personnel and 5,929 officers, resulting in all ships in commission being manned at less than 80 percent complement. Four of the Navy's 15 battleships were in the inactive reserve fleet, and others were approaching obsolescence. The Navy's essential service force for overseas operations was almost nonexistent. To most League members and the other navalists of that era it seemed to be a time of unremitting despair. But such sentiment did not take into account the Chairman of the House Committee on Naval Affairs, Carl Vinson.

The Georgia Congressman's efforts to restore the Navy began in the last year of the Hoover Administration. In January 1932, with the country mired in the depth of the Great Depression, Vinson introduced a 10-year ship construction bill that would fund the building of 120 Navy ships of all types at a total cost of $616 million. Although chances for the bill being passed by Congress and signed into law by President Hoover were minimal, Vinson developed considerable bipartisan support for the bill, maintaining that providing for an adequate Navy was not a partisan issue. Surprisingly, Secretary of the Navy Charles Francis Adams supported the bill during committee hearings, as did Chief of Naval Operations Admiral William Pratt. The committee endorsed the bill by a 17-2 vote.

In the end, Hoover's opposition, based not only on budgetary considerations but on the President's hope for still more arms-reduction agreements doomed the bill. But Vinson's careful planning and well-executed public-relations campaign set the stage for new shipbuilding legislation that he would introduce the following year with a new occupant in the White House.

Less than one month after his sweeping victory over Hoover, Roosevelt had a lengthy meeting with Vinson. The shrewd combination of practical politics and instinct for the common touch that was to be the hallmark of the new administration was evident in this initial meeting between the two leaders. Rather than developing plans to rebuild the Navy to treaty limits, as expected, the President-elect and the chairman agreed on a $100-million reduction in the Navy's budget. Their joint statement indicated an immediate goal would be the building of a Navy that, although below treaty limits, would be sufficient to meet the country's needs.

Roosevelt and Vinson both wanted a much bigger shipbuilding budget, and a much larger Navy, beyond treaty limits. But the President was constrained by both the economic situation and the fact that many pacifist arguments of the 1920s were still popular in the 1930s. In addition, many of the new administration's most powerful proponents were also peace advocates from the progressive days of the Wilson Administration and the President had to be careful in advocating a naval rebuilding program to maintain consensus within his administration to execute the multi-faceted program enacted to attack the Great Depression.

Vinson recognized Roosevelt's dilemma as a political one. Only four weeks after their meeting, the chairman wrote a long letter to the incoming President designed to give Roosevelt a face-saving way, without breaking his campaign promise to cut government spending, to return to the "big-Navy" views he had espoused as Assistant Secretary of the Navy in the Wilson Administration. In the letter, Vinson spelled out his own views concerning the Navy and pointed out the large, and still growing, disparities between the U.S. Navy and the navies of France, Great Britain, and particularly Japan.

Additionally, the chairman added two political arguments. The first was that a well-planned and properly managed long-term naval shipbuilding program need not be overly expensive and would save millions of dollars. The second was that a major shipbuilding program would create jobs—hundreds of thousands of jobs, not only in areas where the ships were actually being built, but deeper inland, where the raw materials to restore the Navy had to be mined, harvested, processed and transported to shipyards and fleet homeports.

Vice Admiral Emory S. Land,USN

In press releases, floor speeches, and one-on-one meetings with editors and reporters, Vinson praised President Roosevelt for the latter's well-known belief in "an adequate national defense." The chairman's effusive rhetoric, picked up and repeated by the Navy League, gave the President-elect useful cover for a future change of course on naval appropriations. Vinson also tackled the national security issues involved by noting that the possession of a strong U.S. Navy would be "cheap insurance for a country like ours."

Vinson's personal salesmanship and dogged hard work still might have been in vain had it not been for the jobs argument, and the equally hard work done by the Navy League. Realizing that one of Roosevelt's highest priorities after taking office would be to get Americans back to work, the chairman worked with Rear Admiral Emory Land, chief of the Navy's Bureau of Construction and Repair, to develop data needed to persuade the Congress and the American people that building Navy ships would be a uniquely effective way to provide meaningful work while at the same time strengthening the nation's defense posture.

There was one final hurdle to overcome, opposition not from the President himself, but from a key Roosevelt Administration official. Shortly after taking office, the Director of the Budget, Louis Douglas, slashed 1934 appropriations for the Navy from $330 million to $260 million and proposed putting up to one-third of the fleet in a "rotation reserve." Chairman Vinson, seemingly at odds with the administration, asked for help from the Navy League to get the budgetary decision reversed and the rotation idea scuttled.

Not aware of the grander designs of these two skilled practitioners of the art of politics, the League appealed directly to the President, and, as reported in the *Chicago Daily Tribune*, the organization "which fought the celebrated 'abysmal ignorance' battle with President Hoover fired a first salvo today across the bow of the Roosevelt ship of state."[32] But learning from its previous mistake of personally attacking a President, the League focused its ire this time, not on Roosevelt, but rather on his budget director:

> With immensely complicated problems confronting him the President must necessarily rely largely upon the director of the budget and other non-naval advisors. Are these latter giving him sound advice on naval affairs? The Navy League thinks not. If the President and the nation come to a full realization of the effects of what the director of the budget is forcing the Navy to do, it won't be done.[33]

Subsequently, newly elected League National President Nathanial Hubbard Jr. got a statement, endorsed by Navy leadership, into the hands of 3,000 newspaper editors. A month later the League issued two more statements in support of Vinson's robust shipbuilding plan.

Hubbard's statement, and several pamphlets and press releases, won the day. Using graphs and word text that approached fleet expansion in the same jobs context used by Congressman Vinson, the League showed that naval construction would be "the perfect instrument for recovery by providing both security and employment." According to Hubbard's figures, Vinson's shipbuilding plan would provide jobs for 260,000 persons from 116 trades, using materials made, mined, or manufactured in 48 states. An estimated 85 percent of the total cost of construction would be for labor.[34]

The Navy League's persuasive argument was just what the President needed to carry out his intentions. Roosevelt and his "big-Navy" allies on Capitol Hill were able to begin measures to rebuild the fleet within the context of stimulating the moribund national economy through a program of job creation and material purchases. The restoration was accomplished in two steps, first through Title II of the National Industrial Recovery Act of 1933, and second through passage of the

"The Navy is dependent upon public opinion translated into votes in Congress, and the Navy League is the only organization that develops public opinion on naval affairs."

Vinson-Trammell Act of 1934. Section 202 of Title II, termed "Public Works and Construction Projects," authorized loans, "if in the opinion of the President it seems desirable" for "the construction of naval vessels within the terms and/or limits established by the London Naval Treaty of 1930."[35] This translated into a public works program to build 32 ships worth $238 million, to be divided between public and private shipyards; included in the program was nearly $40 million for two new aircraft carriers, *Yorktown* and *Enterprise.*

Roosevelt received the political and public credit for the National Industrial Recovery Act of 1933, but from a naval and League perspective it was Carl Vinson who had insisted that shipbuilding be inserted into the act. The Navy also considered the League deserving of credit because of its work with the press and the public at large. In congressional testimony, Rear Admiral Ernest King, serving in 1933 as Chief of the Bureau of Naval Aeronautics, offered his opinion that "the work of the Navy League must go on." "The Navy is dependent upon public opinion translated into votes in Congress," continued the future five-star admiral, "and the Navy League is the only organization that develops public opinion on naval affairs. In other words, the work of the Navy League is essential to the interests of the United States."[36]

The passage of the Vinson-Trammell Act authorized the Navy in the following four years to grow up to the full strength authorized by the London Naval Treaty. This resulted in construction beginning on 102 new ships, enough to bring the Navy up to treaty limits by 1942, as well as more than 1,000 aircraft, split between the Navy and the Army Air Corps. The League came out strongly in support of the Vinson-Trammell Act, declaring that the United States Navy was "third rate" and in "particular need" of full funding of the act in view of the size and capabilities of the navies of Great Britain and Japan.[37]

Taken together, the National Industrial Recovery Act and Vinson-Trammell Act signaled a new intent on the part of Washington; both bills were more than just initiatives taken to address unemployment. In his first Annual Report as Secretary of the Navy, Claude Swanson set forth a position, echoing Woodrow Wilson's "second to none" rhetoric that also echoed themes the League had been sounding for most of the preceding decade:

> A weakened position does not serve the cause of peace, but jeopardizes it, because balanced armament fortifies

> diplomacy and is an important element in preserving peace and justice, whereas weakness invites aggressive, war-breeding violations of one's right. ... I believe one of the strongest guarantees for peace and justice is an adequate United States Navy – a treaty Navy second to none.[38]

Meanwhile, the Navy League, its immediate goal accomplished, turned its attention to the recurring problems of low membership, a depleted treasury, and a new one: dissension in the ranks. Several of the League's senior members objected to both the form and content of a letter, critical of British statesmanship, and generously distributed to the U.S. and British press, that National President Hubbard had written to the "Navy League of the British Empire." More than 280 newspapers quoted the letter in whole or in part; 52 papers used it as the subject of editorials, 49 of which agreed with Hubbard's view that British navalists were trying to use the arms-limitation treaties to continue the Royal Navy's dominance at sea throughout the world.[39]

The principal concern of League dissenters was not so much the content of the letter, which more or less echoed their own opinions, but the fact that Hubbard had written it entirely on his own, asking only one person, former National President Gardiner, to review it. Hubbard accepted none of Gardiner's suggested changes and released it as representing the official views of the Navy League of the United States.

The matter was resolved at a meeting of the League's Executive Committee on November 9, 1933, during which, to restore harmony and avoid a future repetition of such situations, a publicity committee was created that would have authority, by a two-thirds vote, over the issuance of future press releases or open letters purporting to be the official positions of the Navy League.

The most significant long-term ramification of this meeting was that it began the iterative process to make the League a more democratic organization, a process that would continue, at various rates of reform, over the ensuing five decades. Until this late 1933 Executive Committee decision, policy on any major naval or national-defense issue was largely at the near-exclusive direction of the National President. And the National President was selected, not by the Navy League's membership at large, but by consensus of the League's current senior leadership. The creation of an independent committee, in this case related to the League's positions in public affairs, and one that in certain circumstances would have veto power over the organization's National President, was a major change to League operating procedures and established an initial precedent for changes in the manner in which the League was to be administered in the coming years.

League President Nelson Macy, who succeeded Hubbard in July 1934, wasted little time in expressing the organization's appreciation for President Roosevelt's

USS *Houston* (CA-30)

support of the fleet. Reacting to a Presidential speech given aboard a Navy cruiser, the Navy League issued a statement over Macy's signature asserting that Roosevelt "has now done his utmost to remove any doubt ... that the program authorized but not appropriated for by the Vinson Act will be carried out to completion in the shortest possible time."[40] The League statement, printed in its entirety in the *New York Times*, noted:

> The significance of President Roosevelt's historic speech on board USS *Houston* (CA-30) in mid-Pacific July 22 can hardly be overestimated. He pledged a Navy built to full treaty strength in three or four years. ... For the first time in more than 12 years the Navy League, in paying this tribute to President Roosevelt, has the satisfaction of congratulating the American people upon the attainment of an adequate and reasonably assured program of naval construction.[41]

Apparently satisfied that the League's major legislative goals in terms of shipbuilding had been achieved, Macy now turned his attention to matters internal to the organization. The Great Depression had affected the Navy League as deleteriously as it had the rest of the nation. All national headquarters employees shared in the financial travails of the organization. At one point the League's national treasury had a balance of $2.74, and the organization kept solvent only through the beneficence of influential people in industry. These were the most difficult fiscal years in the League's existence, and for several months during this period there were no paychecks for headquarters staff.

But in Macy's view the numbers and nature of the League's membership was the problem requiring his most urgent attention. Only 11 members had attended the Navy League's annual meeting of members in 1934; 504 others sent in proxy certificates, but the other 500 or so members did neither.

Although no formal survey was taken, it was apparent to senior leadership that one of the League's major problems was that since *Sea Power* had been discontinued 13 years earlier, most members felt completely divorced from national headquarters. They felt they had no say in the formulation of national policy and, except for the occasional news item or editorial in their local newspaper, knew nothing about the national organization to which they still nominally belonged. And when the actions of League National Presidents, as in the cases of Thompson during World War I and Gardiner during the Hoover Administration, had called into question the very future of the organization, both Presidents had so dominated Executive Committee deliberations on their actions, that many members had come to view the League as simply the tool of whoever was National President.

Macy tackled that problem head-on by making several national tours, largely self-financed, to stimulate the waning interest of old members and attract enthusiastic new ones. The first tour, to 11 cities in the Northwest and Pacific and Gulf Coasts, resulted in some helpful publicity, but little else. The second tour was much more ambitious. Macy set out in October 1934, accompanied by Harold Washburn, the League's Executive Secretary. The two men stayed in the field for 78 days, sat for dozens of interviews, and gave 72 speeches. The results were excellent: 86 news items and six editorials praising the League's patriotic goals and previous accomplishments, as well as one of the most successful West Coast Navy Day celebrations of the decade.

On his third tour, to 12 principal cities of the Midwest, Macy carried with him a letter from President Roosevelt praising the Navy League for its achievements and endorsing the new recruiting drive. Macy traveled from Ohio to Missouri, delivered 100 speeches (23 of which were broadcast over the radio), attended numerous meetings, dinners, and luncheons, and was interviewed by most of the principal newspapers in the cities he visited. The result of Macy's travels was an increase, albeit temporarily, in membership, which soared from 1,011 members on the roster at the end of 1934 to 2,811 members one year later.

The National President's next goal, unanimously approved by the League's directors with certain funding restrictions attached, was to resume publication of *Sea Power*. The first issue of the magazine, in its second incarnation, appeared in May 1935. In it, Secretary of the Navy Claude Swanson cited the Navy League as "a valuable medium of naval information to the American public."[42] Swanson acknowledged the League's advocacy role—one that was denied the uniformed members of the sea services:

> The nature of any military organization is such that its personnel have but little latitude in the public discussion of service needs, or the value of its function to the nation ... That the people of this country are today better informed as to the conditions and function of its Navy is at least in part due to

the service rendered the public by this organization.[43]

Macy reiterated the League's satisfaction with the Roosevelt Administration's shipbuilding policies, noting that the President was "experienced in naval affairs and, thus, thoroughly competent to measure our naval requirements. He has told us that he will build up our naval strength as soon as possible." But Macy also authored an article entitled *Japan and the Naval Treaties* cautioning that "our reduction of our Navy by under-building for a long period did not reduce the building plans of other nations by a single ship. As they had every right to build as they did, we have ourselves to blame."[44]

Macy also began to put more League emphasis on the rebuilding of the U.S.-flag Merchant Marine. At the urging of the National President, the League endorsed the Bland-Copeland Bill to establish a National Maritime Authority and take the initial steps needed to build a bigger and more economically competitive merchant fleet. Again, the League found itself enthusiastically supporting the Roosevelt Administration's position on rebuilding the merchant marine. In an official statement released in September 1934, Macy noted "with warm approval the President's declaration of policy regarding the merchant marine as a corollary to his recent pledge to build a treaty-strength Navy ... As the President has long been familiar with the problems of our merchant marine and Navy, he knows that these two elements of our sea power are interdependent."[45]

Macy followed up with a widely circulated press release, *Our Merchant Marine: Shall It Sink or Swim*?, in which he pointed out the need to build up the nation's commercial fleet not only to carry America's exports and imports but also as a Naval Reserve "fleet in being." Macy also noted the relationship between the Navy and the merchant marine, and the need for cargo ships and tankers to possess speeds within six knots of the cruising speed of the fleet to provide required support.

A second non-League priority on the Macy agenda was to help forge closer and more cordial ties with Great Britain, despite the Hubbard letter that had caused such controversy within the League three years earlier. In what the *London Times* described as a "significant article," the June 1936 issue of *Sea Power* urged the American people to forget their previous differences with the British, awaken to the fact that Western civilization was in grave danger, and recognize that the only force that might deter war would be an Anglo-American naval alliance that could control the seas, world communications, and international commerce.

The League's Navy Day celebrations in 1936 and 1937 continued to expound on the interdependent nature of the Navy and its supporting U.S.-flag civilian fleets, and the latter year featured the slogan "The Navy and Merchant Marine — National Security and Prosperity." The 1937 celebration in New York City was particu-

USS *Constitution*

larly noteworthy for the keel-laying of the first capital ship to be built in the United States in 14 years, the 35,000 ton, 16-inch gunned battleship *North Carolina*. The *New York Times*, acknowledging that the observances were "arranged by the Navy League," noted with pride the "Renaissance of U.S. Sea Power."[46]

The October 1937 Navy Day events were one of the most involved and extensively covered celebrations of the special day to date. Admiral William Leahy, Chief of Naval Operations, addressed a Navy League audience in Atlanta, Georgia, with Rear Admiral Ernest King speaking to a similar audience in Cleveland, Ohio. Rear Admiral Hugh Rodman, late of Herbert Hoover's "abysmal ignorance" commission, spoke at Terre Haute, Indiana, and a live program in Boston was broadcast from the decks of the frigate USS *Constitution*. Nelson Macy, who had turned the national presidency back to Nathan Hubbard in May 1936, but remained chairman of the Navy Day celebration nationwide, addressed the nation for 15 minutes in the evening from a New York City radio studio.

With the European continent drifting toward war again, the Vinson-Trammell Act of 1938 was the final major shipbuilding act prior to America's involvement in World War II. Building on the foundation of its predecessor, it increased the Navy's tonnage by 20 percent, authorized overhauls and modernizations of older ships then in the active fleet, and put increased focus and emphasis on naval aviation and construction of naval bases and air stations to handle the burgeoning fleet.

More than satisfied with such progress, Hubbard, the only League National President to serve non-consecutive terms, was succeeded in 1938 by H. Birchard Taylor. But while progress on rebuilding the fleet continued apace, the League's overall state of health was succinctly summarized by an embarrassing February 1936 *Christian Science Monitor* headline which declared that a Congressional investigation had found the Navy League " ... Innocuous and Lacking in Cash."[47] Still suffering from the lingering depression, membership varied up and down during both Hubbard's and Taylor's tours; the League finished the 1940 fiscal year showing a deficit of $870. Various fundraising and recruiting ideas were suggested, considered, and then either rejected or not implemented by the League's directors.

Part of the League's membership and financial plights could be blamed on the depression, but another reason was the American public's reaction to ongoing events in Europe and the Far East. Despite the Roosevelt Administration's commitment to rebuilding the Navy, it is worth recalling just how "anti-war" and unprepared the United States was in 1940. In December 1939 a poll indicated that more than two-thirds of the American public was opposed to taking sides in a war that had begun three months before.[48] In the summer of 1940, with its Army ranked 17th in the world in total manpower and modern weapons, the House of Representatives extended, by a margin of one vote, the Selective Service Act to continue a peacetime draft.[49]

As the new decade began, the Navy League, with limited resources and flagging membership totals, faced the same challenges as President Roosevelt: First, how to prepare a reluctant nation for its certain involvement in the global conflict. And second, when the nation was finally brought to war, how to fight and win it.

American societal changes in response to world developments were slow, but nonetheless happening. In July 1940, with Europe at war and Nazi Germany seemingly triumphant everywhere, a $10 billion defense appropriations bill was signed into law by the President. Roosevelt signed the Lend-Lease Act in March 1941, and froze German and Italian assets in the United States three months later. The convoying of lend-lease assets to England started in July. On September 1, 1941, the President issued a "shoot on sight" order to the Navy, freeing commanding officers to fire on foreign vessels threatening American ships.

During this same time frame the Navy League, now (and for the next five years) headed by Chicagoan Sheldon Clark, began, as it had in 1916, carrying out its own prewar preparations. A major internal overhaul was implemented that reorganized the League's headquarters staff and appointed Evelyn Collins as Executive Secretary of the Navy League, a position she was to hold for the next 27 years.

Clark, continuing a trend since the 1920s, gave more responsibility and authority to the councils, and established 13 national regions, each with a certain number of states assigned to it. Each region was headed by a vice president, and each state by a chairman, both appointed by the League's Board of Directors. With national leadership primarily focused on issues revolving around events in Washington, it was easy to overlook the independent League councils located throughout the United States and overseas. Too often, their vital contributions were ignored at national headquarters. The reorganization of the League, which took place in the summer of 1941, resulted in better contact between, and improved supervision and recognition of, the councils.

Clark also instituted several other changes. A Women's Division, similar to that in World War I, was created to assist in the "Bundles for Britain" program; publication of *Sea Power* on a monthly vice bimonthly basis was resumed; and a recruiting drive was initiated with the slogan, "If you can't join the Navy, join the Navy League."

Because of the tense international situation, traditional open-house visits in 1941 by the public to sea-service ships and stations had to be curtailed, but the League still made an effort to attract new members at the limited observances permitted. But even with limited ship visit opportunities, there were 300 Navy Day banquets, principally sponsored by the Navy League, throughout the country. All of them featured President Roosevelt, speaking over all three national radio networks from the Mayflower Hotel in Washington, D.C., to address members of the Navy League and their guests.

German World War II submarine

The theme of his remarks, as reported in the *Washington Post* was "the increasing size and importance of the country's 'first line of defense.'"[50] But more than that, the President's Navy Day speech revealed his explicit intent to use the economic and military power of the United States to destroy the Nazi regime in Germany, proclaiming that "freedom of the seas is now, as it has always been, a fundamental policy of your government and mine." Roosevelt went on to reveal, in terms and characterizations easy to understand by the American people, his orders to the Navy to "shoot on sight" the "rattlesnakes of the sea," as he described the Nazi submarines and surface raiders preying in the North Atlantic.[51] As befitted the Navy Day occasion, the President lavished praise on his favorite service:

> It can never be doubted that the goods will be delivered by this nation, whose Navy believes in the tradition of 'Damn the torpedoes: full speed ahead!' ... The lines of our essential defense now cover all the seas; and to meet the extraordinary demands of today and tomorrow our Navy grows to unprecedented size. Our Navy is ready for action. Indeed, units of it in the Atlantic Patrol are in action. Its officers and men need no praise from me.[52]

Concurrent with the President's speech, the League launched still another membership drive. These and other efforts to prepare the organization for the trying times ahead came not a moment too soon. Less than six weeks after Navy Day, the Japanese attacked Pearl Harbor, the United States was at war, and the Navy League was among the first national organizations to offer its services, "for the duration," to the commander in chief, to the nation, and to America's sea services.

The decade that had opened with the crash on Wall Street was now closing to the sound of guns half a world distant. But when the strike came that destroyed America's neutrality and reluctance to face fascism, it came in a place and location hardly expected, and surprised with devastating destructiveness President Roosevelt's favorite service, and the one that Americans had accepted as the nation's best prepared and its first line of defense: the United States Navy.

EXTRA!!
The Odessa American EXTRA
U.S.-JAPS AT WAR!
JAPS BOMB PEARL HARBOR IN HAWAII
U. S. NAVY INTO ACTION

Chapter V
A World at War
1941-1945

Yesterday, December 7, 1941, a date which will live in infamy-the United States of America was suddenly and deliberately attacked by naval and air forces of the empire of Japan ... The facts of yesterday speak for themselves. The people of the United States have already formed their opinions and well understand the implications to the very life and safety of our nation ... Always will we remember the character of the onslaught against us. No matter how long it may take us to overcome this premeditated invasion, the American people, in their righteous might, will win through to absolute victory ...[1]

With these stirring words, Franklin Roosevelt asked Congress on December 8, 1941, for a declaration of war against the "Japanese Empire" following the devastating attack on the fleet at Pearl Harbor. The reluctance and unwillingness of the 1920s and hesitation and uncertainty of the 1930s were washed away in a singular moment. Secretary of War Henry Stimson would write in his diary, "When the news first came that Japan had attacked us my first feeling was of relief that indecision was over and that a crisis had come in a way which would unite all our people."[2] Playwright Arthur Miller noted, "Everything changed. Immediately. Finally, the whole country had a purpose."[3] In the first week after Pearl Harbor, the U.S. Army, Navy, and Marines signed up almost 25,000 recruits.[4]

World War II would be unlike any the United States had ever fought. A popular President would explain in simple terms how the sacrifices of the global conflict were tied to the higher good of democracy and freedom, and ultimately to America's national security. Similar arguments had been voiced in the last World War, but whereas Woodrow Wilson failed to carry the public with him, Franklin Roosevelt succeeded, no doubt aided by the commonly accepted "treachery" of the Japanese attack on Pearl Harbor. As the President had asserted in his address to Congress December 8, the American people would always remember the character of the onslaught against them and their Navy.

As reported in the January 1942 issue of *Sea Power*, at the Navy League's December 19, 1941, annual meeting, all attendees took the following pledge:

> The treacherous action of the Japanese nation in attacking the island possessions of the United States places an obligation and a responsibility upon all persons whose security has been made possible by those principles upon which the United States of America were established and have been continuously administered. The obligation is not limited to those patriotic citizens who have joined the armed forces of our country, but must be shared by all citizens whose age or sex does not permit active participation.
>
> We American citizens associated under the name of the Navy League of the United States, for the purpose of furthering our naval preparedness, pledge this association to the acceptance of these responsibilities during the present war:
>
> FIRST: To render to the naval service the Navy League's fullest support and assistance in bringing about complete victory.
>
> SECOND: To render to the officers and men of the naval service all possible aid and assistance—supplementing that extended by the National Government—in the hope of lessening the sacrifices they are called upon to make.
>
> THIRD: To render to their families a neighborly hand and association so that they may know and realize their personal sacrifices are appreciated and, we hope, lessened thereby.
>
> FOURTH: To render to the American Merchant Marine the fullest support in order that American ships will be available to sail the seas which the Navy is now freeing.

> FIFTH: To render to the American youth and their parents a report of the American principles for which the Navy is now fighting to preserve and permanently secure.
>
> SIXTH: To render such other aid and assistance as the needs may warrant or require from time to time.
>
> We make this pledge and assume these responsibilities as our contribution to the national welfare and to the Navy which we have always sought to keep ever prepared for any and all emergencies.

The League's commitment was more than just a patriotic gesture. What followed the broad statement of support in the pledge was a list of specific duties and responsibilities, including providing assistance in various ways to sea-service personnel, helping families of those serving in uniform (with particular focus on those killed or wounded in action), educating the public about "American principles" and the history and needs of the sea services, and providing other aid and assistance that might be needed to win the war.

In one aspect, the surprise attack December 7, and Hitler's subsequent declaration of war against the United States, made both President Roosevelt's—and by extension the Navy League's—situation much easier than that faced by their predecessors in 1917. Once the Axis powers declared war on the United States, Americans had no patience with arguments that Germany might have had legitimate grievances arising out of World War I or that uncertain diplomacy in the Far East had incited the militarists in Tokyo. The American public increasingly understood that its own naiveté in international affairs had contributed to the attack on the U.S. fleet now lying in the mud of Pearl Harbor.

But in that disaster, with almost 3,000 Americans dead, one of the Navy League's first (and thereafter most important) wartime tasks was among the saddest as well: helping, both financially and in many other ways, the families of the servicemen who were killed, wounded, or missing in action. That heart-rending task started the second week of December 1941, and continued to and beyond the end of the war. The Navy Relief Society did as much as it could to help the families of those killed or wounded at Pearl Harbor, but its financial resources were limited. The League stepped in and committed itself to raising $5 million to meet the Society's immediate needs. As the war progressed and financial as well as human costs continued to escalate, the League raised millions more, all of which were turned over to Navy Relief.

Another family-assistance program was initiated to purchase gifts and household necessities for naval and military families. The assistance program, headed by Mrs. Robert Kelley, started with the New York Council but soon spread to a host of other councils throughout the country. With millions of men in the armed services, American women entered the workforce in unprecedented numbers and supported the war effort in a myriad of other ways. To assist, the League's leaders established a Women's Auxiliary that by war's end had established almost 90 councils of its own. Active in purchasing gifts and other items for those who were left behind, the program became so extensive that in New York alone there were more than 2,200 shopping orders daily. Another Auxiliary assignment was to counsel women who had been left behind on how and where to find the jobs they needed to support their families while their husbands were serving on active duty.

The Auxiliary councils worked with the League's already existing councils on a long list of other tasks, including recruiting blood donors, establishing and operating a transport service to drive service people on official business, obtaining and distributing books and athletic equipment to sea-service personnel on deployed ships or assigned to bases overseas, taking convalescent patients from naval hospitals on excursion cruises, finding housing for sea-service families transferred from one city or state to another, and promoting the sale of war bonds to help defray the cost of the war. To pay for these and many other programs, the Navy League sponsored dances, dinners, recitals, and lectures in cities from Maine to California.

Originating with the Philadelphia Council, and spreading throughout the organization in 1942, was a particularly active group of Navy League women known as the "Nells." They wore attractive dark blue uniforms and dark blue hats, both of which were emblazoned with the Navy League emblem. The Nells devoted much of their time and talents to planning dinners and other fund-raising events, the proceeds from which were used to help service personnel and their families.

In addition to joining the Auxiliary or the Nells, League women volunteered in hospitals to replace nurses and other health-care professionals who were serving on active duty, and as in World War I, made or donated clothing items to sea service members or their families (along with similar volunteers from the Navy Relief Society, the Seamen's Church Institute, and the Society for Seamen's Children). League women set up and ran free canteens and doughnut stations for service personnel, drove young men and women to sea-service recruiting stations when no government transportation was available, gathered books, newspapers, magazines, and other reading materials for distribution to those serving on active duty, and collected binoculars (250 pairs alone, in early 1942) to help outfit Navy, Coast Guard, and U.S.-flag Merchant Marine ships being built in record numbers.

One particularly innovative program created by League women in the Baltimore area involved the issuing of "pathfinder cards" good for free meals and entertainment in various clubs and United Service Organization establishments. When a Navy vessel came to Baltimore, the port director would come aboard and distribute the cards to every sailor aboard, with explanations for their usage provided via the ship's general announcing system. With a decided decline in the frequency and severity of incidents ashore requiring employment of the shore patrol, Baltimore's port director observed:

> Every port is full of honky-tonks and street girls, but here in Baltimore we have a set-up that is hard to beat. The Navy League offers decent entertainment and makes it attractive ... We feel that if we can get the men to go to the Navy League their first night ashore, our troubles are over ... The splendid work of the Navy League in Baltimore has attracted the attention of the Navy Department. Recently, ships have been sent to Baltimore solely for the purpose of giving the crew recreation. I am sure that many more sailors will say, as I do, that 'I'm completely sold on the Navy League.'[5]

Complementing the Baltimore Council's effort, in Philadelphia the Navy League created a Convalescent Service in five Army and Navy hospitals for soldiers, sailors, airmen, and Marines of any allied nation who had been injured or wounded in action. Navy Leaguers involved with the Convalescent Service took appreciative servicemen and women to the countryside or seashore for picnics and recreation. One soldier, in a thank-you note to his hostess, wrote, "It's people like you who make guys like us want to give all we have."[6]

Despite the fact that ship and station open houses had been cancelled for the duration, the League's Navy Day celebrations during World War II were among the biggest and most spectacular ever. In 1942, more than 1,000 dinners and other Navy Day events and activities were attended by almost 4,500,000 people. In 1943 that number swelled to almost 6,000,000 Americans taking part in an estimated 7,000 lunches, dinners, receptions, school assemblies, and parades. There were more than 16,000 Navy Day programs of various types, with more than 6,000,000 participants throughout the country in 1944, the last full year of the war.

Secretary of the Navy Frank Knox

Supporting the Navy's training establishment was another primary League mission of major significance to the service's combat readiness. Here, League President Sheldon Clark, an avid yachtsman and former secretary of the Chicago Yacht Club, presented to Navy Secretary Frank Knox a plan to establish an inland training program on Lake Michigan to replace the summer training cruises previously enjoyed by the 27 universities having Naval Reserve Officer Training Corps on campus. The League, allied with the National Defense Committee of the Lake Michigan Yachting Association, recruited 140 owners to make their yachts available to the Navy for the training of more than 1,000 newly commissioned officers in the use of navigation instruments, seamanship, and at-sea safety practices.

A much larger and equally innovative program in which the Navy League played a key role involved the establishment and operation of specialized training schools where women volunteers received instruction in such essential tasks as parachute rigging, cryptographic analysis, automotive repair, and radio maintenance and operation. Many Navy League members worked with active-duty personnel in conducting training sessions and handling the administrative and other support chores involved.

Even while accomplishing multiple tasks under the aegis of the Department of the Navy, National President Sheldon Clark felt strongly that the League could not ignore its primary mission of educating the American public and its elected officials. In July 1942, he admonished the League's directors that they "were not a relief or welfare organization." Clark espoused the value of the "large view" and never permitted short-term tasks, willingly accepted for the war's duration, to obscure the organization's more important long-term objectives.[7]

To further accomplish of those objectives, and to handle the tremendously increased activity and correspondence occasioned by the war, Clark hired Evelyn Collins's niece, Jane Collins to become a member of the national headquarters staff, working in support of both her aunt and the national leadership. Jane Collins Grover would work for the League for the next 44 years, eventually replacing her aunt as Executive Secretary, serving 20 different national presidents. It was a degree of continuity unmatched, except for the position of judge advocate, on the national staff.[8]

With restrictions on travel and a necessary focus on supporting the war effort, National President Clark continued to push as much responsibility and authority as possible down to the local council level. Of particular importance in light of future League leadership, in March 1942 local Navy Leaguers and members of the "Navy Council of Illinois" merged to form the Chicago Council of the Navy League, with a charter dating from March 2, 1942. In its 25th anniversary program, reflecting on its creation and largely ignoring efforts by national leadership dating from almost a decade earlier, the Chicago Council noted that "not until 40 years had passed — years of fighting public apathy and years of struggle with a pitifully inadequate budget — did the Navy League officers decide to strengthen their ties with the members and provide for local autonomy through the formation of local councils."[9]

By mid-1942 the goal of building a bigger U.S. Navy already had been achieved, or was on the way to being achieved, thanks primarily to the support of the Roosevelt Administration, the legislative acumen of House Naval Affairs Committee

"Let no blandishment, nor any arguments of economic nature, nor any dreams of partnership with other nations, persuade us in peace time, to let go the mighty sea power we possess today."

Chairman Vinson, and the continued support of the Navy League. In June the chairman introduced a bill authorizing construction of 1.9 million tons of aircraft carriers, cruisers, and destroyers. A month later, with little debate, both houses of Congress passed the new act along with a companion bill funding construction of 1,200,000 tons of auxiliaries shipping. The 1942 Navy Expansion Act permitted Secretary of the Navy Knox to place orders for 14 carriers, 33 cruisers, 100 destroyers, and 420 destroyer escorts.

In his study of the politics of naval expansion during World War II, Joel Davidson observes of this record construction authority for 570 combatant ships: "This legislation proved to be the last naval expansion act passed during the war. So great were the forces authorized that no further similar acts were necessary, especially because Congress had included a provision allowing automatic replacement of losses."[10] The fleet "second to none" that Woodrow Wilson had promised three decades earlier, long championed by the Navy League through the rocks and shoals of the Roaring '20s and the Great Depression, had at last become reality.

By mid-1942, all of the nation's armed services were significantly larger in size and immensely more combat-capable, by any standard of measure. The October Navy Day celebration that year in New York City, witnessed by 300,000 spectators on Fifth Avenue, had 10,000 sailors, a large contingent of British sailors and marines, and, as noted by the *New York Times*, an "unprecedented number of women in uniform."[11]

Still, as National President Clark reminded audiences in print and speeches, America's armed forces had been unrivaled at the end of World War I, and that had not prevented the disarmament and deterioration of the 1920s and consequential rise of the dictators and fascism in the 1930s. Given this reality, he and other League officers issued a series of warnings throughout the war, usually in the pages of *Sea Power*, reminding the American people and their elected leaders of the risks the nation would face if it were to precipitously dismantle the Navy and the other sea services after winning the war. "Let no blandishments, nor any arguments of economic nature, nor dreams of partnership with other nations," Clark wrote in early 1943, "persuade us in peacetime to let go the mighty sea power we possess today."[12]

The League President followed up with an even stronger and more specifically detailed warning the same year, when U.S. and international peace groups were urging the creation of another international body that, unlike the League of

Nations, would keep the peace in a postwar world. But the League was careful, in view of the Roosevelt Administration's position, not to campaign specifically against the evolving international organization, nor did it urge any withdrawal from postwar global responsibilities. However, the League maintained that the peace that would follow after the defeat of Germany and Japan would be so fragile that U.S. military forces would still be needed to protect America's overseas interests as well as maintain peace in areas of the world not traditionally areas of concern or interest to the United States. Numerous articles in *Sea Power* urged the postwar retention of a worldwide network of U.S. overseas bases built during the war, adoption of measures required to maintain the economic viability of the U.S.-flag Merchant Marine, and congressional approval of a sufficient level of funding to keep the U.S. defense industrial base intact and ready for mobilization in future times of war or other national emergency.

At the League's annual meeting at the Biltmore Hotel in New York City in December 1944, Sheldon Clark, re-elected for a third consecutive term as National President, asserted that the only guarantee of a safe future for America in the postwar era lay in "maintenance of her powerful naval and merchant fleets."[13]

Foreseeing a global role for the United States beyond the defeat of Germany and Japan, and in marked contrast to the League's position on the Versailles Treaty and League of Nations in 1919-1920, National President Clark asserted:

> The battle is for the American Merchant Marine, for the extension to countries overseas of our beneficial national influence and our stimulating trade and for the support of proper policies in the field of diplomacy and finance, to the end that America may achieve her destiny as a world power and as a leaven to civilization on universal democracy.[14]

Admiral Ernest King, USN

In 1945 the League increasingly focused attention, in speeches, radio addresses, press releases and in *Sea Power*, on the postwar requirements of the sea services. Memories of the naval disarmament treaties immediately after World War I were evoked as a reminder of the perils of relying on good intentions codified in treaties as opposed to proven combat capability and sufficient force levels to carry out the will of the American people.

But, unlike the mixed messages on preparedness and national defense evident during and after World War I, ensnarled in the imbroglio of the Treaty of Versailles and League of Nations, Navy League and Department of the Navy public statements were now in full agreement.

Fleet Admirals William Leahy and Ernest King, Secretary of the Navy James Forrestal, and others contributed authoritative articles to *Sea Power* during the war, reinforcing the basic Navy League message that a large and powerful U.S. Navy would continue to be a national necessity for years to come. Other articles reinforced a complementary goal that the League had been vigorously pursuing, the retention of the vast complex of overseas U.S. bases and stations that had been built to carry the war to the Axis powers.

Secretary of the Navy
James Forrestal

The League campaigned for the postwar retention of a significant percentage of the most seaworthy ships and combat-capable Navy and Marine Corps aircraft built during the war, concerned that most of them would be scrapped, or sold to other nations after the cessation of hostilities. The League also pointed out that, regardless of the size of the retained fleet and air arm, the sea services would need a pool of highly trained personnel distributed throughout the Naval and Marine Corps Reserves who could be quickly mobilized to man those ships and aircraft if their future reactivation became necessary.

The November 1945 issue of *Sea Power*, the last "wartime" issue, included an article by Secretary of the Navy Forrestal that established the theme of the League's postwar agenda:

> One year ago I said that, 'when the history of the war is written, one indisputable fact will stand out: The victorious nations held the mastery of the sea.' That still stands. Now I add, 'in the peace which lies ahead, one indisputable fact will stand out: The nations which have set out to guarantee a lasting peace must hold the mastery of the sea and of the air above it.'[15]

Forrestal, who soon would become the nation's first Secretary of Defense, could not have found a more attentive audience for his valedictory summation of what had been accomplished by the wartime Navy and what he believed would be its future missions and responsibilities. The League not only was attentive, but in a superb position to carry out Forrestal's injunction to press for the retention of a powerful Navy that was fully combat-ready and immediately available for any postwar missions. The fleet of the future would have to be not only versatile, mobile, and able to carry out a broad spectrum of responsibilities, but also large enough to protect American political and economic interests worldwide.

Whatever its concerns regarding America's postwar defense posture, the League was not worried during the war about its own postwar status. In fact, the League's future had never looked so bright. Membership was at an all-time high. Leadership had worked throughout the wartime years, not only to recruit new members, particularly in midwestern states, but also to establish new councils within the 13 League regions that had been formed in the 1941 reorganization plan. The success of these efforts, strongly supported by the Navy through naval district public information offices, was reflected in record membership at the end of 1945: 18,781 members enrolled in more than 250 councils.

Moreover, the League's financial position had never been more secure. At the end of the war the budget books showed an unprecedented fiscal condition for the League: a cash surplus of $30,013.37, in addition to another $30,000 invested in U.S. Savings Bonds![16]

Fiscal solvency was just one of several intangibles that contributed significantly to the League's growth, and augured well for additional membership increases in

PFC. Robert L. Keller

Tank-borne infantry moving up to take the town of Ghuta before the Japanese can occupy it. The men are members of the 29th Marines.

the future. World War II had served as a great awakening for the American people. They had toiled, bled, and sacrificed through nearly four years of war. Nazi Germany and Imperial Japan had not been merely checked or defeated, but completely vanquished. There was a sense, in 1945, that there was no going back; America's outlook on issues of world affairs and military preparedness had changed forever, and in a direction fully in consonance with the League's views on preparedness espoused since its 1902 founding.

Another intangible was the fact that at the peak of the war 12,000,000 Americans were serving in uniform and millions more were working in shipyards, aircraft factories, weapons plants, and other defense industries directly related to the war effort. Most Americans, in or out of uniform, who lived through the war years 1941-1945 had a much greater appreciation and understanding of sea power, from Pearl Harbor to Guadalcanal, the Philippine Sea to Tokyo Bay, as a prerequisite to the nation's attainment and exercise of global power and responsibility.

League membership figures, statistics, and speeches and editorials on the opinion pages of the nation's newspapers supported these views. But with the death of Franklin Roosevelt in April 1945 the fleet and League's most ardent supporter since the turn of the century was gone. In his place was a relatively unknown Missourian and a nation eager to put the war behind them. It was to be an uncertain time ahead, for both the United States Navy, and the Navy League.

General Douglas MacArthur signs peace treaty on board USS *Missouri* (BB-63).

Chapter VI
Victory's Aftermath
1946-1949

In the immediate postwar years, the League's educational mission should, seemingly, have never been easier. America's triumph, particularly in the Pacific Theater, was largely won by the U.S. Navy and Marine Corps. The number of ships alone that comprised the entire Navy on VJ (Victory in Japan) day staggered the imagination. Present in almost every region of the world were more than 100 aircraft carriers, 5,000 ships and submarines, and 82,000 vessels and landing craft. As characterized by Secretary of the Navy John Lehman a half-century later, it was, without qualification, the "largest Navy in the world, manned by experienced citizen sailors and led by aggressive and seasoned admirals." Clearly, "the Navy had been given pride of place by President Franklin D. Roosevelt."[1]

Fortunately, particularly in light of subsequent events, the Navy League, recognizing this huge fleet could not be kept on active duty in toto, endorsed the Department of the Navy's nascent program to establish a Ready Reserve of both Navy and Marine Corps assets. Within 24 months of the end of World War II, more than 1,000,000 men and women were in the reserve forces and available for recall in a national emergency. More than 2,200 warships were laid up, complemented by more than 2,000 oilers, Liberty ships and other support craft. All were scientifically protected against the elements.

Vice President Harry Truman succeeded to the nation's highest office in April 1945 with the death of Franklin Roosevelt. Though largely a novice at foreign affairs, Truman was a quick study and, sizing up Soviet leadership in several meetings and conferences, quickly decided that the postwar spread of communism had to be contained. In 1946 he sent both the battleship USS *Missouri* (BB-63) and newly commissioned aircraft carrier USS *Franklin D. Roosevelt* (CV-42) to the Eastern Mediterranean to show American support for pro-Western governments in both Greece and Turkey in suppressing communist insurgents and resisting the overt pressure of Stalinist Russia.

Speaking at the Navy League New York Council's Navy Day dinner in October 1946, Fleet Admiral William F. Halsey noted that the deployment of the aircraft carrier "followed logically" from the nation's long-term commitment to protecting American interests in the Mediterranean and hailed the Truman Administration's traditional employment of sea power in a world thought by many to be irretrievably changed by the development of atomic weapons:

> The Navy will use whatever weapons it needs to meet the challenge of modern warfare ... As a university was once considered a collection of books, later to be recognized as a collection of men and ideas, today's Navy is not one weapon or group of weapons but a group of men trained in mind and body to use the tools best suited to its mission.[2]

In March 1947 the Truman Doctrine was declared before Congress, with the President stating that the policy of the United States would be "to support free peoples who are resisting attempted subjugation by armed minorities or outside pressure." A month later American financier Bernard Baruch asserted, "Let us not be deceived — today we are in the midst of a Cold War."[3]

"In the future, as in the past, the key to victory and to freedom of this country, will be in control of the seas and the skies above them."

Yet, even with problems multiplying around the world, from Northeast Asia to the Mediterranean, continued justification for maintaining a significant portion of the naval force that had won the war became problematic. The problem faced by the Navy was not one of America lacking an enemy to justify a continued strong defense; a Stalin-lead Soviet Union was clearly going to be a future threat to the United States and its European allies. Rather, it was the method and enormity of America's naval victory in World War II that posed the central challenge to continued strength of the sea services. The scope of victory saw no nation in the world able to challenge American naval power; there was simply no major opposing Navy left to fight.

House Committee on Naval Affairs Chairman Carl Vinson sensed the irony of the Navy's victory placing its own future at risk when he had asked Secretary of the Navy James Forrestal toward the end of World War II, with the certainty of triumph over the Axis powers evident, "Why should we maintain any Navy after the war?" Forrestal, as documented in his diaries, replied:

> First, the outstanding lesson of the last quarter of a century is the means to wage war must be in the hands of those who hate war. The United States should remain strong. The Navy is a major component of that strength. In the future, as in the past, the key to victory and to freedom of this country will be in control of the seas and the skies above them.[4]

In the wake of total victory, the role played by air power made it easy to believe that the key to future victory against any enemy would lie largely in the air, not on the sea. The destruction of Hiroshima and Nagasaki by strategic air power allowed its advocates to argue convincingly that atomic weapons had made large fleets obsolete, and for diminished future roles for Navies and Armies in securing America's security. By the late 1940s, that is what many Americans, including President Truman and his new Secretary of Defense, Louis A. Johnson (who succeeded Forrestal in March 1949), accepted as the future course for America's armed services.

Close ties between Johnson and Truman had been forged in the 1948 Presidential campaign, when Johnson was a major fundraiser for the Democratic Party incumbent and a key aide on the President's famous "Whistle-stop Campaign" that had won him a second term in the White House. Johnson had served as Roosevelt's Assistant Secretary of War, and both Truman and Johnson had served in the Army in World War I. Both were forceful leaders and, while supporting a strong national-defense program, were also committed to containing defense spending.

The new Secretary of Defense shared the President's opinion that "huge sums were being wasted on defense spending" and both leaders "distrusted generals and admirals when it came to spending money."[5] Both men also agreed with the prevailing view that the principal building blocks of U.S. military power in the postwar era were nuclear weapons, air power, a well-trained and well-equipped modern Army, a capable but not overly large Navy focused primarily on antisubmarine warfare, and a much smaller, less versatile Marine Corps than the one that had grown markedly in size and capability throughout the war in the Pacific.

With the minds of the President and Secretary of Defense tilting in a non-sea service direction, the likelihood increased that Congressman Vinson, other congressional supporters, and the Navy League would soon be fighting several major postwar organizational and roles-and-missions battles. The first and in many ways most important battle, largely settled before Johnson assumed the office of

Secretary of Defense, involved the unification of the War and Navy Departments into a single Department of Defense that would have direct operational control of the Army, Navy, Marine Corps, and Air Force. The latter would be a separate service, and nominal department, succeeding the Army Air Corps. The service secretaries would no longer be members of the Cabinet; instead, that seat at the table would go to a newly created position, the Secretary of Defense.

The second major issue was about air power. From the perspective of fervent air power enthusiasts, all U.S. military assets, including both carrier and shore-based naval aviation, regardless of the current arrangement, should come under the purview of the Department of the Air Force. But that perspective was not shared by career naval officers, particularly naval aviators, the Navy League, or Carl Vinson and several other members of the House and Senate Naval Affairs Committees.[6]

Issues regarding service unification were being openly discussed at both the Pentagon and on Capitol Hill more than a year before the end of World War II. The staggering cost of the war and duplication of effort in many theaters argued that at least some consolidation could be carried out without harming combat capabilities. In addition, the belief that future combat operations would almost always require close coordination of land, sea, and air forces had convinced many military professionals that closer cooperation — in planning, training, and procurement — would be required.

It was the Navy's opinion that this desirable unity of effort could be achieved without full amalgamation. While he was still Secretary of the Navy, Forrestal not only concurred with the creation of a new Department of the Air Force but suggested that it be a Cabinet post, joining the War and Navy Departments. Coordination between and among the services, he said, could be accomplished by the newly formed National Security Council and the Joint Chiefs of Staff.

The Navy League supported Forrestal's recommended alternative through articles in *Sea Power*, press releases, and letters to Congress. In an open letter to Senator Edwin Johnson, acting chairman of the Senate Military Affairs Committee, League National President Sheldon Clark urged that an impartial examination into the unification issue should be carried out before any final legislative action.

One of Clark's principal points in opposition was that giving any one person, no matter how wise, talented, or objective, control of all of the nation's naval and military forces would be exceedingly dangerous. Clark followed up his open letter by sending a telegram to President Truman urging him not to disturb the current naval/military organization without full consideration of both short- and long-term consequences. In strong language Clark assailed a "military clique which is now using the word unification as a means of attaining its end." The League's National President further asserted that the proposed merger of the Army and the

Navy "under a single dictatorship is patently a grab for power, although this purpose is well disguised. It will prove to be not a merging but a submerging of our first line of attack and defense, namely sea-air power."[7]

Truman never replied directly to Clark, who was succeeded in December 1945 by Ralph Bard, a former Under Secretary of the Navy and close associate of Forrestal. But the President did send a message to Congress the same month that endorsed a unification plan already supported by Army leadership. A Navy Department order sent out after the Truman message forbade naval personnel from speaking out against unification unless their opinions were specifically requested by Congress.

National President Bard and other League leaders continued to contest the unification issue for several months, but to no avail. Sensing continued opposition would do both the organization and the Navy more harm than good, on June 27, 1946, Bard announced a cessation of League efforts to resist the move toward unification.[8] After Congress adjourned in August it was announced that the Naval and Military Affairs Committees of both houses would be merged into Armed Services Committees.

With unification of the principal defense committees in both houses of Congress a *fait accompli*, unification of the armed services was a foregone conclusion. The National Security Act of 1947 was passed in the first session of the new Congress. Fortunately, through efforts by Congressman Vinson and Secretary Forrestal the previous year, several provisions particularly objectionable to the Navy Department had been dropped. In addition, guarantees were provided that the Marine Corps and carrier aviation would remain under Navy control.

Several of the improvements in the bill evolved, according to Navy League records, from a March 1946 Board of Directors meeting at the Navy Department with Forrestal and other Navy Department officials. It was decided at that meeting that a report on key unification issues requested by Forrestal and written by Ferdinand Eberstadt — a League vice president and long-time friend of the Secretary — should be released, not through the Department of the Navy, but rather through the Navy League. The *Eberstadt Report* was one of the principal documents used by the high-level tri-service group that in January 1947 produced the final draft of the legislative proposal that later became the National Security Act of 1947, unifying the armed services into a single national defense establishment.

Coincidentally, Ralph Bard turned the national presidency over to Frank Hecht in June 1947. Hecht had played a key role in the League's highly successful 1943-1945 recruiting campaign, and like Bard and Clark, was from the Chicago area. One of Hecht's first actions was to have the Board of Directors restore the slogan of the Navy League as the "Civilian Arm of the Navy," which had been dropped in September 1946 in an effort by his predecessor to de-emphasize the connection between the League and the Navy. Hecht began meeting frequently with the Navy's district commandants and members of the public affairs community. He traveled almost constantly, logging an estimated 50,000 miles in his first year as League National President, telling the Navy and Marine Corps story at luncheons, banquets, and public as well as private meetings. Adopting a more aggressive posture than Ralph Bard on broad issues of concern to the Department of the Navy, Hecht asked the League's national directors and state and regional presidents to approve a more proactive educational campaign directed at Congress.

The need for such a campaign, which was approved by the League's Board of Directors on November 30, 1948, was validated two months later when the League's new Committee on Public Information, charged by the Board of Directors with "the continuous dissemination of authentic information pertaining to the Navy,"[9] delivered a report that it had worked on in collaboration with Navy officials. This report addressed the future of naval aviation, the continued existence of which was once more under attack by those who believed that all U.S. aviation assets should be under the operational control of the U.S. Air Force. Active-duty naval officers firmly believed that the Navy could not accomplish its postwar missions without aircraft, and the League Board of Directors, realizing the gravity of the situation, approved the expenditure of $100,000 per year for five years to do what the Navy could not do for itself: disagree with Truman Administration and Defense Department policies and fight to keep naval aviation in the Navy. Secretary of the Navy John Sullivan, aware of the collusion between the Navy and the League, approved of this effort.[10]

The debate over post-World War II roles and missions of the armed forces, combined with budget cuts in early 1949 that threw the entire defense establishment into chaos, increased competition for shrinking defense funds. This volatile mix of fiscal constraint and service importance in the post-World War II national security environment came to a climax in the spring and summer of 1949 over the relative merits of the flush-deck, 65,000-ton supercarrier *United States* vs. the intercontinental B-36 bomber. When accounts of the intra-Defense Department feud were fed to the press, largely by the Navy, the House Armed Services Committee convened public hearings that revealed a profound depth of discord within the Pentagon over weapons, strategy, and the issue of unification.

The first shot in what was to become a long and bitter fight between the Navy and the Department of Defense was fired by Secretary of Defense Johnson. On April 23, 1949, less than one month after taking office, and following a vote demanded in the Joint Chiefs of Staff "tank" by the Air Force over the issue of continued funding of *United States*, he abruptly cancelled the Navy's highest shipbuilding priority, considered by naval leadership to be essential to the future of naval aviation. The Secretary's action in canceling the contract was taken without informing either Secretary of the Navy Sullivan or Chief of Naval Operations Admiral Louis Denfeld.

Congress had already authorized and appropriated funds for the supercarrier, which had twice been approved by President Truman. The keel for the new ship, tentatively designated the *United States*, had been laid at the Newport News Shipbuilding and Dry Dock construction yard on April 18, 1949.

Secretary Sullivan, who believed he had a commitment from Secretary Johnson to discuss the carrier decision with him before taking any precipitate action, submitted his resignation to President Truman. His letter, given to the press by the Navy, cited Secretary Johnson's "unprecedented action ... in so drastically and arbitrarily changing and restricting the operational plans of an Armed Service without consultation with that service." The letter also cited concerns that Johnson's decision "will result in a renewed effort to abolish the Marine Corps and to transfer all Naval and Marine Aviation elsewhere."[11]

Johnson's cancellation decision only accelerated League efforts on behalf of the beleaguered sea service. Distribution of 20,000 copies of a speech by House Armed Services Committee Chairman Vinson criticizing the reduction in the Navy's budget was followed by dissemination of 18,000 copies of an interview in *U.S. News and World Report* with Fleet Admiral William Halsey that explained why the Navy needed aircraft carriers. Additional articles and open letters from National President Hecht criticized the Secretary of Defense not only for his arbitrary actions but also for his attempt to impose a "gag rule ... a step down the road trod by Hitler, Mussolini, and Stalin" over all active-duty and retired military and civilian employees of the Defense Department.[12]

By the summer of 1949, Navy uniformed leadership was convinced that, rather than being an objective and nonpartisan overseer of all of the nation's armed services, the Secretary of Defense was so Air Force-oriented that he was determined to prevent the Navy from sharing the Air Force's strategic-bombing mission or, as it was oftentimes referred to, the "atomic blitz." Chief of Naval Operations Denfeld and Vice Chief Arthur Radford wanted to share in the execution of the atomic blitz strategy and sought a larger role for naval aviation and carrier task forces in the execution of strategic air warfare in general. But the Air Force outmaneuvered the Navy at every step, not only within the Pentagon and the White House, but also on Capitol Hill and with the nation's print and broadcast media. Additional budget cuts were coming and Navy leadership recognized that many of them would be directed at naval aviation.

Secretary Johnson, acknowledging the damaging political implications of his actions and seeking to mollify sea service advocates, on June 21 announced that he was approving the Navy's request to modernize and upgrade two Essex-class carriers, using the $130,000,000 released by cancellation of the *United States*. That same

USS *Essex* (CV-9)

day, Dan Kimball, the new Secretary of the Navy, wrote to League President Hecht informing him of the decision and suggesting that Secretary Johnson's favorable action, combined with a conciliatory speech he had given at the National War College, answered "practically all the questions that have been bothering the Navy League."[13] From Hecht's perspective, Kimball's letter, originating from a Navy Secretary more supportive of the Defense Secretary than the sea service, was more reassuring than the facts warranted. The Navy League elected to present its concerns on Capitol Hill.

In July 1949, the League National President testified, at Chairman Vinson's invitation, before the House Armed Services Committee. He bluntly asserted that because of Secretary Johnson's dictatorial decisions, Congress should not give additional statutory authority to the Secretary of Defense. He also stated the League's opposition to pending legislation creating the position of Chairman, Joint Chiefs of Staff.

The League was not reluctant to carry the fight for naval aviation beyond the venue of Congress, and, in a particularly strong letter released to the media, Hecht assailed the Air Force Association's position that the Air Force alone should be responsible for all air operations:

> A modern fleet can neither defend itself nor destroy an enemy fleet without control of an air arm. The carrier, with its air-striking potential, has replaced the battleship as the capital ship of the fleet ... To deprive the Navy of its air arm would render it weak, ineffectual, and incapable of fulfilling its mission.[14]

As still further indication of the diminished position of the Navy in the post-World War II era, Secretary of Defense Johnson cancelled all special observances by the services of individual days of celebration and instituted the third Saturday in May as "Armed Forces Day." The Navy League, which had consistently used Navy

Day since its 1922 inception to celebrate the fleet as well as its own contributions as the "Civilian arm of the Navy," initially declared that it would ignore the Secretary's directive and continue the traditional October 27 observance of Theodore Roosevelt's birthday as "Navy Day." But under pressure from Department of the Navy leadership, and with the ordered withdrawal of any naval units from participation in the celebration, in September 1949 National President Hecht sent a letter to Secretary of the Navy Matthews indicating the League was "reluctantly" abandoning its annual celebration of Navy Day.[15]

The assault on the Navy, and naval aviation in particular, continued into the autumn, in a period that would subsequently come to be known as the "Revolt of the Admirals." There was no denying that the stakes were high; from the shared perspective of senior uniformed Navy and League leadership, "at stake was the Navy's survival as something more than a mere transport service."[16] Sources within the executive and legislative branches of government indicated that Truman Administration budget plans for fiscal year 1950 called for reduction to a six aircraft carrier Navy, with only one "fleet" carrier being assigned to the Pacific Ocean!

On October 5, 1949, Congressman Vinson opened hearings on national defense policy. Navy and Marine witnesses asserted that the needs of the sea services were being ignored by the Truman Administration and attacked the B-36 as an inferior airplane. They also criticized as militarily unsound the concept of strategic bombing and stated that Secretary Johnson's termination of the *United States* posed a grave threat to national security.

Admiral Denfeld's testimony was particularly pointed:

> The entire Navy is gravely concerned whether it will have modern weapons, in quality and quantity, to do the job expected ... at the outbreak of a future war. We have real misgivings over the reductions that are taking place ... Our concern is with arbitrary reductions that impair, or even eliminate, essential naval functions.
>
> It is illogical, damaging, and dangerous to proceed directly to mass procurement of the B-36 without evaluation to the extent that the Army and the Navy may be starved for funds and our strategic concept of war frozen about an uncertain weapon.[17]

In response, the Air Force challenged Navy testimony regarding the capabilities of the B-36 and shifted focus toward criticizing the Navy for both its advocacy of *United States* in light of the proven efficacy of land-based air power and its refusal to be a team player in the Department of Defense. Air Force Major General H.J. Knerr even questioned the need for a large Navy in an atomic age against an opponent, the Soviet Union, impervious to sea power: "To maintain a five-ocean Navy to fight a no-ocean opponent is a foolish waste of time, men, and resources."[18]

Particularly damaging to the Navy's case, given the thrust of Admiral Denfeld's statement, was the testimony of America's first Chairman of the Joint Chiefs, Army General Omar Bradley. The general maintained that the real issue was not the B-36 versus the *United States* but a much broader issue, civilian control of the military:

> When the authority of the President and the Secretary of Defense over the armed forces are challenged this amounts to open rebellion against civilian control ... We have here a group of 'fancy Dans' who won't hit the line with all they have on every play, unless they can call the signals ... The Navy in spirit as well as deed refuses to accept unification.[19]

In the wake of the Chief of Naval Operations' testimony on Capitol Hill, on October 27, 1949, Secretary of the Navy Matthews fired Admiral Denfeld for "inability to conform to Defense Department policies." At a subsequent press conference, President Truman indicated he approved of the Navy Secretary's action "as a move to restore discipline."[20] In response to the firing, League National President Hecht issued a statement describing the Chief of Naval Operations as "the Number 1 victim ... [of] the new thought control in the United States."[21]

In December 1949, when Johnson ordered the decommissioning of 35 Navy and Marine Corps aviation squadrons, Hecht and other League leaders again spoke out against the cutbacks and reductions, but, cognizant of Denfeld's fate, did so in restrained terms without embarrassing the Navy further or breaching the close working relationship between the Department and the Navy League that had started before World War II. By this time, several traditional civilian supporters of the League viewed with concern its strident opposition to Defense Department policies, and some senior naval officers, in the wake of Admiral Denfeld's relief, felt that "the League's activity was doing more harm than good by creating the impression that the Navy was anti-everything."[22] In November 1949, at the League's annual meeting in Saint Paul, Minnesota, Secretary of the Navy Matthews indicated that the Navy "was satisfied with its position in the defense setup" and asked the League to modify its program of opposition.[23]

The final report of the House Armed Services Committee on the *United States* versus B-36 hearings was released in March 1950. It took note of the Navy's opposition to the B-36/atomic blitz strategy and directed the "National Military Establishment" to ensure that conventional forces were mobile, flexible, and tailored to a particular mission and properly funded. The House directed the Defense Department to reconsider its strategy "so that all services will have confidence that the decisions represent a meshing of views, not the imposition of a one-service or two-service concept upon a third service."[24]

In conclusion, the House report supported Secretary Johnson's decision to scrap the *United States* and fund the B-36 as the "best weapon for strategic bombing." But, reflecting Chairman Vinson's concerns, and to mollify aggrieved naval leadership, the report added that "experts" such as the Chairman of the Joint Chiefs and the Air Force Chief of Staff were not qualified to determine for the Navy the best weapons to ensure control of the sea.

The "Revolt of the Admirals" had failed. A historian of the Joint Chiefs of Staff would later conclude, "For one of the few times in history, the Navy had been routed ... the Air Force was vindicated ... and the Army seemed clearly in charge of the American high command."[25] But while the League shared in the Navy's fate, the principal issues involved, including strategy, roles and missions of the armed forces, and the merits of sea-based versus land-based air power, were soon to be overtaken by events half a world away.

U.S. Marine tanks scramble around blown out bridge south of Koto-ri. Note: Chinese communist prisoners at left being herded to rear for questioning. "C" Company, 1st Battalion, 7th Regiment patrol.

Nothing stops the U.S. Marines as they march south from Koto-ri, fighting their way through Chinese communist hordes in subzero weather of the mountains. Despite their ordeal, these men hold their heads high.

U.S. Marine Corps air and ground integration during fighting with Chinese communists in Korea. U.S. Marines move forward as close air support clears an area ahead during fighting near "Frozen Chosin" Reservior in early December, 1950.

Chapter VII
The 40-Year War: Confrontation, 1950-1962

In 1949 the Soviet Union exploded its first atomic bomb. *Life* magazine, devoting an entire issue to Soviet military capabilities, noted that while six percent of America's national income was going to defense, the Soviets were spending 25 percent of theirs on military hardware. Concluded the popular weekly, "War Can Come; Will We Be Ready?"[1] In December, Deputy Secretary of Defense Robert Lovett pronounced, "We must realize that we are now in a mortal conflict. It is not a Cold War; it is a hot war."[2] Speaking at the first observance of Armed Forces Day, May 19, 1950, President Truman, reflecting on the advent of the Cold War and the mounting military and industrial strength of the Soviet Union, declared that despite America's victory in World War II, the world now lived in an atmosphere where "some people only understand a fist."[3]

Just how "hot" the Cold War was to become was evident little more than a month later, when, on June 25, 1950, massed North Korean forces invaded the Republic of Korea. They would have completely overrun and occupied the nearly defenseless nation in short order had it not been for the delaying actions provided by U.S. Marine Corps air and ground units and air strikes launched from the carrier USS *Valley Forge* (CG-50) in early July. The F-9F Panther fighters launched by the aircraft carrier were the first Navy jet aircraft ever to enter combat, and Navy and Marine propeller-vintage ground-attack aircraft, which had performed similar missions in the Pacific during World War II, made the North Korean Army, and its T-34 tanks, pay a high price for their advance.

In response to the proven utility of sea-based tactical aviation in stemming the advance of communist forces, Navy League President Frank Hecht immediately recommended to Defense Secretary Johnson that he authorize the recommissioning of 20 aircraft carriers from the mothballed inactive force. Four years later the wisdom of the League's 1946 position in support of maintaining both the force and personnel in a reserve status was seen: 665 combat ships, 540 supply and sealift ships, and 225,000 naval reservists were recalled to active duty between 1950 and 1954.

The Korean War "saved" the U.S. Navy. In the early months of the war there was an almost complete change in the collective congressional mindset on the need for sea-based carrier aviation. Under Secretary of the Navy Kimball remarked in late November 1950 that Vinson and many other members of Congress had become "more than ever convinced that we not only have to have a more modern aircraft carrier, but we must have a number of them." And Chairman Vinson oftentimes reminded Air Force officers in Washington that the Navy and Marine Corps viewed close air support with far greater enthusiasm than *they* did, stressing rapid response and close coordination with the ground commander.

With a shooting war on his hands, reverses on the battlefield, and the American public, through media reports, appalled by the deteriorated state of the American military, Truman fired Secretary of Defense Johnson in September 1950, to be replaced by Truman confidant and World War II hero General George C. Marshall.[4] Francis Matthews continued as Secretary of the Navy for another year, and then accepted appointment as U.S. Ambassador to Ireland. Under Secretary Kimball succeeded Matthews as Secretary of the Navy.

The Navy League, recalling problems in dealing with the Wilson and Hoover Administrations, had been a player in the issues involved in the late 1940s unification and naval aviation battles, but had been careful to ensure that its conduct had the tacit approval of the Department of the Navy. But with a shooting war now ongoing in Northeast Asia, and an intransigent Soviet Union firmly in control of a significant portion of the Eurasian landmass, the League adopted a strident tone, more in keeping with past National Presidents Thompson and Hubbard, but now enunciated by National President Hecht. At a meeting of the California Club in Los Angeles in early October 1950, Hecht unleashed a vitriolic attack against the Truman Administration, alleging serious mistakes in the Departments of State and Defense. The National President then returned to the arguments the League had been making since the end of World War II, with direct reference to the period of the Revolt of the Admirals and Omar Bradley's oft-quoted characterization of Navy admirals as "fancy Dans":

> Korea vindicated the Navy and the Marine Corps and proved to the American people that there was no cheap one-punch knockout blow that the Air Force could deliver in war ... The man who belittled these same Navy and Marine Corps victors in Korea as 'fancy Dans' is in the saddle with added rank. Therefore there is grave doubt whether Korea has proved anything to guarantee this nation an adequate Navy and Marine Corps essential to the national defense.[5]

With the war in Korea perceived in the United States as degenerating into a stalemate, the League continued on the attack. An editorial in the December 1950 issue of *Now Hear This!* decried a "new outbreak of defeatism and old-fashioned isolationism in this country." But considerably more serious was a speech given to the Navy League directors by National President Hecht in April 1952. Reprinted in a May issue of *Vital Speeches of the Day*, Hecht was unrestrained in his criticism of "outsiders dictating how the Navy will fight."[6] Hecht was highly critical of the House Appropriations Subcommittee for deleting funds for a second Forrestal-class aircraft carrier, starkly stating, "I suspect that this is another of the evil fruits of the implacable opposition of some zealots, not all of whom are now in uniform, who say that naval aviation is an unnecessary duplication of the Air Force."[7]

Hecht closed his remarks with a clear statement of the League's position on naval aviation and issued a clarion call to arms:

> The Navy League is not opposed to the presently-approved plans for the expansion of the Air Force ... We also believe that naval aviation is an important integral part of 'Air Power,' and that the Navy, within agreed budgetary limits, should have the decisive voice in the determination of the size, shape, and scope of naval aviation. We definitely do not believe that the Air Force should ever attempt to exercise a veto power over naval aviation ...
>
> Therefore, I call upon all of the officers and directors of the Navy League to join in an active, vigorous campaign by the Navy League for the upbuilding of its membership this year so that we may make our influence felt in the next session of Congress. There is no other organization that can do the job that should be done by the civilian friends of the Navy.[8]

Hecht was not yet done with the Truman Administration. Six months after his speech on saving naval aviation, and less than two weeks before the national election, Hecht publicly defied the Defense Department by announcing the League's intent to celebrate the traditional Navy Day on October 27 "despite lack of U.S. sanction," in the words of the *New York Times*.[9] In a press release, Hecht noted that more people would be celebrating Navy Day in 1952 than in any year since 1949, when it was "officially" abolished by Secretary of Defense Johnson. In the League's view, the increasing interest in celebrating Navy Day by the general public "reflects the growing number of American business and political leaders as well as ordinary citizens who recognize that a war cannot be won without a powerful Navy."[10]

Content with the outcome of the national election, which saw Dwight D. Eisenhower triumph, the League, with its own 50th anniversary approaching, pondered its future and looked back at the past. The organization had come close to bankruptcy several times, and its membership recruiting and retention had been a continuing problem from 1903 on, except during wartime. Nonetheless, the Navy League had always found a way to carry out its basic mission of educating the American people and their elected leaders, as well as the nation's press, about the importance of seapower, naval as well as commercial. Of almost equal importance, and one that would assume a greater role in League matters in the second half-century of its existence, were programs of support for the personnel of all of the nation's armed services and their families, particularly in times of war.

It was fitting that in the month of the League's Golden Jubilee the keel of the 70,000-ton supercarrier *Saratoga* (with a displacement 5,000 tons greater than the stillborn *United States*) was laid, validating all of the organization's efforts of the previous fifty years. In 1952 as in 1902, the Navy League's goal was the same: to build and maintain a fleet adequate to defend America.

Appropriately enough, the Navy League's first half-century of service to the nation was celebrated with the greatest fanfare where the organization had started: New York City. The handsomely packaged program for the League's Golden Anniversary Dinner on October 27, 1952, at the Hotel Astor started with a personally signed *Foreword* by Fleet Admiral Halsey.

Fleet Admiral William F. "Bull" Halsey, USN

The chairman for the dinner was John J. Bergen, a future National President. Francis Cardinal Spellman offered the invocation. Among several guest speakers were Secretary of the Navy Kimball, Chief of Naval Operations Admiral William M. Fechteler, and Major General William "Wild Bill" Donovan, director of the World War II Office of Strategic Services, predecessor to the Central Intelligence Agency.

The program also included brief situation reports by Marine Corps Commandant General Lemuel Shepherd Jr. on the evolving warfighting capabilities of the Marine Corps and retired Admiral John Towers on the current combat successes and future missions of naval aviation. There also were several photo pages of Navy ships and aircraft in the program as well as a three-chapter

"Yesterday," "Today," and "Tomorrow" mini-history of the Navy League.

Halsey's *Foreword* set the tone for the evening. The fleet admiral led off by saluting the Navy League for having always "preached the policy of well-balanced, efficiently trained, and well-equipped forces ... [and for] consistently fighting to keep our legislators informed [about sea-service needs]."[11] Halsey then addressed what he and those present at the dinner fully realized, that the United States and other countries of the "Free World" were faced with a new war against an implacable enemy, the Soviet Union. Because there had been, so far, only a few isolated shooting incidents but no major military conflict between the two nations (excepting Korea, where Soviet logistical support was suspected, but actual participation in combat operations unproven at the time), diplomats and the media continued to refer to the U.S.-Soviet confrontation as a "Cold War."

However, Halsey rejected the label as inappropriate when Americans were fighting and dying on the Korean Peninsula. "There is no such thing as a Cold War," he asserted in the program *Foreword*. "When men die on any battlefield for a principle, that is war, no matter what the degree of heat. ... Let us not delude ourselves into believing we can engage in a conflict of half peace and half war."[12]

"We cannot afford to lose," Halsey continued, referring to the situation in Korea. "The price of defeat is too great. Let us face it, we are engaged in a shooting war, not with Koreans or Red Chinese, but with Communism." And that war, he said, "is no téte-â-téte. It is a slugfest between two diametrically opposed ideologies, one free and the other slave." After shifting focus to address problems caused by highly placed "amateurs" who believed that future wars could be won by land-based airpower alone, the admiral dryly observed, "They have a peculiarly one-track mind, with strong beliefs in a one-weapon defense."[13]

Halsey closed with the following mandate addressed to the entire Navy League:

> You must continue, more strenuously than ever, to combat the forces, within and without our country, who would cripple our defense. You must continuously keep before our people the need for an up-to-the-minute Navy in our team of well-balanced Armed Forces. Today, our Navy is good. Let's make it better, and keep it so.[14]

While the Navy League was ready and willing to carry out Halsey's mandate, seven years after the end of World War II it was not sure exactly what to do that it was not already doing. League membership had increased modestly following the outbreak of the Korean War, but the organization had not formulated a detailed road map for the future that would tell the American people precisely what the organization stood for and where it was going.

As would become apparent over the ensuing decade, the focus of the Navy

League would shift. The elimination of the cabinet-level ranking of the Secretary of the Navy, and the advent of the Department of Defense fundamentally altered the playing field on which the League and other preparedness organizations would play in the second half of the 20th century. Though not immediately apparent in the aftermath of the Korean War, by the end of the 1950s, while retaining its public education goals, the League's focus had clearly shifted to areas only peripherally touched during its first half-century of existence: involvement with America's youth, and substantive ties with the defense industry. Both initiatives would signal a fundamental reorientation in League goals and processes.

But this reorientation would only emerge slowly during the 1950s, and was not a course immediately adopted by national leadership. Initially, the League was undecided as to just what the Navy expected it to do. One reason for this indecision was that uniformed leadership, particularly under Chief of Naval Operations Admiral Forrest P. Sherman, who had succeeded the fired Denfeld during the Revolt of the Admirals, was reluctant to set forth for public consumption a new naval strategy that stressed the central role of carrier task forces, amphibious ships, and submarines in operating offensively against enemy bases and areas. Eventually, Admiral Sherman recognized the need to market the Navy's strategic concept to the American public, but his untimely death in July 1951 terminated such efforts for several years.

But even given the lack of a marketing plan for the Navy, the reality was that, thanks to the Korean War, the fleet had doubled in size between 1949 and 1952. Statements from both soldiers and Marines, as well as North Korean prisoners of war, attesting to the combat effectiveness of "the blue airplanes" flying from Navy aircraft carriers, rendered mute proponents of eliminating naval aviation as a needless duplication of combat capability.[15]

Rather than the Navy facing elimination as a service, by the mid-1950s its aircraft carriers, battleships, and cruisers were being sent on a routine basis to trouble spots around the world. Forward-deployed, offensively-oriented naval forces, generally built around aircraft carriers, became symbols of America's global leadership and commitment to its allies, particularly in the Mediterranean and Western Pacific. In recognition of the increasing strategic value of oil and the volatility of Middle Eastern politics, a small force of destroyers and support ships was even deployed to the Persian Gulf.

By 1953, the United States was a nation far different from the proud, powerful, but untried actor that had strode on the international stage in 1908 with the flamboyant dispatching of the Great White Fleet to circumnavigate the world. The Navy League, too, had changed in the decades since its founding. It was moving with the times through numerous changes in its governance rules, a reorganization of national headquarters, and an unprecedented delegation of program authority and responsibilities to League councils.

These changes, begun back in the early 1930s, were deemed necessary to improve and increase the organization's effectiveness. But there were other reasons, specifically related to members' concerns. Navy Leaguers not living in the nation's capital felt that for most of its existence the League had been too Washington-oriented. And while the League had benefited immensely in its first half century from strong leadership provided by talented and dedicated National Presidents, many felt that it had become too autocratic, and too dependent on the political influence, personal fortunes, and persuasive capabilities of its national officers.

The perception among many League members was that concentration of power at the top was not only hurting the Navy League, but also limiting its ability to help the sea services. This perception would continue throughout the decade, and result in significant changes in League procedures, particularly in the early 1960s.

Armin Rappaport, writing in the early 1950s, sensed the frustration of the rank-and-file and summarized the situation in the concluding chapter of his fifty-year history of the Navy League:

> The nature of the League's organization served to discourage prospective members and dampen the ardor of old ones. Authority was lodged in a half dozen people on the national headquarters level — the Executive Committee, the Executive Secretary, and the President. The membership was rarely consulted on matters of policy. Only occasionally was the opinion of the rank and file solicited by means of polls or questions submitted at the Annual Convention (at which rarely more than ten percent of the members were present). Most often, members became aware of policy only after reading about it in the League magazine or in a publicity release.[16]

Another major organizational problem was that, unless they were personally close to one of the national officers, League members at large had almost no voice in the selection of the League's policy-making officials. The National President and other members of the Executive Committee were appointed by the League's Board of Directors to indeterminate terms. Some vice presidents served in office as many as 13 years with many of their responsibilities largely undefined. The succession of presidents was determined by a small Nominating Committee at the direction of the outgoing National President; timing for incoming presidents was non-existent, with some taking office the day they were elected. The allocation of directors was not specified and left to the Nominating Committee, which had no specified procedures; the alleged bylaws of the organization were subject to "instant" change. Annual meetings had become largely electioneering campaigns, with little direct connection to League programs or determination of issues.[17] The Navy League had, in effect, become a closed-loop society.

A post-World War II start on changing League bylaws and headquarters operating procedures was made during the presidencies of Ralph Bard and Frank Hecht. In his December 1946 *Report to Members of the Navy League*, Bard strongly recommended that local councils "provide tangible help," separate from any nationally-driven program, to local authorities in setting up naval reserve units and the attendant supporting infrastructure such as training quarters, armories, and docking facilities for training vessels.[18]

Hecht, becoming National President in 1947, particularly appreciated the importance of League councils, and traveled more than 50,000 miles during his tenure to interface with Navy Leaguers throughout the country. Partly because of the discussions he had with council presidents and other members, he took a number of steps to improve communications between headquarters and the councils and reinvigorate the League's Navy Day celebrations. He also worked with the Navy Department to establish a new League program that would assist in obtaining Navy speakers for civilian audiences throughout the United States.

Establishment of the speakers program was suggested by former Secretary of the Navy Kimball, who became one of the Navy League's strongest advocates and most active members. Hecht reported at the League's 1953 Spring Meeting that the former Navy Secretary, already serving as chairman of the League's Membership Committee and as a national vice president, had agreed to direct the speakers program as well.

For his part, the National President sought to provide much-needed private-sector assistance to the Navy in its public-relations attempts to win over the hearts and minds of the American people during the postwar budget battles. He spoke out more forcefully than the Navy itself could about the nation's need for nuclear-powered submarines and, later, nuclear-powered aircraft carriers and other surface ships. Hecht also was a persistent and persuasive advocate for building the Navy's new line of supercarriers, beginning with USS *Forrestal* (CVA-59).

But Hecht also insisted that any public positions taken by the Navy League, particularly with members of the U.S. Congress, be only those approved by the Executive Committee and the National President. He wanted to ensure tight control of the League's message as discussed in the April 1953 *Report of the Meeting of the National Directors and Council Presidents*:

> The function and purpose of the Navy League of the United States is to have an informed public familiar with the place and needs of the Navy in our national preparedness program. It is not the function or purpose of the Navy League to be active in politics of any type because such activity will result in the Navy League's educational tax exemption being terminated. In the

> event and if at any time the Navy League can be of assistance to Congress in any of its proposed legislation, that function is specifically reserved to the President of the Navy League ... No member of the Navy League, in his official capacity, shall communicate with any department of the government on general policy matters without the approval of the President or the Executive Committee.[19]

As the League's principal spokesman, Hecht used the occasion of the April 1953 League meeting, and its Washington, D.C., location, to call on President Eisenhower and clarify for him the organization's stance on many issues that had been raised, most often personally by Hecht himself, in the controversial period of the Revolt of the Admirals and early months of the Korean conflict. By this time, Eisenhower's demand that the Joint Chiefs be "team players," and his displeasure at having administration policies on military and national security issues debated in public venues was well known in the nation's capital and among its military leaders. Navy League leadership, in the personage of its National President, hastened to let the new President know of its loyalty, as well as its understanding of the "new" rules to be followed.

At the League's Washington meeting, Hecht discussed his April 27, 1953, visit at the White House with President Eisenhower. During his session with the President, the combative National President pledged the Navy League's support for the administration's "efforts to maintain national security without serious impairment of the country's economy." Hecht said that he also emphasized to the President, who undoubtedly knew of the League's acrimonious positions, personified by Hecht himself, on both service unification and naval aviation, that the "Navy League was for all the armed services," was "not a contentious or political organization," and was "earnestly seeking to keep the public informed about preparedness and in particular the essentiality of sea-air power."[20]

Admiral Robert B. Carney, USN

Four months after Hecht's meeting with President Eisenhower, Admiral Robert B. Carney succeeded Admiral Fechteler as Chief of Naval Operations. Carney was not only an experienced fighter at sea and fleet commander, but also a strategic thinker and budgetary expert. Early in his tour he became concerned about the rapidly shrinking capabilities of the U.S. defense industrial base, particularly those companies closely associated with the shipbuilding industry.

Demonstrating his concern, at the League's 1953 annual meeting in New Orleans, Louisiana,

Carney challenged the assembled members to become more proactive, rebuild membership to mid-1940s levels or higher, serve as a more effective voice in educating the American public on the importance of seapower, and form close working ties not only with the U.S. shipbuilding industry but also with those in other industries that depended on seaborne commerce to sustain their existence.

Reflecting the Chief of Naval Operations's desires, the League adopted 13 resolutions in New Orleans, including ones favoring maintaining "at all times" three combat-ready Marine divisions and three combat-ready air wings "as authorized by law," and continuing a "long-range naval building program to include at least one Forrestal-class aircraft carrier each year." But, reflecting the rancorous period of the Revolt of the Admirals and Louis Johnson's tenure as Secretary of Defense, and despite Hecht's assurances to Eisenhower of the League's desire to be "on the team," resolutions were also approved opposing "the use of public funds for the observance of Armed Forces Day," use of appropriation bills legislation or amendments "affecting the basic structure of any of the armed forces or the strength thereof," or the development of "a one-weapon concept of national defense." Finally, a resolution was approved "in favor of the continued observance of Navy Day under the sponsorship of the Navy League."[21]

Ironically, it was Admiral Carney, and not the Navy League, that would run afoul of the Pentagon's civilian leadership as well as the President.[22] But by the time Admiral Arleigh A. Burke, his relief, became Chief of Naval Operations in the summer of 1955 the situation faced by his three immediate predecessors had significantly shifted at the strategic level and in the highest councils of the government.[23] And while the basic realities of war in the nuclear age would remain defined by weapons of undeniable destructive power, the sentiment that the Navy was largely irrelevant to the "big fight," and required only for certain niche missions at sea, had been totally discredited by events in Northeast Asia.

photo by PH@ Koralewski

The nuclear-powered guided-missile frigate USS *Bainbridge* (DLGN-25).

The proof was in the budget numbers. During Admiral Carney's tenure as Chief of Naval Operations, the Navy's shipbuilding budget had more than doubled. For fiscal year 1955, Carney's final year in office, it was

$893,000,000. In 1956 it would increase to $1.4 billion and rise to $1.8 billion by 1959.[24] The Navy got its supercarriers, and for more than just "atomic blitz" missions. The world's first nuclear-powered aircraft carrier, USS *Enterprise*, (CVN-65) was commissioned in 1958, termed by Navy leadership as "the largest ship of any kind ever built by any nation."[25] These "acres of United States real estate at sea" and their attendant surface ships would remain on the front lines of America's national defense for the remaining four decades of the Cold War.

In addition to the supercarriers, guided-missile frigates arrived in the fleet in 1956; the world's first nuclear-powered surface ship, the cruiser USS *Long Beach*, (CGN-9) in 1957; the world's first nuclear-powered guided-missile frigate, USS *Bainbridge*, (DLGN-25) in 1959. In 1960, the development of a seaborne ballistic missile was realized when a Polaris missile was fired from the submerged fleet ballistic missile submarine USS *George Washington* (SSBN-598).

Perhaps more than any prior Chief of Naval Operations, Admiral Burke emphasized the "long-range view," which in his mind encompassed far more than just building what he termed in public addresses "The New Navy." But with President Eisenhower insistent that Burke, unlike the recalcitrant Carney, in the President's view, be a "team player" and devote the bulk of his effort to shaping military policy on the Joint Chiefs of Staff from a maritime perspective, the new Chief of Naval Operations realized that both he and the Navy would need assistance outside the chain of command to meet the sea service's goals. And Admiral Burke decided that the institution that could provide the most help was the Navy League of the United States.[26]

Burke asked the organization to take a position of increased advocacy, both nationally and in the nation's capital, and realize the full potential of its restored watchword, "The Civilian Arm of the Navy." His suggested direction to the organization began the "rebirth" of the Navy League in the second half of the 20th century. Not only did the League begin working much more closely with the nation's defense industries, but this rebirth at the national level was accompanied by an enhanced role for local councils in the organization's planning/decision-making/implementation process, and eventually by the drafting of bylaws that fundamentally changed the character of the organization. And coming to power in council, state, regional, and national offices, was a new generation of extraordinarily talented men and women, many of whom had served in combat during World War II.

E.V. Richards, who succeeded Hecht as National President in December 1953, expanded significantly on the latter's efforts to work more closely with the councils in carrying out the League's mission. Owner of a prosperous chain of movie houses, he immediately initiated another recruiting program in an attempt to restore the membership ranks that had declined to fewer than 10,000 from a postwar peak of almost 19,000 in 1945.

At an April 1954 meeting of the Board of Directors in Annapolis, Maryland, Richards announced initiation of three major new programs. The first was the "Navy Buddy Program," a youth-oriented program first suggested by Secretary of the Navy Robert Anderson as a way for naval reserve officers to undertake to mentor young men and tutor them in the lore and knowledge of the sea services. Intended to interest those of high-school age in a possible career in the Navy, the program was League-wide and considered a success. Council leaders and youths toured ships, took cruises, worked on naval aircraft, and became involved in almost everything that sailors did. The program demonstrated that young people were interested in the naval service, discipline, and patriotism.

The second new program was the Advisory Council on Naval Affairs in which, working in close cooperation with the Navy Department, numerous councils were established to assist commandants of naval districts and commanding officers of major shore activities in the United States in their community affairs and public-relations activities. Advisory Councils were intended, as explained by National President Richards, to assist the Navy in maintaining a "closer relationship between the civilian components and the naval establishment" and membership was to "be representative of a cross section of the community selected in collaboration with the senior officer present and/or commanding officer in each community."[27]

In an implementing instruction signed by the Secretary of the Navy, the Advisory Councils were to act "as civilian advisers on naval affairs at both the local and national levels, as requested." Members were to be appointed by the naval district commandants and were "not necessarily members of the Navy League."[28]

The third new program was one stemming from the preparation, by Navy Rear Admiral J.P. Womble at the direction of the Secretary of Defense, of a report examining the causes of low morale among all military personnel, and their pessimism regarding prospects for a profitable, long-term career in America's armed forces. Based on the report's findings and recommendations, the League embarked on a major citizen-awareness program by creating Womble Committees within participating local councils. Led by a young industrialist, Frank Gard Jameson, the committees had as their purpose the education of the American people as to the need "to strengthen the defense mechanism of our nation and to build higher public esteem for and greater interest in our military establishments." National President Richards maintained that the desired strengthening of the nation's defense could best be achieved by "attracting the best young men and women to the military services for their careers," but admitted that "some correction is needed to reinstate the traditional benefits and meet competition of industry" for these select individuals.[29]

Of note, at the April meeting, Richards turned away suggestions from his predecessor, Frank Hecht, that the Navy League take official stands regarding the United

States leaving the United Nations, withdrawing diplomatic recognition from the Soviet Union, and opposing creation of the United States Air Force Academy. In a pointed March 15, 1954, letter to Hecht preceding the Board of Directors meeting, Richards declined to sanction any such resolutions and indicated that he intended, unless overruled by the board, "that our entire efforts nationally be put behind" gaining new members and the three new initiatives he intended to bring forward for consideration.[30]

Such sentiments on the part of the National President were in keeping with overall League cooperative efforts with other defense organizations and associations. Despite previously expressed reservations in 1953 regarding public funds being expended for Armed Forces Day celebrations, President Eisenhower's desire for "team players" was evident in the Navy League, Air Force Association, and Military Order of the World Wars being joint sponsors of the 1954 National Armed Forces Day Dinner in Washington. League National President Richards had the honor of giving the welcoming speech; President Eisenhower was the principal speaker.

Secretary of the Navy Robert B. Anderson, left, turns over title to the captured Nazi submarine U-505 to Robert Crown, center, and Carl Stockholm, representing the Chicago Museum of Science and Technology.

For health reasons, Richards turned over the national presidency to Carl G. Stockholm, who was elected at the annual meeting in Detroit, Michigan, in December 1954. Stockholm, a former Olympic athlete, sports columnist, and veteran of both world wars, had been instrumental, along with fellow Chicagoan Robert Crown, in forming the committee that succeeded in getting the German submarine U-505, captured off the West Coast of Africa in June 1944 by Chicago native Rear Admiral Daniel Gallery, donated to the Museum of Science and Industry in 1953. The difficulties overcome in getting the submarine to Chicago were indicative of the energy and vitality Stockholm would bring to the national presidency.

The German submarine U-505 is a focal point of the Museum of Science and Technology in Chicago.

Because the Navy refused to cover the cost of the move, the League, working closely with other private groups and the city, raised $250,000 to make the project feasible. The funds permitted sufficient repairs to enable the submarine to complete the voyage to its new home. Navy League member Arnold Sobel, a World War II Coast Guard veteran and Chicago Council member, managed the 3,000-mile journey from Portsmouth, New Hampshire, through 28 locks of the St. Lawrence Seaway and four of the five Great Lakes, arriving at the Chicago waterfront June 26, 1954. U-505's journey ended on the night of September 2, 1954, when it safely navigated, via an elaborate rail and roller system, an 800-foot transit across Lake Shore Drive. On September 25, the German submarine was dedicated as a war memorial and a permanent exhibit at the Museum of Science and Industry.[31]

Stockholm's hard work and financial contribution to make the U-505 idea a reality played a significant role in his being elected National President. Like his predecessors, Stockholm paid his own expenses as National President, and also made several generous donations to keep the organization afloat during difficult times. Overcoming fears of a precipitous drop in membership, he persuaded the Executive Committee to raise the annual League dues to $10. The increase did not keep citizens from joining the League; membership climbed more than 5,000 during Stockholm's tenure, largely due to the superb efforts of John J. Bergen, who had been placed in charge of the membership drive.

Adopting Richards's approach to League resolutions and public statements, Stockholm largely kept leadership focused on the three programs started by his predecessor: the Buddy Program, the Advisory Council on Naval Affairs, and the Womble Committees (to be renamed the "Career Program"). He did further define the Advisory Council's purposes as assisting retiring personnel to secure employment, aiding the Navy in real estate negotiations, hosting receptions for officers joining the service as well as those entering retirement, and training naval personnel to be better recruiters. Chief of Naval Operations Admiral Robert Carney was particularly pleased with the work of the Advisory Councils, citing their workings as "very sound psychologically" and affording "no better way to further Navy-wide public relations."[32]

The National President also decided to assume writing and editing of the monthly publication to League membership addressing the manpower and hardware needs of both the Navy and Marine Corps. Stockholm and Executive Secretary Evelyn Collins personally wrote much of the material and pasted up, proofread, and mailed issues of the "new" *Now Hear This!* Through his personal efforts, Stockholm sought to raise the periodical above what he termed its "hodge-podge" nature, and began the process which would result, three years later, in development of a truly first-class monthly magazine.

The Navy League, under Stockholm's leadership, also made one of the organization's most ambitious and far-reaching decisions ever: to establish, and manage, an annual naval/maritime exposition featuring state-of-the-art Navy, Marine Corps, and Coast Guard platforms, communications, sensors, and combat systems. From its origins in the mid-1950s, the event would evolve over a half-century to become the premier maritime exposition in the world.

The initial step toward what is now widely known throughout the U.S. and international defense communities as the Sea-Air-Space Exposition was taken in 1955 when George C. "Buddy" Gilman, then a lieutenant in the Naval Reserve as well as the new President of the near-dormant District of Columbia Council of the Navy League, was assigned to two weeks active duty for training in the office of Captain John S. McCain Jr., a key aide to Chief of Naval Operations Burke.[33]

McCain took Gilman to see Admiral Burke and the Navy leader challenged the reserve lieutenant to get the District of Columbia Council further involved in promoting the Navy's message and contribution to national defense. From Burke's perspective, the local council in the nation's capital was not doing enough, and Gilman agreed to take the admiral's concerns to council leadership.

There were only 42 members in the District of Columbia Council at the time, including several former Chiefs of Naval Operation and Secretaries of the Navy. However, fewer than a dozen members routinely showed up for the council's meetings. Regardless, at its next session, Gilman addressed Burke's question to the council's leadership. Collectively, they agreed with Admiral Burke that they needed to become more active, and, as an impetus to greater interest and activity, proposed hosting a "Seapower Symposium," open to the press and the public, that would focus on the Navy's embryonic nuclear submarine program.

For legal, political, and budgetary reasons the Navy and Marine Corps could not sponsor such an exposition. However, as an independent, nonprofit, educational organization, with membership restricted to civilians only, the Navy League could sponsor and financially support any event or activity that its elected leaders had determined would benefit the nation's sea services. In this instance, the benefits achieved proved to be far larger, longer lasting, and more varied than originally anticipated.[34]

Active-duty members of the Navy and Marine Corps would be invited to attend the show, at no cost to the government. Some, mostly from Department of the Navy offices and agencies in the greater Washington area, would be asked to participate in limited ways spelled out both in congressional statute and Department of Defense regulations.

The idea, when reported back to the Pentagon, appealed to both McCain and Burke, so Gilman and his "symposium" team plunged into what were uncharted waters for the Navy League, at either the council or national level. The Hilton Hotel at Farragut Square was booked for the one-day event. The LTV Corporation cooperated by flying a dummy missile from Texas to Andrews Air Force Base just outside of Washington, and then trucked it to the hotel for display in the exhibit hall. Demonstrating a knack for free publicity, the League convinced Dave Garroway, host of the National Broadcasting Company's "Today" program, to originate the morning television show that day from the exhibit hall.

The highlight of the one-day symposium, held November 16, 1956, was the luncheon speech by Rear Admiral Hyman G. Rickover, who in his inimitable way told an audience of about 1,000 people of the rationale for, and absolute necessity of, funding a nuclear Navy. Typically, Rickover also took time to chide the defense industry for its numerous shortcomings.

The first Seapower Symposium was viewed by both the Navy and League leadership as a huge success. By the time of the second symposium, held in 1957, which featured a full-scale model of the *Polaris* submarine-launched ballistic missile and other exhibits provided by General Dynamics (builder of the Navy's *Polaris, Poseidon*, and *Trident* strategic-deterrent submarines) and other contractors, the District of Columbia Council had more than 400 members. Most of the new members were from the Washington area offices of the Navy's major contractors. The venue for the event was changed to the Sheraton Park Hotel; subsequently renamed the Sheraton Washington Hotel. Purchased by the Marriott Corporation, it became the Marriott Wardman Park Hotel, where the event is still held almost five decades later.

Moving beyond strategic submarines and missiles, antisubmarine warfare was the theme of the 1958 symposium, which attracted more than 1,000 attendees. The Navy moved major elements of its Antisubmarine Warfare School from Norfolk, Virginia, to the hotel, installed bleachers in the exhibit hall, and ran an actual battle problem in black lights.

National President Stockholm also succeeded in keeping the League away from contentious issues during his presidency. Resolutions were approved in support of building a nuclear Navy, maintaining the strength of the Marine Corps and naval aviation, and aircraft carrier construction. But more controversial positions on issues such as the People's Republic of China's admission to the United Nations, and the leveling of economic sanctions against the Soviet Union, were stillborn within leadership's deliberations at meetings of the Board of Directors and Executive Committee, despite the determined efforts of former National President Frank Hecht to have the League take positions on such issues.

By late 1956, as Stockholm's tenure as National President ended, League membership had climbed to more than 17,000 and the total number of councils to 134. In December, John J. Bergen was elected National President, with the tacit understanding that his opponent in the election, Frank Gard Jameson, would most likely be his successor.

In his civilian life, Bergen, a retired rear admiral in the Naval Reserve, was both a successful businessman and a well known sports figure as President of the New York Rangers and a director of the New York Knickerbockers. He also had considerable political influence and, as President of the New York Council, played a key role in persuading city officials and the Navy Department to stage, in conjunction with the League's 55th Annual Convention, a spectacular *Operation Remember* ticker-tape parade up lower Broadway Avenue in honor of 67 Navy and Marine Corps flag and general officers who had led the sea services to victory in the Pacific Theater. Honoring these Navy and Marine Corps heroes by their presence in port were the aircraft carrier USS *Valley Forge* (CG-50) and 14 other warships, all hosted pierside by Mayor Robert Wagner and the Navy League.

Hallmarks of Bergen's presidency were three initiatives of lasting significance to the Navy League and the nation's sea services: the development of a quality monthly Navy League magazine; the addition of a Marine Corps Activities Committee to the League's organizational structure; and the establishment of the Naval Sea Cadet Corps.

Dissatisfaction with the League's monthly *Now Hear This!* was widespread throughout the organization. Carl Stockholm had tried to rectify the situation, but was simply unable to devote the time on his own to produce a quality periodical. In the view of League leadership, *Now Hear This!* was largely an "aimless news bulletin."[35] Thus Bergen appointed a committee in December 1957 to examine the issue of producing a professional magazine reflective of the organization, containing professional, scholarly articles on issues of the sea services, and managed and directed by a professional staff.

In February 1958, W. Royce Powell was appointed editor and in May the first issue of *Navy-The Magazine of Sea Power* was published, featuring articles by Chief of Naval Operations Admiral Arleigh Burke, Secretary of the Navy Thomas S. Gates Jr., and Marine Corps Commandant General Randolph McC. Pate. The Pate article was notable because it was further recognition that the League no longer would be treating the Corps as merely part of the Navy but as a separate service with its own proud traditions and its own unique manpower and hardware needs.

Another step in the same direction was taken later that year with creation of a Marine Corps Activities Committee. Bergen named Stanley Hope, president of the National Association of Manufacturers and a former president of the Esso-Standard Oil Company, to chair the committee. Its goals were to further public understanding of the basic strategic necessity for a Marine Corps as the nation's force in readiness, and to promote and strengthen recognition of the interdependence of the Navy and Marine Corps in building and maintaining effective seapower.

The third initiative was creation of the United States Naval Sea Cadet Corps, whose antecedents went back almost to the founding of the Navy League of the

United States. The British Navy League, which served as model for the American organization upon its founding, considered the sponsorship of a sea cadet corps one of its most important programs. In the United States, the League had supported various programs devoted to the education of America's young people and the moral and spiritual improvement of their characters, but with the exception of the Bainbridge Squad in World War I, the League did not make the establishment and support of youth programs a major priority until after World War II.

United States Naval Sea Cadets.

By the early 1950s, the Navy's senior leadership recognized that a civilian-sponsored youth program, designed to promote interest in naval careers, would help Navy recruiting. At the request of Secretary of the Navy Robert Anderson, National President E.V. Richards had created the Buddy Program. It had grown for several years, first under former Secretary of the Navy Dan Kimball, and then George Halas, who had headed up the physical training program for naval shore patrol personnel in Hawaii during World War II. Carl Stockholm had commanded the shore patrol organization in Hawaii and knew Halas well, so when he became National President he asked the National Football League Hall of Fame coach, as a friend, to take on what was clearly becoming one of the League's most important programs.

Both Stockholm and Halas were members of the Chicago Council. Another member of the council, and chairman of its Buddy Program, was Morgan L. Fitch Jr., who had worked closely with Halas on the program until the latter returned to coaching. By that time, John Bergen had succeeded Stockholm as National President and he asked Fitch to serve as the League's National Youth Chairman.

Fitch, with the energy that was to characterize his more than half-century involvement with the Navy League, became concerned with the long-term prospects of the Buddy Program, particularly its focus on recruiting for the sea services, and sought to change its approach to dealing with America's youth. On his recommendation, the Buddy Program was renamed "Shipmate." The program's orientation was shifted from individual reserve officers, and recruitment, to local League councils and their assistance in the broadening of knowledge and understanding of both the sea services and the nation's requirement for freedom of the seas. Councils participating in the Shipmate Program directed their efforts toward high school counselors with educational materials and suggestions for conducting essay contests. They also made schools aware of the opportunities available to their students, such as the Naval Reserve Officer Training Corps, United States Naval Academy, and enlistment in the fleet. Selected participants in the Shipmate Program went to Japan, the Caribbean, and Europe aboard non-combatant logistics support ships of the United States Naval Service.[36]

As the League began transition from the Buddy Program to Shipmate, Chief of Naval Operations Burke, on travel overseas, observed contingents of sea cadets associated with their respective country's navies. Not surprisingly, given his typical energy and vision, after one such trip, Burke directed Vice Admiral H. Page Smith, chief of the Bureau of Naval Personnel, to conduct a feasibility study to determine what benefits might accrue to the U.S. Navy from the establishment of a nationwide naval sea cadet program similar to the extensive programs supported by Britain's Royal Navy and the Canadian Navy. Smith appointed Captain William J. Catlett Jr., commanding officer of the Naval Training Center, Bainbridge, Maryland, to evaluate sea cadet programs of both navies.

Catlett traveled to Canada for firsthand observation, and made numerous inquiries regarding other foreign navies' cadet programs. Catlett's report endorsed the idea of forming a sea cadet organization in the United States, but did not recommend that it become an organizational part of the Navy itself. Acting on Catlett's evaluation, Burke and Gates, the former always searching for initiatives to energize and involve the "Civilian Arm of the Navy" in issues beyond actual naval operations, approached National President Bergen regarding the feasibility of his organization establishing, managing, and supporting a sea cadet program on behalf of the U.S. Navy.[37]

Bergen responded positively, and knew he had just the man to work out the legal and practical specifics with the Navy: Morgan Fitch. Fitch, leveraging his knowledge as a patent lawyer, worked to ensure that the Naval Sea Cadet Corps would be financially and legally viable. He directed that the focus of the Sea Cadet Corps be shifted away from employment as a recruiting tool for the Navy, Burke's and Gates's original intent, and toward becoming a youth program more in keeping with the educational mission of the Navy League.[38]

Working directly with Under Secretary of the Navy William Franke and Chief of Information Rear Admiral Charles Kirkpatrick, as well as with Vice Admiral Smith and Captain Catlett, Fitch reached agreement on several principles, the most important of which was that the Sea Cadet program should be federally chartered. Though supported by the Navy League in numerous ways, it would be a separate organization with its own rules, regulations, bylaws, uniforms, and governing body, and remain clear of any League controversies. This would permit the organization to conform to Navy regulations but also exist as a separate entity distinct from the Navy League, which would facilitate the Corps taking advantage of various venues of official Navy support that were not always available to the League as a Section 501(c)(3) corporation.

Fitch also worked to address Navy concerns, including having a single organization, rather than a number of ad hoc youth groups that had sprung up around the country, to deal with. Because regulations allowed base and ship access only to persons over 14 years of age, the charter, required for Sea Cadet access to naval bases, was limited to youths in the 14 –17 year age bracket. To cover the 11–13 year age group, a separate "Navy League Cadet" program would be created. To ensure a formal organization with strictures on conduct and appearance, Fitch and Captain Catlett sat around the latter's kitchen table and wrote the initial training program and Cadet Regulations, with the Navy's own *Bluejacket's Manual* close by. Sea Cadet officer rank was capped at lieutenant commander; there were to be no Sea Cadet "captains" or admirals." A training regimen and curriculum was built, largely modeled on the one employed by the Naval Reserve.

Fleet Admiral Chester W. Nimitz, USN, inspects the color guard of the San Francisco Council-sponsored Sea Cadet Division on board USS *Oriskany* (CV-34).

The idea of establishing and supporting a Naval Sea Cadet Corps was discussed at the League's 1958 National convention and in a Catlett article in the November issue of *Navy-The Magazine of Sea Power*. That same year, the first United States Naval Sea Cadet Corps Division was formed at the Great Lakes Naval Training Center, Waukegan, Illinois.

The first company of Sea Cadets, 78 young men from cities and states throughout the country, participated in a summer training "boot camp" at the Naval Training Command, Great Lakes, Illinois, in 1959, the Sea Cadet Corp's first full year of operation. The training received was a modified version of the rigorous basic training curriculum required of Navy enlisted personnel.

Most Sea Cadet training during the organization's formative years was carried out, during the school year, at local Navy and Marine Corps Reserve Training Centers. The training soon expanded to the Navy's Recruit Training Centers in San

Diego, California, and Orlando, Florida, as well as at Great Lakes. This expansion encompassed not only recruit training, naval orientation, and basic seamanship, but also instruction in an ever-increasing number of naval and military career fields. Training was provided, on a lesser scale, to members of the Navy League Cadet Corps, to give young people ages 11-13 similar educational opportunities.

Commander William Thompson noted, in his 1964 research paper on the League, that the Sea Cadet program was so well received by the uniformed Navy that commandants of naval districts in various sections of the country were encouraging the formation of Navy League councils "wherever there is a Naval Reserve Training Center" just so a local Sea Cadet unit could be formed.[39]

The "new" Navy League of the postwar era, responding to Arleigh Burke's desires, was displaying a strength and energy exceeding that of its prewar predecessor. It also was an increasingly more democratic organization, thanks to several important governance changes. Invigorated by thousands of veterans of all the nation's armed services who had joined its ranks, it became increasingly proactive, innovative, and forward-looking, not only at the national level but at city and state levels as well.

It was also succeeding at continuing to avoid the controversial issues that had led to such problems with the Wilson and Hoover Administrations. National President Bergen continued the policies of his two predecessors, E.V. Richards Jr. and Carl Stockholm, in keeping the League away from activities that would create controversy and call into question the League's non-profit status as an educational institution. The one exception to this policy was the 1958 issue of the reorganization of the Defense Department.

The bill President Eisenhower submitted to Congress in April 1958 for consideration was viewed by many in the Navy, including Chief of Naval Operations Arleigh Burke, as the first step toward service unification and substitution of a single, Prussian-like chief of staff for the combined Joint Chiefs. Burke was sufficiently alarmed, even after testifying in Congress as to his opposition to various elements of the bill, to ask the League for help. Bergen agreed, and in April sent a telegram to all League officers, directors, and council presidents urging them to speak publicly against the legislation under consideration. In May, following a meeting of the organization's Executive Committee, Bergen went public with their agreed position of strong opposition to the bill. Finally, in June, Bergen advised the entire League membership to write their congressmen to vote against the measure.

The League's efforts were for naught, as Congress approved the bill on August 6, 1958, and President Eisenhower signed it into law shortly thereafter. Recalling the lessons learned under his predecessors, Robert M. Thompson and William H. Gardiner, Bergen quickly sent a letter to the White House, pledging the League's continued support and cooperation with both the Department of Defense and the

Navy Department.

In the long run, the Navy's, and the League's concerns were unfounded, as the Defense Reorganization Act of 1958 led neither to a single, unified service, nor a joint staff cast in the mold of a European-style general staff. It did remove the operating forces away from direct control of the service chiefs, shifting that responsibility to the President and the Secretary of Defense, and removed from the service secretaries responsibilities for anything other than the administration of their departments.[40]

In May 1959, as expected, Frank Gard Jameson was elected to succeed John Bergen as National President. Only 35 when elected, Jameson was not only the League's youngest National President but also the first to have been born west of the Mississippi. A Navy veteran with wartime service, his business acumen was amply complemented by his personnel management skills, contagious enthusiasm, and boundless generosity. He persuaded George "Buddy" Gilman, now President of the District of Columbia Council, to take a two-year absence from his job to become Jameson's Executive Assistant at Navy League headquarters.

The decrepit headquarters' office furniture, typewriters, and other business machines were antiquated and obsolete. So Jameson paid for new furniture, air conditioning (much appreciated by the headquarters staff), automatic typewriters, signing machines, and other office equipment out of his own pocket.

And with no provision for funding some of the expenses of the National President, he, like his predecessors, paid for his own travel and other expenses. But Jameson had the wherewithal, and traveled almost constantly in his own plane, upwards of 400,000 miles in two years, visiting as many Navy League councils and Navy and Marine Corps bases and activities during his presidency as possible.

Through the pages of *Navy-The Magazine of Sea Power*, in testimony before Congress, and in numerous speeches and interviews Jameson spread the seapower message, focusing attention on the growth of the Soviet Navy and, in particular, the importance of the *Polaris* ballistic-missile submarine program as the nation's best and most survivable deterrent to nuclear war. Reflecting the change in mindset since the fractious days of the Revolt of the Admirals, he emphasized that the Navy and Marine Corps were members of a larger defense team that included the Army, Air Force, and Coast Guard. Jameson personally visited the headquarters of the Air Force's Strategic Air Command, the Army missile center in Huntsville, Alabama, and the Army training base at Fort Benning, Georgia, for intensive background briefings. In 1960 he sponsored an orientation cruise aboard the newly commissioned carrier USS *Independence* (CV-62) for 80 senior members of the Navy League, the Air Force Association, and the Association of the United States Army. That same year he joined these organizations' presidents in issuing a detailed statement spelling out the "mutual support" of the three groups for "an adequate military posture" and the overall "strengthening of our national security."

The League-sponsored Naval Sea Cadet Corps and Navy League Cadet Corps that had started under National President Bergen continued to grow under Jameson's leadership and Morgan Fitch's direct involvement in every aspect of their affairs. Fitch and others continued to work with the Navy's chief of information and office of legislative affairs on the complicated process of obtaining a federal charter.

With the need to go to Capitol Hill for approval, both the Navy and the League encountered surprising opposition from the Boy Scouts of America, which had a strong base of support in Congress. The Boy Scouts were able to put the legislation establishing the federal charter on "hold," delaying action on the bill. Seeking to ascertain the nature of the Scout organization's concerns, Fitch and Sanford Flint, a League vice president, met with senior leadership of the Boy Scouts in their national headquarters. Fitch relates:

> As it turned out, they were concerned that the Navy would provide uniforms for Sea Cadets and the Scouts would lose revenue from sale of Sea Scout uniforms. Upon assurance that Sea Cadets would not be uniformed by the Navy and that uniforms would be obtained from surplus, the 'hold' was removed.[41]

Finally, rewarding the unflagging enthusiasm and hard work of Fitch, Jameson, and Crown, the continued support of Navy leadership, and the strong advocacy of Illinois Senator Everett Dirksen, on September 10, 1962, the 87th Congress passed Public Law 87-655, "An Act to Incorporate the Naval Sea Cadet Corps." The approved charter reflected the legal and organizational work done by Fitch and the Navy League; the "Objects and Purposes of the Corporation" were stated in Section 2:

> The objects and purposes of the corporation shall be, through organization and cooperation with the Department of the Navy, to encourage and aid young people to develop an interest and skill in basic seamanship and in its naval adaptations, to train them in seagoing skills, and to teach them patriotism, courage, self-reliance, and kindred virtues.[42]

Another member of the League's Chicago Council, Robert Crown, (whose father was a close friend of Senator Dirksen, no doubt helping to expedite the passage of the charter bill) served as President of the Chicago Council before his ascendancy to the national presidency in 1961, and had the honor of seeing the Sea Cadet program's gestation come to fruition during his term. Three years after its founding, the Corps consisted of 29 Sea Cadet Divisions and Squadrons and 19 "Cadet Ships"

"The Naval Sea Cadet Corps has been legally launched. May I remind all who are interested that it is not yet fitted out, finished with the builders trials, manned, shaken down, nor underway."

throughout the United States.

While success of the Naval Sea Cadet Corps during this period was considered a significant achievement of the Navy League as an institution, both Jameson and Crown were adamant in giving the lion's share of credit for the Sea Cadet program's success to Morgan Fitch. Jameson maintained in a May 1967 interview that he "used to get really upset" because the program was, from his point of view, moving along so slowly. "As it turned out," Jameson continued, "he [Fitch] was so right and I was so wrong. If we had gone out like a bull in a china shop and set up ... [units] all over the country, it would have flopped." The "great, great success" Fitch achieved, said Jameson, "is because he ... [proceeded] slowly and really built on rock."[43]

United States Naval Sea Cadets

For his part, Crown attached particular significance to the importance of chartering the Naval Sea Cadet Corps, recalling in a March 1967 interview Fitch's insistence that the Sea Cadets exist as "a separate corporate structure ... independent of the Navy League." If, for financial or other reasons, Crown noted, the Navy League had gone "down the drain," the Sea Cadets would have "continued to exist for the Navy Department."[44]

Crown was clearly proud of the Naval Sea Cadet Corps and considered its granting of a federal charter one of the highlights of his national presidency. But in his final "President's Report" to the League at its annual meeting in San Juan, Puerto Rico, in May 1963, Crown noted that much work remained to be done to ensure the program's success:

> The Naval Sea Cadet Corps has been legally launched. May I remind all who are interested that it is not yet fitted out, finished with the builders trials, manned, shaken down, nor underway. I feel this program to be one of our organization's most important tasks for the future. It is the more remarkable because it is volunteer.[45]

Indicative of the importance Frank Gard Jameson assigned to the Sea Cadets, at least two or more pages of *Navy-The Magazine of Sea Power* were devoted to Sea Cadet and League Cadet news every month during his presidency. U.S. and Canadian Cadets joined forces in 1959 in a ceremonial parade in Sault Saint Marie, Canada, honoring Queen Elizabeth II and Prince Philip. In 1960, a League Cadet unit sponsored by the Western Connecticut Council was inspected by President Eisenhower during the President's visit to the USS *Mitscher* (DDG-57) in Newport, Rhode Island.

Beyond the Sea Cadet program, during the late 1950s the Navy League as an institution received several awards. The Navy Department presented its first-ever Award for Public Relations Achievement to *Navy-The Magazine of Sea Power* editor Royce Powell and Publications Committee Chairman Donald Mackie for their roles in informing the American people and the Congress about Navy and Marine Corps achievements and requirements. R.J. Bicknell, President of the Navy League of Canada, presented an honorary lifetime membership in the Navy League of Canada to League National President Jameson, the first U.S. citizen to receive that honor.

On a less celebratory note, despite the success of the three Seapower Symposiums staged in the late 1950s, the program was held in abeyance in the early 1960s. President Eisenhower's "military-industrial complex" speech toward the end of his second term, combined with a new administration coming to power in the nation's capital, raised concerns among some members of the League's national leadership that the improved working relationship between the League and the nation's defense industries would revive spurious charges of the 1920s and 1930s that the organization was a tool for munitions makers and shipbuilders.

Such concerns were borne out in November 1961 when Kennedy Administration Deputy Defense Secretary Roswell Gilpatric called attention to the relationship between elements of the Defense Department and industry in general. Citing organizational changes instituted by Secretary of Defense Robert McNamara, Gilpatric asserted that industry needed to reconsider its relations with the military services:

> In my opinion there are too many industry associations dealing with military departments with the resulting multiplication of effort both on the part of industry and the Defense Department. We recognize the importance of keeping industry informed of our needs and our problems, but we cannot afford to do this job several times over.[46]

As subsequently reported in the *New York Times* from Department of Defense sources, one industrial supplier to the Navy reported that it "felt compelled to belong to 15 organizations" (including the Navy League), costing it $43,000 in annual dues. Management "agreed with Pentagon authorities that the number of groups was growing out of hand." Specifically cited as a burden driving up costs to the federal government were membership fees, social functions, advertisements in trade journals, and the requirement, in this company's view, of buying "exhibit space at various conventions."[47]

Navy League leadership realized that sentiments of the 1920s and early 1930s were resurfacing. In view of this, and numerous other changes in the way the Pentagon was being administered by Robert McNamara, the organization decided that the timing was simply "not right" to publicize and advocate a defense contractor-laden event such as the "Seapower Symposium."

Of equal concern by the early 1960s was a growing problem in the seven-year relationship between the League and the Advisory Council on Naval Affairs. The problem between the two organizations stemmed from the Advisory Council being able to accomplish anything only "when requested" by the Navy district commandants, and, for their part, the reluctance of district commandants to appoint members to an organization that was sponsored by another. Non-Navy League Council members chafed at the role played by the League in their affairs and resented what they considered interference by the more established and well known League leadership. District commandants remained confused as to who was working for whom, and an attempt by the League to nationalize the program not only further exacerbated the sense of confusion and uncertainty, but created real problems for the parent organization.[48]

Seeking to resolve the issue and give the Advisory Council on Naval Affairs something to do outside of normal League activities, in 1960 it was assigned a significant role in executing and promulgating an anti-communism community awareness initiative called *Project Alert*. This plan, begun in Lubbock, Texas, in the spring of 1959, was but one of several prevalent in the 1950s and early 1960s that through speeches, seminars, and presentations at public gatherings, described "the threat to democracy posed by international communism." It also called for moral leadership to awaken "the consciousness of the nation" and a program of "community education to revitalize the American character." *Project Alert* proponents gave numerous statements warning about moral decay in American society and the importance of "the home, the church and the school" to "teach and mold our youth."[49] National President Jameson enthusiastically endorsed *Project Alert* and assigned to the Advisory Council on Naval Affairs responsibility for disseminating the ideas of the plan throughout the nation by conducting one-day seminars "on methods of combating communism."

But as the seminar message, prepared by the National Education Program of Searcy, Arkansas, became better known, League leadership began to grow increasingly uneasy with the affiliation. Political statements, regardless of intent, gave some national leaders pause, particularly as the anti-communism message grew more strident in the early 1960s. The fact that the Navy League was organizationally linked with the Advisory Council on Naval Affairs, which was in turn involved with *Project Alert* (at the League's direction) in matters regarding anti-communist initiatives, began causing problems for the League with the Navy, the Department of Defense, and Congress.

When *Project Alert*'s leadership, principally two retired Navy admirals, asked Jameson for $75,000 to continue the program, he called a halt to League sponsorship. Recognizing that the League was sailing into dangerous waters, in January 1961 responsibility for *Project Alert* was transferred to another organization, Freedom's Foundation, of which Frank Gard Jameson was a director. The program was no longer officially associated with the League.

But problems with *Project Alert* and the Advisory Council on Naval Affairs persisted into the term of the new National President, Robert Crown. The 59th annual meeting, in which Crown had been elected, had also passed resolutions against admission of the People's Republic of China to the United Nations, as well as support for the House Un-American Activities Committee and resumption of nuclear testing. Suggestions that the League adopt positions on civil defense and protest the removal of Major General Edwin A. Walker from his command in Europe (for indoctrinating his troops on the "menace of communism" and labeling certain Americans as "leftists") had been defeated.

But Advisory Council members, many of them Navy Leaguers, continued to argue for the parent organization to adopt positions on numerous issues that had little to do with the sea services. With *Project Alert* demanding that the Kennedy Administration refuse to negotiate over Berlin with the Soviet Union, withdraw from the United Nations, and support foundation of Christian, anti-communist schools throughout the United States, Robert Crown grew increasingly alarmed with the tone and nature of the rhetoric from organizations still affiliated, in the eyes of many citizens, with the Navy League.

Finally, in early 1962 he issued a statement as National President:

> The Navy League of the United States has a primary interest in matters relating to the defense of the nation. Thus, the Navy League approved the original principles of *Project Alert* in common with many other programs for the education of the American people on the values of the American way of life in opposition to any ideology detrimental to our national security. But keeping the Navy League on target as the Civilian Arm of the Navy, whose purpose it is to help the Navy, and not get involved in peripheral problems is, I feel, of real importance.[50]

This statement was followed by termination of League funds being provided to *Freedom's Foundation* for maintaining *Project Alert*. Crown then directed the Advisory Council on Naval Affairs to return all *Project Alert* materials to the *Foundation*'s Valley Forge, Pennsylvania, headquarters. Despite continued unhappiness from various Advisory Council members, Crown directed that its mission be sharply defined as only one of carrying the message of seapower forward, helping retired military personnel adjust to civilian life, and forming new League councils. Furthermore, the Advisory Council was to operate only in areas where there was no League council; in the event one was formed, the Advisory Council in that area would cease to exist.

Responding to Crown's leadership, the organization got back on course and returned its focus to matters affecting the sea services, moving away from the dangerous shoals of politics and politicians. In his final "President's Message" two years later, Crown noted in a single sentence that the Advisory Council on Naval Affairs was now "concentrating on the dissemination of sea power philosophy and the organization of new Navy League Councils."[51] The 1963 edition of the *Navy League Handbook* omitted all reference to the council and deleted it from its list of affiliated programs. In December 1963 Crown's successor, Robert H. Barnum, confirmed that the program would be allowed "to die."[52]

The entire Advisory Council on Naval Affairs/*Project Alert* episode remained somewhat controversial among senior League leadership for years thereafter. In a March 1967 interview, Crown called *Project Alert* and the League's involvement with it through the Advisory Council on Naval Affairs, a "series of good intentions that ran wild," ending up with "an outlet for a lot of things that weren't very American." He charged that *Project Alert* was allowed to "run loose without any supervision or control" and became involved with "what some people would call the radical right." Crown asserted "there is nothing more difficult to control than a very sincere, emotional patriot ... it almost scuttled the Navy League."[53]

In Crown's view, the League's involvement with *Project Alert* endangered its status as a non-profit educational organization. He saw *Project Alert* as an "organization and its context" being used for "political rather than educational purposes" that struck at the very existence of the Navy League: [54]

> If anybody were going to try to attack the Navy League, it struck me very early that the place to strike it was in its pocketbook, particularly when it was relatively weak. If tax-exemption of contributions and dues were to be removed, I could see the organization drying up; that's why I was so very disturbed when I saw some things, some people, and some organizations getting involved with the Navy League.[55]

Crown admitted that his effort to sever any connection between the League and *Project Alert* (and subsequently the Advisory Council on Naval Affairs) was controversial — "a lot of people were disgusted with me" — but believed his efforts were right: "I could have gone after it [*Project Alert*] and given the League a political connotation ... based on that, gotten rid of the tax exemption ... we were a lot closer to that kind of accusation than anybody realized. I think we treaded a very, very tight rope for a while."[56]

Frank Gard Jameson's perspective on the issue was considerably different from Crown's. In a May 1967 interview, he defended both the League and the Advisory Council on Naval Affairs's involvement with *Project Alert*, maintaining he "didn't have any problems" with the program.[57] He believed, as National President in 1959, that the Navy League should have been involved in more than just "ships and weapons and things like that" because "there was so much apathy" that "we could lose the [Cold] War." Then Jameson, reflecting on the current social turmoil of the mid-1960s, added, "As we see today with these draft card burners, with the people not being behind their government ... we ought to have a little resurgence of patriotism ... That was the reason I threw the Navy League's full support behind it [*Project Alert*]."[58]

Jameson maintained that the problem with *Project Alert* was that "certain people wanted recognition and really hadn't earned it," thinking the program was a "quick way to fame and success." He admitted that he was under a lot of pressure from League leadership over the organization's continued relationship with *Project Alert*, particularly his eventual successor, Robert Crown, who was "very close to the new [Kennedy] Administration."[59]

The May 1961 annual meeting that saw Robert Crown succeed Frank Gard Jameson as Navy League National President would be an event that would prove historical for the administration and operation of the organization in ways far beyond the controversy over *Project Alert* and the Advisory Council on Naval Affairs. Like most League leaders of his era, Crown had seen service in the Navy during World War II. A success in business after the war and well-connected in the political arenas of Chicago and Illinois, his national presidency stands out as one of the most important and influential in the second half-century of the League's existence.

Like Jameson, Crown was an activist President who traveled considerably, visiting and meeting early in his tour with the leaders of the Navy Leagues of Belgium, Canada, France, England, and Germany. He logged more than 100,000 additional miles on his visits to over 200 League councils within the United States. More than 40 new councils, four of them overseas, were chartered during his presidency.

And like Jameson, Crown continued the close working relationship with both the Navy Department's senior leadership and with naval district commandants throughout the United States. Membership continued to grow during his presidency and by 1963 had climbed to over 36,000, almost twice the World War II high of just over 18,000 members.

But what set Crown apart as a Navy League National President was his wholesale revamping of the headquarters staff and fundamental reorganization of the manner by which the organization was run at both national and local levels. He reorganized the League's financial structure, established an Investment Committee, brought in a management evaluation team (which he, not the League, compensated), and significantly revised the League's bylaws.

His rationale for such actions was made clear in a March 1967 interview. Crown maintained that for many years dating to before World War II the League had been run as a "private club." In addition, there was a "lack of financial controls." The net result was that whoever became National President could not only set national policy for the entire organization but could also "do anything he wanted with other people's money" and use League funds to promote and publicize his own personal views.[60]

In practice, most Presidents did consult with other national officers, and frequently with Navy Department officials, before articulating their (and, as was assumed, the organization's) views on important matters of policy. But some instances, notably the anti-Royal Navy views espoused by H. Birchard Taylor in the 1930s, had resulted in considerable unhappiness within the ranks of senior League leadership. Many members continued to feel during the 1950s, as Armin Rappaport had found in the early years of the decade, that the League was being run as an autocracy, a "fiefdom" of national leadership, and that genuine influence on larger policy questions from the rank-and-file was seldom being sought or accommodated.

National Presidents Richards and Stockholm were aware of these sentiments, and both had taken nascent steps to broaden the League's membership base and bring in younger men to serve as national officers. But Crown deemed the earlier initiatives insufficient in view of continuing feelings of alienation between the League at the local and national levels, and sought to remedy the situation in dramatic fashion by asking Morgan Fitch to revise and update the bylaws.

Neither the National President nor Fitch shared the opinion of many that the bylaws were a subject not worthy of serious effort at rewriting. Crown believed that they were "completely obsolete and inconsistent" when he became President.[61] While some changes had been made under his predecessors, Crown maintained they were poorly drafted and indifferently implemented:

> The bylaws had been changed in part, but not in total ... in other words, one bylaw had been modified, but all of the 'chain reaction of

> modification' had not been cleaned up, language-wise. Morgan is the one who cleaned up the bylaws for me. I saw that it needed it. I asked him to do that; he did it. He was a lawyer and he knew the language.[62]

Bylaws delineating infrastructure and procedures have an importance not readily visible to rank-and-file membership. Retired Rear Admiral William Thompson, a student of the League while on active-duty, a League member after retirement, head of the Navy Memorial Foundation for 15 years, and charter member of several other associations, agrees with Crown's emphasis on bylaws as key to changing the organization:

> The Navy League is unique, perhaps one of a kind in its infrastructure and organization. Like all organizations, as long as human beings are involved it is not perfect but it works and is functional. I have found that those critical of its governance procedures are a little short on experience with other non-profits ... It is the bylaws that make the difference, that provide a good structure and appropriate checks and balances.[63]

To make League headquarters more responsive as well as more effective, Crown brought his personal assistant, Lou Levy, to Washington to analyze staff procedures and accounting. As a result, Crown established the position of executive director, first held by Dick Harrison, to serve as the administrative chief of the headquarters staff. Initially, three staff positions were provided for in the bylaws: executive director, executive secretary and the editor of the League's monthly periodical. The bylaws stipulated that all three appointments were to be made by the National President and approved by the Board of Directors annually.[64]

With the approval of the Board of Directors, Crown made three additional organizational changes:

* The Executive Committee was enlarged to 35 members by adding all past Presidents to the committee and a limited number of other new members, including the chairmen of major national committees.
* A Steering Committee was created, smaller in size than the Executive Committee, to consider new policies, programs, bylaws changes, and similar matters before referring them to the Executive Committee.
* $6,000 was appropriated to help defray travel expenses of the National President. This was an important change because it opened the office of National President to a larger number of possible candidates. While neither the Presidents nor any of the League's other national officers were paid a salary, easing part of the financial burden previously imposed made it possible for a large number of eminently well-qualified

men and women to aspire to the League's highest office.

In addition to the bylaws changes, Crown implemented a number of internal fiscal reforms to keep the League financially solvent. Committee chairmen were directed to submit their proposed budgets for the following year to League headquarters in time to permit preparation of a master integrated budget. The national treasurer was directed to examine the various League funds and budget accounts and Crown appointed an audit committee to check the treasurer's annual report. He required the League's weekly income and disbursement reports to be distributed, not only to the National President and national treasurer, but also to the national judge advocate and national vice presidents.

Crown also standardized the awards program, which had begun in 1957. The Awards Committee recommended the creation of five new awards: a Distinguished Service Award, which would be presented annually "to a member who has made outstanding contributions to the Navy League, especially during the preceding calendar year;" and four other types of awards: meritorious citations, scrolls of honor, certificates of appreciation, and honorary memberships. (See Appendix F for a discussion of Navy League Awards.)

The importance and impact of Crown's internal changes to the Navy League were largely transparent to the more than 100,000 spectators who watched the Navy's Blue Angels flight team, and its Chuting Stars parachute team, during the League's 1962 annual meeting in Chicago. Among the principal speakers and other luminaries at the convention were new Secretary of the Navy Fred Korth, new Chief of Naval Operations Admiral George W. Anderson, and his predecessor, now-retired Admiral Arleigh Burke. Motion picture and television star Jackie Cooper, a member of the Beverly Hills, California, Council, and a captain in the Naval Reserve, also attended.

Events in the fall of 1962 shifted the League's focus away from internal issues, and once more highlighted the continuing conflict between the United States and the Soviet Union. John F. Kennedy was the first American President to have served on active duty in the U.S. Navy during World War II. And it was during his presidency that the Navy was most aggressively deployed in a direct confrontation with the Soviet Union.

On two occasions during the first two decades of the 40-year-long Cold War, it nearly got hot, and both were due to Soviet provocations. The first, the 1948 blockade of Berlin, was countered by the massive Berlin airlift ordered by President Truman and did not involve the Navy. However, the second, Soviet Premier Nikita Khrushchev's attempt to introduce intermediate range ballistic missiles into Cuba in 1962, directly involved the Navy and was successfully concluded only because of an at-sea blockade established by ships of the Atlantic Fleet.

Secretary of the Navy Fred Korth, left, with Naval Reserve Captain and motion picture and television star Jackie Cooper and a Hollywood starlet attend the 1962 Navy League annual meeting in Chicago.

The Navy League's involvement in the Cuban Missile Crisis centered on caring for the women and children evacuated from Guantanamo Bay Naval Station. As tensions over the missiles increased, President Kennedy directed that all civilians be evacuated from the base. Because of the numbers involved, this had to be done by sea, mostly on amphibious ships that had large, deep well decks for personal effects as well as bunks and facilities to feed and house the dependents being transported. As the five-day transit began, Chief of Naval Operations Admiral Anderson directed that preparations be made to receive the evacuees at the Little Creek and Norfolk, Virginia, naval stations.

Captain Nelson Watkins, commanding officer at Little Creek, asked his wife to coordinate with other Navy wives in the area and enlist the assistance of Navy League councils in the Norfolk and Hampton Roads areas. The result was an outpouring of food and, most importantly, extra clothing and blankets. When the dependent-laden ships had left Cuban waters the temperature was over 90 degrees but about 50 degrees at the piers in Tidewater Virginia. Because the dependents were arriving from a tropical climate where they had lived for months and years, most had no warm weather clothing, and not much more clothing than what they were actually wearing.

Navy League members met the needs of the families of men still manning the Cold War lines in Cuba. In addition to clothing, League members provided baby formula, donated baby cribs, and drove dependents to Navy Exchanges where they could cash checks and purchase other needed items. As the crisis continued, League members also assisted dependents in getting to airports and rail stations to travel to homes-of-record to wait out the event, which was finally resolved to the mutual satisfaction of both sides, in mid-November 1962.

As he noted in his final "President's Report" at the League's May 1963 annual meeting, National President Robert Crown was proud of both the sea services' and the Navy League's role in the Cuban Missile Crisis:

> Never in the history of our organization has an adequately equipped and trained Navy, Marine Corps, Coast Guard, and Merchant Marine been so vital to the defense, to the very existence, of our country. Think, if you will, of what alternatives would have been open to the President at the time of the Cuban quarantine had we had an inadequate sea power.
>
> Never in the history of our organization has the rapport, the mutual respect, regard, and cooperation between Americans in uniform, the Navy Department and the Navy League been greater.[65]

From the perspective of national security and Cold War realpolitik, both sides learned valuable lessons from the Cuban Missile Crisis. The most important, from the American point of view, was that the Soviet Union would back down when faced with superior power. The Kremlin agreed, for in the sea approaches to Cuba, the superior power, as Khrushchev recognized, had belonged to the U.S. Navy, which had quickly assembled a force of three aircraft carriers, two cruisers, 22 destroyers, and three support ships. For Soviet leadership, the lesson was clear and in the aftermath of the confrontation, the building of a powerful bluewater fleet under Fleet Admiral Sergei G. Gorshkov, Khrushchev's senior naval advisor, became one of Moscow's top military priorities.

At the time of the Cuban Missile Crisis, the U.S. Navy could attain local air, surface, and subsurface superiority in any kind of naval scenario. But from 1962 onward, Kremlin leadership was determined to see that this would not be the case in the future. The U.S. Navy would find out just how well the Soviets had learned the lessons of the 1960s missile crisis when they encountered the Soviet Navy in the Mediterranean Sea in the Arab-Israeli Yom Kippur War of 1973.

But from the perspective of the United States, and the Navy League, the final outcome of the Cuban Missile Crisis was viewed as a clear victory in the Cold War. That was the way it was viewed in the nation's capital, and at the Naval War College in Newport, Rhode Island, where Navy Commander William Thompson completed a research paper entitled, "The Navy League of the United States — A Status of Forces." A fascinating "time-capsule" view of the League and its membership in the early 1960s, the principal thrust of Thompson's work, following a brief summary of the League's six-decade history, was to analyze and summarize results of a survey conducted with both Navy League members and officers in attendance at the Naval War College. The results were interesting in many aspects, including this profile of "Mr. Navy League:"

> [He] is an energetic or professional man with tinges of gray on his sideburns, which suggest his fifty years. For four and

> one-half years he has been a member of what he considers to be an effective, patriotic, educational organization. He is married and has two children, one over 18 years of age ... He earns more than $20,000 a year, is a college graduate, and has done some graduate work. He is a Navy veteran and was attracted to the Navy League because of an interest in the Navy and considers that he can help the Navy through the League's community relations program, his favorite activity in League work. He also thinks it imperative to educate the public about the virtues of sea power and helps in the Sea Cadet program whenever he can.[66]

Other conclusions from Commander Thompson's research indicated the Navy League still had some work to do in increasing knowledge about its existence and mission. Thompson found that "several flag officers have confessed that they had known little about the Navy League until they were actually confronted with it as a Naval District Commandant or in a command position where the League has consistently made its presence known."[67] Among junior officers, surface ship officers had better knowledge of the League and its activities than their more "glamorous" aviator brethren. As expected, the more senior the officer, the greater his knowledge of the League and its missions. And, although a majority of officers considered the League more successful at the local community than national level, 71 percent of the officers surveyed thought the League "did an adequate job in presenting aspects of sea power [and naval power] to the layman."[68]

Commander William Thompson, USN

Thompson summarized his survey results by noting that the "Navy League and its programs are not understood by personnel of the Navy and Marine Corps." He called for a program to "educate sea service personnel on the Navy League and its activities," suggesting the need to "hold school" within the fleet itself on the organization's existence and purpose.[69] But a lack of knowledge of League activities would be the least of the Navy's concerns beyond the Cuban Missile Crisis, as the remainder of the decade would prove in many ways as trying for the sea services and the Navy League as the 1920s.

USS *George Washington* (SSBN-598)

Chapter VIII
The 40-Year War: Détente, 1963-1980

While aware of the essential role played by the Atlantic Fleet during the Cuban Missile Crisis, Secretary of Defense Robert McNamara's personal relationship with Chief of Naval Operations Admiral George Anderson became increasingly strained over issues ranging from conduct of the naval quarantine off Cuba to the admiral's congressional testimony over the acquisition of the Tactical Fighter Experimental, or TFX. Eventually, McNamara's displeasure resulted in the admiral not being reappointed to the senior position of leadership in the Navy, and even his initial two-year tour was cut short by several months. Anderson's acceptance of the ambassadorship to Portugal resulted in vigorous and open questioning of the firing by numerous active duty and retired military leaders until personally stopped by Admiral Anderson himself. Regardless, the incident presaged an increasingly strained relationship between the Navy and senior civilian leadership in the Department of Defense.

But unease with Secretary McNamara and the Kennedy Administration's national security policies was not confined to the Navy. In September 1963, following the announcement of agreement between the United States and the Soviet Union on a treaty regarding banning of the testing of nuclear weapons, the Air Force Association denounced the Administration's efforts. The fact that 95 percent of all Air Force generals were members of the Association caused a considerable stir in the nation's capital. Contrasting the Air Force Association and the Navy League's reactions to the Test-Ban Treaty, a columnist in the *Washington Post* observed that:

"The fly-boys are comparatively new at this. What they put out is like raw whiskey. What you get from the Navy League is fine old brandy."[1]

Unhappiness with the treaty soon receded to the background, however, as the nation's military became involved in the longest and most unpopular war in American history, an intense conflict that split American society along the divides of age, race, and wealth. The Vietnam War would involve virtually every warfighting capability available in the fleet, from carrier air strikes, riverine warfare, and naval gunfire support, to offensive mine laying, maritime blockade, and interdiction.

The principal naval task was the employment of sea-based air power to support land operations in South Vietnam, interdict enemy supply routes to the south and engage in strategic bombing of North Vietnam. The Vietnam War had a tremendous impact on the Navy worldwide, with all other missions and commitments subordinated to prosecution of the conflict in Southeast Asia. Because the government sought to avoid wartime budget austerity in domestic programs, the Navy consumed itself, foregoing necessary maintenance of ships and equipment, research and development, and quality-of-life initiatives for its sailors.

With the exception of nuclear-powered submarines, there was a near stoppage of major surface ship construction. The last fossil-fueled aircraft carrier was authorized in 1963, eventually to be named *John F. Kennedy* (CV-67). But the decision over whether it should have nuclear or conventional propulsion was resolved only after a lengthy argument between the Defense Department, the Navy, and Congress.[2] While the Navy League advocated a nuclear-powered carrier, budget considerations prevailed, and USS *John F. Kennedy* (CV-67) became the last fossil-fueled aircraft carrier to be built in the United States.

Just as important, domestic anti-war sentiment eroded military morale among many wearing the uniform and created a major challenge for the Navy League and other civic and patriotic organizations during the 1960s. Chief of Naval Operations Admiral David L. McDonald quantified the problem and cited its principal cause in a speech before the Navy League in Washington in 1965. The admiral noted that 100,000 sailors were leaving the Navy each year and added, "I do believe that one of the major reasons for these large losses is the unbelievably long absences from home which our Cold War deployments have imposed upon us."[3] Exacerbating fleet personnel and readiness issues was a Soviet Navy, still smarting from its lackluster performance in the Cuban Missile Crisis, growing in numbers and quality, narrowing the capability advantage of the U.S. fleet.

Against the background of these disturbing events, following receipt of his second Secretary of the Navy Distinguished Public Service Award, Crown turned leadership of the League over to Robert Barnum at the close of the League's 61st Annual Convention in 1963.[4] Whereas Robert Crown had put special focus on reforming the manner in which the Navy League was run, Barnum elected to focus his presidency on improving the well-being of sea service personnel. He was passionate about the issue, and signed, along with the leaders of the Association of the United States Army and the Air Force Association in April 1964, a joint message to the Secretary of Defense endorsing his new pay proposal as "a positive step in the right direction" and for establishing a "system of annual adjustments that would keep military compensation comparable with other sectors of the economy."[5]

Barnum made clear in his "President's Report" at the League's 62nd Annual Convention in Dallas, Texas, in May 1964, that in over 100,000 miles of travel and visits to 200 League councils in his first year as National President, he had emphasized four principal points: [6]

* Pay service people rates at least comparable with civil service and other government employee pay scales.
* Stop the erosion, the shrinkage, the pilferage of things that used to help make service life a little more pleasant.
* Provide adequate, decent housing where needed.
* Provide reasonable respect and thought for the dedication of service people.

Barnum continued the campaign in the second year of his presidency. In speeches, "President's Messages," articles in *Navy-The Magazine of Sea Power*, and letters to members of Congress, Barnum buttressed his arguments with facts, statistics, and common sense. More than half of his messages to the League dealt with the issue of military compensation. Typically, his message in the January 1965 issue of *Navy-The Magazine of Seapower*, observed that "the Navy pays newly commissioned ensigns less than a New York City fireman or a probationary patrolman requiring only a high school education." He also identified "poor housing and separation of families," in addition to low pay, as principal reasons why the "services are losing good men daily."[7]

Other issues of League concern during this period, addressed in considerable detail in *Navy-The Magazine of Sea Power*, included the nuclear Navy, Marine Corps aviation, antisubmarine warfare, the continued growth and technological modernization of the Soviet Navy, naval and civilian benefits that could be achieved through a well-funded U.S. oceanographic program, burgeoning problems facing the U.S.-flag Merchant Marine, and the increasingly vital role played by the U.S. Coast Guard.

Almost all of these were less-than-popular causes in the Pentagon of the 1960s. Secretary of Defense McNamara was so unhappy with the Navy League's continual focus on the pay issue that he threatened to bar all League personnel from access to any Navy bases or ships. But, substantiating the wisdom of its founders in maintaining that the Navy League should have no members on active duty in the armed forces, McNamara had little power over individuals within the organization, a freedom the Association of the United States Army and the Air Force Association, with many members still wearing the uniform, did not enjoy. [8]

League President Barnum, accustomed to the corridors of power as a former personal assistant to the chief executive officer of U.S. Steel was not to be deterred. The organization's national leadership, as it had most recently in the Truman years preceding the Korean War, continued telling the American people, members of Congress, and the media what it believed were the true needs of the sea services, regardless of prevailing sentiments on Capitol Hill or in the Pentagon.

Surprisingly, given the increasingly unpopular war in Southeast Asia, the League's net membership increased by more than 5,000 during Barnum's tenure, including 40 new councils. Navy Day, under the leadership of National Affairs Chairman Harold Wirth, was observed in more than 250 cities. National headquarters provided a large assist by distributing instruction booklets, complete with spot announcements for local radio and television stations, to all councils. The Sea Cadet program continued to prosper under the guidance of Morgan Fitch, with 15 new divisions commissioned and another 37 being formed.

Two future National Presidents moved into key leadership positions: James M. Hannan was elected President of the Naval Sea Cadet Corps and Charles F. Duchein became chairman of the Marine Corps Affairs Committee. Duchein continued the *With the Marines* section of *Navy-The Magazine of Sea Power*, and played a key role in establishing the new *General Clifton B. Cates Award*, presented annually to an officer graduate of the Marine Corps' Command and Staff College who had demonstrated superior academic achievement.

Three other new annual national awards were established during Barnum's presidency: The *Sheldon Clark Naval Air Reserve Trophy*, presented to the naval air station or naval air reserve training unit "achieving the highest combat readiness;" the *David Sinton Ingalls Award*, presented to the Naval Air Training Command's "Flight Instructor of the Year;" and the *Donald M. Mackie Awards*, presented to League councils judged to have published the "most outstanding newsletters" during the previous year. (As of 2005, the *Clark* and *Ingalls* awards are no longer active).

During Barnum's presidency, League councils continued to participate in Navy Day as well as Armed Forces Day celebrations and observances, and raised funds for the Naval Aviation Museum in Pensacola, Florida; the Pemberton House, birthplace of the Continental Navy, in Philadelphia; and the Navy-Marine Corps Foundation in Washington, among other worthy causes. Nationally, the League sponsored a *Fleet Admiral Chester W. Nimitz Scholarship for Oceanographic Research* at the University of California, donated $1,000 to the National Navy Relief Society, and enthusiastically supported and contributed to the *Thresher Fund*, established to assist dependents of the officers and men of the nuclear-powered submarine USS *Thresher* (SSN-593), which sank while on a training mission in April 1963.

Thanks in large part to the fiscal reforms and controls instituted by Robert Crown, National President Barnum was able to report at the League's 1965 Annual Convention in Washington, D.C., that the organization's net worth had increased "from over $233,000 [two years earlier] to over $279,000." Moreover, "less than two percent of the League's membership income during the previous year was from business," and "less than 10 percent of the League's total membership was employed in the defense industry," allaying concerns that closer ties with corporate America would make the organization seem but a handmaiden to shipbuilders, aircraft and weapons manufacturers.[9]

U.S. Navy photo by JO1 Lancaster

Members of the 6th Marine Regiment disembark from the amphibious transport dock USS *Dubuque* (LPD-8) upon their arrival in Saudi Arabia as part of Operation Desert Shield.

Further strengthening ties between the Navy and its supporting organizations and associations, in the spring of 1965 Secretary of the Navy Paul Nitze hosted a "Prospectus '65" conference on the status of the Department of the Navy for the Navy League, Fleet Reserve Association, Marine Corps Reserve Officer Association, and Marine Corps League. Rear Admiral William Mack, Chief of Information, suggested to the attendees that the information could be used at the local, hometown level. The wide range of subjects briefed included current fleet operations, Marine Corps activities, anti-submarine warfare, the Merchant Marine, fleet nuclearization and modernization, and personnel. The conference was deemed so successful by its participants that it was held again in the fall of 1965.

Attitudes about national defense — and the relationship between government, the armed services, and the defense industry that had contributed to the League's decision to hold the Seapower Symposium in abeyance in the early 1960s — had changed considerably by mid-decade. While the Cuban Missile Crisis had been peacefully resolved, the pace of the Cold War continued unabated. In addition, the major buildup of U.S. forces in Vietnam had started, and all of the nation's armed forces were feeling the strain caused by having too many commitments and too little in the way of resources.

The Navy and Marine Corps found themselves, as they had in the past, needing the help of the Navy League. Huge increases in defense spending were required, but most additional defense appropriations approved by Congress were earmarked for current operations and for the American air and ground units in South Vietnam, leaving little additional funding for the procurement, research, development, test, and evaluation investment accounts.

The Navy League decided it could best help the sea services meet this challenge by scheduling another, bigger, and more ambitious antisubmarine symposium as the headline event of 1965's National Convention scheduled for late April. In a complementary move, the District of Columbia Council scheduled, at the same time and hotel, a revived Seapower Symposium, and, to avoid confusion with the concurrent antisubmarine symposium, renamed the event a Sea-Air-Space Exposition. Like its predecessor from the late 1950s, it featured a full spectrum of exhibits from U.S. and allied defense contractors.

More than 2,000 League members and guests, including 85 flag and general officers and 20 members of Congress, registered for the antisubmarine symposium, the Sea-Air-Space Exposition, and other feature events during convention week. Chief of Naval Operations Admiral David McDonald officially opened the Exposition, which featured a number of imaginative and educational exhibits provided by 37 participating U.S. and allied defense contractors.

In the aftermath, with the event a public relations and fiscal success, and after numerous committee meetings, prolonged discussion, and resolution of several outstanding issues, League leadership decided to make the Sea-Air-Space Exposition an annual event, largely organized and administered at the national level, using the 1965 experience as the template for future endeavors. This was a significant change for the organization, taking it in a new direction. It solidified the League's ties not only with industry but also with the Navy's shore establishment and infrastructure which was, and is, primarily responsible for providing the ships, aircraft, and weapons systems needed by the operating forces.

The success of the Sea-Air-Space Exposition was indicative of many of the changes occurring in the overall national security establishment following the Korean War. The threat of communism could not be defeated quickly, as had German and Japanese adversaries in each of the World Wars. Now, competing ideologies and defense industries fought for primacy in laboratories, research, development, and test facilities, as well as in the jungles of Southeast Asia and above, on, or beneath the world's seas and oceans.

This reality was appropriately captured, three decades after the League's initial sponsorship of the Sea-Air-Space Exposition, by National President Hugh Mayberry. In words that could hardly have been used in the 1920s or 1930s by a Navy League National President, his "President's Message" of April 1996 saluted the defense industry:

> The principal components of the U.S. defense industrial base are the private-sector U.S. companies and corporations that design, develop, test and build the ships, aircraft, avionics and electronics systems, tanks, armored personnel vehicles and other rolling stock, weapons, and thousands of other equipment items that for more than half a century have given U.S. and allied forces the technological edge that means the difference between victory or defeat on the modern battlefield.
>
> I grew up in an era when the United States was called the 'arsenal of democracy.' It was something to be proud of then, and it is now.
>
> The defense and maritime industries that support all of our nation's armed services deserve a special salute ... They are the unsung heroes of the Cold War. They are the keepers of the peace. They serve, every day, with our nation's armed forces on the front lines of freedom. In short, they have earned our admiration and appreciation. In abundance.[10]

Initial concerns that the evolution of the Sea-Air-Space Exposition would detract from the League's traditional focus on the young men and women of the nation's armed services proved to be unfounded. Rather, it helped considerably, both by bringing in new members and by generating additional income, most of which was used to fund, and expand, the Navy League's awards program, the Sea Cadet and League Cadet programs, and other League activities created to help sea service people and their families.

The Sea-Air-Space Exposition would evolve dramatically over the following four decades into one of the "must attend" events on the calendars of most senior sea service leaders. A number of important changes were introduced as the exposition continued to improve in quality while increasing in size and number of attendees. The initial antisubmarine symposium was replaced by several professional seminars (many of which were classified), focused on single- or multi-service issues, policies and programs. These seminars, several of which were focused on professional aspects important to senior enlisted personnel, became another major Sea-Air-Space Exposition highlight and were scheduled, one or two per day, over the three-day event.

The League's Legislative Affairs office, employing volunteers, began making intensive efforts, through personal invitations, phone calls, and office visits, to encourage attendance by Congressional staff members, particularly at the Legislative Affairs Luncheon. Providing door-to-door service from office building to the hosting Exposition hotel, the League began arranging personal, guided tours of the exhibits for key professional staff members, allowing Capitol Hill visitors the opportunity to meet exhibitors from their home districts and states.

The success of the Sea-Air-Space Exposition for the Navy League was complemented by the League's continued campaign for "comparability" in military compensation. National President Barnum had made this his top priority during his two years in office, and his focus paid off handsomely in the first several months of Morgan Fitch's presidency. House Armed Services Committee Chairman L. Mendel Rivers, who had succeeded Carl Vinson, met with the two League leaders a few days after Fitch had been elected to succeed Barnum. Legislation that Rivers had introduced earlier in the year to increase military pay by an average of 10.7 percent was the principal topic on the agenda.

On June 15, 1965, Fitch, accompanied by Air Force Association President Jess Larson and Association of the United States Army Executive Vice President Walter Weible, testified on Capitol Hill during hearings on the Rivers bill. They also presented Chairman Rivers a joint position paper asserting that "a substantial increase in current pay at this time appears to be the simplest, most effective, and, in the long run, cheapest solution" to the difficult and complex challenge of retaining professional, well-trained personnel in all the nation's armed services.[11]

In response, Chairman Rivers stated, "We will take into consideration the things you have brought to our attention and which you urge, I assure you. You have made a great contribution ... your thinking helped to draft this bill whether you know it or not, and we owe you a debt of appreciation and I want to express it and thank very much each of you."[12]

The House passed the bill in July, 410-to-0. The Senate passed a similar bill shortly thereafter. Reluctantly, President Johnson signed the measure in August. The $1 billion pay raise for military personnel that went into effect almost immediately was twice as much as he and Secretary McNamara had recommended to Capitol Hill earlier in the year.

Chairman Rivers received the bulk of the credit for the pay raise along with Senate Armed Services Committee Chairman Richard Russell. But with no active-duty personnel on its membership roster, the League was considered to have been the most influential of the several defense-oriented associations, not only in advocating significant increases in service compensations but also working to ensure the bill's final passage.

League National President Fitch, another World War II veteran, was a Chicagoan who joined the Navy League by accident. His wife, Helen, related in a May 1967 interview, "After his discharge, he was very busy completing his education and obtaining his doctor of law degree. We knew of the League and its goals and activities, of course. But the invitation to join it was actually addressed to his father and delivered to him by mistake. Anyway, he's been a member ever since."[13]

Fitch was best known, prior to 1965, for his involvement with the League's youth programs, a special interest, according to his wife. He had also worked with Robert Crown in updating and modernizing League bylaws and other governance instruments. Fitch acceded to the office of National President as a result of a genuinely contested candidacy, a first for the Navy League, being popularly elected over Sanford Flint from the Jersey Shore Council and Asa Phillips from Boston.

Emboldened by his time working with Robert Crown, National President Fitch continued an aggressive approach to his new responsibilities. He expanded the organization's horizons in several other ways, working with Vice President for Naval Affairs Harold Wirth, to explore ways in which the League, as had been suggested two decades earlier by then-Secretary of the Navy James Forrestal, could join forces with the Naval Reserve Association, the Fleet Reserve Association, and the Marine Corps League to better support the nation's sea services on Capitol Hill. Fitch also worked with Sanford Flint, one of the men he had run against for the national presidency, and now chairman of the Committee for Liaison with National Civic Organizations, to promote joint council meetings with local Rotary, Lions, and Kiwanis chapters to educate their members on the need for American sea power and the accomplishments of the Navy-Marine Corps Team.

Fitch had long been concerned that the members of the League's Board of Directors were increasingly isolated from, and largely ignorant of, the various activities being carried out by local councils. Though he was fond of saying that the League ran on "two tracks, one the Washington track and one the local council track, and ne'er the twain shall meet,'" he sought to bring those two tracks together, at least in terms of mutual understanding and personal knowledge of both tracks' leadership.

Part coach, part Marine Drill Instructor, National President Morgan Fitch gained the nickname "The Whip" during his tour of office.

Fitch set out to improve the knowledge of the Board of Directors by conducting what he termed "shirt sleeve" meetings in their regions. He came to know almost every national director on a face-to-face, first-name basis, and worked hard to ensure that each director understood his or her responsibilities within the organization. Fitch's approach in working with League leaders was part coach, part Marine Drill Instructor. During his tour in office he would gain the nickname "The Whip," and when he turned over the national presidency after two years the League presented him with a bull whip as a lasting memento of his time in office.[14]

Fitch's travels to various cities and council locations also afforded him the opportunity to recognize the sacrifices of sea service personnel on the front lines in Southeast Asia. By the mid-1960s, as the War grew in scope and casualties, it was an issue the League could not avoid. Fitch began routinely talking about Vietnam in public speeches, in League council visits, and in "open microphone" radio and television interviews. In public appearances at non-League functions, his normal procedure was to arrange for Navy and Marine Corps combat veterans to join with him in meeting various Rotary, Lions, and other civic groups. He would also meet frequently in the company of active-duty flag officers — with the wives of Navy and Marine Corps fliers killed in the skies over Vietnam or missing in action.

The League's evolving view on the war was reflected in Fitch's public statements. Speaking at an El Centro, California, press conference shortly after becoming National President, he observed, "What we are seeing in Vietnam today is a situation where we are not only trying to win over an enemy but to win over a people in a way that they may find their own self determination."[15]

In August 1965, Chief of Naval Operations David L. McDonald wrote Fitch a letter indicating that "as the military effort expands, so must the effort to improve American understanding of the conflict and our role in it be expanded."[16] He then pointedly explained his dilemma, and asked for Navy League assistance:

> Lest a call for such effort be mistaken for a desire for mere self-gratification, let me assure you the reasons are serious and the needs real. The fighting man knows why he is there and why he is fighting ... But, if a lack of public awareness and appreciation among Americans at home is allowed to grow, if the real seriousness of the issues appears to the fighting man to be understood only by him and to mean little to his fellow citizens ten thousand miles away from hostile fire, then morale may well sag and with it efficiency and effectiveness.
>
> As the organization most directly devoted to the task of speaking for the Navy in such matters, the Navy League has its work cut out for it. We will welcome your support in this vital task.[17]

Fitch answered the Chief of Naval Operations' call. He began an aggressive series of speeches, college campus visits, and presentations on the "Navy and Marine Corps Team in Vietnam." In appearances in Ohio on radio programs and before such organizations as the Toledo Club he found most people asking, "How can we help and what can we do?"[18] He was frank with his audiences, in some respects more so than the politicians in Washington, telling an Oregon audience in

"It should not be the Navy League's business to defend or support the policy of being in Vietnam, but it is the Navy League's business to support the sailor or Marine who is ordered to go there."

December 1965, "We are not winning in Vietnam and we will lose a lot more men — and planes and possibly ships — before we do win. It will be a long war. It is time the public faced the facts."[19]

By 1966 his emphasis had shifted from advocating the war effort itself to the strenuous conditions of service being faced by military personnel in a difficult and increasingly unpopular conflict. Frequently alluding to a Marine with "a gun in one hand and a 'Care' package in the other," he asserted in an August speech in New Orleans that the "lack of recognition of the serviceman and what he is doing in Vietnam in the service of his country must be corrected."[20]

Fitch's views were buttressed by those of Charles Duchein, the League's national vice president and national chairman of Marine Corps affairs. In a situation report reflecting the reality of the war in Southeast Asia from a Marine's perspective, Duchein wrote in the recurring column "With the Marines" in the November 1965 issue of *Navy-The Magazine of Sea Power*:

> While defeat of the Viet Cong is vital to the accomplishment of our mission in VietNam ... it has become increasingly clear that force of arms alone cannot insure a lasting peace in that troubled land ... By far the most significant and effective feature of the Marine's civic action enterprise lies in the fact that it is conducted entirely by combat forces ... the same troops have suddenly become benefactors as well as guardians ... [21]

In the last year of his presidency, Fitch's public remarks on Vietnam reflected the fact, that unpopular as it was, the war in Southeast Asia was the policy of the United States government. In a speech before the Brigade of Midshipmen at the Naval Academy in April 1967, he asserted that the "Navy League cannot be categorized as 'hawks' or 'doves.' But since Vietnam is a matter of national policy, the Navy League supports the nation's actions there."[22]

In his final speech as National President before the League's National Convention in Jacksonville, Florida, Fitch told the attendees that the League should not enter the "arena of debate as to public policy" because it largely concerned "political matters."[23] Fitch continued:

> It should not be the Navy League's business to defend or support the policy of being in Vietnam, but it is the Navy League's business to support the sailor or Marine who is ordered to go there.[24]

Fitch's efforts in less contentious matters were more favorably rewarded, and were clearly gains for the Navy League in public recognition. On October 9, 1965, he signed an agreement with the National Park Service, Independence National Historic Park in Philadelphia, Pennsylvania, and the Association of the United States Army for development and administration of an Army-Navy Museum related to the history and traditions of both services between the Revolutionary War and the beginning of the 19th century. The two organizations raised nearly $500,000 to bring the project to fruition; the National Park Service agreed to operate and maintain the building. It was located in the Pemberton House, birthplace of the Continental Navy. The actual structure was a 1960s reconstructed Georgian mansion originally built in 1775 and owned by Joseph Pemberton, a Quaker merchant and fervent supporter of American independence.[25]

Fitch's enthusiasm for hard work was contagious. Thanks in large part to the efforts of Winifred Quick Collins, chairman of the League Membership Committee, the organization recorded a net growth of more than 2,700 new members. A former director of the World War II-era Women Accepted for Volunteer Emergency Service (WAVES), Collins's name had been placed in nomination for a vice-presidency at the 1965 National Convention by Morgan Fitch, in his capacity as head of the Nominating Committee appointed by Robert Barnum. Collins was subsequently elected as the League's first female vice president in almost 50 years. She later served for many years as chairman of the League's Awards Committee, and played a key role in the huge expansion of that program during her tenure.

League membership, national Navy Day observances, and the League's three youth programs, Shipmate, Sea Cadets, and League Cadets, continued to prosper during Fitch's presidency. Both Secretary of the Navy Nitze and Chief of Naval Operations Admiral McDonald praised the League youth programs as "probably the most important thing" the Navy League was doing to support the sea services. Writing in the November 1965 issue of *Navy-The Magazine of Seapower*, in a special section of the magazine devoted to the League's youth programs, Nitze commented:

> When the goal of establishing a Sea Cadet Unit in every Navy and Marine Corps installation ashore is reached, I foresee a continuous line of well motivated, patriotic, and knowledgeable young men entering the sea services as a result of this program ... The progress and growth of the Sea Cadet Program is of vital concern to the Department of the Navy — and one in which I have a personal interest.[26]

But as successful as the League was becoming as an institution accepted by the nation's political leadership in the mid-1960s, some traditional concerns dating from its founding were still evident. The continued expansion of the Soviet

Union's Navy and modern and rapidly growing merchant fleet, concomitant with the Johnson Administration's "economizing" of Navy programs, led National President Fitch to issue a strong warning in his January 1966 President's Message: "If we are to avoid ... being the second greatest *Sea Power* in the world, we must modernize the Navy, maintain our carrier forces, reestablish our sealift capability and merchant marine, and proceed with nuclearization of our surface fleet."

These issues were constant themes of the Navy League throughout the mid-1960s. In numerous speeches, interviews and opinion pieces written for newspapers nationwide, Fitch frequently criticized the Johnson Administration's "bare bones" budgetary approach to the Vietnam War, arguing, as he did in the January 5, 1966, issue of *Navy Times*: "We are fighting a war — and yet we are not at war."[27] Decrying the failure to properly fund ship and aircraft building programs at the same time as the war effort, Fitch cited the loss of aircraft over Vietnam, consumption of munitions, and the wear and tear on fleet personnel occasioned by heightened operating tempos in Southeast Asia. In the *Navy Times* opinion piece he criticized Secretary of Defense McNamara's judgment on these issues as being "far from infallible."

In a caustic speech in Jacksonville, Florida, in April 1966, the League National President rebuked the Johnson Administration for making "the sailor and Marine today a forgotten man." Fitch asserted that the men and women of the armed forces have "gotten little recognition from the President or the Secretary of Defense" who have "fought his raises in pay, restricted his housing accommodations and have ordered him to stand mute as to his plight."[28]

As both Herbert Hoover and Harry Truman did under similar withering blasts from Navy League Presidents, Lyndon Johnson never replied specifically to Fitch's criticisms of his administration's conduct of the Vietnam War. But, sensing the need to remind a presumably "friendly" audience of why America was engaged in a seemingly endless war, he traveled to Manchester, New Hampshire, in August 1966 and addressed the Merrimack Valley and Portsmouth, New Hampshire, Navy League Councils in a speech entitled "Our Objective in Vietnam." Rather than discuss the manner in which the war was being prosecuted, the President stuck to a broader theme in a luncheon attended by numerous senators and representatives from the New England region in addition to Navy League members:

> I think most Americans want to know why Vietnam is important.
>
> I think they know that communism must be halted in Vietnam, as it was halted in Western Europe and in Greece and Turkey and Korea and the Caribbean, if it is determined to swallow up free peoples and spread its influence in that area trying to take freedom away from people who do want to select their own leaders for themselves.
>
> To give the people of Vietnam time to build is one reason that we are all there. There are times when the strong must provide a shield for those on whom the communists prey. We have provided that shield in other countries. We are providing it there. And this is such a time.
>
> Until peace comes, our course is clear: We will keep our commitment, carry on our determination, and do what we can to help protect ... and maintain the stability of Vietnam.[29]

As dominating as the issue of Vietnam was for both the nation and the Navy League in the mid-1960s, there were other subjects and occurrences that could be dealt with in a more successful and less controversial manner. In February 1966, Fleet Admiral Chester Nimitz, the last of the Navy's five-star World War II officers and a longtime friend of the Navy League, died. Shortly thereafter, the Navy League recommended a new nuclear carrier be named after the architect of victory in the Pacific. The initial suggestion, originating with former Secretary of the Navy Robert Anderson, a member of the League's National Advisory Council, was endorsed by a number of other Navy-oriented associations. This was the genesis for the Nimitz-class nuclear-powered aircraft carrier, the world's largest warships, which with their nearly 100 high-performance aircraft have provided the United States with a highly flexible, mobile, and capable instrument of national power for more than a quarter century.

The League's 1966 National Convention in Santa Monica, California, offered President Fitch an opportunity to lay before attendees a detailed summary of the organization's fiscal condition and policy positions and achievements to date. His Annual Report, which he termed "history" in his keynote speech, indicated how far the League had progressed in the 1960s.

The League's net worth had climbed to $324,000 from May 1965 to May 1966, Fitch reported.[30] He attributed the fact that *Navy-The Magazine of Sea Power* readership had climbed to more than 100,000 monthly due to the "outstanding editorship" of L. Edgar Prina. Two other headquarters publications, *Now Hear This!*, a monthly administrative newsletter distributed to national officers and directors, and council presidents, and *Ammunition Locker*, an "as needed" bulletin on sea service and national defense issues mailed to a select list of more than 4,000 Leaguers and other prominent citizens throughout the country, were also well received, significantly narrowing the communications gap between national headquarters and League councils.[31] Fitch also cited his open-ended series of sessions with region and state presidents and the national directors living within each region as providing " ... a more knowledgeable officership and directorship within the Navy League."[32]

The Navy League was supporting the Marine Corps' Civic Action Fund for Vietnam, Fitch reported, and was starting a new program of its own, Active-Duty Assistance Program Team, also related to the war effort. Its purpose was to help those on active duty, or being recalled to active duty, with their personal affairs, by providing advice on mortgages, wills, and insurance programs, and helping their spouses find employment.

During the previous year the League had contributed $1,300 to the United Services Organization in Vietnam, sponsored a number of appearances of the Naval Academy Choir and U.S. Navy Band, prepared and widely distributed slide programs on military pay and the Panama Canal Treaty (a national defense and foreign policy matter of increasing concern), and donated $2,000 to help the Navy Wifeline Association support Navy spouses. In addition, a number of League councils had contributed financially and in other ways to support Navy Relief, local United Service Organization centers, and the Navy-Marine Residence Foundation.[33]

Fitch noted that the League had resolved to expend its effort in promoting four main objectives:

* Telling the basic need of the nation for the seas and the attendant requirement for elements of sea power.
* Improving the understanding and appreciation of American society for sailors and Marines, and improving their living conditions and compensation.
* Providing similar support and recognition for both the Navy and Marine Corps Reserves.
* Educating and training America's youth on the customs, traditions, and opportunities of the Navy and Marine Corps, particularly through the Naval Sea Cadet Corps.

These chosen four objectives were determined by Fitch, but only after he had presented Secretary of the Navy Paul Nitze a list of ten League programs, and asked him to select four the Department of the Navy was most interested in having the organization focus on. After some deliberation, Nitze had declined to make any choices, leaving that option up to Fitch. The National President had done so, and candidly noted in his Annual Report that the "Navy-Marine Corps team has many other problems that [the League] might help in. However, we have limited capability and staff. This necessitates concentrating on a few objectives."[34]

Fitch noted in the report the various topics on which he had spoken in numerous appearances and speeches as well as television and radio interviews. They succinctly indicated the issues the League thought most important in the mid-1960s as the nation slipped deeper into the conflict in Southeast Asia. Fitch's list, as presented to convention attendees, included:

* The image of the sailor and Marine and retention of trained personnel;
* Modernization and maintenance of an adequate Fleet and Fleet Marine Force;
* Building of a modern merchant marine and a faster amphibious force;
* Improved housing and increased incentives to make the Navy and Marine Corps a career;
* A larger carrier force, increased nuclear ships, and more propeller aircraft;
* Oceanography;
* Civilianization of the Navy;
* Erosion of command responsibility; and
* Naval and Marine Reserves.

That was the "history" part of the convention. "Live," from the speaker's lectern, Fitch delivered an address that he considered "talking about the Navy League of the future–where it is going, or at least where it can go"–that, perhaps better than any report, captured the essence of his leadership style and aptly lived up to his nickname of "The Whip."[35]

While expressing pride in League accomplishments in his first year in the national presidency, Fitch added, "I am not content in this and I hope that you are not." He pointed out that the American people still failed to comprehend the importance of seapower to their livelihood and standard of living and held that this ignorance was largely the fault of the League: "If we fail in making the people understand the need for the seas for their own good ... we fail our country." Fitch charged that the League spent "too much time talking to itself ... there is little gain for the Navy-Marine Corps team in selling seapower to Navy Leaguers."

Calling on the League's local council to get involved in ensuring that living conditions and quarters for sea service personnel in their locales were adequate, Fitch held that a "council which is not aware of local conditions for the Navy and Marine Corps is not worth its salt. Oftentimes the council is more concerned with the privileges of the officers' club and the golf course than it is with the conditions under which the officer and enlisted man is serving."

Finally, rejecting any call for increasing the size of the national headquarters staff — "I, for one, am not about to abandon the initiative and direction of this organization to any Washington staff" — he promised, if reelected, to continue at the same accelerated pace as his first year in office. If reelected he "expected far greater undertakings of the national vice presidents or, as far as I am concerned, they can get off the ship now." He closed by noting:

> The continued growth of the Navy League is directly proportional to the degree in which the national vice presidents pick up the ball and run. If they — any one of them — have time to campaign in this next year, they will not be doing their job for the Navy League. I want to make this awfully clear.[36]

In forwarding a copy of this speech to Secretary of the Navy Nitze, Commander William Thompson observed:

> This speech sets a new standard for Navy League activity and industry. The organization is buckling under to Mr. Fitch's hard-working, no-nonsense leadership. With this type of leadership this unique organization should prove increasingly helpful in the achievement of some of our public information/public relations objectives.[37]

Fitch's close liaison with the Department of the Navy continued in the second year of his presidency. In the summer of 1966 he met with Secretary Nitze on several occasions to update him on League activities and solicit the Secretary's desires and advice. In a July meeting, Fitch outlined eight specific objectives the League would put focus on in the next year: [38]

* The education of the American public concerning seapower;
* The refurbishment of the Navy and Marine Corps image in light of the Vietnam conflict;
* Improving housing at the local level for Navy and Marine Corps personnel by involving local League councils;
* The Naval Sea Cadet and Shipmate youth programs;
* Observance of Navy Day with the theme, "U.S. Navy–Mark of a Man";
* Active Duty Assistance Program, an initiative where the League would assist reservists and their families when and if they were recalled to active duty;
* Annual Naval Reserve luncheon; and
* Congressional breakfasts.

To further assist the Department of the Navy in accomplishing some of its public relations objectives, Fitch wrote a letter to Secretary Nitze proposing that a council be formed to provide close coordination among Navy-Marine Corps-oriented organizations in order to further common interests and objectives of the Navy-Marine Corps team. With approval of the Navy Secretariat and Chief of Information Rear Admiral William Mack, the council's first meeting, held in February 1967, was so well attended that it had to be moved from Secretary Nitze's office to the hallway outside his office. Attendees included, in addition to the Navy League, the Naval Reserve Association, the Marine Corps Reserve Association, the Marine Corps League, the Naval Enlisted Reserve Association, the Navy Mothers' Clubs, the Navy Wives' Clubs, and the Fleet Reserve Association.[39] The Navy-Marine Corps Council would serve for several years as a venue to communicate broad Navy policy issues and surface problems and challenges from the perspective of people not directly involved in the chain of command.

Charles F. Duchein, who succeeded Fitch as League National President at the close of the League's 1967 convention in Jacksonville, Florida, was a former member of the Louisiana state legislature, a successful businessman, and a major general in the Marine Corps Reserve. Like Fitch, he had seen combat operations in World War II, and had also served a tour at the Marine base at Da Nang, Vietnam. With Marines playing an increasingly important role in that embattled country, the ties between the Navy League and the Marine Corps became even closer during Duchein's presidency. Symbolic of this closer relationship, the Jacksonville convention focused on "A Day in Vietnam" and had as program participants more than a dozen Navy, Marine Corps, and Coast Guard officer and enlisted personnel who had recently seen combat in Southeast Asia. In a letter to convention participants, Marine Corps Commandant General Wallace Greene Jr. noted that the Navy-Marine Corps Team and the Navy League shared a proud tradition:

> Together, we value our role in guarding the national interest, in maintaining a Naval Service and providing it the tools — material, moral, and spiritual — with which it must fight. The current conflict in Vietnam daily demonstrates the importance of this role.[40]

Continuing his emphasis on the Marine Corps, in his President's Messages and in numerous speeches and press conferences, Duchein had the opportunity to include front-line reports "direct from the combat zone." Because of his active-duty background, Duchein was a vigorous supporter of Navy/Marine Corps amphibious forces, and of the U.S.-flag Merchant Marine. Among his most innovative President's Messages, in fact, was one advocating a merchant marine "Manhattan Project" to rebuild the U.S.-flag fleet. He also was an articulate advocate for maritime research, the nuclear Navy, and a larger shipbuilding program in general.

As National President, Duchein advocated a broad-based national maritime

/oceanic educational program directed not only at the legislative and executive branches of government and the media, but also at the American people. Working with the League's Steering, Executive, and Resolutions Committees, as well as a number of outside consultants, Duchein developed and promulgated "Seven Strategic Safeguards" for long-range national policy:

* Orientation of national strategy seaward;
* Undertaking a major ship-construction program to build up the modern U.S. Navy and merchant marine;
* Conversion of the Navy to nuclear power;
* Creation of an Indian Ocean fleet;
* Stressing the importance of the oceans;
* Establishment of a Secretary of Maritime Affairs at the cabinet level; and
* Reorganization of the Department of Defense to ensure full consideration of the maritime viewpoint.

Like all of his recent predecessors as National President, Duchein traveled extensively during his tour, not only visiting League councils but also attending as many state and regional meetings as possible, during which he was always available for press conferences, interviews, and guest appearances on television and radio. As part of the same outreach process, he worked with the headquarters staff to increase both the size of the media mailing list and the number of press releases distributed. The latter covered a broad range of subjects related not only to the Seven Strategic Safeguards but also to current issues such as the Navy and Marine Corps budgets, Soviet technological breakthroughs, and the Sea Grant College legislation steered through Congress by Senator Claiborne Pell.

Reflecting continued public disenchantment with the Vietnam War, the League grew by only 1,500 members during Duchein's 1967-1969 tour as National President, a lower growth rate than the average of the previous twelve years. But on the positive side was the fact that League councils focused increasing attention on a broad spectrum of programs designed not only to support Navy, Marine Corps, and Coast Guard personnel deployed to Southeast Asia, but also to assist the spouses and children of sea service families left behind. And, as was the case in World War II, special attention was paid to helping the families of those killed, wounded, or missing in action.

In addition, the Navy League was in the vanguard of several patriotic organizations calling attention to the unique problems facing the wives and children of service personnel known or believed to be prisoners of war. The "POW problem," as it was frequently called, was oftentimes avoided by Washington officials because it had become a powerful political tool used by both North Vietnam and anti-war activists in the United States. A number of *Navy-The Magazine of Sea Power* articles by Heather David, Pentagon reporter for Fairchild Publications, on the prisoner of war issue started with a lengthy report on the program initiated by Texas businessman, and Life Member of the League's Dallas, Texas, Council, Ross Perot (later a candidate for President of the United States), to call public attention to the plight of the POWs.

Seeking to broaden the organization's base of both support and influence through fuller employment of League councils on Capitol Hill, articles in *Navy-The Magazine of Sea Power* spelled out for League members the specific jurisdictional and budgetary responsibilities of the House and Senate Armed Services Committees, the defense appropriations subcommittees of the two houses, and the numerous other committees and subcommittees with jurisdiction over U.S. maritime and oceanic affairs.

Complementing this in-house educational effort, councils were urged to invite the House and Senate members from their own states to speak at council luncheons, banquets, and similar events. The councils were requested to ask other patriotic and civic organizations to serve as co-sponsors, whenever possible, of the same event. In addition, individual League members were asked to write to their elected representatives, giving personal views as constituents, on various defense issues.

On Capitol Hill, the greater council involvement at the local level was welcomed. Despite the continuing disenchantment with the Vietnam War, many members of the House and Senate were finding the councils in their home communities to be objective audiences that could be used to air their own views on national defense and foreign policy issues.

In a similar manner Navy League publications during this period frequently served as outlets for congressional views on issues of maritime affairs and national security, particularly on the issue of nuclear power for both submarines and surface combatants in the fleet. Representative William Anderson, former commanding officer of the submarine USS *Nautilus* (SSN-571), wrote several authoritative articles for *Navy-The Magazine of Sea Power* spelling out the immense increase in combat capabilities provided by nuclear propulsion. Senator Henry Jackson, member of the Senate Armed Service Committee and Chairman of the Military Applications Subcomm-ittee on the Joint Committee on Atomic Energy, argued in the October 1964 issue of *Navy-The Magazine of Sea Power* for the construction of additional nuclear-powered surface ships. In doing so, he took a position at odds with the budgetary limitations on new ship construction imposed by the Johnson Administration to pay for the expanding war in Southeast Asia. But Jackson, emerging as a leading authority on defense issues, cited his committee's unanimous conclusion that the Defense Department's cost effectiveness studies were flawed by a "fundamental weakness that negates their validity." The article also cited the committee's conclusion that it is "fundamentally illogical and wasteful to fit our new first-line warships with power plants that are, perhaps, already obsolete."[41]

Jackson later wrote another much-quoted article for the May 1969 issue of *Navy-The Magazine of Sea Power*, that aptly captured the mindset of many Navy Leaguers at the end of a troubled decade. The senator from Washington state asserted that "five prevalent myths need to be dispelled ... if the American people are to come to grips with the real dangers" facing the United States: "We live in a restless and risky world ... Faced with complex issues and understandably hoping for simple answers, it is not surprising that convenient but false myths work their way into some people's thinking." The five myths were: [42]

* The Soviets are on a fixed course toward more peaceful and moderate policies and are ready to leave their neighbors alone.
* The Soviet rulers are becoming progressively more liberal and civil rights conscious, and are about ready to rejoin Western society.
* It is the United States that is responsible for heating up the arms build-up.
* The only way to manage our problems with the Soviet Union is 'instant negotiation.'
* The 'devil theory' of history: the military-industrial complex.

Complementing both Jackson's article and those of a similar vein, largely from Democratic Party senators (in later years these men would be termed "Scoop Jackson Democrats," synonymous with the strongest elected Cold Warriors in Congress), National President Duchein and other officials continued to focus attention on the Soviet Navy, still growing in size, quality, and combat capability, and on several new topics. In a series of articles, the Oceanographer of the Navy, Rear Admiral Odale Waters Jr., discussed various ways in which pure oceanographic research was facilitating improvements in the Navy's antisubmarine capabilities and technology. Another article, authored by Assistant Secretary of the Navy (Research and Development) Robert Frosch, focused on the economic, scientific, and humanitarian benefits to be achieved by investing additional funds in the oceanic sciences.

Regardless of the variety of topics discussed in the pages of *Navy-The Magazine of Seapower*, the United States was still a nation at war and, as a grim reminder, fire on the flight deck of the aircraft carrier USS *Forrestal* (CVA-59) off the coast of Vietnam in July 1967 killed 134 sailors and injured 62 others. Beyond the human cost, the tragedy reinforced the ill-considered practice of relying on "best-case" scenarios in the formulation of budgetary requirements. The Joint Chiefs of Staff were on record that, to carry out all missions it was to be assigned in times of future conflict, the Navy needed a minimum of 15 aircraft carriers. But the Johnson Administration was always reluctant to request the shipbuilding funds needed to maintain that number.

USS *Forrestal* (CVA-59) suffered a fire on the flight deck that killed 134 sailors while the ship was steaming off the coast of Vietnam.

Because the fire occurred early in the ship's deployment cycle (it had been in the Tonkin Gulf only five days), the *Forrestal* tragedy highlighted the fact that there was no replacement carrier immediately available. The Navy filled the gap as quickly as it could by accelerating deployment schedules of other carriers. Nevertheless, as Duchein and other League spokesmen pointed out, the situation would have been much worse if the United States had been involved in major combat anywhere else in the world at that time.

Numerous other issues were the subject of Duchein's "President's Mess-ages," League press releases, and articles in *Navy-The Magazine of Sea Power* in the late 1960s. One of special concern was the status of the U.S.-flag Merchant Marine. In a May 1968 editorial that was picked up by the *New York Times*, the League charged that the Johnson Administration had "tragically failed to deliver" a new national maritime policy and was victim of a "decision-making paralysis in the White House on maritime matters." Perhaps anticipating a Republican victory in the upcoming election, the League concluded that "the fourth arm of defense will have to await the incoming administration and hope for the best from it."[43]

Another issue of continual concern to the League was the controversial revision of the Panama Canal Treaty under which the United States would voluntarily give up its control of the Canal and agree to share it, and a significantly greater share of canal revenues, with Panama. A complementary article by Chief of Naval Operations Admiral Thomas H. Moorer focused on the continuing loss of U.S. air and ground bases overseas and suggested that, if the trend continued the nation would increasingly have to rely on the Navy and Marine Corps to shoulder more of the collective U.S. defense workload.

The Republican Party regained the White House in the 1968 elections, and three months after Richard Nixon took the oath of office, James M. Hannan succeeded Charles Duchein as National President of the Navy League. Hannan had served as President of the Naval Sea Cadet Corps in mid-decade, but his perspective and concerns quickly widened to engage the plethora of problems facing the sea services as the deleterious effects of an unpopular war, societal unrest, reduced force structure, and deferred maintenance became apparent.

While the League maintained its publicly stated position on the Vietnam War, and continued to fervently support America's men and women in uniform, there was disquiet and concern throughout membership's ranks as it became obvious to many members that the conflict had produced little more than defeat, grief, and bitter, divisive anger that was splitting American society.

Navy Leaguers were well aware that nowhere was the war's corrosive impact felt more than in the armed forces. They would have agreed with Marine Colonel Robert Debs Heinl Jr., writing in the last days of the conflict, when he asserted, "The morale, discipline, and battleworthiness of the U.S. Armed Forces are, with a few salient exceptions, lower and worse than at any time in this century and possibly in the history of the United States."[44]

The League's concern over the deteriorating state of America's armed forces was clearly shared by the retired flag officer community, many members of which had been responsible for prosecuting the war. In remarks before the Navy League in San Diego in the summer of 1971, retired four-star Admiral U.S. Grant Sharp, formerly Commander in Chief, U.S. Pacific Command, was highly critical of restrictions placed on the air campaign in *Operation Rolling Thunder* in terms of targets and the numbers of strike aircraft allowed to enter North Vietnamese airspace. Charging that the Johnson Administration's "dilly-dallying with the air war" had allowed the enemy to "take an increasing toll on our planes and pilots," Sharp maintained that, "if we had continued the campaign and eased the restrictions in 1968, I believe we could have brought the war to a successful conclusion."[45]

Complementing League concerns over Vietnam was the reality of a Soviet blue water Navy far superior to anything the Russians had possessed since the May 1905 destruction of their Baltic Fleet in Tsushima Strait that had so concerned Theodore Roosevelt. Six decades later, the League, like Roosevelt, was concerned with the reality of burgeoning Soviet sea power, and with America's seeming willingness to be relegated to secondary maritime status.

The September 1969 issue of *Navy-The Magazine of Seapower* reflected these concerns in an article by retired Rear Admiral Ralph James. The article's central argument was picked up by the *New York Times*, which cited the League's criticism of the "disinterested American attitude toward improving our maritime posture." The League's concern, as reflected in James's article, was stated in stark terms: "We can expect that our own maritime position in the world will soon be eclipsed as a result of [this] massive Russian commercial and naval shipbuilding effort."[46]

National President Hannan continued the argument into the next decade. While expressing relief that President Nixon "was getting us out of Vietnam with honor," Hannan's "President's Messages" expressed concern about the 22 percent drop in fleet numbers under what he termed the Nixon Administration's "defense economy program."[47] Echoing Admiral James's articles, the Navy League President also cited with alarm the dramatically increased level of funding in Soviet military research and development budgets and expansion of Soviet naval power in both the Mediterranean Sea and Indian Ocean. In an article that compared naval capabilities in the "last great vacuum," the Indian Ocean and Arabian Gulf, the League termed "near comical" the Navy's "two ancient destroyers and converted seaplane tender" present in the Gulf.[48]

In a broader strategic context, as the direction of the evolving Nixon Doctrine, articulated by both President Nixon and National Security Advisor Henry Kissinger became apparent, both the Navy and the League became concerned that it was too focused on land forces and the Central European theater of operations, shunning both the Pacific and a more balanced approach to the national security needs of the nation. In January 1971 the League cited Vice Admiral B.J. Semmes's assertion in congressional testimony that the "U.S. fleet's sea control forces had dropped 35 percent" in the past decade and that the Navy feared a return to Eisenhower's national defense investment program which "concentrated resources on nuclear forces and reduced conventional forces."[49] A month later the League expressed a broader concern with the thrust of America's post-Vietnam War national strategy:

Chicago Mayor Richard J. Daley signs proclamation calling upon the citizens of Chicago to observe Friday, October 29, 1959, as Navy Day in Chicago. With the Mayor, left to right: John McGehee, chairman of Navy Day activities for the Chicago Council of the Navy League, Arthur C. Conrad, President of the Chicago Council, and Mrs. Robert Crown, chairman of Navy Day Ladies Committee.

> If only President Nixon and his defense advisors weren't, possibly unknowingly, the prisoners of their own land-oriented staffs and industry pressures, and could hear and understand the maritime options, a 'Blue Water Strategy' could become a reality.[50]

Another reality that the League found disquieting was the pending end of the draft and the soon-to-be-introduced All Volunteer Force. As the term of his presidency drew to a close, James Hannan wrote increasingly with concern over what would happen to the Navy when the draft ended. In his final "President's Message" before the 1971 National Convention, the League National President argued that the All Volunteer Force would fail: "It appears crystal clear that without the draft the force level goals of the President and Secretary of Defense [Melvin] Laird simply will not be met."[51] However, Hannan did hold out hope for the new system, but only with a fundamental reassessment of pay and quality-of-life issues in the armed forces:

> The Navy League believes that, if there is to be an all volunteer force, there must be a transition between it and what we have today. We believe that our country must first show, however, that it means business so far as improving the lot of the military.[52]

It was in such an environment that Hannan, frustrated with the direction national issues concerning the sea services were taking, cited only the "decentralization of responsibility to individual councils" as his principal achievement while National President, as he turned leadership of the League over to Thomas E. Morris in the spring of 1971.[53]

Morris, a successful Massachusetts businessman, had seen naval service in both World War II and Korea, and had served as National Chairman of the Naval Sea Cadet Corps. Although sharing many of his predecessor's concerns over the new national strategy as well as the size of the fleet and ship construction programs, Morris elected to focus the League's efforts on sea service personnel, as well as Navy Leaguers themselves.

An Old Salt talks with a young Sea Cadet

In one of his first "President's Messages" after taking office, and reflecting the reality of a society torn apart by the seemingly never-ending Vietnam War, Morris stated that the Navy League's greatest challenge would be to "bring about a restoration of respect for the men and women who wear the uniform of the armed forces."[54] A month later, as the effects of the Nixon Administration's personnel end-strength reductions combined with an economy tottering on recession became apparent, Morris noted with concern that "we are bringing our young men home from an unpopular war ... and right now the men and women getting out of uniform need help just as much as those now climbing into one."[55]

Within the League itself, membership was just under 40,000 and Morris was concerned with the growing median age of the membership, as well as the reluctance of many councils to get involved in the organization's youth programs. Calling on Navy Leaguers to more aggressively support educational efforts within the nation's middle schools, his September 1971 "President's Message" entitled "Sea Cadets — A Golden Opportunity Is Being Missed," expressed disappointment in the League for only having 122 councils (of a total of 307; 40 percent) sponsoring 173 Sea Cadet units: "I urge non-participating councils as strongly as one can, to involve themselves in this tremendously vital and important program."[56]

Morris raised the issue of the quality of local council leadership several months later, indicating that the League needed younger leaders "who perceive that our goals are inextricably and eternally linked to the security of the United States and 200 million Americans."[57] The National President was specific in the qualities he was looking for in local council leadership positions:

> We want leaders who know that what we hope to accomplish requires more than just a day of effort, or a week of it, and who have the staying power which can help lead us to a position of peace through strength.[58]

To bolster membership itself, he encouraged the councils to embark on a League-wide membership program with a goal of 50,000. Even in the midst of the turmoil of Vietnam, League leadership pulled together, and by the end of Morris's term, the organization had grown to 49,800, just short of the goal. Spearheading the recruiting drive personally, Morris and his wife Rosamond traveled thousands of miles; while he worked the local councils, Rosamond recruited women into the League and helped start several women's councils. The Morris's travels were so extensive, both domestic and overseas, that at the end of his term in office he was presented a "Seat Belt Award" for being the most traveled National President.

Unfortunately, Morris's successful efforts to address issues within the League were overshadowed by the deteriorating situation of manpower within the Navy itself. For the first time since the months leading up to World War I, the Navy League was formally asked by senior Department of the Navy leadership for help in recruiting young men and women into the service; projections forecast a fleet shortage of 8,000 people in 1972.

Morris moved quickly, appointing Ernest A Carrere Jr., a national vice president, to head a League committee to meet with the Secretary of the Navy, Assistant Secretary of the Navy for Manpower and Reserve Affairs, and the Commander of the Naval Personnel Command. Morris personally recommended raising the Commander, Recruiting Command, rank to vice admiral (O-9) to show the importance the Navy was placing on meeting the personnel challenge; Secretary of the Navy John Warner thought it was a good idea, and directed the change.

Former Secretary of the Navy, Senator John Warner, speaks at a Navy League event.

At meetings with Department of the Navy senior leadership, the League was asked to provide assistance in two specific areas: recruiting enlisted personnel for the nuclear propulsion program and the nurse corps. Speaking at the League's National Convention in Charleston, South Carolina, Secretary of the Navy Warner began his remarks by enjoining, "I'm here tonight to impress you into service as recruiters for the United States Navy and the United States Marine Corps."[59]

The League accepted the challenge, and results were almost immediate, as the organization's efforts resulted in fulfillment of over 100 percent of the annual quota in those two specialty ratings. But while Morris hailed the League's achievements as "dramatic evidence that the Navy League can make a marked contribution in this sensitive and vital sector of endeavor,"[60] he recognized the enormity and longevity of the challenge facing the sea services in the post-Vietnam era:

> The Navy League must continue to aid in recruiting young people for a Navy which, for perhaps the first time in memory of most of us, is facing more difficulty in attaining its recruiting goals than any of the other services.[61]

Half a year later, Morris could report that, thanks to League efforts, the Navy's overall recruiting goal had been met, but indicative of the times, only 65 percent of enlisted inductees were high school graduates; the Navy's goal had been to have 75 percent of incoming recruits in possession of a high school diploma. The National President concluded, "The road is a lot longer than we perhaps had thought it would be. But I am completely confident the Navy League will travel it successfully. ... "[62]

To meet the recurring challenge of recruiting, in 1973 the League joined with the Navy in forming Navy Recruiting District Assistance Councils in several parts of the United States. Not surprisingly, Boston, Massachusetts, was the location of one of the first councils, with (by then) former National President Morris as its chairman. The councils consisted of Navy Leaguers, reservists and active-duty personnel, retirees and any other interested persons. Members assisted recruiters in opening doors within the local community, including high schools, and arranged for interviews with prospective sailors; some councils established awards programs to recognize outstanding recruiters for their efforts. The effort, successful from its onset, continues today.

National President Morris's focus on personnel issues within the fleet and the League did not result in his overlooking issues of maritime power and fleet size. Articles reflecting League concerns about the Soviet Navy operating with impunity in regions as disparate as Indonesia's Malacca Strait, in the Red Sea and Mediterranean adjacent to anchorages for the Suez Canal, and in the Caribbean Sea astride the sea lines of communication passing through the Panama Canal. Surveying the reality of Soviet naval power in early 1972, Morris concluded:

> The time has come to quit taking for granted our ability to maintain freedom of the seas. There are doubts now that we have that ability. Unless our forces are increased and modernized, soon there will no longer be doubts; it will be a certainty that we cannot.[63]

Morris's concerns were shared by many during the Vietnam War-era regarding the condition of the fleet. When combat operations finally ended in 1973, there was no denying that the Navy was in deep trouble. Morale was corrosive, racial problems abounded, and ships and aircraft were in deteriorated material condition after a decade of deferred maintenance and repair.

Notwithstanding growing Soviet naval power, Chief of Naval Operations Admiral Elmo R. Zumwalt Jr., appointed to the post by Richard Nixon in 1970, decided to retire 500 ships to save the huge deferred cost of maintaining them. This more than 40 percent reduction in total ships was accompanied by increased funding to buy new ships and weapons and invest in new technologies; in fiscal year 1973, the Navy's shipbuilding budget was increased by more than $500 million. Both Zumwalt, and his successor, Admiral James Holloway, also embarked on a series of dramatic reforms within the post-Vietnam War Navy, broadening the fleet's focus beyond projecting power ashore (as in both Korea and Vietnam) to include sea control, deterrence, and regional presence.[64]

In the League's view President Nixon's budget for the Navy in 1974, even with increased monies, fell far short of what was required. In a March 1973 "President's Message," Morris decried the continued inadequate funding of the fleet:

> The Administration says that the President's budget is all the traffic may bear. It may well be. Even so, it leaves the Navy at its lowest level of capability in years, and fails to take all those

> steps towards modernization that even Congress has agreed must be taken.[65]

A month later, in a letter to the editor of *Sea Power* endorsing recent League positions advocating coordination of all maritime arms, as well as increased budget levels for all the sea services, retired Admiral Arleigh Burke wrote, " ... excellent — right on — thousands of Navy people ought to be writing similar [articles] so millions of people will know what is really happening to us in the international arena."[66]

"What was really happening" to the sea services was a dramatic reduction in funding, as post-Vietnam War economies were exacted on both men and material; the increases in shipbuilding accounts looked good on paper, but underneath a cancer was eating away at the fleet. Promotion delays for officer and enlisted personnel, curtailment of reenlistment bonuses, and postponement of personnel transfers within the fleet were causes for concern, along with the seemingly relentless buildup of the Soviet Navy.

The May 1973 issue of *Sea Power* lamented that "having already paid the price for the Vietnam War in blood, in labor, and in family separations, personnel are now also paying part of the price in dollars."[67] The same issue predicted that the Soviet Navy would have "12 aircraft carriers in ten years," and in an article entitled "The Postwar Follies," decried the fact that "for the third time in one wracked generation, the United States is repeating the same mistakes of the recent past [as after World War II and Korea]."[68]

Personnel issues were clearly at the top of senior Navy leadership's concerns in early 1973. Testifying before Congress, Admiral Zumwalt, noting a $75 million reduction in the Navy's personnel budget for that year, voiced his concern over "the long-term toll exacted from morale, retention, recruiting, and readiness" of the force by such Congressional actions.[69]

Writing in June 1973 as the new National President, Ernest A. Carrere Jr., a native of New Orleans and World War II veteran of convoy duty in the North Atlantic, combat operations off Omaha Beach, and operations in the Pacific during the closing months of the war, voiced similar apprehensions:

> We may find ourselves faced with the unusual spectacle of having produced the finest fighting machines in the world, then having them on the ground or alongside piers because there aren't enough competent people in uniform to maintain them and then get them underway.[70]

From budget reductions, to an increasingly aggressive Soviet Navy, amnesty for Vietnam War deserters and conscientious objectors, race riots, sit-downs, and strikes aboard Navy ships, the early 1970s were not a pleasant time for either the sea services or the Navy League. The contentious issue of amnesty was discussed at length at the League's April 1973 National Convention in Washington, D.C. Members voiced a wide spectrum of opinion, from forgiveness to incarceration, for those who had avoided the military draft. Many of these discordant views were reprinted in the June issue of *Sea Power*. But in the end, the Navy League sent a telegram to President Richard Nixon that read: "The Navy League of the United States, in Annual Convention, pledges to you its wholehearted and continuing support of your stated position with respect to amnesty."[71] In essence, there was to be none.

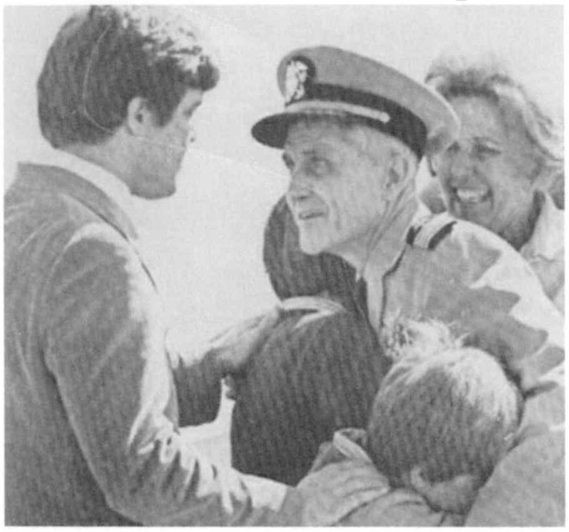

Captain James Stockdale reunites with his family in 1973 after seven years in a North Vietnamese prison camp.

One notable exception to the general atmosphere of angst and concern, and for many attendees an event they would never forget, was the May 1973 Sea-Air-Space Exposition. That month, shortly after the initial release of prisoners of war from the Vietnam War, Navy Captains Jeremiah Denton and James Stockdale, following initial hospitalization and treatment, made their way to Washington and the Sea-Air-Space Exposition. The ballroom was packed with more than 2,600 attendees, who remained standing for 15 minutes in a sustained ovation when the two officers were introduced. Following a chronicling of their hellish years spent in captivity in North Vietnam, which brought forth strong emotions and tears among many in the audience, the Navy promoted both officers to rear admiral.[72] For its part, the Navy League awarded both officers with its *John Paul Jones Award for Inspirational Leadership*"for their own magnificent courage and leadership while imprisoned by the North Vietnamese and as a symbol of that demonstrated by both military and civilian prisoners of war during their years of incarceration under the most difficult and trying circumstances."[73]

However brief, the stygian darkness of the Cold War was occasionally broken by a ray of light, and one such event occurred in 1972. Early that year, Secretary of the Navy Warner completed a long series of negotiations with Fleet Admiral Vladimir Kasatonov, vice chief of the Soviet Navy, that led to the *Incidents at Sea Executive Agreement*. The agreement was designed to put an end to dangerous at-sea confrontations that were occurring with increasing frequency between ships of the U.S. and Soviet Navies, and was considered at the time to be a potential "turning point" in the Cold War. Warner signed the agreement on behalf of the United States. Signing the agreement for the Soviet Union was Fleet Admiral Sergei Gorshkov, commander in chief of the Soviet Navy and first deputy minister of defense of the

Soviet Union.

Sea Power (in 1971 the League's magazine had returned to its simpler title, implying broader concerns than just the Navy) interviewed Secretary Warner shortly thereafter. One of the questions asked during the interview, a summary of which appeared in the July-August 1972 issue of the magazine, was "What's next on the agenda? An exchange of port visits between the two navies?" Warner replied, "Yes, that is one of several ideas we are considering." His statement was picked up by the wire services and much of the Pentagon press, and added to the general impression that a thaw in the Cold War might be in the offing.

The Nixon Administration's 1972 restoration of relations with China, the 1973 disengagement from Vietnam, and the initiation of strategic arms limitation talks with Moscow were the high points of the period that became known as *détente*. But while largely shifting focus to internal societal issues, Kremlin leadership was not reluctant to attempt to win various non-aligned "Third World" nations to their side, resulting in similar efforts on the part of the western alliance.

Despite seeking a more practical approach to international relations as symbolized by the *Incidents at Sea Executive Agreement*, the "on-again, off-again" nature of relationships between Washington and Moscow — and, thus, the issue of reciprocal port visits — became "off" again in late 1973 as U.S. 6th Fleet and Soviet 5th Operational Eskadra naval forces confronted each other in the eastern Mediterranean during the Arab-Israeli Yom Kippur War.

At its peak, during which President Nixon ordered the Pentagon to Defense Condition 3, the confrontation involved two American task forces and 48 ships, including three aircraft carriers, versus 95 Soviet ships, including 11 submarines and several cruise-missile-firing cruisers and destroyers. Although the crisis would subside by mid-November, it was clear that the unchallenged naval superiority the U.S. Navy had enjoyed during the Cuban Missile Crisis 11 years earlier was no longer either clear or unchallenged. More than a year later, Admiral Zumwalt would observe, "Facing these kinds of odds in that particular set of circumstances, the odds were large that the United States would have been defeated in a conventional war in that area."[74]

The specter of a resurgent Soviet Union that understood the importance of sea power was made clear by senior Navy leadership in testimony on Capitol Hill and in speeches throughout the country. Admiral Zumwalt, noting the impact continuing budget cuts were having on shipbuilding accounts, testified that 1973 was "the year that the United States Navy fell behind in what had always been its number one position."[75] By the end of the year, in the face of demonstrated Soviet "gunboat diplomacy" in the Eastern Mediterranean during the Yom Kippur War, Zumwalt would add, "We have disastrously lost more ground at a faster pace. The Soviets have passed the United States Navy in strength — and continue to build furiously to widen the lead."[76]

With such pronouncements from active duty leadership, it was little wonder that the Navy League, in its November 1973 issue of *Sea Power*, would declare: "Today, in 1973, the short-lived *Pax Americana* swiftly wanes, and is being succeeded by the graveyard peace of *Pax Sovietica*."[77]

Admiral James L. Holloway III relieved Admiral Zumwalt as Chief of Naval Operations in 1974. Many in the League welcomed the change in senior Navy leadership. Some members viewed with increasing concern the effects that Admiral Zumwalt's tradition-flaunting "Z-Grams," cancellation of directives deemed "Mickey Mouse," and personnel reforms in areas such as personal grooming, civilian clothes aboard ship, and race relations were having on the overall good order and discipline in the fleet. Coincidently this was a concern shared by many senior admirals serving under Zumwalt.[78]

But the passing of the charismatic, precedent-breaking admiral January 2, 2000, prompted a reappraisal of his period of leadership. *Sea Power* Editor in Chief Jim Hessman maintained that "the challenges Zumwalt faced as Chief of Naval Operations were, it is now recognized in hindsight, among the most daunting encountered by any to hold that office in the post-World War II era."[79] While a few subsequent letters to the editor remained critical of Zumwalt's stewardship of the service, particularly revealing was a remembrance by retired Rear Admiral William Thompson: "His selection as Chief of Naval Operations had an abrupt, cyclonic effect on the naval establishment. This brilliant, articulate, charismatic, leader blew away the cobwebs that stifled naval thinking."[80]

But in 1974, many Navy Leaguers, captured by Admiral Hyman Rickover's rapturous vision of the future Navy, viewed Zumwalt's retirement as an opportunity to call for substantial new investments in nuclear power, particularly for surface combatants such as cruisers and destroyers. In welcoming Admiral Holloway's appointment to the senior position of leadership in the service, the Navy League noted approvingly that he "would be the first Chief of Naval Operations to have commanded a nuclear powered ship, and for this reason it is believed that ... he will be instrumental in bringing into the fleet greater numbers of nuclear ships."[81]

Even stronger in its endorsement of nuclear power for the Navy's ships, was author John Norris's article in the May 1974 issue of *Sea Power* which, in comparing the warfighting capabilities of a nuclear versus fossil-fueled carrier, found the latter sorely deficient. Norris concluded, in what could well have represented the position of the Navy League on nuclear power:

> Admiral Rickover is completely right when he says that the Navy now sorely needs a constant, consistent long-range program to convert the fleet from oil to nuclear power, rather than the on-again, off-again haphazard and unplanned 'program' of the last quarter-century.[82]

Other topics meriting the League's interest and concern were the All Volunteer Force, which continued to earn the League's profound skepticism, and the disestablishment of the military draft. An April 1973 editorial in *Sea Power* termed the initiative "a sort of military-personnel utopia ... a utopia that could become a 'Pandora's box.'"[83]

In view of the ongoing United States withdrawal from Vietnam, and a building sense that America had "lost" its first war, geopolitical issues to redress the defeat were explored and discussed at length. These included the need for increased naval presence in the Indian Ocean, construction of repair and communications facilities on the British-owned island of Diego Garcia, the challenge of maintaining the right of passage in the Suez Canal given increasingly difficult relations between the United States and the Arab world, and the decline by more than 50 percent in overseas naval and air facilities.

National President Carrere was particularly interested in energy issues, a subject occasioned by the Arab oil embargo during the Yom Kippur War. Many *Sea Power* articles throughout 1973-1974 focused on the resultant energy crisis, scarcity and price of fuel, and the broader issues of national security that reliance on foreign sources of supply entailed. A February 1974 article entitled "Energy Overview: Obstacles and Opportunities" was authored by the President and Chief Executive Officer of San Diego Gas & Electric.[84] Some issues of *Sea Power* more resembled *Petroleum Intelligence Weekly* than a magazine focused on the sea services, a point brought out by an annoyed reader in a letter to the editor entitled "Too Much Energy" in the April 1974 issue.[85] But Carrere persisted, and from oil reserves to the expanded use of coal and natural gas to power the American economy, *Sea Power* covered it all. That the energy challenge persists more than a quarter century later is testimony to the validity of Carrere's concern and interest. What appeared perhaps as a temporal issue in the mid-1970s is a vital factor in America's national security equation of the 21st century.

In the summer of 1974, J. William Middendorf became Secretary of the Navy, as John Warner was appointed by President Nixon to coordinate the celebration of the United States Bicentennial and direct the federal role at events in all 50 states and in 22 foreign countries. In his first interview with *Sea Power* magazine, Middendorf was asked about the feasibility of building more nuclear-powered surface ships. In the context of an expanding Soviet fleet, and recurring fiscal challenges prevalent in the post-Vietnam Congress, Middendorf gave little solace to those who foresaw nuclear power as the future of the Navy's propulsion systems:

> I'm just not now sure we can go all nuclear. ... The nuclear surface ships are going to come to $300 million or more ... and what we need are numbers. We're way behind [the Soviets] in numbers. You can build four or five patrol frigates for the same money.[86]

Six months later the Navy Secretary still voiced concern over the expanding Soviet Navy. In an article in *Sea Power*, he reminded his audience that whereas in 1962, at the time of the Cuban Missile Crisis, the Soviet Navy was largely a "coastal defense navy," now "they have gone to sea. Today there are Soviet ships circumnavigating Hawaii, exercising in the Caribbean, and operating near the strategic oil routes of the Indian Ocean."[87]

Secretary of the Navy J. William Middendorf with Evelyn Collins, Executive Secretary of the Navy League.

Still, even in the midst of a perception of escalating tensions and renewed competition in the international arena, the idea of mutual port visits between American and Soviet warships would not die. And in the spring of 1975, the idea moved from concept to execution, with the Navy League assuming a major role in the proceedings.

Though not publicized at the time, the Navy League's Eastern Massachusetts Council played an important behind-the-scenes role in the eventual exchange of ship visits. In April, former National President Thomas Morris, a member of the council, received a phone call from "a senior naval official." This official apprised Morris of the possibility of "foreign ships" coming to Boston in about three weeks, contingent on U.S. ships being allowed to visit a port of "this nation." The "senior naval official" wanted to know if the council could sponsor a reception for visitors from, as it soon became clear, the Soviet Union. But the nature of the visit and identity of the visitors had to be kept secret until the official announcement of the exchange was made in Washington.[88]

"There was no difficulty on the Navy League side," said Ivan Samuels, then President of the Eastern Massachusetts Council. It was quickly decided, he said in an after-action report to Navy League headquarters that "the ideal place" for the reception "would be at the Wellesley Hills home of Tom and Rosamond Morris. That way, the Soviets would not only be able to relax in a less formal setting but also have a chance to see an American home." With only three Eastern Massachusetts Council members knowing the actual identity of the possible visitors, invitations to other council members and Boston-area special guests to attend a "Reception for Foreign Naval Officers" were sent out. Acceptances "poured in, with almost no questions about the identity of the mystery guests," Samuels noted.

Early on May 12, 1975, half a world away, two U.S. Navy ships, the guided-missile destroyer leader USS *Leahy* (CG -16) and the guided-missile destroyer USS

A *Tattnall* gunner's mate explains the features of the Tartar Missile to Soviet naval cadets during the ship's visit to Leningrad.

Rear Admiral A.M. Kalin, senior Soviet Navy representative from the destroyer *Boykiy*, passes through sideboys dressed in historical uniforms aboard the sail frigate USS *Constitution* in Boston Harbor.

Tattnall (DDG-19), entered the harbor of Leningrad, second city and leading port of the Soviet Union. With reciprocity assured, two Soviet guided-missile destroyers, *Boykiy* and *Zhguchiy*, in company with the guided missile-cruiser USS *Albany* (CG-10), Commander U.S. Second Fleet, Vice Admiral Stansfield Turner embarked, entered Boston Harbor, escorted by the Coast Guard cutters USCGC *Sherman* and USCGC *Cape George*. It was the first official visit to Boston by Russian/Soviet ships since the American Civil War.

For security reasons the reciprocal visits deliberately had not been announced in advance. The officers and crews of all the ships were well briefed and on their best behavior. There were no major incidents in either port, and thousands of Americans flocked to Boston to welcome the visiting Soviet sailors. In Leningrad, despite the fact that the crowds were carefully controlled by local authorities, Soviet citizens went out of their way to extend their own unofficial greetings of friendship to the American sailors.

The political significance of the twin visits was obvious. Among the numerous personages flying into Boston to extend official greetings on behalf of their countries were Soviet Ambassador to the United States Anatoly F. Dobrynin and U.S. Chief of Naval Operations Admiral James L. Holloway III, both of whom later described the visits as major successes.

Navy-chartered buses took the Soviet visitors 12 miles inland to Wellesley Hills on regular highways through industrial and residential areas, to the amazement of the Soviets who were permitted unrestricted viewing of, in their words, "everyday America." Even though each group of officers and sailors, intent on not giving up their hats, was accompanied by a Soviet State Security [KGB] agent, the reception at Wellesley Hills went well, Samuels also said in his report, and "set the tone for the entire week."

While the Soviet ships were open to visitors, off-duty Soviet crew members were in town, shopping, sightseeing, walking the "Freedom Trail," visiting Lexington, Concord, and other Revolutionary War sites in the greater Boston area, "and having just a wonderful time for themselves." Some of the visiting sailors even attended a Red Sox game, "where they received a standing ovation from the fans," Samuels noted.

At a final reception aboard the *Boykiy*, the Russian commanding officer acknowledged the role of the Eastern Massachusetts Council in making their visit a success, noting that the "Navy League and what they did was like making pancakes; usually you throw out the first batch; but that first night in Boston the pancakes were perfect."

The following morning, Council President Samuels, after receiving permission from the Second Fleet staff accompanying Vice Admiral Turner in USS *Albany*, was permitted to ride *Boykiy* out to sea, only to disembark with the pilot at the end of restricted maneuvering waters. Samuels noted that he would have liked to have remained aboard for an extended cruise, but *Boykiy's* next port-of-call was Havana, Cuba, not a hospitable locale for an American citizen in the midst of the Cold War.

Writing soon after the exchange visits were concluded in both nations' ports, *Sea Power* editor Jim Hessman noted that the event was "part of the constantly shifting mosaic in the balance of naval and maritime power between the United States and the Soviet Union."[89] More than two decades later, a September 1996 article in *Sea Power* about the Navy League's role in the reciprocal visits maintained that "the improved relations resulting from the ship visits, was responsible, at least in part, for the beginning of the end of the Cold War." The article's author was Admiral Igor Kasatonov, son of the Soviet fleet admiral who had worked with Navy Secretary John Warner to complete the final details of the 1972 *Incidents at Sea Executive Agreement*. This agreement, and the success of the first ship visits, Kasatonov maintained, led to later expansion of the ship-visit program, "an increase in the exchange of naval delegations," and the start of "combined exercises and maneuvers" in the Mediterranean between the U.S. and Russian navies.

But the Cold War still had almost 14 years to go when the Soviet ships cleared Boston harbor. No one in the Navy was deceived as to the finality of this slight thawing in the icy relationship between the two superpowers, and certainly the Navy League was unwilling to let its Cold War guard down.

This point was emphasized by Vice President Gerald Ford who was the featured speaker at the 1975 National Convention held in New Orleans, Louisiana. Seconding the League's continuing concern over the size and capability of the Soviet Navy, the Vice President observed: "There is no doubt about it. The Soviet Union understands the importance of sea power. The Russians built up their navy while we permitted ours to shrink and they know how to show their flag."[90] But Ford was careful not to promise more than the Nixon Administration, wracked by the Watergate scandal that would force the President from office in August, could deliver:

> Unfortunately the double blows of inflation and recession, along with other drains on government revenues, are occurring at precisely the time that we should be putting more funds into ships ... Department of Defense expenditures in the next fiscal year will present slightly less than six percent of the gross national product, the lowest point since the pre-Korean demobilization.[91]

For the Navy League, with Defense Department budget issues well beyond its ability to affect, there was much work to do in areas where the organization could actually make a difference. Reflecting the times and dramatic advances by women in all facets of American society, in the early 1970s a pilot program had been approved by League leadership, and selected councils had been permitted, to enroll limited numbers of young women in the Naval Sea Cadet program. Public Law 87-655, the legislative charter establishing the United States Naval Sea Cadet Corps, was amended in November 1974, when the wording was changed from "boys" to "young people" to permit enrollment of young women in the Naval Sea Cadet Corps.

The spring of 1975 saw the League welcome a new National President, as World War II and Korean War Navy destroyer and subchaser veteran DeWitt James Griffin took over leadership of the organization. But regardless of the health of the Navy League, and it was remarkably robust in the traumatic post-Vietnam War/Watergate era despite a drop in membership, severe problems were affecting the sea services and the nation itself. In a June 1975 opinion piece entitled "The Lessons of Vietnam," Griffin wrote that "perhaps those in positions of leadership today can help restore our confidence in ourselves by willingly acknowledging there's a lot to learn from history ... and right now there's also no place to go but up."[92] And ironically, given events in the 21st century, the accession to the office of Secretary of Defense in the Ford Administration by Donald H. Rumsfeld in the fall of 1975 did not receive an overwhelming vote of confidence from League leadership. Writing in the December issue of *Sea Power* which profiled the Defense Secretary, Griffin lamely noted, "We are assured that the new 'member of the team,' Mr. Rumsfeld, will espouse the cause of defense just as vigorously as his predecessor. Perhaps he will."[93]

Though largely ignored at the time of its publication, a January 1976 *Sea Power* article by Secretary of the Navy Middendorf established a benchmark for required fleet size that would resonate in the corridors of power in Washington for the next decade. Summarizing the results of the Navy's *Sea Plan 2000*, worked out largely by Admiral Holloway's staff, the Secretary noted that the "key to carrying out Navy and Marine Corps functions, wherever the national command authority shall dictate, is having a balanced fleet."[94] Then the Secretary continued in words that warmed the hearts of Navy Leaguers who knew their history:

> We project a need for a balanced fleet of 600 ships by the mid-1980s ... a multi-year authorization concept, much like the Vinson-Trammell Act of the 1930s, would improve the potential for increased efficiency which is inherent in long term stable shipbuilding programs.[95]

The supporting analysis that determined 600 ships as the proper size of the fleet may have been sound, but League National President Griffin was profoundly skeptical that the political will existed within the Ford Administration, embarking on a re-election bid, to press the issue with Congress. A month after Middendorf's article was published, with the Administration's defense budget submitted, Griffin could scarcely conceal his disappointment and concern that the shipbuilding goal had been so widely missed:

> Certainly what the President and Secretary of Defense Rumsfeld say about the priority of the defense of our country is plain old American horse sense. Then why, we ask, did these men then present to Congress a 5-year shipbuilding plan that is far below the 30-35 ships per year Admiral Holloway already has stated are his minimum needs, and in which his superiors in and out of uniform concurred?[96]

Unease with the Ford Administration's unwillingness to adequately fund the Navy remained a League concern throughout America's bicentennial year of 1976. Though few Navy Leaguers would go as far as the anonymous contributor to the June issue of *Sea Power* who opined that the "Navy shipbuilding program may be the only item in the Defense Department budget not an issue in this year's Presidential campaign" because "Jimmy Carter has indicated he thinks more money must be spent on ships,"[97] the League remained unhappy with the Ford Administration's naval program. Though National President Griffin would get entangled in a fleet size and shipbuilding argument with Representative Les Aspin of the House Armed Services Committee in the August and November issues of *Sea Power*, accusing the Wisconsin Democrat of casting "serious aspersions of character on our naval leaders and their civilian superiors,"[98] the League reserved most of its ire for the incumbent leadership in the White House.

Reviewing the Defense Department budget machinations after President Gerald Ford was defeated by his Democratic challenger, *Sea Power* editor emeritus L. Edgar Prina was unsparing in his criticism. But as events would subsequently prove, he was mistaken in thinking that new leadership in the White House would resolve issues in the Navy's favor:

> It goes without saying but it must be said anyway: Secretary Middendorf and Chief of Naval Operations James L. Holloway III were bewildered and bitterly disappointed by the President's decision ... the suspicion is that Secretary of Defense Donald Rumsfeld waged something less than an all-out battle for the carrier ... President-elect Carter may be a peanut farmer, but it is a good bet he is not anywhere near as naîve about the Soviets as some American intelligence 'experts' appear to be. The country will know for sure 'ere long.[99]

The problem from the League's perspective was that it did not know which direction on shipbuilding and other issues affecting the sea services the new administration was going to take. Four months into the new President's term, League National President Griffin could only state that "a great degree of uncertainty still exists" but that from early indications the "Navy appears to be the biggest loser among the maritime services." Griffin concluded that the "Ford Administration's 600-ship Navy still appears to be a valid goal, but it won't be sailing the seas until the 1990s."[100]

What Griffin could state with utmost certainty was that the League was in trouble. In one year there had been a net loss of 6,000 Navy Leaguers, and Griffin asserted there were two principal reasons for the drop in leadership: First, the failure of local councils to adequately involve their membership in their activities, failing in some instances to even communicate with their own members; and second, the Navy League's institutional unwillingness to stand up and be counted. In Griffin's view, this second reason could be directly laid at the doorstep of national leadership, as disgruntled members believed that "no progress was being made in making the Navy League's presence and purpose better known and respected."[101]

For the drop in membership, and corresponding failure to become more effective in the national arena, Griffin felt that both local councils and national leadership were at fault. Assessing the reasons behind members quitting the organization, Griffin concluded that "there is a need for what the Navy League stands for, but Americans will not continue to support an organization if they cannot be involved as participants in achieving the goals it has set for itself. The lesson is clear. It must be heeded."

To "heed" that lesson, Griffin proposed that the League embark on a "program of legislative education," as authorized by the Board of Directors, with the caveat that the program be implemented "when the League's operating budget permits."[102]

Griffin concluded his *1977 President's Annual Report* in a resigned tone:

> My view is that the Navy League, to be effective, must be heard. When it does speak, it is listened to, but in my view it has not been willing to speak as forcefully, or on a broad enough front as it should have in times past, either as an organ or through its individual members. ... In this arena, much, much more is needed.[103]

Griffin may have been too harsh on himself and the League councils, for the difficulties the organization was experiencing, not unlike those after World War I and during the Great Depression, were largely not of its own making. In the post-Vietnam, post-Watergate political environment in the White House and on Capitol Hill, defense budget cuts had become fashionable, and prospects for funding increases not politically feasible, regardless of what the League said or did. Chief of Naval Operations Holloway, never one to shy away from a fight or to strongly advocate what he believed was right for his service, later would indicate that the challenge he, and other defense leaders, faced in the mid-1970s was more than just a "Washington problem":

> We didn't have a tough time getting defense increases through the Congress; we had a tough time getting the increases past the people. After Vietnam the American people were just sick of the military. They didn't want to hear about defense spending.[104]

In such a climate, when the Carter Administration's direction on naval forces became evident, it was not one that the League found palatable. Significantly slowing the renewal and rebuilding of the fleet effort that both Admirals Zumwalt and Holloway had advocated, modernization was cut back, pay was frozen, and fleet numbers dropped to 467 ships, the lowest number since 1939.

This was the situation that Vincent Hirsch, a 9th Infantry Division World War II veteran who had fought in the Battle of the Bulge inherited when he succeeded DeWitt James Griffin as National President at the League's 1977 National Convention. Active in the Navy League for more than two decades, he had served as a national director since 1963, and had been a national vice President 1970-1976.

Hirsch agreed with Griffin's proposal regarding the League developing a "program of legislative education," and began immediately working with the headquarters staff to provide the funding needed. He also initiated a search for the right person to head the effort and hired retired Marine Colonel Warren Baker to lead the initiative as the League's first staff assistant for legislative affairs.

From 1977 onward, the League would maintain a more visible presence on Capitol Hill. Principal among the responsibilities for the legislative affairs assistant were maintaining contact with the offices of legislative affairs for the sea services, and the congressional staff committees with jurisdiction over defense matters, and distributing League press releases, white papers, annual resolutions, and maritime policy statements.

From its inception, other duties and responsibilities accrued to the staff assistant for legislative affairs. These included coordinating with the District of Columbia Council congressional receptions and breakfasts on Capitol Hill, and promotion of the Sea-Air-Space Exposition, League seminars, and similar events for members of Congress and their staffs. Beyond the District council, the assistant for legislative affairs facilitated League councils in maintaining close contact with their respective senators and representatives, answering inquiries from Congress about the League's position on various policy and budgetary matters, and assisting the National President in the preparation of testimony before congressional committees.

As the new National President, Hirsch was well prepared for the challenges he and the Navy League would be facing throughout his entire term. In internal affairs, the principal concern was to keep the League financially solvent and stem the continuing loss of members that Griffin had highlighted in his *1977 Annual Report*. Membership losses would level off beginning in 1978, but were still a principal source of concern at senior levels of the League's national leadership. On a more positive note, increased fiscal discipline, complemented by increased revenues from both the annual Sea-Air-Space Exposition and advertising in *Sea Power* averted any major budget problems during Hirsch's two years and enabled proper funding of the legislative education initiative.

The League National President also heeded his predecessor's view that the organization needed to take a more forceful, publicly articulated view of issues of national defense affecting the sea services. Working closely with Executive Director Vincent Thomas throughout his presidency, he crafted a series of "President's Messages" spelling out what he considered to be ill-advised Carter Administration decisions and initiatives in the fields of foreign policy and national defense. Many of these, accurately reflecting the seriousness of the issues, were considerably longer than the one- or two-page "Messages" issued by previous National Presidents. Several were long enough to serve as League position papers.

Reflecting broad-based national security concerns beyond traditional maritime issues (and, ironically, in view of the League's stance on the purported shortcomings of the Air Force B-36 bomber during the Revolt of the Admirals period), the

June 1977 Carter Administration decision to cancel the Air Force's new B-1 bomber resulted in a lengthy message from the National President in the August issue of *Sea Power*. Hirsch spoke out against the decision in a carefully constructed argument, pointing out that the cost savings cited could not possibly be as high as projected. He also took issue with what he considered an over-optimistic timeline for modernizing the Air Force's aging B-52 bomber, an initiative employed by Carter Administration appointees to justify the B-1 cancellation. The League National President also noted that deferring B-1 production might seriously jeopardize the viability of the land-sea-air strategic triad strategy to deter nuclear war, and argued against a solely defensive posture arrayed against the Soviet military, concluded his argument by stating, "We wish the President and his Secretary of Defense would act to ensure we have the best possible offense."[105]

Similar concerns regarding maritime forces appeared in the following issue of *Sea Power*. L. Edgar Prina wrote that the Carter Administration's budget cuts threatened Navy and Marine Corps air and ship programs and promised to "turn the U.S. Navy into a sea control/show-the-flag force ... with the power projection mission allowed to atrophy."[106]

But far and away the most contentious Carter Administration proposal from the League's perspective was the return of the Panama Canal to Panama. Branding the proposed treaty as "too far and too fast" in the September 1977 issue of *Sea Power*, Hirsch criticized the "steamroller tactics" being employed by Carter and called for outright defeat of the treaty in the U.S. Senate.[107] All subsequent issues of the League's periodical through the end of the year contained at least one critical essay or snippet reflecting negatively on the treaty.

It soon became apparent that Hirsch had stirred the passions of League membership at large. And it was also evident that not everyone was agreeing with the League's strongly worded opposition to the treaty. The National President acknowledged this in his first "President's Message" of the new year:

> Within the Navy League, no writing on any subject in the past decade has evoked more of a response than the President's Message on this subject in the September issue of *Sea Power*. That response has ranged from laudatory telegrams to a thoughtful and erudite 4.5 page letter from a former Ambassador to Panama who is now a Navy League Council President to the hastily scribbled note on the back of a membership renewal notice which said: "In view of what you wrote in September about the Panama Canal Treaties, I quit."[108]

Having taken such a stance, Hirsch was careful to ensure, unlike some past National Presidents in the 1930s, that he had the full backing of senior League leadership. The January 1978 issue of *Sea Power*, while acknowledging the opposition of many League members, also reproduced, in toto, the December 3, 1977, Board of Directors Resolution on the Panama Canal Treaties made at the winter meeting at Litchfield Park, Arizona. The Resolution identified seven specific questions that the Board of Directors had on the treaty:[109]

* How do the treaties provide for vital use and defense of the canal beginning in 2000?
* How can the United States move expeditiously and effectively to defend the canal — in light of Article IV [which required such decisions to be taken by a joint U.S./Panamanian committee]?
* How can an additional payment of over $15 billion to Panama be justified to U.S. taxpayers when at the same time we are making a gift of a $5 billion asset?
* Why do we give up our rights to what may well be a most critical option — another location for a new canal?
* How do we justify giving away our existing rights to deny enemy ships entry and passage in time of war, as being in the best interests of the United States?
* Why do so many of our retired senior military officers oppose ratification of these treaties?
* How can oral amendments or modifying agreements be binding?

A view from the bridge of the Mine Countermeasures Support Ship USS *Inchon* (MCS-12) as it passes through the locks of the Panama Canal.

Hirsch noted that the Board of Directors had asked "in a formally adopted resolution, that the treaties not be ratified until satisfactory answers to these questions be provided by means of alteration, revision, or amendment of the treaties."[110]

Interestingly, in an October 1977 interview with the Carter Administration's Secretary of the Navy, William Graham Claytor, the Secretary had only been willing to cite his view, "along with the Joint Chiefs," that the treaty was "a tremendous step forward from the standpoint of our national defense ... a big step toward maintaining the security of this hemisphere."[111]

Far more combative and aggressive was Claytor's response to concerns about the size of the fleet. Dismissing claims from Representative Les Aspin that a 600-ship Navy was "absurd," he was equally critical of attempts by pro-Navy partisans to have the Carter Administration specify a particular fleet size by a particular time: "Nobody knows exactly how many ships we're going to have in seven years. [Aspin] doesn't know, we don't know, nobody else knows. I just think it's an exercise in semantics."[112]

But what the League did know was that its hopes for a more "maritime friendly" administration, in that the President himself was a Naval Academy graduate, had run aground on the shoals of budget austerity and analysts within the Department of Defense that harkened back to the early 1960s and Robert McNamara's "whiz kids." The administration's emphasis on land-oriented defense strategies, the Central European front, and relegation of offensively-oriented sea forces, particularly aircraft carriers, to second-tier status, had finally become clear by early 1978 with the issuance of a draft "consolidated guidance" submitted for review within the Department of Defense. Keeping in mind DeWitt James Griffin's advice that the League had to "forcefully" present its views, National President Hirsch voiced the concern of many members over the philosophy of the "consolidated guidance" in his "President's Message" of February 1978:

> With the Carter Administration giving the distinct impression it does not wholly understand, much less support, the seapower tenets of Alfred Thayer Mahan — and, as a matter of fact, causing us to wonder whether it heeds at all the advice of Navy leaders — it now falls to the Congress to ensure that the fleet is something more than a modern rowboat Navy.[113]

Ironically, the next salvo to be fired against the "consolidated guidance" came from within the Department of the Navy itself in no less a personage than the Secretary of the Navy, William Graham Claytor. In a letter to Secretary of Defense William Perry, which Claytor maintained was "not intended just to be the customary effort by a service secretary to try to get more for his service," the Navy Secretary argued that "the naval forces section of the consolidated guidance requires a complete re-writing ... from scratch."[114] Claytor continued:

> The naval equivalent of the Maginot Line has been constructed — betting that the future is so predictable that the Navy can be sized for a specific scenario without regard for a global strategy and the uncertainty of the real world ... Changing the offensive striking power of the U.S. Navy to a static convoy defense will give the initiative over to the Soviet Union.[115]

In covering Claytor's letter to Perry, *Sea Power* headlined the service Secretary's unhappiness as "Claytor Fires Back; Disputes New Defense Strategy." Two months later, in his *1978 Annual Report*, National President Hirsch noted with pleasure Claytor's retort, and then added one of his own: "Not one of the shipbuilding programs Carter has submitted to Congress even remotely reflects the known beliefs of the Navy concerning the shape and size of the fleet of the future."[116]

But despite the impassioned rhetoric, the League lost repeated battles to reverse the continued cutbacks in defense spending ordered by President Carter. Carter's first five-year shipbuilding plan, unveiled in March 1978, provided for a total of 70 ships to be built, as opposed to the Ford Administration's last plan, which had projected construction of 156 ships over the same time period. Chief of Naval Operations Holloway maintained that implementing the Carter Administration's shipbuilding plan would result in a 420-ship Navy by 2000. Holloway deemed such a fleet size sufficient for defensive operations to protect America's sea lines of communication, but not enough to maintain peacetime forward deployments worldwide.

Holloway's concerns were justified in the League's views, and to many in Congress. And concerns over the future of the Navy were exacerbated when the Carter Administration decided to cease construction of big-deck, nuclear powered Nimitz-class carriers and return to smaller deck, oil-fired "medium-sized" carriers. Although a majority of the House and Senate found the Carter shipbuilding program inadequate, the President vetoed the congressionally approved plan that included a Nimitz-class carrier; the veto was sustained in the House.

In his "President's Message" of October 1978, National President Hirsch, reflecting on the Carter veto failing to be overridden, commented, "It is our fervent hope that the Administration's views toward maritime superiority will not prevail; if they do, we fear for the future of our nation."[117]

On a more positive note, it was also during this period that the Navy League embarked on one of its most successful initiatives in preserving America's naval heritage, the creation of the Intrepid Sea-Air-Space Museum at Pier 86, 46th Street and 12th Avenue, in New York City. The idea was first discussed at a breakfast in November 1978. Lamenting the fate of the soon-to-be scrapped Essex-class carrier USS *Intrepid* (CV-11), a ship that symbolized American air power that won the war in the Pacific, a group of 20 prominent businessmen in New York City decided to see if they could do something to reverse its intended fate. As one breakfast attendee put it, "How can we cut up our own history for razor blades?"[118]

One of those present at the breakfast, Zachary Fisher, renowned for his generosity to service members (and others) as a private citizen, vowed to save the *Intrepid* from the scrappers' torches. After touring the ship in Philadelphia, where she had been rusting away since serving as official host ship of the Navy and Marine Corps during America's Bicentennial, Fisher created the Intrepid Museum Foundation in February 1979. Upon being convinced that Fisher possessed the financial wherewithal to adequately fund the effort, Congress in April 1981 transferred the aircraft carrier to the Foundation.

Meanwhile, the New York Navy League Council worked the politics on the homefront. Winning Navy, city, and state approval, as well as meeting building code standards required the considerable effort and support of three New York Council Presidents: John Bergen, John Will and James P. McAllister. Fortunately, New York City Mayor Edward Koch envisioned the *Intrepid* as a centerpiece of the city's planned West Side development. He ordered the restoration of Pier 86 on the Hudson River as the ship's new berth. Koch's support, private donations from Fisher and many others, the sale of bonds, a loan from the city, and the teamwork provided by the New York Council, senior Navy officials, and the National Maritime Historical Association, saw *Intrepid* modified at Bethlehem Steel's Hoboken Shipyard from February to June, and arrive pierside June 12, 1982. On August 4, 1982, the Intrepid Sea-Air-Space Museum had its opening day.

Photo courtesy of Christopher Kavamagh

USS *Growler* (SSN-577) sits at her permanent berth next to the aircraft carrier *Intrepid* (CV-11 and the destroyer *Edson* (DD-946) on the Hudson River in New York City. These three ships comprise the remarkable Intrepid Sea-Air-Space Museum, a focal point for the annual Fleet Week co-sponsored by the Navy League's New York Council.

For more than two decades the museum has been one of the top tourist attractions in New York City, hosting more than 500,000 visitors annually. Its hangar deck houses three World War II aircraft, and its flight deck modern Navy, Marine Corps, and Air Force aircraft, as well as aircraft from the United Kingdom, France, and Poland.

Ten years after the opening of the Intrepid Sea-Air-Space Museum, the Navy League honored Zachary and Elizabeth Fisher for "their years of support of the United States sea services and the Navy League." In presenting the League's *Resolution of Appreciation* to the Fishers in New York City, National President William C. Kelley Jr. thanked them for "their public-spirited support of numerous Navy League of the United States programs, particularly the annual essay and scholarship programs, to which they have contributed so generously." Among the many acts of generosity and patriotism cited by Kelley were "the establishment of the Intrepid Sea-Air-Space Museum, the building of the Fisher Houses at major military and naval hospitals, and their invaluable help in starting and supporting Fleet Week New York-New Jersey."[119]

But although the fate of *Intrepid* represented a major victory, other challenges were not so easily resolved. Ironically, for an Administration that was stressing the importance of the land campaign in Europe at the expense of forward-deployed, sea-based forces, in early 1979, the first international crisis faced by the Carter Administration required extensive employment of the very sea-based combat capability they were trying to diminish.

Despite this, the Administration's second five-year shipbuilding plan submitted in February 1979 called for only 67 ships to be built, with a single conventionally powered, short-takeoff-and-landing carrier. Again the House and Senate Armed Services Committees demanded another nuclear-powered Nimitz-class carrier, and rewrote the President's plan so as to include it. This time, however, the President did not veto it.

Coming to the end of his term as National President, and despite significant achievements such as the now operational formal education program with Capitol Hill on sea service issues, Vincent Hirsch summarized the challenges facing the League, and by extension the Navy, in pessimistic tones in his *1979 Annual Report*:

> This Administration has manifested a startling lack of initiative in proposing and supporting actions that would strengthen our maritime forces, and as a consequence the potential for disaster in years to come continues to grow in geometric progression.[120]

Not unlike his immediate predecessor, a frustrated Vincent Hirsch turned over the national presidency of the Navy League to John J. Spittler in the spring of 1979. A Navy veteran of the Second World War, Spittler had subsequently graduated from law school at Ohio State. While a corporate lawyer, he had joined the Navy League, eventually holding every League office at local, state, regional, and national levels except judge advocate and treasurer. Upon becoming National President he was challenged almost immediately by another period of declining leadership. But he also decided it was time to purchase a permanent home for the Navy League, and made that, along with reversing the membership decline, his top priorities.

Spittler's renewed focus on internal League issues did not mean he would passively accept what the Carter Administration was doing to the Navy. In a severely worded October 1979 "Open Letter to the President of the United States," Spittler minced few words:

> The reports that I have read appall and frighten me. ... I implore you to pay more than lip service to the terribly serious needs of the Navy ... Throughout the country I hear those who ... are convinced the Navy is deliberately, systematically, and ruthlessly being decimated against the recommendations of your senior naval and military advisers. Act now to reverse this suicidal trend.[121]

Two months later, with the United States enmeshed in the American hostage crisis in Iran, the Soviet Union invaded Afghanistan. But though increasingly under fire at home for perceived weakness in defense issues, the Carter Administration submitted its third five-year shipbuilding plan calling for construction of 83 ships. While 15 more than the previous submission, it was still considerably below what many in Congress, and the Navy League, thought required. The House and Senate again rebelled, and the bill that went to the President for signature contained an additional $3 billion worth of ship and aircraft additions, including two additional submarines, two frigates, and reactivation of an Essex-class carrier and the battleship USS *New Jersey* (BB-62). The President signed the defense authorization bill.

Against a backdrop of the failed Iranian hostage rescue attempt, continued Soviet aggression in Afghanistan, and a Soviet Indian Ocean Squadron — matching in numbers, if not capabilities, the American forces already operating there — Spittler sounded a particularly pessimistic note in his survey of the nation's sea services in his *1980 Annual Report*:

> What of the future. I wish I could be more optimistic. But I can't. Because there is no hard evidence that the leadership of our country will face reality on the world scene. It is inconceivable that the President of the United States ... could publicly proclaim that he learned more about the Soviets from the Afghanistan invasion than from anything else in three years in office. Why does he ignore the lessons of history?[122]

But the lessons of history were being learned, in real time and on a daily basis. For the remainder of his time in the White House President Carter kept two carrier battle groups operating continuously off Iran, and routinely sent 1,800-man Marine Amphibious Units to operate in company with them.

Spittler's *1980 Annual Report*, in addition to its decrying the state of the Navy and national defense in general, also contained the good news that League membership had climbed 1,589 people in one year. But it only hinted at a major sea change that would occur over the next 16 months, as the League, for the first time in almost eight decades, was finally going to purchase its own headquarters building.

In January 1981, Spittler alluded to what he was working on in the pages of *Sea Power* by reporting that one of the top challenges facing the League was "the problem of finding a permanent home for our headquarters." Identifying this task as "an absolute must because of soaring rents in Washington," Spittler indicated that a new headquarters building would "allow the staff to cope with increasing demands of service," make the Navy League "better known to members of the services it supports" and finally, support "a broadening of the League's legislative activity."[123]

The task was daunting, as Spittler acknowledged in 2005 in a letter to Janet Mescus, the League's senior director of communications. Many of his predecessors had tried similar efforts over the years, but too often divergences of opinion on the Board of Directors had denied the National President the freedom to act. Spittler admitted, "As a matter of fact, there was [still] a minority group of board members unalterably opposed to real estate ownership, arguing that it would dilute the Navy League purpose and in times of economic depression could bring about the demise of the League."[124]

Vince Thomas, then Executive Director, had oftentimes worked with his counterpart at the Association of the United States Army, retired General Bob Cochran, availing himself of the state-of-the-art office equipment that the League could not afford. It seemed logical that a location near the Army organization would prove ideal, because of its proximity to both the Pentagon and Washington's mass transit system; unstated, but a near certainty because of rising property values in the Northern Virginia area, was the fact that it would undoubtedly prove a profitable investment.

Thus, when a property centered on Wilson Boulevard in Arlington, Virginia, came available, at a $1 million asking price, an immediate decision needed to be made. National Vice President John Clark, who chaired the search committee, was supportive. A sales contract was drawn dated April 9, 1981 whereby the Navy League agreed to buy the building at 2300 Wilson Boulevard, Arlington County, for $950,000. John Spittler, as National President, signed the contract, but the vendor, Menswear Services, Inc., did not. The contract was not consummated.

While events toward purchase continued, Charlie Hale, President of the Mexico City, Mexico, Council, suggested the formation of an internal Navy League group, to be known as the "Commodores" to help finance the initial payments on the building. Spittler supported the initiative, and subsequent membership reached nearly 500 members.

But while events were proceeding on a positive, beneficial track within the League itself, the sea services were operating for extended periods of time in regions notorious for some of the worst operating conditions in the world. The result was a precipitous drop in the Navy's personnel retention rate, as morale sagged and sailors and Marines "voted with their feet."

This was not an unexpected development among top Department of the Navy leadership. In his October 1977 interview with *Sea Power*, Secretary Claytor had earlier indicated that personnel matters, particularly the issue of "pay," were his top priority. Two years later, Admiral Thomas Hayward, who had relieved Admiral Holloway as Chief of Naval Operations a year earlier, sent a letter to Secretary of Defense Perry that indicated the full depth of his concern:

> It is no exaggeration to say that we are rapidly approaching a crisis. The highly trained officers and petty officers who are leaving the Navy represent a vital asset acquired at great cost, which can be replaced only over a period of many years by rebuilding our base of experienced personnel. ... We must stem this outflow of essential talent now.[125]

But President Carter rejected the advice of his Defense Department leadership regarding an increase in pay and other quality-of-life issues. In March 1980 he responded to Secretary Perry's oft-voiced concerns by sending him a letter which read in part, "Stop complaining about the morale and combat readiness problems ... you should assess other factors involved in re-enlistment problems. When I was in the Navy, pay was not a major factor." The President's response, when it became known in the fleet, was viewed with considerable disquiet, and commanding officers and squadron commanders on the waterfront and at air bases worked hard to dispel any public displays of unhappiness with the commander in chief that active duty personnel were routinely voicing aboard ships and in squadron ready rooms.[126]

Problems continued to mount for the sea services in the summer and fall of 1980. The cover of the July 21, 1980, issue of *Forbes* depicted an aircraft carrier going aground on rocks and shoals and posed the question "U.S. Naval Power, How Strong? How Vulnerable?" The six-page article, unusual in a business/finance magazine, was replete with statistics of decline and obsolescence; charts depicted the current employment of the fleet, and tables delineated Soviet and U.S. force structure profiles. These tables, in particular, were remarkably similar to those the League had used in the 1920s to compare U.S., British, and Japanese fleets. The caption of a picture of Admiral Hayward highlighted his pronouncement, "We are trying to meet a three-ocean requirement with a one-and-a-half-ocean Navy." *Forbes* concluded, "Reversing Teddy Roosevelt, then, Jimmy Carter is speaking loudly and carrying a very short stick."[127]

With the nation consumed by the campaign for the White House, the League carefully tracked what each nominee was saying about defense and naval issues, but in keeping with the Section 501(c)(3) strictures it operated under, refused to publicly endorse either candidate for national office. But such self-imposed restraint could be abandoned after the election results were known, and National President Spittler wasted no time, declaring in the December 1980 issue of *Sea Power* that "there is great cause for rejoicing among the multitudes who believed far more needed to be done to strengthen our armed forces than had been accomplished under President Carter."[128]

Lest his "President's Message" be overlooked, *Sea Power*'s full color cover was the evocative image of two sailors at sunset aboard USS *Blue Ridge* (LCC-19) operat-

ing in the South China Sea, with the photo caption reading that while it was sunset in South-east Asia, "Halfway around the world it is sunrise — a time for hope during a period of transition in the government, and in attitudes toward national defense."[129]

Inside the December issue, an article aptly titled "A Sea Change in Congress?" analyzed the "scope and dimensions of the Reagan landslide" and forecasted that the conservative Republican's election would result in the "largest turnover in policymaking and upper echelon managerial jobs in the history of the United States."[130]

Just what effect that turnover would have on the sea services was undetermined by the end of the year, but one thing was certain. In January 1981 a new leader would arrive in the White House, one decided in his views, confident that he was right, and one who considered the Soviet Union an "evil empire." Things were about to change!

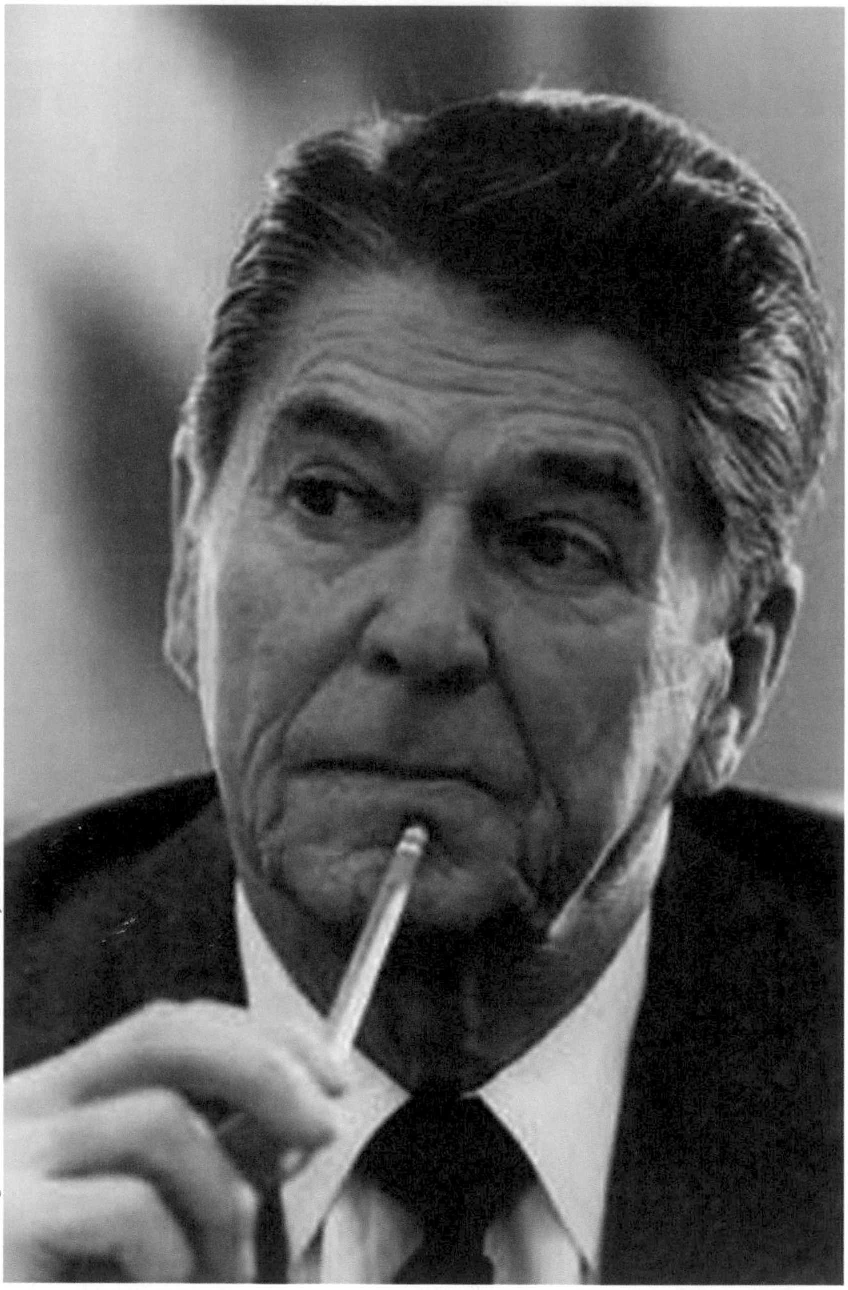

Ronald Reagan Presidential Foundation and Library

President Ronald Reagan at a cabinet meeting in the White House in November, 1983.

Chapter IX
The 40-Year War: Victory 1981-1990

When President Ronald Wilson Reagan took office in 1981, he quickly rejected both the *realpolitik* policies of détente practiced by the Nixon Administration and the defensiveness espoused by the Carter Administration. From its first days in power, the Reagan Administration set about reversing the precipitous decline in military, particularly naval, strength that had occurred in the previous decade. Embarking upon the largest peacetime military buildup in American history, nowhere was the increase in force structure, combat capability, and intent more evident than in the restoration of the United States Navy. It was the halcyon days of Franklin Roosevelt and Carl Vinson revisited.

The Navy League, attuned as it was to the moribund condition of the sea services, was almost rapturous in its hailing of the new Administration, even before the principal Defense Department nominees had been announced. The January 1981 issue of *Sea Power* had a picture of the launching of the submarine USS *Atlanta* (SSN-712) on the cover with the inside front cover caption, "Navy supporters hope the incoming Reagan Administration will 'launch' the Navy itself into a new and more prosperous era."[1]

Inside, League National President Spittler was positively buoyant, declaring that the "Back to Mahan philosophy of President-elect Reagan ... is cause for rejoicing by our countrymen, our maritime services, and our allies." Concluded Spittler, "The principal thrust of Reagan's defense policy is aimed at rebuilding the Navy ... the only questions now are 'how?' and 'how fast?'"[2]

Just "how fast," given the magnitude of the challenge was a legitimate question. Traumatized by the Vietnam experience, America had let its maritime power erode in the 1970s, a period, in the view of many of the new Administration's leaders, of virtually unilateral disarmament. The League had voiced its concerns throughout the decade, but the quantitative scope of the decline, across all the services, still surprised many people. Real defense spending had fallen by 22 percent and the Navy had dropped from over 1,000 units in 1970 to only 479 battle force ships when Ronald Reagan took office. By 1980 only 12 aircraft carriers remained from a force of 23 a decade earlier.

This downward trend in the Navy's ability to fight and win occurred at the same time the Soviet Union funded a tremendous expansion of military might. As Navy Secretary Middendorf had forecast at mid-decade, what had once been largely a coastal defense force at the time of the Cuban Missile Crisis was now an offensively minded, true "blue water" navy. In the July 1980 *Forbes* article, Admiral Hayward had noted this change with concern: "They're building our kind of navy. The difficulty is they're building it faster."[3]

Recognizing the gravity of the situation, President Reagan embarked upon a major program to reorder national priorities and rebuild America's naval strength. Succinctly expressing his views almost two years after taking office, the President made clear his intention of restoring the United States Navy to its rightful place on the high seas:

> Freedom to use the seas is our nation's lifeblood ... Maritime superiority for us is a necessity. We must be able in time of emergency to venture in harm's way, controlling air, surface, and subsurface areas to ensure access to all the oceans of the world.[4]

Almost immediately after taking office, President Reagan nominated John F. Lehman Jr., to become Secretary of the Navy. Combative, assertive, and comfortable in the political "give-and-take" of the nation's capital, Lehman believed that command of the seas was indispensable to America's survival as a maritime nation. He concluded his confirmation hearing on Capitol Hill in typical fashion:

> I believe that the Navy's former narrow margin of superiority is gone ... Our national security demands maritime superiority and nothing less; no euphemism, no fancy academic hedge words.[5]

For Lehman and his President, "maritime superiority" meant two numbers, dating from the Navy's *Sea Plan 2000* of almost a decade earlier: 15 carrier battle groups and a 600-ship naval force.

Shortly after his confirmation, the new Navy Secretary, sitting for an interview with *Sea Power*, left few doubts as to what direction he intended to take the Navy. Reflecting Admiral Hayward's previously voiced concern, Lehman agreed that the Navy's "very first operational need was to get the retention problem solved." He also signaled his intent to ask Congress for another nuclear-powered Nimitz-class aircraft carrier "at the earliest possible date." But then, moving beyond immediate issues, he hinted at a fundamental re-making of the Navy's strategy that had yet to be made public: "If we are serious about regaining superiority the key to it is being able to prevail in those high-threat areas against the maximum Soviet threat in the areas of vital interest to us."[6]

Joanne S. Crown, National Director Emeritus, of the Navy League of the United States, with National President Jack Spittler

The League responded almost immediately, entitling its April 1981 *Sea Power* cover story "Firing Off a New Naval Strategy." In his "President's Message" National President Spittler cited the "utmost importance that all Navy Leaguers be fully aware of this situation and that we get off our apathy and educate." L. Edgar Prina, citing the proposed Reagan defense budget as "the largest peacetime growth for defense in United States history" was particularly enamored with the new Secretary's "brilliant extemporaneous explanation of the Navy's new/old strategy of going in Harm's Way."[8] In Prina's view, the Forward Maritime Strategy, as it would soon be called, marked a "major change in naval strategy from the 'low-threat pulled back' fleet scenarios postulated by the Carter Administration to a commitment to restore naval superiority ... and defeat the Soviet challenge."[9]

To make the Forward Maritime Strategy more than just a slogan, Lehman sent to Capitol Hill a five-year shipbuilding, conversion, and reactivation plan that proposed acquisition of 147 new ships, the modernization of three active aircraft carriers, and the procurement of 1,917 aircraft. Seeking to rebuild the air arm of the fleet, the most controversial aspect of the plan was a proposal to build two nuclear aircraft carriers at the same time, saving $750 million in construction costs. Washington was "astounded"; veteran Hill watchers and former Carter Administration political appointees remarked on the "audacity of making such a request in peacetime."[10] But the critics were silenced when Lehman, after a hard fight, got his aircraft carriers.[11]

For the Navy League, accustomed to a decade of budget cuts, declining force structure, and poor morale affecting the sea services, the first four years of the Reagan Administration were reminiscent of the first four years of Franklin Roosevelt's presidency. John Spittler succinctly captured the League's upbeat posture in his final message as National President in May 1981: "This last year has concluded on the most hopeful note of the past decade."[12]

There was also good news for the League itself, as Spittler laid out in his *1981 Annual Report*. Regular membership had increased by 2,088 in two years, a 15 percent gain. The number of League councils was at an all-time high, with more new councils formed than in any two-year period over the preceding two decades. Corporate membership had increased to 102, a gain of more than 100 percent; Sea Cadet enrollment had topped 7,500, up from 6,000 two years earlier, with a total of 172 Sea Cadet divisions and 26 League Cadet ships, an all-time high for the Corps.[13]

Against this backdrop, so markedly different from the decade that preceded it, the Navy League evidenced renewed energy and focus, buoyed by the new spirit and enthusiasm permeating the sea services. John Spittler's successor as National President was John M. Rau, whose attitude toward the League presidency was not unlike that of John Lehman's toward his role as Navy Secretary. Both were aggressive "lead from the front" types, who had a vision of their respective organizations' futures, and set about making those visions a reality.

Rau was elected League senior vice president in November 1980 by the Board of Directors at the winter meeting in New Orleans. In January 1981, as the new senior vice president, Rau attended a conference in the U.S. Virgin Islands that focused on several issues of naval and maritime importance. During the conference, he witnessed William Graham Claytor, now Deputy Assistant Secretary of Defense, "explode" when a Carter Administration appointee made his presentation on the Navy. Rau would later remark that the "four years of frustration as to how the Navy and Marine Corps had been treated by the Carter Administration" was evident in Claytor's response. "He was so angry he was positively shaking."[14]

Upon becoming National President, Rau secured permission from Chief of Naval Operations Admiral Thomas Hayward, on his first visit as the new League National President, to "tour the world of the Navy" and "get down on the deck plates with the sailors." Shortly thereafter, with invitational orders in hand, Rau spent three weeks in the Indian Ocean aboard every ship in the forward-deployed battle group, and then visited the island of Diego Garcia, followed by stops in the Philippines, Okinawa, Japan, and Hawaii. As he had promised Admiral Hayward, Rau was careful to talk not only to admirals and commanding officers, but also spend time in the chiefs' and first-class petty officers' messes.[15]

Upon his return to Washington, Rau addressed the Navy's Public Affairs Officer Conference at Chief of Information Rear Admiral Bruce Newell's insistence and subsequently memorialized his trip in a 16-page interview in *Sea Power* magazine.

"The Almanac is designed to be an encyclopedia compendium of facts and commentary covering every aspect of the broad spectrum of seapower."

The Navy reproduced 4,000 copies of the interview and distributed them on Capitol Hill and throughout the nation.

Next, Rau asked the Commandant of the Marine Corps, General Robert Barrow, if he could tour the "world of the Marine." Impressed with the National President's articles, interviews, and testimony before Congress, the general, after reading a special issue of *Sea Power* devoted to the Marine Corps, issued Rau a set of orders. Though originally destined for the Mediterranean, he ended up north of the Arctic Circle, his escort through the snowy Norwegian landscape being then-Colonel Carl Mundy, a future commandant. As before, upon his return, Rau reported, in an interview in *Sea Power*, the wealth of experiences he had gained — and following the Navy's lead, the Marine Corps obtained and distributed several thousand reprints in the nation's capital.

Rau soon had another set of permissive orders, this time at the behest of the Commandant of the Coast Guard, to tour the "world of the Coast Guard," which included several weeks at McMurdo Sound, a trip to the Scott-Amundsen base at the South Pole, and a dip in near 0° Lake Vanda, where the "membership" requirement was full immersion! As before, Rau's Coast Guard experience was related in a subsequent issue of *Sea Power*—this time, though, written by a reporter rather than in an interview format. Rau's subsequent testimony on Capitol Hill as to the material condition of engineering plants of Coast Guard icebreakers he had been aboard in Antarctica helped secure additional funding for the service.

Based on this series of world tours, and reflecting the excitement and expansive nature of the early Reagan years for the sea services, in 1982 it was announced that the League would be publishing an annual *Almanac of Seapower*. League President Rau and *Sea Power* Editor in Chief James Hessman said that the new publication would cover a wide range of pertinent sea service topics, especially relevant in view of the U.S. Navy's expanding roles and missions vs. the blue water capability of the Soviet Navy. The *Almanac* would focus on essays and reports on major sea service activities as well as industry trends, and include an encyclopedic reference section of facts and figures on America's sea services.

Thanks to the National President's vision and Hessman's editorial background, the first *Almanac of Seapower*, a 282-page hardbound book compiled and edited primarily by Thomas B. Allen, was published in 1983. In his *Foreword*, Rau set forth the League's intent:

> *The Almanac* is designed to be an encyclopedic compendium of facts and commentary covering every aspect of the broad spectrum of seapower ... With its publication the Navy League takes another major step forward in informing and educating our citizens about the need for and complexities of sea power. That is the cause to which we have dedicated ourselves for more than eighty years, and for which we shall continue to work.[16]

The book included 16 essays, on topics ranging from consideration of the individual sea services to the Soviet Navy and the North Atlantic Treaty Organization, as well as regional coverage of the Mediterranean, Middle East, and Pacific and Indian Oceans. Five special reports were devoted to such diverse topics as the Law of the Sea and the Politics of Defense.

Rau's personal aggressiveness was also reflected in his approach to securing funding for a new headquarters building. At a June 26, 1981, steering committee meeting, he was authorized to buy the building at a price not to exceed $1,100,000. Now Rau had to come up with the money to secure the title transfer to the League.[17] With the League having talked about buying a new building for at least three decades, gifts from several Navy Leaguers in the mid-1960s had started a building fund. By the early 1980s it had increased to more than $100,000.

Rau hired a professional fund raiser, Elsa Jablonski, and directed the League's business manager, Kenneth Cornell, who had been brought on board the national headquarters staff by John Spittler, to be in charge of the remodeling and furnishing effort once the building had been purchased. Rau and Jablonski began the campaign with a personal approach, including the drafting of a series of individualized letters, many with a personal note written by Rau himself.

The results were gratifying, with nearly 100 percent participation from past National Presidents, the League Steering and Executive Committees, and Board of Directors. More than 20 percent of the League's Life Members, of whom there were about 7,000 at the time, participated, and the New York and District of Columbia Councils each contributed $125,000. Membership contributions were augmented through fund-raising events initiated and executed by Jablonski resulting in numerous grants from maritime-oriented corporations.

Negotiation of terms with the building vendor, Menswear Services continued, and the building was purchased September 1, 1981, for $975,000. On April 4, 1982, after 80 years of renting, and periodic moves, Mrs. John M. Rau christened the new national headquarters building at 2300 Wilson Boulevard in Arlington, Virginia, with a bottle of champagne. Attendees at the ceremony, which coincided with that year's Sea-Air-Space Exposition, numbered more than 200, including the Commandant of the Coast Guard, the Vice Chief of Naval Operations, and the Assistant Commandant of the Marine Corps. Finally, the national headquarters of the Navy

League of the United States had a permanent home.

The successful efforts to purchase and move into a new headquarters building did not slow Rau's vigorous efforts to carry the Navy League's message forward. He attended a high-level conference of the North Atlantic Treaty Organization, the Navy's own seminal Current Strategy Forum in Newport, Rhode Island, and two World Affairs Council meetings. In the tradition of all his predecessors he gave over 600 speeches during his two-year term; moreover, at his request, any visit to a League council had to be accompanied by an opportunity to speak to a non-Navy League group or organization, and/or to be interviewed by local radio/television media personalities.

Internal to the organization, Rau initiated a Past National President's Dinner at the League's Annual Convention, an event that continues to this day. He also actively solicited, in writing, the opinions of members of the National Advisory Council (including past National Presidents, retired uniformed and civilian leaders of the Department of the Navy, and other key League members), on issues such as the League's long-range strategic plan. While meetings of this Council, when called in Washington at national headquarters, had seen poor attendance, and observations and opinions of limited value, solicitations in writing by mail saw an almost 100 percent response, particularly by retired Navy flag officers such as former Chief of Naval Operations Robert Carney and Atlantic Fleet Commander Isaac Kidd.[18]

John M. Rau was succeeded by Albert Friedrich as National President in 1983. Friedrich, a gifted speaker and writer, directly involved himself in initiating a number of programs to improve the League's public image, particularly in the local District of Columbia area. He sponsored an essay contest in District high schools to encourage youth support and involvement with the sea services, and saw the local Dahlgren Division of the Sea Cadets increase in membership from 39 to over 100 cadets in two years. He also developed a specialized series of scholarships for deserving students who wanted to enter the United States Naval Academy and initiated a forum between Coast Guard admirals and senior League leadership to develop a better dialogue and enable the League to better address the needs of the service.

In 1985 Bernard Bennett assumed presidency of the League, and one of his first concerns was to revitalize the organization's program of education and involvement with Capitol Hill. Bennett invited Lou Kriser, a veteran professional staff member on the House Armed Services Seapower Subcommittee, to become chairman of the League's Legislative Education Committee and "give top priority to the League's ability to communicate with Congress."[19]

Upon joining the League's national hierarchy, Kriser (who had not been a Navy League member before, but had worked with and admired the organization) found that the program was largely dormant and lacked substantive legislative initiatives. To revive the program, he brought on board a staff legislative affairs professional, S. Peter Huhn, "to make himself known on the Hill on behalf of the League and to open doors when necessary and make the League's policies known to the professional staff."[20] At national headquarters, Kriser and other staffers began revising and updating the League's "key contact network"– Navy Leaguers with close ties to their legislators – originated by John M. Rau years earlier when he was national vice president.

The network was intended to enhance the League ability to influence Congress and legislation, an opportunity made possible when the Internal Revenue Service issued a ruling that a Section 501(c)(3) corporation could retain its tax-exempt status as long as the funds expended on legislative matters did not exceed 15 percent of the organization's budget. Rau's efforts to set up a key contact network were successful, and during his presidency had been utilized quite effectively a number of times by Rear Admiral Thomas Kilcline, head of the Navy's Office of Legislative Affairs.

Both Kriser and Huhn felt that, if used judiciously to raise specific issues of concern to the League, the network could be particularly influential, but its effectiveness depended directly upon the involvement of council members and their relationships with their elected representatives on Capitol Hill.

Kriser, while admitting that many Navy Leaguers "had little interest in, or knowledge of, Congressional affairs,"[21] sought to facilitate the efforts of those who did want to be involved. Directives were sent from national headquarters requesting that each council make a special effort to engage their representatives or senators while they were in their home districts or states. Kriser's recommendations included inviting and getting to know local congressional staff personnel (other than those assigned to offices in Washington, D.C.) at League activities and social events and keeping them informed of League issues and concerns regarding the sea services. When in the nation's capital, Navy Leaguers were encouraged to visit their state representatives' offices and to provide them with informational material prepared and packaged by national headquarters.

Executive Secretary Evelyn Collins, with National President Bernard Bennett, center, and Secretary of the Navy John F. Lehman, Jr.

Lou Kriser eventually would turn over responsibility for legislative affairs to others, but remained as chairman of the Resolutions Committee. From that position he suggested that the process for drafting League resolutions on issues of importance for the sea services be changed: chairmen of each of the sea services committees were subsequently added to the Resolutions Committee, and the ad hoc format of the resolutions was changed to generate a formal *Maritime Policy* document, which to this day remains the principal document published by the League stating the League's position on key sea service issues.[22]

In addition to improving relations on Capitol Hill, National President Bennett also decided to address the recurring issue of again revising the League's bylaws. For this in many ways thankless task, he selected former National President Morgan Fitch as the chairman of the committee to make it happen. Fitch, never one to shy away from a challenge, particularly one he felt so strongly about, elected to conduct a complete overhaul of the bylaws, picking up where he and Robert Crown had left off in the 1960s. A structured questionnaire was sent to each national director, enjoining them to carefully read the existent bylaws and come back with suggested changes and additions. Fitch received a large response to his queries.

Subsequently, at the winter meeting in Honolulu, Hawaii, in November 1985, he took the floor for eight hours to propose, and receive approval, for several changes in the bylaws. When insufficient directors were present, he dispatched a "posse" to nearby beaches and golf courses to "recover" absent directors, ensuring a quorum for voting purposes. With the possibility of having to conclude the winter meeting's business at the evening dinner an unpalatable option, everyone got down to work, and with the assistance of Calvin Cobb, then the League's judge advocate, new League bylaws were enacted, the principals of which were the following:[23]

* Bylaws amendments would require advance notice to provide adequate consideration by the National President and the Bylaws Committee.
* Maximum tenures of office were established for national officers; national vice presidents were limited to six (or other) consecutive one-year terms, to provide training for potential future National Presidents; the number of vice presidents was limited to ten, and their respective responsibilities were left to the National President to determine.[24]
* Provision was made for the election of a senior vice president to allow that person adequate time to arrange personal affairs before his/her presumed future election as National President.
* Provision was made for financial support for the National President to enlarge the universe of candidates able to afford the term in office.
* The constitution of the Nominating Committee was made more specific to give broad representation to the directorship and restrict the National President's control over succession.
* The selection of national directors was substantially removed from the control of the national Nominating Committee and allocated to the regions

for determination, with the national Committee arbitrating conflicts. The number of directors allocated for each region was to be determined in accordance with its membership numbers, but a limited number of "floating directors" could be appointed by the National President.

* An amendment was approved providing for a volunteer to be elected corporate secretary, and for this individual to be both an officer of the organization and a member of the Steering Committee. (The first corporate secretary was elected at the 1986 National Convention.)

The 1986 annual meeting in San Francisco saw the departure of another League stalwart, Jane Collins Grover. Coming to the headquarters staff in the early, dark days of World War II to assist her aunt, Evelyn M. Collins, Jane, in the words of the League's resolution passed July 2, 1986, had "faithfully served the purposes of the Navy League for forty-four full years." In words not dissimilar to those expressed about her aunt eighteen years earlier when she had retired, senior League leadership was frank in its acknowledgement of the indispensable nature of her contribution: "No Navy League National President could have functioned as effectively without her firm guidance and wisdom in the intricacies of the Navy League and its manifold facets."[25]

Jane Collins Grover was designated corporate secretary emeritus, and in the words of the resolution, "throughout her lifetime" would be "invited as a guest of the League to be present at all major fore-gatherings, national, sectional, regional, of the Navy League to add her counsel and contribution to the League's purposes ..."[26] Fittingly ending her "active" tour of duty, not only did Jane Collins Grover receive the League's President's Award presented by Bernard Bennett, but also the Secretary of the Navy's Distinguished Public Service Award and the United States Coast Guard's Distinguished Service Award. Her replacement was Linda (Trump) Hoffman.

The years 1981-1988 were good ones for the sea services, and issues of *Sea Power* were largely devoid of the apocalyptic articles that had seemed to permeate almost every issue in the 1970s. The services felt good about themselves and their leadership. Pay was significantly increased, with double-digit pay raises in each of Ronald Reagan's first two years in the White House. An aggressive program to build new, and overhaul existing, officer and enlisted personnel living quarters began, and maintenance and material budgets were funded to levels unprecedented in peacetime. When San Francisco Mayor Diane Feinstein issued an official proclamation announcing the city's first official Fleet Week in more than 30 years, the sailors in California, Hawaii, and the Pacific Northwest knew that times had really changed.

By the mid-1980s it was clear that Ronald Reagan meant what he said about restoring the United States Navy to its former glory. In the Navy League's lifetime, only two other American Presidents, both sharing the surname Roosevelt, had demonstrated Ronald Reagan's faith and commitment to the sea services. Commented one long-time observer of defense budgetary issues and their fate on Capitol Hill: "The success of current naval programs must in large part be credited to the civilian leadership of the Navy and the Administration."[27]

But to Ronald Reagan, "success" meant more than just hulls in the water and full ammunition bins. He wanted to *win* the Cold War, and to do so had to have a Navy "second to none," one that would leave no doubt in the Kremlin as to the final outcome of any encounter at sea. Thus, to complement a 15 carrier battle group, 600-ship Navy, a Mahanian strategic approach to seapower was required. The Forward Maritime Strategy, with antecedents dating to Admiral Forrest Sherman in the years after World War II and now being publicly articulated by John Lehman and new Chief of Naval Operations Admiral James Watkins, put the Soviet Navy on the defensive. While some questioned the wisdom of such an aggressive strategy, a leading historian of the Cold War, writing more than a decade after the fall of the Berlin Wall, noted:

> The Maritime Strategy created a sensation. Not since the late 1940s had the Navy explained what it would do in wartime ... [but] the Soviets understood. Their naval exercises began to concentrate on home defense against an attacking U.S. fleet rather than on open-ocean attacks on Western shipping. They strengthened their coast defenses — which meant reducing the threat they could deploy against the NATO army on the Central Front.[28]

Ronald Reagan left the White House in January 1989; less than ten months later, and half a world away, on November 9, 1989, the Berlin Wall, detestable symbol of communist tyranny and a divided Germany, passed into history. Its unanticipated collapse unleashed forces that ultimately liberated all the captive peoples of the Soviet Empire.

The peacefulness of the Cold War's resolution belayed the intensity of the struggle; no prolonged Versailles Conference with heretofore allies at each others' throats or European capitals reduced to rubble and Asian cities incinerated, radioactive, or both. Yet, as one who lived through the entire conflict, either in uniform or as a civilian directly involved in national security issues, Thomas Reed, Secretary of the Air Force during the presidency of George H.W. Bush, succinctly summarized the four decades of conflict:

> The Cold War was real, make no mistake about that. It was a fight to the death: at the top, between contending ideologies and national interests; around the globe, with propaganda and

> money; and in the laboratories and factories with blood, toil, sweat, and tears. In the jungles and deserts it was fought hand-to-hand, with bayonets, napalm and high-tech weapons of every sort — save one. It was not fought with nuclear weapons.[29]

What was the role of the United States Navy in the final collapse of the Soviet Union and victory in the Cold War? Writing from the perspective of 15 years later, Reagan White House speechwriter Peter Robinson offered his opinion in a March 2005 *Wall Street Journal* editorial:

> Our 600-ship Navy, the invasion of Grenada, support for freedom fighters in Afghanistan and Latin America, the Strategic Defense Initiative — the revolution of 1989 was soft as velvet because the United States had spent eight years being hard as steel. There's nothing quite as important to the cause of human liberty as the armed forces of the United States.[30]

Ronald Reagan had fulfilled both his vision and his pledge to the American people. As Thomas Reed states, "President Reagan put the pieces in place to end and win the Cold War ... [his] contribution was to rearrange the chessboard of history in a whole new way."[31]

Fifteen years after leaving the White House, Ronald Wilson Reagan was honored by his nation in the commissioning of the Navy's ninth Nimitz-class aircraft carrier, the first to be named after a living U.S. President. Speaking at the ceremony, Vice President Richard Cheney made clear the debt the Navy and the nation owed this great leader:

> The Navy we have today is in many ways a monument to the vision and the convictions of Ronald Reagan. He came to the presidency with a clear understanding of the tools our Navy would need to protect the American people, to honor our commitments to allies, and to maintain command of the seas.
>
> Today we send forth a great American ship bearing a great American name. More than two decades ago on his first voyage on an aircraft carrier, the USS *Constellation* (CV-64), President Reagan called that ship 'a powerful force in an uncertain world.' A generation later, we can say that about the ship that we've now named for him.[32]

America's naval renaissance, led by Ronald Reagan, and executed by John Lehman, was a key part of a broader national effort in defense that contributed immeasurably to the unexpected demise of Soviet communism, the society that supported it, and the disintegration of the 1,700-ship Soviet Navy without a shot being fired in anger. It was a fitting testimonial to the vision and beliefs of the 40th President of the United States.

John Lehman left the office of Secretary of the Navy in February 1987, in his own words "knowing that the objectives of maritime supremacy had been achieved."[33] In a final interview in *Sea Power* that ran almost 16 pages, interviewer Jim Hessman prefaced the Secretary's remarks by referring to the period 1981-1987 as "what naval historians undoubtedly will describe as 'the Lehman era.'"[34]

And the portents of that era were almost all positive from the perspective of the Navy League; it was difficult to find fault with anything senior military leadership was saying about the status of their services. Testifying on Capitol Hill, Chief of Naval Operations Admiral Carlisle A.H. Trost, who had relieved Admiral Watkins in 1986, told Congress, "The state of the Navy is sound ... On January 1st there were 555 ships in commission in the fleet, up from 479 six years earlier ... the Navy is demonstrably more ready than ever to meet national security objectives and will remain so for the near term ... our 600-ship goal will be reached in 1989."[35] The Commandant of the Marine Corps, General P.X. Kelley, was adamant: "The Marine Corps readiness to go to war today is the highest it has been in our peacetime history."[36] A month later, in his farewell address before retiring, General Kelley unequivocally stated, "Today's Marines are the best ever."[37]

In his *1987 Annual Report* to the Navy League, Bernard Bennett was also able to find almost nothing but good things to say about the League ... and the condition of the sea services:

> The Navy League, I am proud and happy to report, is in excellent condition, financially sound, and making almost daily gains across a broad front, from publications, our legislative education program, and the annual Sea-Air-Space program ... to the very important Sea Cadet program.
>
> Much more important than the health of the Navy League, though, is the fact that the nation's sea services are probably in the best shape today that they have ever been. Superior leadership is evident at all levels ... Considerable credit is due to the Reagan Administration and its forward-thinking, forward-deployment strategy — and to the brilliant enunciation and implementation of that strategy by such outstanding public servants as Defense Secretary Caspar Weinberger and Navy Secretary John F. Lehman Jr.[38]

Bennett was succeeded as National President at that year's National Convention by Jack H. Morse. And while the new President sought out the highest military officers and officials in government to determine what course the League should take in the next two years, he remained particularly concerned about the plight of the U.S.-flag Merchant Marine. While agreeing with his predecessor's upbeat assessment of the Navy and Marine Corps, the new National President, in one of his first "President's Messages," noted that of the nation's four sea services, only one, the Merchant Marine, "is in shoal waters and in danger of sinking." Noting that the 1967 merchant fleet of 1,000 or more gross tons, which numbered 1,113 ships, had declined 20 years later to only 460 ships, of which 100 were currently inactive, Morse pledged "to go the extra mile, and yet another one if needed, and to do everything possible to muster the support of the Navy League of the United States in a campaign to save the Merchant Marine."[39]

Morse's focus was evident, as almost every issue of *Sea Power* during his term in office had a detailed discussion of the plight of the Merchant Marine, and the risk entailed in letting the "fourth arm of national defense" wither. The League's concern, along with many others, led to the creation of the Commission on Merchant Marine and Defense, chaired by Alabama Senator Jeremiah Denton. But L. Edgar Prina, a veteran of reporting on many such efforts in the past, noted in December 1987 that "every President since World War II has asserted his support of a strong U.S. Merchant Marine, but for the most part such statements have been little more than rhetoric."[40]

Realizing that Prina was right, Morse's opening "President's Message" of 1988 still indicated his unwillingness to give up the fight:

> The fact that we now have nearly lost our merchant fleet, not through enemy action but as a result of our own lethargy, may rank as one of the greatest economic and military blunders our country has been guilty of since World War II.[41]

But the plight of the Merchant Marine was overshadowed a month later when Secretary of the Navy James H. Webb Jr. resigned on February 22, 1988. A highly decorated Marine officer with extensive combat experience in Vietnam, and also a successful writer, he had not adjusted well to the political give-and-take in the Washington trenches, an environment his predecessor relished and excelled in. With concerns over the mounting federal budget deficit and what one defense commentator termed "the post-Lehman attitude that the Navy got what it wanted and now it's our turn"[42] leading to naval force reductions, Webb resigned.

The League had not even had a chance to publish an interview, previously conducted, with Secretary Webb before he left office. So when it ran in the April 1988 issue of *Sea Power*, the article lead with the title "... Interview with [Then] Secretary of the Navy James H. Webb Jr." The same issue contained an editorial from National President Morse, lamenting Webb's resignation, and noting that it "should not be taken lightly, particularly in view of the proven difficulties at this time in persuading men and women of high caliber to accept appointments to government service."[43]

National President Calvin H. Cobb Jr. with Marine Corps Commandant General Alfred M. Gray Jr. USMC.

Jack Morse was succeeded as National President in 1989 by Calvin H. Cobb Jr., who had been the League's National Judge Advocate for the previous 14 years. He was a Washington, D.C., lawyer who had served as a combat information center officer on a cruiser in the Pacific for the last year of World War II. That year the change in League leadership occurred in Cobb's hometown, as 611 members attended the National Convention in the nation's capital. Opening ceremonies were conducted on the west steps of the Capitol, with John Warner, now a United States Senator from Virginia, and Representative Charles Bennett, providing welcoming remarks.

Senator Warner was particularly gracious in public greetings to his boyhood friend, Calvin Cobb, the incoming National President. This presaged a continuing warm relationship between the League and both the executive and legislative branches of government.

Then Navy Leaguers were escorted into the House Chamber, to be personally greeted by Congressman Jim Wright, the Speaker of the House. After everyone was seated, the Speaker gave a presentation on the history of the House of Representatives and its procedures. Leaguers subsequently attended a House committee session with members and staffers to address legislative matters and procedures, then spread throughout Capitol Hill offices to meet with their respective representatives and senators. Each member carried with him or her, a red, white, and blue tote bag that contained pertinent League material for distribution to congressional members, including the League's position papers on matters considered critical to the sea services. A dinner at the Capitol Hill Hyatt Regency was held later, with numerous congressmen, senators and professional staff attending; Representative (later Senator) John McCain was the banquet speaker. A subsequent briefing by Admiral Isaac C. Kidd, commander in chief of the Atlantic Fleet, was attended by over 200 congressional staff members as well as by Navy Leaguers attending the National Convention.

The autumn of 1989 afforded the Navy League — specifically the Baltimore,

Maryland, Council — an opportunity to demonstrate again its support of the sea services. On October 22, Hurricane Hugo devastated Charleston, South Carolina, with heavy rain and winds over 120 miles per hour. Declaring the downtown area "dead," Charleston's mayor pleaded for help. A few days later, the USS *William V. Pratt*, an Oliver Hazard Perry-class frigate, arrived in Baltimore, while enroute to its homeport of Charleston, to render assistance. Baltimore businessman and Baltimore Council President Bruce Copeland contacted the ship's commanding officer and asked what the Navy League could do to help. He replied, "Load my ship with roofing and building materials so that we can go home to Charleston with what they need to rebuild their lives."[44]

Copeland contacted another Navy Leaguer, Alan Walden, whose job as a local news anchor and commentator on WBAL radio enabled him to voice an on-air appeal for assistance. Within hours a steady stream of family vehicles, semi-trailers, and flatbeds began showing up at the berth where *William V. Pratt* (DDG-44) was tied up, offloading their contents onto the pier for further transfer to the Navy frigate. After the ship was filled to capacity with tons of building and roofing materials and other donated supplies, Baltimore's mayor added a gift of $10,000 from the city of Baltimore. The following morning, secured for sea, with her decks and helicopter hangar overloaded with building and restoration materials, *William V. Pratt* sailed for Charleston, arriving safely two days later with materials needed to begin rebuilding one of America's oldest and historically important cities. Additionally donated material was forwarded by truck.

President Cobb had as his personal philosophy for League leadership the maximum dissemination of maritime information to the public. The League had as a primary mission, as he would write in the April 1991 magazine of the U.S. Naval Academy Alumni Association, quoting one of the League's 1902 founders, "to enlighten the people on naval matters."[45] Consistent with this theme, Cobb established a national essay-writing contest for high school students writing on matters of maritime interest, with scholarships awarded for the best entrants.

Throughout his presidency, Cobb continued hammering home, mostly through his "President's Messages" in each issue of *Sea Power*, the fact that despite the collapse of the Soviet Union and reduction of tensions in Europe, the world was still a dangerous place. The need for retaining sufficient sea service force structure and sea-based combat capabilities, and in particular a viable Merchant Marine, had not diminished with the collapse of the Soviet empire.[46]

The verities of which he spoke became clearly evident in the summer of 1990, as reality once again intruded, and seemingly dissipated the oft-discussed "peace dividend," which many had assumed as a "given" following the end of the Cold War. In the early months of 1990, Iraq's despotic President, Saddam Hussein, had initiated an anti-Western propaganda campaign and called for the withdrawal of the

Navy's Middle East Force from the Arabian Gulf. By mid-summer, brandishing his considerable military capability to intimidate neighboring Arab nations, specifically Kuwait and the United Arab Emirates, he had massed 30,000 Iraqi troops along the Kuwaiti border. By August 1, the number had swelled to about 100,000, and early

Members of a U.S. Coast Guard Law Enforcment Detachment boarding party leave the guided-missile destroyer USS *William V. Pratt* (DDG-44) to inspect vessels and assist the Maritime Interdiction Force enforce sanctions against Iraq during Operation Desert Storm.

on the morning of August 2, 1990, Iraqi troops swarmed across the border and by the end of the day had overrun most of the small country.

With the exception of limited facilities in nearby Bahrain, the United States did not have a single military base in the region. Moves by Iraqi ground forces to seize ports in northern Saudi Arabia and deny the United States and its allies access, were forestalled by the prompt arrival of two aircraft carriers, USS *Independence* (CV-62) and USS *Dwight D. Eisenhower* (CVN-69). The ships, and their accompanying battle groups, were on station in the North Arabian and Red Seas respectively, and, along with a handful of Air Force tankers and control aircraft, provided initial cover for the airlift that brought Marines of the 7th Expeditionary Brigade and 1st Marine Expeditionary Force from California and Hawaii to Saudi Arabian ports on August 14. A day later the Marines "married up" with their mechanized equipment, ammunition, and other supplies carried from Guam and the Indian Ocean island of Diego Garcia by vessels of Maritime Prepositioning Ships Squadrons 2 and 3.

In his message to the League in October 1990, "On the Way, Sir!", Cobb delineated five lessons from the rapid naval and military response to Iraq's invasion of Kuwait, lessons that would serve as touchstones for maintaining and deploying sea-based combat capabilities throughout the remainder of the 20th century:[47]

* The world is a dangerous place and the United States would be unwise to reduce its military force structure too much, too soon.
* The only U.S. forces able to respond immediately to oversea crises threatening America's national interests are the nation's forward-deployed Navy and Marine Corps task forces.
* National security cannot be bought 'on the cheap.' ... Those still agitating for massive cutbacks in the defense budget are out of touch with reality as well as forgetful of history.
* To protect its global interests the United States must continue for the foreseeable future to rely on forward-deployed forces and needs overseas bases to support those forces.
* The most important component of U.S. military strength is manpower, the young men and women in uniform on the front lines today.

By early 1991, *Operation Desert Shield* had positioned American and coalition forces in Saudi Arabia and surrounding nations. The Navy had moved 124 — six aircraft carrier battle groups, two battleships, and a 31-ship amphibious force — to positions in the eastern Mediterranean, Red Sea, Arabian Gulf, and North Arabian Sea. More than 75,000 naval personnel were at sea, 73,000 Marines deployed ashore, and another 18,000 embarked aboard amphibious ships. It was the largest buildup of naval forces since World War II.[48]

League National President Cobb, notwithstanding the imminence of hostilities, decided to honor in mid-January his long-standing commitment to deliver the Navy League of the United States message in speaking engagements at the Royal Australian Navy Staff College in Sydney, Australia, and in five other cities, as a guest of the Australian Navy. He particularly wanted to recognize Australia as the only country in the world that had stood with the United States as an ally in its major combat commitments in the 20th century. Although somewhat embarrassed at being touted "down under" as an "expert on maritime affairs in the United States," Cobb felt an important function of the National President was to "develop an image of the Navy League of the United States with foreign countries."[49]

And another such commitment was coming, for it was clear to Cobb that America and its coalition allies, on land, sea and air, were shortly to be in combat operations for the first time in nearly two decades.

U.S. Marine Corps photo by Sgt. Brad Mitzelfolt

A U.S. Marine sights a target with his M-249 squad automatic weapon during Operation Desert Storm.

A plane director guides a S-3 Viking aircraft onto a catapult on the flight deck of USS *Independence* (CV-62) during *Operation Desert Shield.*

Chapter X
Beyond The Berlin Wall 1991-2000

Early on the morning of January 17, 1991, *Operation Desert Storm* commenced. In the next 100 hours, 42 combat divisions of Saddam Hussein's vaunted army would be destroyed and American troops would be on the banks of the Euphrates River. At the actual commencement of hostilities six aircraft carriers, including four operating in the Arabian Gulf, were launching aircraft against Iraqi targets.

For the United States, the military effort — which, including the air campaign preceding conventional ground operations, lasted little more than six weeks — was not nearly as conflicting and traumatic as the domestic political struggle on the defense budget that had preceded the war, and was subsequently joined again, after final victory in Southwest Asia. Even within the construct of a flurry of "*Desert Storm* Lessons Learned" white papers, monographs, seminars, and Washington think-tank conferences, the salient factor remained, as League National President Cobb asserted in the March 1991 issue of *Sea Power*, that "if the United States is to continue to wear the mantle of leadership, as the President has said, it will have to maintain a naval/military force structure equal to the job."[1]

Plowing ground previously furrowed by his predecessors after World War I, World War II, and Korea, Cobb reviewed the pending defense budget requests with a gimlet eye. In words and phrasing that could easily have been issued by Frank Hecht inveighing against the Truman Administration in the late 1940s, Cobb reviewed the 1985-1995 budget authorizations, current requests and future projections (resulting in a cumulative real decline of 34 percent) and minced few words in expressing his concern:

> Cutbacks of that magnitude in today's circumstances seem unwise, unwarranted, and inconsistent with the demanding responsibilities facing our nation's armed forces for the foreseeable future ... These cutbacks reflect unwillingness on the part of government today, unlike the early 1980s, to provide our armed forces with all the resources necessary for them to discharge the global responsibilities assigned to them. ... The United States does wear the mantle of global leadership — and does bear too heavy a share of the collective defense burden. But it cannot be otherwise for the foreseeable future. We simply cannot afford to be a bystander.[2]

The March 1991 Sea-Air-Space Exposition afforded the Navy League the opportunity to host the victors of Southwest Asia, both the men and women of America's armed forces and the people of the defense industry that had given them the tools needed to do the job. National President Cobb was quick to point out that the victory in Kuwait and Iraq "was the real pay-off of the investment the American public had made in national defense in the 1980s."[3]

But League awareness of recurring talk of significant defense budget reductions also resulted in one of six scheduled professional development seminars to be entitled, "Navy Budget Realities — 1991 and Beyond." League Executive Director Dudley Carlson, reporting on the just-concluded symposium in the May 1991 issue of *Sea Power*, noted with concern: "This destructive downward spiral could easily bode ill for America's ability to respond as quickly and as successfully as it recently did when faced with the next threat to democracy and to its own vital national interests."[4]

The previous month, *Sea Power* printed the change-of-command speech of new Chief of Naval Operations Admiral Frank B. Kelso II as he succeeded Admiral Carlisle A.H. Trost. Kelso sought to allay the concerns expressed by Cobb, Carlson, and many others regarding pending budget cuts and force structure reductions, noting that "the world has changed dramatically, and changed dramatically again in the past year. Our defense strategies will be shaped by the need to address these changes."[5]

Positing that, with the demise of the Soviet Union, "we can expect a significant period of forewarning before a true global threat emerges" the new Chief of Naval Operations asserted that the Navy of the future "will need a force of about 450 active and reserve ships to meet national strategy goals."[6] Aware of concerns voiced both by Navy League membership and by other defense and preparedness groups, Kelso proposed a bold departure from Cold War deployment patterns, accelerated introduction of advanced technologies into the fleet, and furtherance of coalition efforts among the world navies, a hallmark of the *Desert Storm* maritime campaign. Noting that "many people are skeptical that we can maintain our national security with this size Navy," he continued, "I believe with the right mix of assets, continued support of vital personnel programs, improved efficiency, and sufficient research and development, we will maintain maritime superiority."[7]

U.S. Navy photo by PH1 Flynn

Marines wait with their gear on a ramp leading to the well deck of the amphibious assault ship USS *Nassau* (LHA-4) during *Operation Desert Storm.*

National President Cobb was not so easily swayed. In his May 1991 "President's Message" to the League, he noted that *Operation Desert Storm* "marked the 53rd time since 1980 that the Navy and Marine Corps had been ordered into an area of potential conflict ... [and] not one of those crisis operations involved a Soviet-U.S. confrontation."[8] Cobb viewed with considerable skepticism the pending changes in naval force structure, asserting that the "reduction in numbers will seriously affect the Navy's future flexibility and ability to carry out all of its missions."[9]

League concerns, as expressed at its May 1991 National Convention in Anaheim, California, were not quite as strident. The *Navy League's 1991-92 Resolutions* accepted Kelso's views in broad terms. Employing language borrowed from President George H.W. Bush's view of global events beyond both the Cold War and *Desert Storm*, the League encouraged national leaders to "allocate resources to the sea services commensurate with the additional burdens to be imposed upon them in preserving the 'new world order.'"[10] But, reflecting outgoing National President Cobb's concerns, the League did not endorse the 450 ship number as the "correct" size for the fleet and decried, with the pending retirement of the last of the Navy's battleships recommissioned during the Reagan-Lehman era, "a total lack of the powerful naval gunfire support needed by the Marines ashore."[11]

During his tenure, 1991-93, National President William C. Kelley Jr. was faced with a number of challenges including the continuing contentious issue of the "peace dividend" and the loss of America's forward base in the Republic of the Philippines. He also was confronted with the collapse of the Soviet Union and the subsequent freedom and independence of the nations of Eastern Europe.

Kelley kept members informed of world developments and adopted "America — A Maritime Nation" as a theme for the League in a time of dynamic change. In his "President's Messages" in each issue of *Sea Power*, he frequently emphasized that the primary mission of the Navy League was one of educating the American public about the continued need for a strong national defense program, with particular emphasis on forward-deployed seapower. From Kelley's perspective as

National President, the League's community education program had to be given top priority. Addressing the Executive Committee meeting in August 1991, Kelley asserted that the League's education message was imperative: "The public must be made aware that strong U.S. sea services are needed to protect American political, military, and economic interests around the world."[12]

In meeting that educational mission, the League issued its White Paper on *Operations Desert Shield* and *Desert Storm* in the summer of 1991. Authored by Vincent C. Thomas, editor for many years of *The Almanac of Seapower* series, it examined in detail the roles and missions of the Navy, Marine Corps, Coast Guard, and U.S.-flag Merchant Marine during both *Operations Desert Shield* and *Desert Storm*. Sections of it were read into the *Congressional Record* by Representative Charles Bennett, chairman of the House Armed Services Committee's Seapower and Strategic and Critical Materials Subcommittee, who praised the Navy League in his introduction:

> The Navy League has no superior as our nation's staunchest supporter of the maritime services — the U.S. Navy, Marine Corps, Coast Guard, and Merchant Marine ... Through wartime and peacetime, through times when the sea services had adequate funding and those with funding shortfalls, the members of the Navy League have told the maritime story.
>
> The Navy League is an active, forward-thinking organization dedicated to ensure the quality of our sea services is maintained and recognized. As educators, first and foremost, Navy Leaguers inform the public about our nation's dependence on maritime superiority ... I salute the Navy League's efforts, and their preparation of this report.[13]

USS *Iowa* (BB-61)

The League's White Paper lauded the Navy, not only for the newest weapons in its arsenal — like Tomahawk land attack missiles — but also for the "weapons and techniques of yesteryear, foremost among them being the 16-inch guns of the Navy's last two battleships, which fired more than two million pounds of ordnance."[14]

The League noted that "paramount in the ultimate success of *Desert Storm* were a Navy organization tried and tested over the past decade ... enhanced by more than 40 years of operational experience in the Middle East, and the absolutely magnificent performances by tens of thousands of sea service men and women, regular and reserve, afloat and ashore." The Paper also cautioned that, of the 124 fleet combatants and support ships participating in *Operations Desert Shield* and *Desert Storm*, no fewer than 39, including six cruisers and most of the ships in the amphibious force, were 20 years of age and older.[15]

The issue of "support ships" was explored in exhausting detail in the June 1991 issue of *Sea Power*. An article authored by retired Navy Captain Robert W. Kesteloot pointed out that the decline in the "Fourth Arm of Defense," the U.S.-flag Merchant Marine, was so great that, "if reliance had been placed solely on it," the required combat and combat support equipment would not yet be — six months after the conclusion of hostilities — in Saudi Arabia! [16]

Kesteloot highlighted the issue of America's moribund Merchant Marine, and the need to maintain a sufficiently sized force to meet future naval and sealift requirements. The status of the Merchant Marine, too often viewed as an "orphan" sea service, had been a concern of the Navy League's since the organization's founding.

At the end of World War I, the December 1918 issue of *Sea Power* had argued that the "most important current work" for the League would "unquestionably" be support of "the American Merchant Marine."[17] The League strongly supported the 1920 Jones Act which required maritime commerce within the United States be limited to U.S.-flag vessels that were built in American shipyards, owned and operated by U.S. citizens, and manned by an American crew. But government support and public concern for the fate of the merchant fleet dissipated over high labor costs and stringent government-mandated safety standards in the 1920s; these factors, plus subsidies provided by their own governments to foreign-flag merchant ships, made it almost always cheaper to charter and operate those ships to carry U.S. cargoes in international trade. The U.S.-flag Merchant Marine withered and almost died in the throes of the Great Depression.

As tensions built in the 1930s, and the likelihood of another war became increasingly more probable, the Navy League renewed its call for the rebuilding of the U.S.-flag Merchant Marine. Its advocacy of the Copeland Bill in the mid-1930s earned the personal thanks of the bill's sponsor, New York Senator Royal Copeland, both in a personal letter to League National President Hubbard and acknowledgement in a nationally broadcast radio address. Navy Day celebrations during the 1930s frequently stressed the importance to the nation of a strong Merchant Marine.

U.S. Navy photo by PH2 Savage

Dock workers steady a pallet of supplies as it is hoisted aboard the Military Sealift Command combat stores ship USNS *Sirius* (T-AFS-8).

FDR certainly did not need the League's help to further his understanding of the numerous elements comprising seapower. But, as was true throughout his presidency, Roosevelt and the Navy League were largely in agreement on the salient national issues affecting the sea services.

His Administration secured passage of the Copeland Bill, as the Merchant Marine Act of 1936. The League later also supported the Merchant Ship Sales Act of 1946, which created the National Defense Ready Reserve Fleet and Ready Reserve Force, and the Cargo Preference Act of 1954. Efforts to repeal or modify the 1920 Jones Act in the ensuing four decades had been turned back on Capitol Hill, with the Navy League often arguing the strategic importance of the Merchant Marine.[18] Notwithstanding such support, the League had failed, as had Merchant Marine interests in general, to convince the American public at large about the need for a strong, viable, and numerically large U.S.-flag merchant fleet.

Now, with the end of the Cold War, the decline in overseas base infrastructure, and the increasingly "expeditionary" nature of U.S. armed forces, the need for a significant sealift capability, available on short notice, to sail in harm's way had been verified by *Operations Desert Shield* and *Desert Storm*. Author Kesteloot noted that 88 percent of the total tonnage required by U.S. forces in the combat theater had been delivered to Southwest Asia by early February 2001, and the total percentage continued to rise to 95 percent during the sustainment phase of combat operations. Yet during that month, of 168 dry cargo ships in use, 74 were foreign-flag ships and only 25 were privately-owned U.S.-flag ships.[19] Vessels of the U.S. Military Sealift Command comprised the balance, including Maritime Preposi-

The value of underway and vertical replenishment cannot be overstated.

tioning Ships dating from the Carter/Reagan Administrations, Fast Sealift Ships and ships of the Ready Reserve Force and Afloat Prepositioning Force. These ships were largely crewed by more than 3,000 mariners, recruited from the relief crews that regularly sailed in U.S. commercial ships, from the ranks of retired mariners, and from a large population of unemployed and under-employed seafarers in the depressed U.S. maritime industry.

Kesteloot posed a number of scenarios, from a sea-going Iraqi combat capability to lack of international support to oust Hussein from occupied Kuwait, that would have severely reduced foreign-flag ship availability. Also, a severely degraded material condition of U.S. government-owned ships, as would have resulted from earlier attempts (opposed by both the Navy League and the U.S. Transportation Command) to reduce or eliminate funding for the Maritime Prepositioning Ships and Afloat Prepositioning Force, would have impeded the coalition ground campaign. Noting that Chief of Naval Operations Admiral Frank Kelso had directed that feasibility studies be initiated for ship designs for a new class of sealift ship, Kesteloot suggested consideration of a less costly alternative — namely the rebuilding of a strong U.S.-flag Merchant Marine that would be available for military use as well as help maintain the U.S. maritime industrial base.

While Kesteloot's calls for "an all-encompassing national sealift policy" would not be specifically endorsed by the Navy League, the organization's concern with the material condition and numbers of ships in the Merchant Marine would result in President William J. Clinton signing into law, in October 1996, the Maritime Security Act. This law authorized the establishment of a maritime security fleet, owned and operated by U.S. citizens, and manned by American seafarers that would meet the sealift needs of the nation's armed services and also provide a competitive seaborne presence in America's international trade. While not fully restoring the U.S.-flag Merchant Marine to robust health, the Maritime Security Act did represent a rare victory for the Navy League, and for others concerned about the viability of, and long-term prospects for, the "Fourth Arm of Defense."

Sufficient sealift ships, albeit with a large percentage under foreign flag, did enable *Operation Desert Storm*, a singular triumph for the United States at the beginning of the 1990s. Another one would become apparent a few months after victory in the deserts of Southwest Asia. President George H.W. Bush was still in office when the United States again emerged a winner, this time from a conflict begun decades earlier in the ruins of postwar Europe. In his memoirs, the American President noted the end of the 40-year war in simple, matter-of-fact prose:

> Mikhail Gorbachev contacted me at Camp David on Christmas morning of 1991. He wished Barbara and me a Merry Christmas, and then he went on to sum up what had happened in his country: the Soviet Union had ceased to exist. He had just been on national

> television to confirm the fact, and he had transferred control of Soviet nuclear weapons to the President of Russia. 'You can have a very quiet Christmas evening,' he said. And so it was over. It was a very quiet and civilized ending to a tumultuous time in our history.[20]

Quiet perhaps, yet for those who expected a huge peace dividend, and a return to the Washington Treaty milieu of the early 1920s, the decade of the 1990s would be a profound disappointment. Despite academic theories, politicians' speeches praising America's victory in the Cold War, and the prospect of no global peer competitor in the offing for two or more decades, the U.S. Navy had scarcely returned from *Desert Storm* when it became very well acquainted with stability operations in the Balkans, East Timor, and Haiti, as well as a continual presence in the Arabian Gulf to demonstrate continued U.S. resolve. The sea services enforced embargoes, sanctions, and quarantines, and conducted anti-piracy and drug interdiction operations from Southeast Asia's Lombok and Sunda Straits to the Caribbean Sea.

Regardless of such sea service commitments, the clamor for a reduction in defense spending was nearly continuous when the decade of the 1990s commenced. As Secretary of Defense Richard B. Cheney pointed out in a speech in August 1991, the Defense Department had already "fundamentally transformed" its national security strategy "to reflect the kinds of changes that we have been witness to now over these past two years."[21] Cheney pointedly observed:

> Spending reductions already imposed on the Defense Department by Congress over the past several years, combined with the additional self-imposed reductions that are incorporated in the current budget projections, mean that by the middle of the decade — 1995 or 1996 — we will have cut U.S. defense spending to the lowest percentage of federal spending ... in more than 50 years, since before Pearl Harbor.[22]

U.S. Navy photo by PH1 Allen

Two marines wearing M-17A1 field protective masks man a fighting position on the perimeter of their camp during *Operation Desert Shield*.

In an extensive, wide-ranging interview in the October 1991 issue of *Sea Power*, Chief of Naval Operations Admiral Frank Kelso defended many of the budget and force structure reductions the Navy was undergoing, stating that a base force "of about 450 ships" was right, but that it was not a "magic number." Rather than focus on a finite number, Kelso, in an argument that would become increasingly common throughout the post-Cold War period among all of America's service chiefs, asserted instead the greater need for a balanced force possessing the full spectrum of combat capabilities needed to meet America's maritime interests around the world:

> We have to remember we have never been very able in the West to define what the next need for military force is going to be ... Balance in our naval forces is critical because we don't know what we might need exactly the next time around, and whether circumstances may dictate a need we can't see right now. We may shift our resources more in one direction than in another temporarily as we embark on major procurement programs, but we had better be careful before we get completely out of one area and limit our ability to respond.[23]

But as the number of fleet ships began to drop precipitously, seemingly in free-fall, the League's concerns were not assuaged, and articles and "President's Messages" in *Sea Power* expressed increasing concern over having, at a future date, to once again learn the lessons of 1941 and 1950. Aptly reflecting League sentiment, in a 1992 speech before the Richmond, Virginia, Council, Gilven Slonim, President of the Oceanic Educational Foundation, hardly minced words in decrying the fact that the Navy built by John Lehman under Ronald Reagan's leadership was being dangerously "shrunk" and that the reality of *Operation Desert Storm* was that "despite the spectacular victory our combined arms achieved, the reality remains; we reacted to Saddam Hussein's aggression six months after the fact."[24]

Slonim reminded the League of Theodore Roosevelt's precept that the United States should always "carry a big stick" and asked if Hussein's invasion of Kuwait would have occurred if "there had been a carrier striking force poised in the Persian Gulf to give teeth" to the U.S. Ambassador's words of caution to the Iraqi dictator.[25] He closed with an admonition for the League to recall that a strong Navy requires a fleet operating routinely beyond America's own shores:

> The premium remains fixed squarely on sustained mobility and global readiness ... The reality remains deterrence derived from poised power alone–convincingly conveying readiness, determination and a will of steel–with ready reinforcement to prevail–that's

> the hallmark of the world leadership the Nation must aspire to maintain in the 21st century.[26]

But such sentiments and beliefs fell on an American public that saw in America's twin victories in the Desert and the Cold War an opportunity to scale back defense expenditures, force structure, and readiness levels. Anxious to earn the so-called "peace dividend," many armchair strategists, or as John Lehman oftentimes referred to them, "parlor-room Pershings," entertained thoughts of drawing down Marine Corps end-strength to eventually merge the sea service into the Army to save money on personnel and equipment.

The Navy League, aware of such musings, was quick to take up the Marine Corps' cause in a seven-page White Paper authored by Vincent Thomas Jr. that ran in the September 1992 *Sea Power* and was widely distributed on Capitol Hill. Posing a question at the beginning, "What kind of Marine Corps should be created to permit it to carry out its clearly defined mission and to conform to the requirements of the National Military Strategy?"[27] Thomas then explained in considerable detail in the following six pages the uniqueness of the Marines as the nation's principal expeditionary force in readiness, and the basic difference between its role in the nation's military strategy, and that of the United States Army. Concluded Thomas, and thus the Navy League: "It is our firm belief that this is no time to be penny wise and pound foolish with regard to the capability of that arm of our armed forces that inevitably will be the first ordered into action in time of conflict."[28]

The League, joined in chorus by supporters of the Marine Corps, were eventually successful in turning back efforts to meld the sea service into the Army. But by the time Evan S. Baker became National President in 1993, even relatively modern naval vessels were being scrapped or sold off at an alarming rate. As had happened after both World Wars and Vietnam, the Navy was being "right sized," and the League, as in the issue of saving the Marine Corps, again joined in the fight to retain an adequate degree of maritime power to keep the nation secure in uncertain times.

Baker was a seasoned veteran, in and out of uniform, in the realities of Washington politics and the Navy League. As a naval officer he had served on both destroyers and submarines, then for Admiral Arleigh Burke as part of both his Navy War Plans and Strategic Plans Divisions in the Pentagon, focused exclusively on interfacing with the Joint Staff. In both billets, he had worked with more senior officers who had been with (then) Captain Burke during the Revolt of the Admirals. Following release from active duty at his own request, he worked in private industry for a decade, and also joined the Navy League. He had been chairman of the Sea-Air-Space Exposition in both 1971 and 1973, the latter held in conjunction with the National Convention. He had also been District of Columbia Council President from 1974-1976.

"The Navy is rapidly, and seemingly inexorably, being reduced in size to a point where it may not be able to fulfill its historical role."

In the late 1970s, when Baker was chairman of the Strategic Planning Committee, concerned "that stagnation at the national level in League leadership had become a problem," his committee evolved a reorganization plan that sought to "improve the ready flow of leaders and ideas back-and-forth" and serve as a catalyst to facilitate the turnover of League leadership.[29] Though the Strategic Planning Committee's national strategic plan was only tepidly endorsed initially, it did serve as the impetus for organizational reforms that restructured senior leadership and brought the League forward into the remaining years of the 20th century.

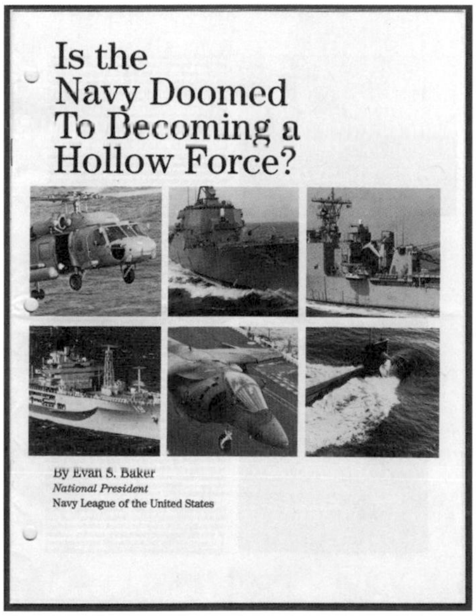
Is the
Navy Doomed
To Becoming a
Hollow Force?
By Evan S. Baker
National President
Navy League of the United States

Baker was now the League's National President, one of the youngest to ever hold the position. His first editorial piece in *Sea Power* criticized the Clinton Administration's Secretary of Defense, Les Aspin, a former League sparring mate from a decade earlier, but that was only the opening skirmish in what was to become a concerted assault on the nation's Defense Department leadership.

Concerned about the realities of the oft-publicized and now expected "peace dividend" among Clinton Administration political appointees in and out of the Department of Defense, Baker, in collaboration with Vincent Thomas, authored a White Paper in the spring of 1994 entitled "Is the Navy Doomed to Becoming a Hollow Force?" He had spent several preceding months traveling to, and talking with, the commanders in chief of the worldwide unified commands and fleet and force commanders to "discuss with complete candor what they are doing now to meet operational and budgetary shortcomings and what they fear in the months ahead."[30] In language as incisive and critical as any League document of the inter-war years or during the trying times of service unification and the "Revolt of the Admirals," Baker unequivocally asserted that the Navy "is rapidly, and seemingly inexorably, being reduced in size to a point where it may not be able to fulfill its historical role."[31]

Citing with concern a fleet strength reduced to 387 ships, Baker recounted the lessons of cutting the Navy budget and strength after both World Wars and maintained that "with the Cold War behind us, we once more are reducing our military strength too rapidly, and thereby inviting a potential theater/world aggressor to prepare for yet another bold thrust against the free world."[32] Of equal concern, Baker cited a perception among men and women in uniform that their benefits were at risk, resulting in fewer numbers willing to either join or stay the course of a career in the sea services. He also was skeptical of the nascent Base Realignment and Closure Commission process (which in 1993 shuttered 75 naval installations and realigned 17 more) in its stated promise to generate significant long-term savings, but only incurred with substantial up-front costs that had to be paid by reducing other accounts. Baker was hardly politic in his closing paragraph: "At this juncture we must ask: Do the words 'national security' have any real meaning to either the President or Congress?"[33]

A year later, in a hardly less sanguine follow-up entitled "A year ago we asked: Is the Navy Doomed To Becoming a Hollow Force? Today, our assessment is: Yes, unless ..." Baker authored (again in collaboration with *Almanac of Seapower* Editor Vince Thomas) another White Paper. Referencing the assertions of the earlier effort, Baker did not back away from the frank, strong wording previously employed. Restating his concerns regarding the Navy becoming a hollow force, given the realities of the budget, the National President was equally blunt in his new assessment: "Sadly, in the year since that forecast was made, those trends not only have continued, but will do so for at least another year."[34]

This follow-up White Paper, half the length of its predecessor, focused particularly on the force structure and shipbuilding accounts, noting that, while three Base Realignment and Closure Commission findings had reduced infrastructure by "about 25 percent," the "size of the fleet had been reduced 35 percent." Presciently, Baker predicted, "the Navy could see a fleet below 300 ships"[35] and ended on a hardly less optimistic note: "Clearly, national security is being jeopardized by present budget pressures, and if they are permitted to continue there is no doubt it will be endangered."[36]

Both White Papers and an accompanying "Hollow Force" video were given wide distribution to members of Congress, Department of Defense leaders, League members, and the media.

Baker's "President's Message" in the League's *1994 Annual Report* sounded many of the same concerns regarding issues of national security and the sea services. But, he also noted the strengthening of League ties with members of Congress and their staffs, giving full credit to the Office of Legislative Education. Baker also cited increased emphasis on the League's growing scholarship program (including the Naval Sea Cadet Corps Scholarship program) and the "essential interface" the League was providing, through the Sea-Air-Space Exposition and other venues, between the private sector and the sea services. And, not unlike virtually every

League National President before him, Baker stated that, "once again, our principal internal challenge is to increase our membership."[37]

Hugh Mayberry became National President in 1995, and the tumultuous times so ably decried by his predecessor in office continued with cost cutting and wholesale reductions in military and Coast Guard spending. Mayberry established "Pride, Service, Patriotism" as the new League slogan and also instituted *The Navy Leaguer*, a quarterly publication to be distributed to all members of the Navy League, providing timely information on activities of individual councils and focusing on local events and activities. Mayberry also subsequently introduced another method of formal communication, *The Watchkeeper*, issued from national headquarters, as a periodic message on how the League was achieving its goals.

U.S. Navy photo by C2 Hatzakos

Litter bearers carry a wounded Marine across the helicopter pad at a Fleet Hospital during *Operation Desert Storm*.

In the spring of 1996 Mayberry announced a new League "Highline" program designed to provide job-hunting and other assistance to sea service men and women transitioning from active duty to civilian life. Mayberry asserted that, particularly given ongoing force structure reductions and end-strength drawdowns in the Clinton Administration's second term that were expected to affect more than 1,000,000 active duty personnel and their families through 1998, the Highline program would "start immediately" and grow "just as fast as we can sign up council points of contact in every community in which we have a Navy League Council." Jack M. Kennedy, National Vice President for Navy and Marine Corps Affairs, added that the new program would provide Navy Leaguers a "unique opportunity to help sea service people, and their families, in the most meaningful way possible ... The opportunity to assist these fine, highly qualified men and women ... is a call to duty that we as Navy Leaguers must answer."[38]

Things were changing dramatically in the Navy during this time. The global order defined by the Cold War was gone. What remained were shards of communist empires, recurring ethnic conflicts in unfamiliar areas of the world and shadowy networks and international arms dealers. In this markedly changed environment the primary purpose of forward-deployed naval forces became, as it had been during the Korean and Vietnam Wars, the projection of American power from the sea to influence events ashore in the littoral regions of the world.

Nearly continual force strength reductions forced the Navy to begin to address several post-*Desert Storm* realities. One trend that had been a concern in the later years of the Cold War was exacerbated in the years after it was over. In 1988, 50 percent of America's combat force structure had been permanently stationed overseas. By 1996 this percentage had dropped to 30 percent. In contrast the number of ships forward deployed had remained relatively constant, while actual fleet force structure had dramatically decreased. In 1992, as the Navy drew back from *Desert Storm* commitments of a fleet of 526 ships, 126 ships were deployed at any time. By 1993, with a fleet reduced to 466 ships, 95 were deployed at any time.

By 1996, the downward spiral of force structure, which League National Presidents Cobb and Kelley had repeatedly inveighed against from the beginning of the decade, was beginning to exact its inevitable toll on the men and women of the fleet. With a total force declination to 356 ships, overseas force-level deployments increased to 103 ships, or 29 percent of the total fleet. Clearly, a shrinking American presence in geographically "fixed" locales worldwide (a concept that Admiral Frank Kelso had been opposed to in 1991, but one still largely extant five years later, reflecting bureaucratic inertia occasioned by four decades of Cold War deployed fleet patterns) was placing an increasing premium on naval forces with their inherent flexibility, sustainability, graduated-response capabilities, and, when required, combat striking abilities.

National President Jack Kennedy, left, with Secretary of the Navy John Dalton.

In recognition of this reality, Mayberry's successor as National President, Jack M. Kennedy, 1997-1999, continued a strong program of advocacy for the sea services, seeking to ensure that the nation and its leaders would never forget, even with the end of the Cold War, that the United States was a maritime nation. Kennedy endorsed an aggressive shipbuilding program to replace vessels being scrapped or relegated to inactive ship facilities, and repeatedly expressed concerns that the paucity of defense spending by the Clinton Administration was doing unforeseen damage to United States military capability. When repeated questions arose as to the reality of purported "increases" in monies being appropriated for defense,

Kennedy demanded an end to the "smoke and mirrors" and called for "defense leaders, uniformed and civilian alike, testifying before Congress this year to provide an accurate and honest assessment of our naval/military budget requirements."[39]

A less traditional focus for the National President, and unique in Navy history, was an initiative undertaken, in conjunction with the Navy and the National Geographic Society, to send more than 100,000 posters to every school in the nation announcing a first-ever "American Student Ship Naming Competition," to name an oceanographic survey ship then being built in Mississippi. With the League encouraging students to learn about the maritime sciences and oceanography, participants formed teams to decide on a proposed name, and developed complementary projects to support their nominee.

By December 1997 more than 1,600 proposals had been submitted to the Navy. Top entries were reviewed by a panel of nine judges, comprised of Navy and civilian historians, authors, teachers, and ship operators, and in June 1998 Secretary of the Navy John Dalton announced that a group of nine fifth-grade students from Oak Lawn Elementary School in Cranston, Rhode Island, had won the contest. They proposed naming the ship for the late Bruce C. Heezen, a geologist, oceanographer and marine investigator whose discovery of the Mid-Atlantic Ridge and pioneering work in plate tectonics had done much to further man's understanding of ocean floors.

Another unique initiative during the Kennedy presidency was meeting the League's traditional mission of education in a non-traditional manner. The impetus for what eventually became a professionally produced, award-winning videotape, presented to Secretary of the Navy Richard Danzig in March 2000, came from retired Rear Admiral Larry R. Marsh, chairman of the Navy heritage oversight group. In the May 2000 *Sea Power*, Marsh, who had served as deputy director of the Bureau of Naval Personnel when on active duty, noted that "most young men and women entering the Navy today have only a 'hazy knowledge' of naval history." He related that the need for some sort of educational tool became evident to Navy leadership when "several young sailors at the Great Lakes Naval Training Center were asked if they knew the significance of December 7th and Pearl Harbor and they answered, 'No sir!' without hesitation."[40]

With Corporate Secretary Jerry Rapkin playing a key role in convincing League leadership that a naval history video could help remedy the situation, as well as organizing numerous fundraising efforts, the organization enlisted the help of Life Member Robert Rositzke, President of Empire Video, Inc., to professionally script, film, and produce a videotape for distribution to training facilities and accession points throughout the Navy. Rositzke worked with the Navy History Center, including Director of Naval History Dr. William Dudley and Naval Historian Dr.

Edward Marolda, to produce a one-hour video chronicling more than 220 years of the Navy's history and heritage: "Our Navy Story: A Legacy of Honor, Courage, and Commitment."

"Our Navy Story" producer Bob Rositzke flanked by Navy Leaguers Don Sacarob, Director of Marketing, left, and Executive Director Charles Robinson.

The video was completed in January 2000 with oversight and approval of both the director of naval history and the Navy's Chief of Information. Following review, the Vice Chief of Naval Operations directed it be distributed to all ships and stations and made a part of the training curriculum at the Great Lakes Naval Training Center. Subsequently, Rositzke and Empire Video, Inc. were awarded a *Telly* and the *Worldfest Houston Award* in 2000 based on the content and production quality of the video.

Executing more traditional responsibilities, National President Kennedy worked hard to maintain the League's sound financial footing and introduced significantly improved automated and multimedia systems to national headquarters. The 1990s also saw a significant increase in both numbers of attendees and the importance of the Sea-Air-Space Exposition. By the end of the decade, the three-day count was upward of 10,000 attendees, many of whom also signed up for such special events as the "Secretary of the Navy Luncheon," the "Chief of Naval Operations Luncheon," and the "Sea-Air-Space Banquet." Several Secretaries of Defense, senior members of Congress, chairmen of the Joint Chiefs of Staff, Marine Corps and Coast Guard Commandants, and other key Washington personages served as featured speakers and special guests of honor at various Sea-Air-Space Exposition events and activities.

But even with increased interest and attendance at such events in the nation's capital, clearly evident by the end of the decade was the negative impact of funding cuts, enacted in the Bush and Clinton Administrations, on the readiness of the United States military. National President Kennedy was sufficiently concerned about the continuing downward trend to write a remarkably prescient editorial in the April 1999 issue of *Sea Power* entitled "The Day of Reckoning":

> There eventually will be a day of reckoning. It could be along the De-Militarized Zone in Korea, in Kosovo ... or an outbreak of terrorist attacks here at home–in downtown Chicago, or San Francisco, New York City again, or even in Washington, D.C.

> When it happens we will have little or no warning, and we will almost assuredly not be as ready as we should.[41]

Pennsylvania Congressman John P. Murtha with National President Jack Kennedy and the President's own Marine Corps Band at opening ceremonies of the 1999 Sea-Air-Space Exposition.

A month later, based on reports that the Navy was running critically low of Tomahawk land-attack missiles due to expenditures during *Operation Allied Force*, the North Atlantic Treaty Organization land, sea, and air campaign against the Serbian dictator Slobodan Milosevic, Kennedy again expressed concern over the Clinton Administration's approach to national defense, finding fault, evident in shortages of expensive "smart" weapons, with its "seemingly automatic assumption — in virtually every international crisis it has faced over the past six years — of a best case, lowest-cost outcome of any potential combat scenario."[42]

And even though retired Navy Rear Admiral John Fisher succeeded Jack Kennedy as League National President in the summer of 1999, the drumbeat of editorial concern continued. Three months after taking office, Fisher issued a "Call to Action," asserting that "no matter how euphemistically it is worded, current U.S. defense policy is deliberately, knowingly, consciously based on mortgaging the future to pay for shorter-term needs."[43]

Taking a longer, though certainly no less pessimistic, view of the decline of America's sea-based combat capability, the September 1999 *Sea Power* contained an analytical piece on possible military strategies for the new century that put into stark terms the situation the Navy found itself in at the end of the decade:

> Little more than 13 years ago, with the public release of the United States Maritime Strategy, then-Secretary of the Navy John F. Lehman Jr. effectively argued that a 600-ship Navy was necessary to meet a U.S. national security requirement for maritime superiority. Remarkably, the Navy today is on the threshold of falling below 300 ships — the smallest fleet since 1931.[44]

Four months later, in his introduction to the *Almanac of Seapower 2000*, Fisher voiced the League's concern that America's defense structure was the "leanest it has been in the post-World War II era." Noting the "steady decline in the size, and

USS *Cole* (DDG-67) returns to the United States on board the Norwegian heavy salvage ship MV *Blue Marlin*.

therefore, responsiveness, of the vital U.S. vital defense industrial base" and a Navy "cut almost in half" from the Reagan-era, Fisher charged "America's defense decision members" with "culpable negligence." Accurately foretelling a future no one could envision, he noted, "It is not foreordained that the so-called 'American century' that has now ended will be extended by another uninterrupted period of U.S. economic and military dominance."[45]

But however late, the end of the decade finally saw an upturn in funding for all the military services. The tide had started to turn back in late December 1998, when Navy League friend and acquaintance, Virginia Senator John Warner, upon becoming new Chairman of the Senate Armed Services Committee, had declared, "I think greater emphasis has to be placed on maritime mobility and strategy."[46]

Ten months later, with tales of warfighting shortfalls in the Balkans echoing in the corridors of power months after the fighting had ended, President Clinton signed legislation marking the first sustained increase in defense spending in more than a decade. And signaling a new mindset in Washington, Secretary of Defense William S. Cohen told *Sea Power* in early 2000 that "we have been living off the buildup from the early 1980s, and the 'peace dividend' is over. We must start investing in the future."[47]

What that future portended became tragically evident on October 12, 2000, when terrorists in a small craft attacked and inflicted significant damage on the USS *Cole* (DDG-67), an Arleigh Burke-class guided-missile destroyer, then in Aden, Yemen, refueling following a tour of operations in the Arabian Gulf. The attack, blowing a 40-foot by 40-foot hole in the side of the ship, killed 17 members of ship's company and injured 39 more. As Chief of Naval Operations Admiral Michael G. Mullen would remark on the fifth anniversary of the attack, the attack on *Cole* "marked the beginning of the war on terror for the U.S. Navy."[48]

Members of the Hampton Roads, Fort Lauderdale, and New York Councils made particularly generous donations to a fund established by the Navy-Marine Corps Relief Society, and the Navy, to help families of the victims of this terrorist attack. Navy League members from throughout the eastern United States participated in the memorial service at the Norfolk, Virginia, Naval Station honoring both those who had fallen and those who had survived.

On December 24, 2000, secure within the cavernous hold of the Norwegian heavy salvage ship MV *Blue Marlin*, USS *Cole* (DDG-67) returned to the Mississippi shipyard — where it had been built — for extensive repairs. League members of the Pascagoula-Moss Point, Mississippi, Council, many of them shipyard workers, stood in silent tribute, then got to work. Less than two years later, these same League members celebrated the guided-missile destroyer's return to active duty. But there was other urgent work still to perform. For once again the clarion call to duty had been sounded — after the most grievous attack on American soil since Pearl Harbor six decades earlier.

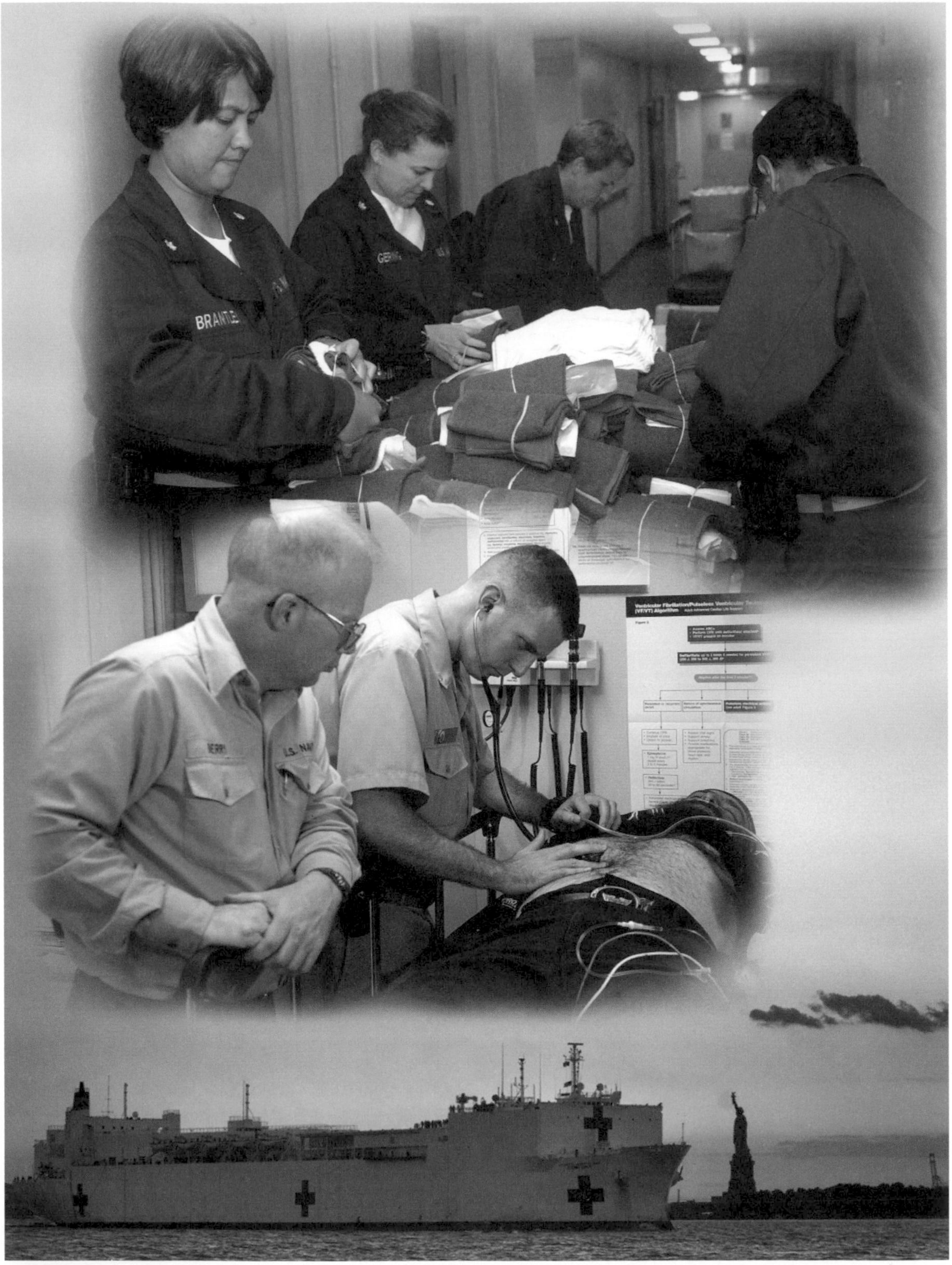

The Navy's hospital ship USNS *Comfort* (T-AH-20) arrived in New York Harbor shortly after the terrorist attack on the World Trade Center, providing vital life-saving support to New York firefighters and others.

Chapter XI
Challenge of a New Century
2001-2005

> Tuesday, September 11, 2001, dawned temperate and nearly cloudless in the eastern United States. Millions of men and women readied themselves for work. Some made their way to the Twin Towers, the signature structures of the World Trade Center Complex in New York City. ... For those heading to an airport, weather conditions could not have been better for a safe and pleasant journey.[1]

So begins *The 9/11 Commission Report*, a narrative of the event, causes, and recommendations stemming from a day that, along with December 7, 1941, will forever be etched into the collective psyche of the American public. By 10:29 a.m. that morning, the United States had "suffered the largest loss of life in its history — 2,973 — on its soil as a result of hostile attack. The New York City Fire Department suffered 343 fatalities — the largest loss of life of any emergency response agency in history. The [New York] Port Authority Police Department suffered 37 fatalities — the largest loss of life of any police force in history."[2] The nation, its Navy, and the Navy League were to be thrown into war against a "sophisticated, patient, disciplined, and lethal" enemy, whose "hostility toward us and our values is limitless."[3]

This was not the expected way ahead for the new century, and the dramatic change in the nation's course occasioned by the terrorist attacks of September 2001 are still affecting events and policy half a decade later. At the end of the 1980s, with the Berlin Wall in ruins, many had argued that the paramount issue in the post-Cold War era would be "endism" — the central tenet being that all bad things were coming to an end — hence, there would be much less need for any armed forces. In the ensuing decade, *Desert Storm*, Somalia, Bosnia, and Kosovo had put the lie to those optimistic assumptions, but few long-range planners considered that the first years of the 21st century would see "war" and "conflict" through a strikingly different lens than in the aftermath of the Cold War.

For planners and strategists, while the new century promised to be considerably different from the Cold War years that preceded it, the sea services would remain the foundation of "Pax Americana." No other forces were so well and singularly positioned to deal with a full range of global challenges, and no other services possessed their capacity to sustain combat operations with minimum personnel risks.

So Chief of Naval Operations Admiral Vern Clark laid out a largely conventional vision of the Navy's future in his address to the Navy League at the Sea-Air-Space Exposition on April 12, 2001. Asserting that for "now and the near term, there is no more powerful, no more capable platform, anywhere in the world, than America's large-deck aircraft carrier,"[4] the admiral affirmed the reality of the Navy's current maritime superiority, but cautioned that the public's assumption that this superiority would continue unchallenged into the future was not prudent.

Commenting on the value of a forward-deployed force to overcome the time-distance problem — "being there certainly is better than trying to get there" — he issued a note of caution, maintaining that the Navy "was getting to the point where business as usual and marginal changes aren't going to get the job done." He asserted that the Navy does not have "the resources required to continue into the 21st century with the strategy and the force structure that has been identified for us."[5] Clark warned the Navy League audience of the operational and strategic risk that would flow from having a smaller Navy dictated by fiscal constraints:

> The nation must understand that a smaller and/or less capable Navy will lead to greater risks in the form of less security for seaborne trade, less flexibility in response, limited response time due to proximity and availability, and more difficult access.[6]

For itself, the Navy League anticipated an eventful 2001, but only in terms of scripted events. The year was to mark the beginning of a celebration of the organization's centennial. With the year-long theme "Citizens in Support of the Sea Services" prominently displayed at the June convention in Reno, Nevada, National President Jack Fisher announced plans for a series of events and programs sponsored by Navy League councils around the world, to be capped by a 100th National Convention to be held in the place where it all began, New York City.

National headquarters issued a "Centennial Council Kit" filled with special press releases, suggested interview formats, and a "How To" list for obtaining local media coverage of a particular council and locale. Fisher also restated the Navy League's intent: "We are a maritime nation and for nearly a century the Navy League has been there to support the men and women of the sea services and their families. Today we pledge that we will continue to be there for those brave patriots, every day, for the next century and beyond."[7]

A year later the League did celebrate its Centennial, which included a formal dinner of both celebration and remembrance in New York City. Simon Roosevelt, Theodore Roosevelt's great-grandson, greeted members at the opening ceremony on June 29, 2002. In his remarks, new National President Timothy O. Fanning considered the League's first century "only a prelude to the future."[8]

An important part of that future was construction of a new headquarters building. Fanning had become President in the summer of 2001, and after concentrating on setting up a course to train council officers nationally and initiating the Navy and Marine Corps Caucus on Capitol Hill, he turned his attention to the headquarters issue.

The League's fundamental aim in purchasing another headquarters building was different from that during the Spittler/Rau era a quarter century earlier. In the 1980s the intent had been to simply obtain better quarters and working conditions for the national staff, eliminate the rent payment burden, and present a better image of the League itself to visitors and Washington's political leadership. But by the early 21st century, a move to another headquarters location was viewed as a strategic financial move to develop an income-generating real estate property to support operations of the national headquarters staff and provide a substantial League educational endowment for future years.

Ground is broken for the Navy League's new permanent home at 2300 Wilson Boulevard in Arlington, Virginia. From the left: Lieutenant General Robert Magnus, USMC, Assistant Commandant of the Marine Corps; Vice Admiral Thomas J. Barrett, USCG, Vice Commandant of the Coast Guard; Admiral Vern Clark, USN, Chief of Naval Operations; Christine Todd Whitman, Administrator of the Environmental Protection Agency; Timothy O. Fanning, Navy League National President; Bruce Carlton, Acting Deputy Administrator, U.S. Maritime Administration; and Paul Ferguson, Member of the Arlington County Board.

National President Fanning oversaw a development team that, through several real estate transactions, accumulated an entire property block directly across the street from the Courthouse Metro Station in Arlington, Virginia. In April 2003 a groundbreaking was held for the Navy League's new headquarters building at 2300 Wilson Boulevard. The 214,000 square-foot building would be the first "green" building in Arlington County, maximizing both environmental and energy conservation processes through innovative use of modern technologies. Its appearance was to be striking both outside and within, a notable departure from the prior headquarters building. There were to be balconies on most floors and a large conference room on the ground level for the use of tenants.

Fanning, speaking at the groundbreaking ceremony along with Bush Administration Environmental Protection Agency Administrator Christine Todd Whitman, noted that the League "elected to construct a green building because it is reflective of the Navy's commitment to be publicly responsive and technologically advanced in pollution prevention and conservation." Then, reflecting the fiscal objective of the headquarters move, Fanning added that, while the building stood "as an example of good environmental stewardship," it also would generate "a steady stream of revenue that will be used to support Navy League programs for many years to come."[9]

But the celebratory nature of the League's headquarters groundbreaking ceremony could not conceal the reality that the United States was a nation at war. Subsequent military operations during *Operations Enduring Freedom* (Afghanistan) and *Iraqi Freedom* indicated that there would be a different set of requirements to successfully conduct "warfare" in the 21st century than the skill set necessary to fight and win in the context of the late 20th century. Chief of Naval Operations Admiral Clark drafted a vision for the future, *Sea Power 21*, to serve as a template to transform the Navy into the force required for the nation's security. As a naval officer involved in the development of the template noted, "The terrorist attacks on the World Trade Center and the Pentagon woke us up to the reality of 21st century threats and the immediate need to protect the homeland in ways that we had not previously understood."[10] Clearly, while no other nation possessed the military power to directly confront the United States in the first years of the 21st century, a diverse set of adversaries posed a security challenge every bit as threatening to the nation's security as the Soviet Union was during the Cold War.

The Navy League's response to the 9/11 attacks was immediate — the first League component to respond was the Naval Sea Cadet Corps. Soon after the attacks on the World Trade Center, as rescue workers began their sad task of finding the living and removing the dead, specially trained dogs were brought in to assist. But the dogs needed rest and food just like the hundreds of aid workers, so New York-based Sea Cadets volunteered to help by assuming the responsibility of caring for the dogs. Their efforts enabled the animals to return to duty as soon as they were properly rested and fed, and freed other workers for more specialized rescue and recovery work.[11]

Several members of the Navy League were directly involved in the tragic events surrounding the attack on New York City's World Trade Center. One New York Council member, Detective Steven McDonald, was paralyzed while conducting rescue operations. In December 2001, the Navy League's New York Council, in association with the New York Police Department Navy Association, paid tribute not only to Steven McDonald, but to one of its own, Police Officer Stephen Driscoll of Emergency Service Unit Truck 4, who gave his life at the World Trade Center. Presenting a check on behalf of the Navy League to Police Officer Driscoll's widow Ann and son Barry, New York Council Treasurer Rick Kenney addressed brief remarks to the "little guy in this room":

> You know, Barry, after a lot of years thinking about it, I've decided the best definition of a hero is, quite simply, an ordinary person called upon to do extraordinary things. ... A real hero decides to 'give back' however much or how little he has to offer to his neighbors, by becoming a police officer. A real hero gives everything he's got to his son, because you are all he can leave behind in life that's a part of him. Barry, let me tell you, when the chips were down, like they were on 9/11, everyone there looked up to that ordinary guy, and he was as tall as those Twin Towers! Barry, I could only call him Steve. You were lucky — you could call him 'Dad!'[12]

From a national security perspective, senior League leadership noted in the pages of *Sea Power* the enormity of the new task at hand, as well as the continuing role of the nation's sea forces in all aspects of the war on terror. National President Fanning wrote several strong editorials supporting the Bush Administration's positions on Afghanistan and Iraq, and the prolonged struggle against global terrorism. In the *2003 Almanac of Sea Power*, Fanning favorably compared the preemptive action against Saddam Hussein's regime in Iraq advocated by President George W. Bush with that taken by John F. Kennedy four decades earlier in the Cuban Missile Crisis, quoting the late President: "We no longer live in a world where only the actual firing of weapons represents a sufficient challenge to a nation's security to constitute maximum peril."[13]

Through the pages of *Sea Power*, League members were kept updated on the Navy's contributions to operations in Afghanistan and Iraq. Such operations in support of ground operations, both conventional and precedent-breaking, were extensive. They included providing aircraft carriers for use as afloat forward-staging bases (USS *Kitty Hawk* (CV-63) during *Operation Enduring Freedom* served as a mobile sea base for Special Operations Forces and Marines); interdiction of time-sensitive targets at sea and on land; expanded maritime interdiction operations against vessels suspected of being involved in terrorist activity; and the protection of shipping choke points.

Combat actions in Afghanistan proved the mettle of the Navy and Marine Corps Team, allowing the projection of thousands of combat forces more than 600 miles inland — the farthest inland campaign fought by a sea-based force in history. Once again, America's ability to project power around the world was dependent upon seapower, and this mission was directed at a nation totally land-locked, hundreds of miles from the nearest salt water!

As it had since World War I, the Navy League responded to another overseas combat deployment of the U.S. sea services by providing aid and comfort on the home front. The dramatically increased call-up and utilization of reservists to prosecute the war on terror saw the League involved at an early stage of the hostilities in support of families unaccustomed to extended overseas commitments. And, because so many reservists were from regions in the United States without a strong active-duty presence or military support network, League involvement was essential in many circumstances to assist dependents.

The Twin Cities, Minnesota, Council was particularly active in this regard, inviting returning reservists and veterans to local meetings to relate their experiences in Southwest Asia as well as the challenges faced by their spouses and families remaining behind in the United States. In December 2003 the Twin Cities Council formed a Military Affairs Committee to facilitate coordination with the Minnesota State Government in its effort to provide support and create a sense of community among Minnesota National Guard personnel and reservists.

Again, it was the nature of the war on terror in relying so much on reservists that made the effort particularly welcome. Robert Faust, chairman of the Twin Cities Council's Military Affairs Committee summarized the unique needs of Navy reservists who were normally being activated on an individual basis, because of their specialty, rather than the entire unit to which they were assigned: "It can be an incredibly isolating event."[14] Throughout 2003 and 2004 the League worked hard to reduce or eliminate that feeling of isolation — particularly among newlyweds, pregnant dependents, or those with small children — and also worked with the civilian employers of reservists called to duty to ensure their employees' family needs were being met.

In areas like Hampton Roads, Virginia, with one of the largest military facilities in the world, local League councils still found plenty of work to do in support of both active-duty and reserve families. Many families were financially hurt by the extended deployment to Southwest Asia, and the League assisted them by helping to meet emergency needs and defray unexpected expenses. Being careful not to duplicate services being provided by the Navy's extensive Fleet Family Services organizations, the Hampton Roads Council focused on efforts to assist spouses and/or other family members obtain jobs in the local area to augment civilian income lost because of the reservist call up. Other assistance provided included help in resume writing, baby-sitting, household maintenance, and transportation.

Other League councils throughout the nation rushed to assist the sea services. The Kingsville, Texas, Council donated 500 two-hour phone calls to crew members of the USS *Theodore Roosevelt* (CVN-71)to allow them to stay in touch with family members while at sea. The Channel Islands, California, Council hosted baby showers with donated clothing packaged as "Baby's First Sea Bag" and given to young service families. The council also collected funds to assist in paying baby-sitting costs, giving young parents the time needed to attend training or workshop classes provided by Navy Family Services in the Port Huene-me/Point Mugu area of California.

Nancy Reagan christens the ship named for her husband in ceremonies at Newport News, Virginia.

In recognition of the fact that the percentage of forward-deployed military members with families was the highest in the nation's history, *Operation Homefront* was founded in 2002 with the specific goal of aiding families of deployed members of all the nation's armed services. The Navy League was the first major organization to establish a relationship with the nascent effort, with several League officials from various councils taking active, leading roles in getting *Operation Homefront* off and running. Although initially concentrated in Southern California, with major synergies established with the Orange County and San Diego Navy League Councils, the effort subsequently expanded to 30 chapters in 20 states and one in Europe.

As in its work with the Navy's Family Service Centers in areas of fleet concentration, the League was careful not to duplicate or compete with services offered by *Operation Homefront* to all U.S. service members. Because so much of the funding and support services were provided by the local business community, many of which were unfamiliar with the nature of a service organization, the Navy League found a special niche in providing training and suggested procedures to *Operation Homefront* participants. League members proved particularly adept not only in providing their professional counsel and suggested contacts, but also in their ability to show donors how their services were being put to use. As an ancillary benefit, these efforts provided an opportunity for councils to expand individual membership and bolster their Community Affiliate programs.

Ernie Leidiger, executive director of *Operation Homefront* (and a Navy League Life Member) noted the invaluable nature of the League in support of the program:

> The Navy League can provide access to bases, ships, or people. Service providers can see, touch, and feel the people they are helping. ... It's a win-win situation for everyone. We get the benefit of the Navy League's experience and access along with the services of the donor companies, the Navy League has an opportunity to increase its ranks and Affiliates base, and the providers get to see their services in action.[15]

Efforts in support of sea service personnel, as well as assisting the work of newly formed service organizations such as *Operation Homefront*, did not deter the Navy League from engaging in traditional activities that have been its forte for more than a century. In a League first, the Santa Barbara, California, Council joined forces with the Hampton Roads, Virginia, Council, in co-hosting a weeklong series of activities and events culminating in the July 12, 2003, commissioning of the USS *Ronald Reagan* (CVN-76), a 97,000-ton/1,100-foot aircraft carrier built in Newport News, Virginia. With the Navy prohibited by law from using appropriated funds for any but the most austere celebrations of ship christenings and commissionings,

the willingness of League councils from the East and West Coasts to fund a celebration more worthy of the man who won the Cold War was an excellent example of how the organization continued to do for the Navy what it could not do for itself.

The President of the Santa Barbara Council, Connie O'Shaughnessy-Los, was the major driving force behind the entire commissioning effort. Already recipient of the Department of the Navy's Meritorious Public Service Award in May 2002 for forming "a unique bond between the Santa Barbara community and thousands of active duty sailors and Marines,"[16] Ms. Los came up with a novel idea that spawned one of the most successful fund-raising events in League history. Knowing of former First Lady Nancy Reagan's fondness for teddy bears, she sponsored creation of a "Ronnie" Beanie Baby by the Ty Company, creator of the popular line of "Beanie Babies." The light gray bear — with a "Date of Birth" of February 6, 2003, dressed out in a Navy collar, blue scarf, and white sailor hat, and sporting the logo of the Navy League and the USS *Ronald Reagan* (CVN-76) designation — was an immediate hit with the public as well as avid Beanie Baby collectors. The attached heart-shaped tag noted that all of Ty's profits from the original purchase would be "donated to the Navy League of the United States, Santa Barbara Council, to support those serving our nation throughout the world." A Navy League logo, with the annotation "Citizens in Support of the Sea Services," was placed immediately below Ty's promise.

Proceeds from sales of "Ronnie the Bear," which debuted in the spring of 2003, were almost $500,000, with 100 percent of the profits from the original sale of the bear being donated to the Santa Barbara Council. Commented Santa Barbara Council Vice President Faye Eson, "The effort not only has provided funds that we need, but has gotten the word out about the Navy League and enhanced the knowledge not only of who we are, but what we do, and that's just as important."[17]

In the spring of 2005, celebrating the efforts of the men and women of the sea services, the Navy League, in a joint effort with the Navy-Marine Corps Relief Society, published *Our Navy-Marine Corps Team, Defending Freedom*, a compilation of military photographs detailing America's warriors engaged in *Operation Enduring Freedom* and *Operation Iraqi Freedom*. This collection vividly captured the heroism, courage and compassion of American men and women in uniform who were opposing terrorism and its heinous acts of hatred and violence. In his introduction, Secretary of the Navy Gordon England observed, "These photos capture the next great generation of Americans as they fight terrorism and strive to bring security, stability, liberty and democracy to nations around the world."[18] The book was accompanied by two digital video discs containing hundreds of photos and by a video capturing the opening hours of *Operations Enduring Freedom* and *Iraqi Freedom* as well as a depiction of the power of winning teamwork on the battlefields of Southwest Asia.

The nature and character of the men and women of the sea services were never better demonstrated than in the last month of 2004 and the first several months of 2005. On December 26, 2004, a tsunami ravaged parts of the Indonesian island of Sumatra and other areas of southeast and southern Asia, claiming lives as far away as Somalia, on the horn of Africa. Huge ocean waves, generated by an earthquake off Sumatra, killed more than 175,000 people in eleven countries and left almost 50,000 others missing and hundreds of thousands homeless. Navy ships, already present in Asian waters, were dispatched to the scene of the disaster. From ferrying food and water supplies ashore, to airlifting stranded victims to safety and critical medical care, the United States took charge of coordinating all international military and commercial ships conducting relief operations offshore.

The inherent flexibility of sea forces to quickly shift from presence and deterrence operations to humanitarian relief operations in the Indian Ocean pointed to the continued utility of sea forces in the 21st century, over and above those required to prosecute the war on terror. But the specter of a continuing decline in the size of the fleet, coupled with increasingly unanticipated naval operations of undetermined longevity in distant corners of the world, had many in the Navy League as well as Congress concerned, particularly after the duration of the war on terror became evident in early 2003.

The issue of the size of the Navy was older than the Navy League itself. Regardless of its pedigree, the reality was that at the end of 2003 there were 295 ships in the force, a decrease of 50 percent from the 594 ships on the waterfront in 1987, and the lowest number since the mid-1930s. Senior Navy leadership understood and recognized the challenge posed by the "arithmetic" of fleet numbers. In an October 2002 interview in *Sea Power*, Admiral Clark maintained that "we need a fleet numbering about 375 ships." While admitting that "we will continue to refine the number as we go," he also observed the well-known truism, "You can only be in one place at one time with one ship, and so numbers do matter. Numbers have a quality all their own."[19]

In April 2003 Admiral Clark stated that the force of the future should be "about 135 combatants, 12 carriers, 55 submarines, and, since it is going to be a more distributed force, we'll need a larger logistics force."[20] However, when those numbers were endorsed by neither the Secretary of the Navy nor senior officials in the office of the Secretary of Defense, concern grew as to just how realistic such projections were, given the lack of advocacy by civilian leadership of both departments.

Anticipating such challenges, with the full support of the Navy League, a 92-member Navy and Marine Corps Caucus had been formed on Capitol Hill in early 2002 to inform members of the "significant contributions to national security made by the sea service team and the various ways to demonstrate their own support of this team through a strong national defense program."[21] Commenting on the importance of the caucus to the sea services, National President Timothy O. Fanning observed:

> This is an especially important time for all Americans, including members of Congress, to support all of the nation's armed services ... not only because of their front-line role in the war against international terrorism but also because of the huge deficits in acquisition and procurement funding that have developed over the last decade.[22]

From the left: General Michael W. Hagee, USMC, Commandant of the Marine Corps; General Thomas Collins, USCG, Commandant of the Coast Guard; National President Sheila M. McNeill; the Honorable Gordon R. England, Secretary of the Navy; and Admiral Vern Clark, USN, Chief of Naval Operations.

Lest the sea services' efforts, as well as force structures and budgets, be focused to near exclusivity on the war on terror, Fanning also warned, in his last "President's Message," that there were a host of nations and adversaries other than terrorists to be concerned about, and that "the bulk of the combat burden," regardless of where it would occur, "would fall on forward-deployed U.S. naval forces."[23]

It was in this context that a new National President took office. A League member since 1966, Sheila M. McNeill had been a member of the Brunswick Glynn Council, and then moved to the Camden-Kings Bay, Georgia, Council in the mid-1980s. She served as president of that council 1993-1994. She subsequently served as vice president for legislative affairs, reinvigorating the program that Lou Kriser and S. Peter Kuhn had created in the mid-1980s. She was the first woman to be elected to the top leadership position.

As National President, McNeill decided to concentrate on the education part of the League's mission, emphasizing its legislative affairs aspect. McNeill and her vice president of legislative affairs, Randy Hollstein, sat down with each of the services' chiefs of legislative affairs, as well as their Coast Guard and Merchant Marine counterparts. A plan for engagement with Congress was drawn up in a two-page agenda paper focusing on the top issues of importance to the sea services.

Concomitant with this effort in legislative affairs and furthering the League's educational mission, McNeill re-launched the League's "Sea Power Ambassadors Program," a grassroots effort in coordination with the American Shipbuilding Association, to educate the public and Congress about the issue of fleet size. In announcing the effort, she noted that, "Our Navy League goals today are identical to the goals of the Navy League one hundred one years ago: To educate the Congress and the American people on the need for strong sea services and to support our men and women in uniform."[24]

But, having failed to gain support for his "about 375" number from the civilian leadership of either the Departments of Navy or Defense, Admiral Clark abandoned advocation of a finite number of ships, and subsumed the issue in a plethora of initiatives and new ideas. From repackaging of fleet strike units into Carrier and Expeditionary Strike Groups to creation of a "Fleet Response Plan," and development of "Sea Swap," and "Optimal Manning" concepts, he sought to recast the issue as one of more than just numbers. As a *Sea Power* article succinctly observed in December 2003, "the Navy has stopped arguing for 'presence' and 'numbers' in favor of 'presence with a purpose' and for a fleet that is measured in terms of its capability rather than hulls."[25]

The Navy League was forced to tread a delicate line between official Department of the Navy policy and what many members thought about such a basic issue as the size of the fleet. Just how carefully that line was being walked was evident in November 2004 when the League withdrew its support from the "Sea Power Ambassadors Program" because of "differences over the tactics to be used in advocating for the maintenance of a strong maritime force in America."[26] In announcing the termination of the relationship in the recently renamed *Seapower Almanac 2005* issue, National President McNeill noted, "We share many goals with the American Shipbuilding Association, and will continue to work with them on issues of mutual concern, but we have at times found their approach to issues too narrow and their tactics too divisive."[27]

But in the same issue of the *Almanac*, McNeill also noted in her lead-off editorial that "few issues in official Washington attract more heat and less light than the annual release of the Navy's plan for new ship construction." Continuing with the same theme she observed, "Shipbuilding is a volatile issue in part because there is no stability in the shipbuilding program ... Congress, the Office of Management and Budget, and the Navy have struggled for years to bring a measure of constancy to naval shipbuilding. Their results are difficult to discern."[28]

But some Navy Leaguers saw the issue of shipbuilding and fleet size in black and white rather than shades of gray. The February 2005 issue of *Seapower* (formerly *Sea Power)* included not only a lengthy examination of the issue of shipbuilding with two industrial leaders and a staff member of the Congressional Research Service, but also a short, pithy letter to the editor that cut to the core of the issue:

> Over the past five years, I believe the Navy League has endorsed the Navy's declining shipbuilding program by printing interviews with admirals and civilian Secretaries without a contrary comment.
>
> The Navy League's publishing policy of passing on the Navy Department's public relations message that 'our force reductions are over' and 'our future shipbuilding program is approved' is not responsible if it does not represent the concerns of Navy League leadership or membership.
>
> I ask that our organization now speak up on this topic and no longer print 'powder-puff' interviews on shipbuilding. The litmus test should be: What would Theodore Roosevelt do?[29]

The following month, Richard Macke, the League's National Vice President for Sea Services and a member of the Maritime Policy Committee, wrote in the Honolulu, Hawaii, Council magazine *Fore 'n Aft*, that "if the shipbuilding requested in the current budget before Congress is continued, it will guarantee well less than 300 ships and the Navy League is convinced that is too small a force ... that number begins to erode our credibility as a reaction force around the world."[30]

Reflecting Macke's concern, the League's *Maritime Policy 2005* advocated, as an official position, "a Navy force structure of 55 submarines and well over 300 surface ships. ... The Navy must build, on average, over 10 ships per year for the next several years in order to restore the fleet to the numbers required by today's global threat environment."[31,32]

Sensing that the issue of force structure had become a pressing concern, in one of his first speeches after becoming Chief of Naval Operations in the summer of 2005, Admiral Michael G. Mullen abandoned the "range of ships" argument that his predecessor had frequently voiced in public. To an all-services audience at the National Defense University he indicated that one of his first duties was "to build the right Navy for the future — a fleet, a discrete number of ships and aircraft and submarines — a truly decisive naval force."[33]

The new Chief of Naval Operations continued this theme in his *CNO Guidance for 2006, Meeting the Challenge of a New Era*. Listing the building of a fleet for the future as second only to sustainment of combat readiness in his hierarchy of priorities, in a personal message to Navy flag officers and senior executive service officials, he asserted that he would be "focused keenly" on an alternative shipbuilding plan, and then added a personal note: "We simply must set about the task of building a fleet large enough and capable enough to deal with the dynamic security environment before us."[34]

In late October 2005, Senator John Warner, chairman of the Senate Armed Services Committee, called for an increase in the rate of shipbuilding, creation of a separate allocation of funding for shipbuilding outside of the normal defense budgeting process, and expressed concern not only over numbers of ships in the fleet, but the overall warfighting capability of the service. "It is time for the Navy to begin a down-to-earth, long-term shipbuilding program to try not just to restore numbers, but to bring the elements of the fleet up to where they can continue to defend this nation and our interests abroad," Warner admonished.[35]

Along with the issue of the Navy's force structure, the other subject of considerable League interest in the immediate post-9/11 environment was the size, manning, funding, and effectiveness in the new security environment of the U.S. Coast Guard. This concern was particularly evident in *Seapower*, where no fewer than 13 articles in a period of 20 months (April 2003-December 2004) focused on various topics, from funding to new missions, involving the Coast Guard.

Such focus made particular sense in fighting the war on terror, with increased emphasis on the security of America's 95,000 miles of Atlantic, Pacific, and Gulf of Mexico coastline and 361 ports. In addition, two large Coast Guard cutters, a buoy tender, eight patrol boats, four port security units, and more than 1,250 personnel deployed overseas in 2003 to join coalition naval forces in support of *Operation Iraqi Freedom*, where their support was termed "pivotal" by Vice Admiral Timothy Keating, commander of the U.S. Fifth Fleet and Commander, U.S. Naval Forces, Central Command.[36]

The reality of homeland defense as a mission of great importance had been clearly signaled on March 1, 2003, when the Coast Guard was transferred from the Department of Transportation to the newly created Department of Homeland Security. But expanded homeland security missions could not mean abandonment or degradation of the Coast Guard's traditional missions such as emergency preparedness and response and maritime law enforcement. Faced with a growing list of missions and a fleet of ships and planes increasingly worn out from overuse, the service began a concerted effort on Capitol Hill, backed by the Navy League, to seek additional force structure, personnel, and new technology to identify potential ship-borne threats to the United States.

The Coast Guard addressed the issue through inauguration of the *Deepwater* Program, the largest acquisition and modernization program in the service's history. It sought, and received in three years, a net growth of 30 percent in funding and more than 4,000 additional personnel.

But the challenge was considerable. In testimony on Capitol Hill, Coast Guard Commandant Admiral Thomas H. Collins commented that, "if the Coast Guard is to meet the nation's future maritime needs, its aging assets, support systems, and infrastructure must be recapitalized with a due sense of urgency."[37] In an interview with *Sea Power* Editor in Chief Richard Barnard in August 2004, Collins was frank about the poor condition of his fleet:

> We've got ships, planes, helicopters, and sensor systems that are at the end of their service life. They're old, they're tired, and they break down. They're breaking down at the very time that we are using them at a high operational tempo. Every index shows you that we are in dire straits.[38]

In his June 2005 luncheon address at the League's National Convention in Norfolk, Virginia, Admiral Collins noted the challenge of employing the "39th oldest fleet of the 41 Coast Guard services in the world; only Mexico and the Republic of the Philippines have older fleets in service." But he was also effusive in his praise for the Navy League's strong advocacy of both the Coast Guard's transformation efforts and for its work in furthering the service's legislative processes on Capitol Hill on such issues as port security and the *Deepwater* project.[39]

USCGC *Tampa* sits high and dry at the Coast Guard Yard, Curtis Bay, Baltimore, Maryland, during a 9-month major systems refurbishment as part of the Mission Effectiveness Project (MEP) funded by the *Deepwater* Program.

The issuance by the Bush Administration of *The National Strategy for Maritime Security* in September 2005, with its emphasis on maritime domain awareness, including relevant information about every vessel traveling above and below the ocean, renewed the importance, from a Coast Guard perspective, of the *Deepwater* Program. Speaking at the 2005 Maritime Security Exposition on September 20, 2005, the Coast Guard Commandant pointedly observed, "*Deepwater* is Maritime Domain Awareness."[40]

Additionally, in the context of the war on terror, the security of entryways of seaborne commerce into America took on added importance. In her "President's Message" of September 2003, National President McNeill warned that the Maritime

Transportation Security Act of that year could become "a hollow law, long on promise and short on impact." McNeill asserted that "resources are woefully inadequate to the task of tightening security at the nation's ports."[41]

Almost a year later, the League's National President would again return to the issue of homeland security, criticizing Congress for levying excessive bureaucratic reporting requirements on a department composed of 22 government agencies having to report to 88 different congressional committees. McNeill noted that "the largest reorganization of the federal bureaucracy in 57 years" required "similar retooling on Capitol Hill."[42]

Also critical of the government's failure to address the vulnerability of U.S. ports was John Lehman, a member of the 9/11 Commission. He testified on Capitol Hill in October 2004 that 90 percent of the Government's transportation security funding was allocated to aviation safety, and only 10 percent toward port security and similar efforts. Echoing National President McNeill's message, Lehman, returning to a theme he had voiced often when Navy Secretary, asserted that much of the problem with inadequate port security funding and support lay with Congress and "the 80-plus committees and subcommittees that want a piece of the action in homeland security."[43]

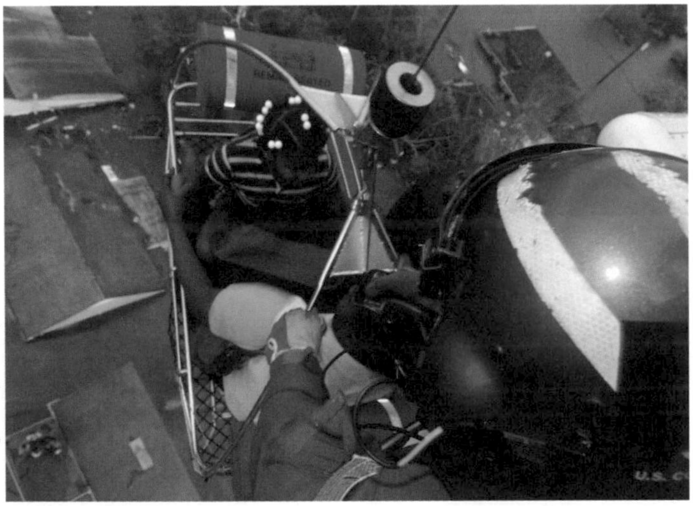

USCG photo by PO2 Kyle Niemi

Petty Officer Steven Huerta hoists two children to safety into a Coast Guard rescue helicopter in New Orleans following Hurricane Katrina.

Ironically, unexpected support came for the Coast Guard in the context of another tragic loss of life in America, as Hurricane Katrina ravaged the Louisiana and Mississippi Gulf Coasts and surrounding environs in late August 2005. As a primary first responder, the U.S. Coast Guard initiated a massive rescue effort which at its peak included 43 helicopters, 30 cutters, eight airplanes and hundreds of small boats. More than 33,000 Americans were rescued, including more than 24,000 plucked by helicopter or rescue boats from the rooftops of their flooded homes and neighborhood buildings; more than 9,000 hospital patients were evacuated to safety by air and sea. For a service that normally saved on average 5,500 people a year, the Coast Guard basically accomplished five years work in less than two weeks, with assets from as far away as Kodiak, Alaska, and Hawaii involved in rescue operations.[44]

With such heroic performances being televised throughout the nation on a daily basis, in late September the House of Representatives passed a nonbinding resolution lauding the Coast Guard's performance. Then, in recognition of the age and material condition of much of the equipment used in the rescue effort, the resolution called for increased funding for the service. The result was a House-Senate conference agreement September 29, 2005, to provide $933 million to the Coast Guard for its *Deepwater* recapitalization and replacement effort. Commenting on the agreement which almost doubled the amount of funding previously approved by the House, Representative Harold Rogers, chairman of the Homeland Security Appropriations Subcommittee praised the Coast Guard's "heroic" actions in responding to the plight of thousands in the Gulf Coast region, and noted that "there has never been a point in the service's history where it saved so many people at one time."[45]

The stakes for the Coast Guard in the new 21st century environment were high, as they were for all the sea services by mid-decade. On March 23, 2005, Chief of Naval Operations Clark noted in his remarks at the Sea-Air-Space Exposition that "my acid test for what America should be investing in goes along in line with the 'three Rs.' My three Rs are readiness, responsiveness, and relevance. My view is that this nation should invest in pieces of force structure that meet all those requirements." The admiral asserted that a transformation in the way the Navy looks at the world was required, and advocated changing the "way we think about the world ... and the challenges we are going to face, the real enemy that we *have*, not the enemy that we *had*."[46]

But even in a 21st century world transforming, some time-tested certainties remain. In a page that could have been taken directly from Alfred Thayer Mahan's *The Influence of Sea Power Upon History*, Admiral Clark observed:

> We are still an island nation. And we still live in a world where globalization has already occurred and will occur at ever-increasing rates in the future ... We still live in a world where over 95 percent of the trade and 80 percent of its value moves by sea. We understand that the economic underpinning of our world will not be correct if we do not have, and are not able to command, the seas.[47]

> *"We are aware that the burden has fallen almost solely on the shoulders of the uniformed military and security services and their families. We have used that in our calls to action by our members. We have said, 'We are at war. What have you done lately?'"*

Admiral Clark retired in July 2005 and Admiral Michael G. Mullen became the new Chief of Naval Operations. In his initial message to the Navy, Mullen cited

From the left: Al J. Bernard, Chairman, National Capital Council of the Navy League; Rear Admiral Patrick Stillman, USCG; Chief of Naval Operations, Admiral Michael Mullen, USN; Lieutenant Commander Henry E. Mooberry, U.S. Sea Cadet Corps; Commandant of the Marine Corps General Michael Hagee, USMC; Senator John Warner; the Honorable Gordon England, Secretary of the Navy. The occasion: The National Capital Council's Second Congressional Sea Services Award Ceremony. After receiving the Sea Services Award, Senator Warner participated in the ceremony where the National Capital Council's Sea Cadet Division was renamed to honor Commander Mooberry.

three principal challenges faced by the Navy in the years ahead; the second one — "building a fleet for the future, one of the proper size and mix of capabilities to deter or defeat the enemies we may face tomorrow ... a fleet that will ensure the security of our grandchildren and great-grandchildren" — was certainly in keeping with Navy League sentiments and the concerns repeatedly expressed by both national leadership and the rank-and-file.[48]

But also of increasing League concern were the prolonged war on terror and its affect on the men and women in uniform. To many Navy Leaguers it seemed that just as in the Vietnam War four decades earlier, only the men and women in uniform were being asked to sacrifice for a war garnering limited public enthusiasm.

In his first "President's Message" after succeeding Sheila McNeill as National President in June 2005, John A. Panneton challenged Navy Leaguers to respond to questions from their friends and neighbors "on wanting to do something to help win the global war on terror" by encouraging them to "join the fight by joining the Navy League."[49] Executive Director Stephen Pietropaoli continued this theme in an interview published in the *New York Times*. Addressing the issue of a military on the front lines of the war, with little involvement or sacrifice demanded of the

National President John A. Panneton addresses Navy Leaguers at the 2005 Winter Meeting.

American public in general, he asserted that the Navy League recognized the issue:

> We are aware that the burden has fallen almost solely on the shoulders of the uniformed military and security services and their families. We have used that in our calls to action by our members. We have said 'We are at war. What have you done lately?'[50]

But regardless of American society's interest in the continued war on terror, there was little indication that the sea services' commitments would be lessened. This was clearly evident when, even with the Navy's disaster response to Hurricane Katrina in late August 2005 that totaled more than a dozen ships, hundreds of helicopters and involved thousands of personnel, including 2,600 Marines, the war effort in Southwest Asia did not skip a beat.

Speaking at the 17th International Seapower Symposium at the Naval War College in Newport, Rhode Island, September 21, 2005, Admiral Mullen, while noting the effects of Katrina on crippling a "critical node of the world's economy," maintained that the most serious threat to maritime and international security was not a random act of nature, but rather the lawlessness of man: "... irregular and unrestricted warfare — warfare with no rules, with nothing forbidden."[51]

Speaking largely to leaders of the world's navies, Admiral Mullen pointedly observed, "When our careers began, nobody spoke of the threats from transnational networks, environment attack, human trafficking, and failed states" and asked for "assistance from like-minded nations interested in using the sea for lawful purposes and precluding its use for others that threaten national, regional, or global security."[52]

The Navy League's 2005 Winter Meeting, held in Arlington, Virginia, in November, received up-to-date briefings from each of the sea services. The common precept throughout all the presentations was the manner in which each sea service was dealing with both the war on terror and the series of natural calamities that had struck the United States in the summer and early autumn. From the perspective of each speaker, the only thing constant in the first decade of the 21st century would be change.

Yet also clear was the reality that while service employments and technologies were transforming and adapting to a new era, the mission of the sea services remained largely the same as at the Navy League's founding 103 years earlier: to ensure the national security of the United States of America and the freedom of the American people.

"When our careers began, nobody spoke of the threats from transnational networks, environment attack, human trafficking, and failed states" and asked for "assistance from like-minded nations interested in using the sea for lawful purposes and precluding its use for others that threaten national, regional, or global security."

Admiral Michael G. Mullen, USN
Chief of Naval Operations

U.S. Marine Corps photo by Brian Wickliffe

Scouting for possible enemy attacks, a Marine from E Company, Battalion Landing Team 2/1, 15th Marine Expeditionary Unit, creeps along a fence line in support of *Operation Iraqi Freedom*.

CONCLUSION

One of the most notable characteristics of seapower is its capacity over the years to adapt to changing circumstances. In 1915, 1921, 1941, and 1950, and for 16 years after the fall of the Berlin Wall and subsequent implosion of the Soviet Union, the sea services grappled with the consequences of a rapidly changing global environment. Doubtlessly, the first decades of the 21st century will be much different than the years, and the century, preceding them, but that was as true in the 1920s and 1950s as it is today.

Like the sea services, the Navy League has adapted to the realities of a new time. The issues that Timothy Fanning and Sheila McNeill, and now John Panneton, have faced in the first half-decade of the 21st century are different in both content and context than those addressed by Robert Thompson, Nelson Macy, and Robert Crown in prior years. But for the Navy League, the differences are largely of tactics and procedures, time and circumstance.

For at its core, the founding principles for which the organization was created remain as valid at the beginning of the 21st century as they were at the dawn of the 20th. The Navy League of the United States continues to believe in the sea services' vital role in America's national security, both at home and abroad. The educational mission to explain that role in a new century, with naval presence in the heartland declining as reserve centers are consolidated and sea service activities reduced, remains as important today as it was in the 1930s when Nelson Macy was carrying the same message of the need for a strong Navy and the importance of seapower to depression-ridden Great Plains and Rocky Mountain regions far removed from areas of fleet concentration on both the coasts.

In its more than 100 years of existence, and in support of the sea services during two world wars, a "police action," a 40-year protracted conflict, and now a war on terror with unforeseen and undefined challenges, the Navy League has maintained a clear imperative throughout: the need for well-educated, well-trained, and well-compensated men and women in uniform to protect the interests of the United States at sea and on land. The premium placed on finding the highly qualified personnel necessary to man, equip, and operate the sea services remains as important as ever. John Paul Jones's dictum that "men mean more than guns in the rating of a ship" remains as true in the 21st century as it did in the days of wooden decks and black powder.

Through all its programs and supporting initiatives the League has sought to ensure the right kinds of tools are put into the hands of the people it supports, the greatest sailors, Marines, and mariners the world has ever seen. And while capabilities and technologies will play a pivotal role in future conflict, those who go down to the sea in ships know it is the fire, spirit, and determination of the men and women in uniform that will win the day if combat becomes necessary.

The legacy of service and sacrifice that the Navy League honors today celebrates standards established at the republic's founding. The sailors in the Navy, Coast Guard, and U.S.-flag Merchant Marine, and Marines on guard for more than two centuries, have had the strength to face evil ... and the courage to stand against the brutal logic of dictators.

What the nation has witnessed over the past four years is no different from that experienced in 1918, 1942, 1968, 1991, and the years in between: the sacrifices of a free people to ensure both their, and their children's, future. As Pericles reminded the Athenians centuries ago, a nation has no other character than that which its own people give it from generation to generation.

The Navy League of the United States continues to believe, as it has from the earliest days of its existence, in the men, women, and institutions of the sea services. And it has maintained, through good times and not, spanning more than a century, that its primary responsibility is two-fold: to educate the American people as to the need for seapower and continued freedom of the seas, and to give all of America's sea service Sailors and Marines the tools needed to prevent, but if necessary, to fight and win the next war, whatever its nature, wherever its location, whoever the enemy. They and the society they seek to preserve and protect deserve nothing less.

APPENDICES

A. Evelyn Mary Collins

During the summer of 1925 an event occurred internal to the Navy League which was to have repercussions for the next 43 years. Answering a position for a stenographer at a monthly salary of $75 at League headquarters was a nearly 17-year-old Washington native, Evelyn Collins, recently graduated from Saint Dominic's Business School. At this time there were but three permanent staff; with her hire, Evelyn became the fourth.

Evelyn may have thought she was hired just to take dictation, but she was soon doing more. Over the ensuing months and years her job was expanded to include just about everything that had to be done in the national headquarters office to keep the League alive. One day it was working on the League magazine, then working into the night typing and folding dozens of letters. She particularly enjoyed the League's educational mission and often intimated to her niece, Jane Grover, that it was great to be working in an office full of bright people "working to make a difference."

Although initially uncertain of working in an office filled with older men, she began a 43-year career, and her final job description listed 27 different responsibilities she had, ranging from production of the Steering Committee agenda to advising the National President." Throughout good times and bad, peace and war, Evelyn Collins was to earn the undying admiration, respect, and support of a legion of co-workers, League and Navy leaders.

At one point during the Great Depression, the League's national treasury had a balance of $2.74, and the organization was kept solvent only through the beneficence of influential people in industry. Evelyn Collins's niece, Jane Grover, recalled in a 2005 interview that "the League was so poor in those years. But Evelyn could get the right person on the phone on Wall Street if the rent was coming due and we needed the money."

In 1941 major internal overhaul was implemented that reorganized the League's headquarters staff and appointed Evelyn Collins as Executive Secretary of the Navy League, a position she was to hold for the next 27 years. During World War II, the increasingly essential nature of the work she was doing quickly became evident. While continuing to put in 50-70 hours a week at national headquarters, having worked for the League since 1925 she was now much more than just a talented employee. To League staff, congressmen and senators, officials in the Roosevelt Administration, and active duty personnel in the Department of the Navy, Evelyn Collins was literally "the voice" of the Navy League. She was the first person any incoming caller, by phone or in person, encountered. She was personally known to Navy Secretaries and Chiefs of Naval Operation on a first name basis, and knew most of the important personages in the sea services in the nation's capital. When a piece of legislation needed the League's personal attention or advocacy, Collins always knew the right people to call in the corridors of power on Capitol Hill. Collins's critical support role in headquarters was just one of several intangibles that contributed significantly to the League's growth, and augured well for additional membership increases in the future.

In 1959 Secretary of the Navy Thomas S. Gates awarded the Navy's highest civilian award, the Distinguished Service Award, to Evelyn Collins. In the history of the award, she was only the fifth woman to receive it. The citation read in part:

> The Secretary of the Navy takes pleasure in presenting the Distinguished Public Service Award to Evelyn Mary Collins ... for her outstanding services to the Department of the Navy in the fields of public information and education ... [She] has served as a principal point of liaison between the Department of the Navy and the Navy League of the United States during the terms of office of 13 Secretaries of the Navy and 12 Presidents of the Navy League.
>
> During her long association with the League, and as National Secretary since 1941, Evelyn Collins has been a devoted friend and a tireless advocate of service to the Navy and its personnel. With no thought of personal aggrandizement, she has perpetuated and strengthened the true relationship of harmonious dependence between these two great organizations.
>
> Her loyal dedication, support, and cooperation, combined with her personal warmth and understanding, have earned for Evelyn Collins the affectionate admiration and gratitude of thousands of Navymen throughout the world. I know they join me in this expression of appreciation and in approving this award this twenty-third day of April 1959.

In 1968, ending a career that spanned the Roaring '20s, the Great Depression, World War II, and the Cold War, Executive Secretary Evelyn Collins finally retired on the last day of the year, becoming the League's first Executive Secretary Emeritus. At the time of her retirement, Chief of Naval Operations Admiral Thomas H. Moorer presented her with a gold bracelet adorned with four stars to express the Navy's appreciation for her many years of service. The baton of Executive Secretary was passed to her niece, Jane Collins Grover, who remained, as she admitted years later, never hesitant to "call Evelyn ... she'll know what to do."

The League's 66th Annual Convention in Honolulu, Hawaii, in 1968, unanimously adopted a "Resolution in Appreciation to Evelyn Mary Collins." Signed by

National President Charles Duchein, it read in part:

> Whereas, Evelyn M. Collins has faithfully served the purposes of the Navy League for 43 full years ... and selflessly contributed to the respected posture of the Civilian Arm of the Navy;
>
> Whereas, 'Miss Navy League' through firmness of purpose and personality is recognized as a significant element of the status enjoyed by the Navy League throughout the Nation and within the maritime nations worldwide;
>
> Whereas, no Navy League President could have functioned as effectively without her firm guidance and wisdom in the intricacies of the Navy League and its manifold facets;
>
> Whereas, Evelyn M. Collins has provided the sinew of strength for the organization through periods of both trials and triumphs, even foregoing her salary when the exigencies of the fiscal situation required;
>
> Whereas, Evelyn M. Collins is to retire from her position of Executive Secretary of the Navy League of the United States in January of next year;
>
> Therefore be it Resolved that the Navy League of the United States express its heartfelt appreciation, its respect, its recognition to Evelyn M. Collins...

In 1989 Evelyn Collins was unanimously selected to become the first member of the Navy League's then-new Hall of Fame.

The year 2000 was the last year Evelyn Collins graced the Navy League with her presence. After supposedly retiring, she had frequently returned to help out in the national office and attend the League's National Conventions and winter meetings (by actual count she attended a total of 71 National Conventions between 1925 and 1999, as well as numerous winter meetings and sessions of the Board of Directors). When she passed on in January 2000, she was described by National President John R. Fisher as a "one-person corporate board ... [she remembered] everything and everybody and was always available to anyone who needed her."

Similar sentiments were expressed by several other former National Presidents in a special tribute page in the March 2000 issue of *Sea Power*. Jack M. Kennedy, National President 1997-1999 commented on Evelyn's "encyclopedic knowledge of the Navy League" and characterized her as "an irreplaceable resource." John M. Rau, National President 1981-1983, termed her "the Empress of the Navy League" and asserted that "without her sacrifice and devotion — many months she took very little and sometimes no pay — the Navy League would not have survived the Depression of the 1930s." Bernard Bennett, National President 1985-1987, observed on her passing, "Evelyn Collins was the heart and soul of our organization. She provided strength and guidance ... through difficult times and turbulent waters. We shall miss her — she was one alone."

Evelyn Collins was not just a talented woman who worked at the Navy League. Over the years, her peers, seniors, and subordinates, both in uniform and civilian attire, recognized her as a rare individual, literally the essence of the Navy League for almost a half century. The success the organization enjoys today as a powerful, influential voice in support of the sea services can claim many important contributors, but none more so than Evelyn Mary Collins. Her work and example served as a standard of excellence that left an indelible imprint on the legacy and heritage of the Navy League of the United States.

B. Navy League Presidents

Benjamin F. Tracy	1903-1907
Horace Porter	1907-1915
Robert M. Thompson	1915-1918
W. Cameron Forbes	1918
Henry A. Bishop	1918-1919
Henry L. Breckinridge	1919-1921
Robert W. Kelley	1921-1926
Walter Bruce Howe	1926-1928
William Howard Gardiner	1928-1933
Nathaniel Mead Hubbard Jr.	1933-1934
Nelson Macy	1934-1936
Nathaniel Mead Hubbard Jr.	1936-1938
H. Birchard Taylor	1938-1940
Sheldon Clark	1940-1945
Ralph A. Bard	1945-1947
Frank A. Hecht	1947-1953
E.V. Richards Jr.	1953-1954
Carl G. Stockholm	1954-1957
John J. Bergen	1957-1959
Frank Gard Jameson	1959-1961
Robert Crown	1961-1963
Robert H. Barnum	1963-1965
Morgan L. Fitch Jr.	1965-1967
Charles F. Duchein	1967-1969
James M. Hannan	1969-1971
Thomas E. Morris	1971-1973
Ernest A. Carrere Jr.	1973-1975
DeWitt James Griffin	1975-1977
Vincent T. Hirsch	1977-1979
John J. Spittler	1979-1981
John M. Rau	1981-1983
Albert H. Friedrich	1983-1985
Bernard Bennett	1985-1987
Jack H. Morse	1987-1989
Calvin H. Cobb Jr.	1989-1991
William C. Kelley Jr.	1991-1993
Evan S. Baker	1993-1995
Hugh H. Mayberry	1995-1997
Jack M. Kennedy	1997-1999

John R. Fisher	1999-2001
Timothy O. Fanning	2001-2003
Sheila M. McNeill	2003-2005
John A. Panneton	2005-

C. Navy League Publications and Information Technology Resources

The original League publication, *The Navy League Journal*, was first issued in July 1903. The 96-page Volume I, No.1, was introduced with a photograph of President Theodore Roosevelt and featured his March 10, 1903 letter to Navy League President Benjamin Tracy. The letter congratulated Tracy and the League and wished the fledgling organization well.

The Navy League Journal was published from July 1903 until December 1906 when, largely due to a lack of fiscal resources, it was replaced by *The Navy*. This monthly periodical, although edited by a League vice president, was not an official League publication. Nonetheless, League news was included as a special section. The periodical *Seven Seas*, begun in June 1915, replaced *The Navy* a year later, but the League subsequently severed any official relationship with the periodical.

A national publication for the Navy League returned in 1916 with *Sea Power* which, with changes in style and content, continued until July 1921. But the League's declining fortunes and membership in the 1920s again resulted in a cessation of publication. Reflecting the decline in the Navy's fortunes after World War I, minutes from a 1921 Board of Directors meeting dryly stated, "Since 'sea power' has ceased to exist, there isn't much reason for keeping one [*Sea Power* magazine]."

That situation would exist for 14 years. Finally, in May 1935, publication of *Sea Power* was resumed, in a relatively thin, 16-20 page quarterly format, but in fairly substantial quantities, with 7,000 copies rolling off the press on the initial run.

With the fleet rebuilding, and the war tocsin sounding, monthly publication of *Sea Power* resumed in October 1941 and continued throughout the war years. But, as after the First World War, declining membership and revenues, combined with postwar apathy and exhaustion, resulted in discontinuing publication of *Sea Power* in June 1947.

The League attempted, with varying levels of success, to replace it with *Know Your Navy*, published from September 1947 through August 1952, and *Now Hear This!*, first distributed as a monthly in December 1949, and thereafter functioning more as a newsletter than a magazine.

This tenuous situation existed until early 1958, when National President John Bergen decided publication of a monthly periodical would be the best instrument to carry on the League's challenging educational mission in the Cold War. The result was *Navy—The Magazine of Sea Power*. The May 1958 first issue was 48 pages, had nine advertisements, and included articles by Secretary of the Navy Thomas Gates, Chief of Naval Operations Admiral Arleigh Burke and Commandant of the Marine Corps General Randolph McC. Pate.

In August 1971, at National President Thomas Morris's suggestion, the League's Executive Committee approved resurrecting the simpler title *Sea Power* for the League's flagship periodical. As announced in the re-named September issue, the committee reasoned that the title *Sea Power* was "more in line with the Navy League's endorsement of an overall maritime concept which includes the Navy, Marine Corps, Coast Guard and merchant marine and all phases of development of the oceans."

In 1983, the League began publication of *The Almanac of Seapower*. National President John M. Rau noted in his Foreword to the first edition that it was the League's intent that *The Almanac* should "become the most important reference work for everyone working in, studying, writing about or otherwise concerned with naval and maritime affairs." The League's objective has been well served. *The Almanac*, now distributed to Navy League members as the January "Special Edition" of *Seapower*, is considered by many to be the most authoritative and comprehensive unclassified reference annual published on the state of the U.S. sea services. It is widely used within the national and international naval communities.

In 1996, to supplement *Sea Power* and its coverage of issues of national and international import, the League began publishing *The Navy Leaguer*, a quarterly for Navy Leaguers about Navy Leaguers, dealing with strictly internal League issues such as council and membership news, public relations work shops, legislative agendas, and upcoming events.

Several councils also publish their own monthly periodicals or newsletters, some of which can run up to 24 pages or more. The League has established a special awards program to recognize these efforts.

As communications technologies have transitioned from print to the electronic medium, the Navy League has kept up with the times. In 1996, in addition to several style and layout changes to *Sea Power* (new logo, more readable typeface, new section headings, and shorter feature articles and situation reports), the League's Internet Home Page was created, allowing anyone with internet access to gain a wide range of information on League activities, programs, and events. Six years later the League's website was redesigned to include feature articles from *Sea Power*, online membership processing, and the ability to register for several of the League's national events. For members only, an Online Community was also created to include news, council home pages, a membership directory, and calendars of future events.

In December 2004 the League's flagship publication was again made over. In addition to changing its title to a single word, "*Seapower*," the magazine was restyled with another new logo, more modern typefaces, and a new, cleaner design to make it easier to read and more quickly find particular areas of interest and import. For its February 2005 cover, the magazine was named a winner in the "2005 American Graphic Design Awards."

But, the magazine remains true to the League's original intent. As Editor in Chief Barnard noted in announcing the changes in 2004, "We'll still talk with the top people ... and continue to focus on the individuals, strategies, and technologies that promise to make a difference for the sea services ... As always, *Seapower* is the defense magazine that covers the future."

D. Navy League 2005 councils

Following are Navy League Councils in the United States, listed by State or Territory, followed by our international Councils. For more information about the Navy League Council in your area, please visit our website at *http://www.navyleague.org/councils/council_locator.php*

Councils in the U.S.	State / Province
Alabama	
Mobile	Alabama
Alaska	
Anchorage	Alaska
Juneau	Alaska
Arizona	
Phoenix	Arizona
Tucson	Arizona
Yuma	Arizona
Arkansas	
Conway-Central Arkansas	Arkansas
Ozarks	Arkansas
California	
Alameda	California
Bakersfield	California
Beverly Hills	California
California Central Coast	California
Channel Islands	California
Co-Mar Waves	California
Contra Costa	California
Corona Riverside	California
Coronado	California
Fresno	California
Greater Kings County	California
Greater Los Angeles Women	California
Hollywood/Los Angeles	California
Humboldt Bay	California
Imperial Valley	California
Indian Wells Valley	California
Lake Merritt	California

Long Beach	California
Malibu	California
Marin County	California
Monterey Peninsula	California
Napa Valley	California
Newport Beach	California
Oakland	California
Orange County	California
Palm Springs	California
Pasadena	California
Placer County	California
Sacramento	California
San Bernardino	California
San Diego	California
San Diego Women	California
San Francisco	California
Santa Barbara	California
Santa Clara Valley	California
Sonoma County	California
Stanislaus County	California
Stockton	California
Tri-City	California
Vallejo	California
West Contra Costa	California

Colorado

Colorado Springs	Colorado
Denver	Colorado

Connecticut

Bridgeport	Connecticut
Eastern Connecticut	Connecticut
Hartford	Connecticut
Waterbury	Connecticut
Western Connecticut	Connecticut

Delaware

Wilmington	Delaware

Florida

Boca Delray	Florida
Broward County	Florida
Cape Canaveral	Florida
Central Florida	Florida
Clearwater	Florida
Daytona Beach	Florida
Everglades	Florida
Fort Lauderdale	Florida
Jacksonville	Florida
Key West	Florida
Mayport	Florida
Miami	Florida
Palm Beach	Florida
Panama City/Bay County	Florida
Pensacola	Florida
Saint Augustine	Florida
Saint Petersburg	Florida
Santa Rosa County	Florida
Sarasota-Manatee	Florida
Space Coast	Florida
Sun Coast	Florida
Tallahassee	Florida
Tampa	Florida
Treasure Coast	Florida

Georgia

Aiken-Augusta	Georgia
Atlanta Metropolitan	Georgia
Camden-Kings Bay	Georgia
Golden Isles	Georgia
Savannah	Georgia

Guam

Guam	Guam

Hawaii

Barbers Point	Hawaii
East Oahu	Hawaii
Hilo	Hawaii

Honolulu	Hawaii
Kauai	Hawaii
Kona	Hawaii
Maui	Hawaii
Windward-Oahu	Hawaii
Idaho	
Boise	Idaho
Illinois	
Aurora	Illinois
Champaign	Illinois
Chicago	Illinois
Glenview	Illinois
Joliet	Illinois
Lake County	Illinois
Naperville	Illinois
Springfield	Illinois
Indiana	
Crane Area	Indiana
Indianapolis	Indiana
South Bend	Indiana
Iowa	
Cedar Rapids	Iowa
Des Moines	Iowa
Dubuque	Iowa
Kansas	
Greater Kansas City	Kansas
South Central	Kansas
Kentucky	
Central Kentucky	Kentucky
Louisiana	
Baton Rouge	Louisiana
Bayou	Louisiana
Greater New Orleans	Louisiana

Maine	
Casco Bay	Maine
Penobscot	Maine
Maryland	
Annapolis	Maryland
Baltimore	Maryland
Central Maryland	Maryland
Eastern Shore	Maryland
Frederick-Hagerstown	Maryland
Patuxent River	Maryland
Massachusetts	
Berkshire	Massachusetts
Massachusetts Bay	Massachusetts
Michigan	
Battle Creek/Kalamazoo	Michigan
Detroit Women	Michigan
Greater Oakland County	Michigan
Huron Valley	Michigan
Inland Seas	Michigan
Macomb County	Michigan
Metropolitan Detroit	Michigan
Traverse City	Michigan
Tri-County	Michigan
Minnesota	
Twin Cities	Minnesota
Western Lake Superior	Minnesota
Mississippi	
Meridian Area	Mississippi
Pascagoula-Moss Point	Mississippi
Southwest Mississippi	Mississippi
Missouri	
Mid-Missouri	Missouri
Saint Louis	Missouri

Montana	
Helena-Greater Montana	Montana
Nebraska	
Cornhuskers	Nebraska
Nevada	
Carson City	Nevada
Elko	Nevada
Fallon	Nevada
Las Vegas	Nevada
Reno	Nevada
New Hampshire	
Portsmouth	New Hampshire
New Jersey	
Atlantic City	New Jersey
Central New Jersey	New Jersey
Jersey Coast	New Jersey
Jersey Shore	New Jersey
Lakehurst	New Jersey
Merchant Marine & USN Armed Guard	New Jersey
North Jersey	New Jersey
Trenton	New Jersey
Trenton Women	New Jersey
West Jersey	New Jersey
New Mexico	
New Mexico	New Mexico
New York	
Central New York	New York
Long Island	New York
New York	New York
Niagara Frontier	New York
Rochester	New York
Schenectady/Upper Hudson	New York

North Carolina	
Asheville	North Carolina
Charlotte	North Carolina
Coastal Carolina	North Carolina
Piedmont Triad	North Carolina
Triangle	North Carolina
Wilmington	North Carolina
North Dakota	
Dakota	North Dakota
Ohio	
Akron-Canton	Ohio
Cleveland	Ohio
Dayton	Ohio
Greater Cincinnati	Ohio
Greater Columbus	Ohio
Toledo-Erie Islands	Ohio
Western Reserve	Ohio
Oklahoma	
Oklahoma City	Oklahoma
Tulsa	Oklahoma
Oregon	
Blueback Submarine	Oregon
Coos Bay	Oregon
Oregon's Rogue Valley	Oregon
Portland	Oregon
Pennsylvania	
Altoona	Pennsylvania
Central Pennsylvania	Pennsylvania
Harrisburg	Pennsylvania
Philadelphia	Pennsylvania
Pittsburgh	Pennsylvania
Southeastern Pennsylvania	Pennsylvania
Puerto Rico	

Eastern Puerto Rico	Puerto Rico
San Juan	Puerto Rico
Vieques	Puerto Rico
Rhode Island	
Newport County	Rhode Island
South Carolina	
Beaufort	South Carolina
Charleston	South Carolina
Columbia	South Carolina
Hilton Head Island	South Carolina
Upper South Carolina	South Carolina
Tennessee	
Greater Chattanooga	Tennessee
Knoxville	Tennessee
Memphis	Tennessee
Nashville	Tennessee
Texas	
Alamo	Texas
Corpus Christi	Texas
Dallas	Texas
El Paso	Texas
Fort Worth	Texas
Greater Central Texas	Texas
Greater Houston	Texas
Ingleside Area	Texas
Kingsville	Texas
Utah	
Northern Utah	Utah
Provo	Utah
Salt Lake City	Utah
Vermont	
Green Mountain	Vermont
U.S. Virgin Islands	

Saint Croix	Virgin Islands
St. Thomas-St. John	Virgin Islands
Virginia	
Atlantic Shore	Virginia
Charlottesville	Virginia
Fredericksburg Area	Virginia
Hampton Roads	Virginia
Lynchburg	Virginia
Northern Virginia	Virginia
Richmond	Virginia
Roanoke	Virginia
Shenandoah Valley	Virginia
Williamsburg-Yorktown	Virginia
Washington	
Bellingham	Washington
Bremerton-Olympic Peninsula	Washington
Capitol	Washington
Columbia Basin	Washington
Everett	Washington
Gig Harbor	Washington
Lake Washington	Washington
Oak Harbor	Washington
Seattle	Washington
Spokane	Washington
Tacoma	Washington
Vancouver	Washington
Washington D.C.	
National Capital	Washington D.C.
West Virginia	
Huntington-Ashland	West Virginia
Kanawha	West Virginia
Wisconsin	
Fox Valley	Wisconsin
Madison	Wisconsin
Milwaukee	Wisconsin

Wyoming	
Wyoming	Wyoming
International Councils	**Country**
France	
French Riviera-Monaco	France
Provence	France
Italy	
Naples	Italy
Rome	Italy
Japan	
Commodore Perry	Japan
Sasebo	Japan
Korea	
Korea	Korea
Mexico	
Acapulco	Mexico
Lake Chapala	Mexico
Mexico City	Mexico
Mexico City Women	Mexico
Puerto Vallarta	Mexico
Netherlands Antilles	
St. Maarten	Netherlands Antilles
Panama	
Panama	Panama
Singapore	
Singapore	Singapore
Spain	
Andalucian	Spain
Barcelona	Spain
Levante	Spain

Madrid	Spain
Palma de Mallorca	Spain
Valencia	Spain
Thailand	
Thailand Eastern Seaboard	Thailand
United Kingdom	
United Kingdom	United Kingdom
Venezuela	
Caracus	Venezuela

E. Navy League Membership

Source: Navy League Membership Department

1903	166	1937	1,041	1971	47,305
1904	4,000	1938	2,519	1972	49,556
1905	3,747	1939	2,405	1973	45,840
1906	4,258	1940	1,300	1974	44,496
1907	4,769	1941	4,335	1975	45,872
1908	5,280	1942	6,944	1976	40,356
1909	5,791	1943	8,408	1977	38,878
1910	6,300	1944	14,515	1978	38,310
1911	6,640	1945	18,781	1979	39,899
1912	6,980	1946	16,834	1980	41,987
1913	7,520	1947	8,600	1981	43,409
1914	7,560	1948	8,168	1982	44,909
1915	8,000	1949	8,080	1983	49,678
1916	8,450	1950	7,670	1984	51,576
1917	8,900	1951	8,217	1985	53,477
1918	9,350	1952	9,341	1986	57,086
1919	9,800	1953	9,503	1987	62,726
1920	10,250	1954	10,593	1988	69,270
1921	10,700	1955	13,696	1989	73,510
1922	3,100	1956	17,190	1990	73,785
1923	3,891	1957	20,342	1991	73,136
1924	4,682	1958	24,027	1992	69,725
1925	5,473	1959	29,270	1993	67,787
1926	5,101	1960	29,666	1994	67,093
1927	4,824	1961	31,112	1995	71,300
1928	4,547	1962	33,476	1996	69,534
1929	4,221	1963	36,431	1997	69,931
1930	3,131	1964	38,722	1998	68,106
1931	2,640	1965	39,244	1999	69,036
1932	950	1966	39, 481	2000	74, 279
1933	859	1967	41,963	2001	77,720
1934	1,011	1968	42,345	2002	75,736
1935	2,811	1969	42, 421	2003	70, 451
1936	1,926	1970	43,942	2004	66,095

F. Navy League Awards

The League Awards Program, started on a modest scale in 1957, has become over the years one of the League's most important ways of publicly recognizing the men and women of the nation's armed forces and thanking them for their service to the nation. The Navy League Awards Program is administered by the National Awards Committee, currently chaired by former Secretary of the Navy J. William Middendorf, and assisted by the national headquarters staff. For certain awards, awardees are selected by a specially appointed awards committee or by responsible national committees other than the National Awards Committee.

Many awards are given on an annual basis and usually are presented at the Awards Luncheon at the League's National Convention. The League arranges, and pays for, hotel accommodations and meals for the awardees and their spouses, at the convention location. (Awardees, however, must pay for travel costs for their spouses). Awards are arranged in six broad categories: Navy and Marine Corps selections, Coast Guard selections, U.S.-flag Merchant Marine selections, Youth Awards, Other Awards (awardees from naval and national defense war colleges, etc.), and Special Awards.

The first five of what are termed *Professional Excellence Awards*, dating from the 1957 awards program founding, are presented to persons who have excelled in civilian leadership, inspirational Navy and/or Marine Corps leadership, scientific progress, literary achievement, and operational competence:

* The *Robert M. Thompson Award*, named for the "Father of the Navy League" is awarded to a civilian for outstanding leadership in contributing to the furthering of the importance of sea power through his or her efforts.

* The *John Paul Jones Award*, named for the indomitable sea fighter and "Father of the U.S. Navy," is awarded to a Navy officer who has made an outstanding contribution to the high standards of leadership traditional in the naval service.

* The *Rear Admiral William S. Parsons Award* is awarded to a Navy or Marine Corps officer, enlisted person, or civilian who has made an outstanding contribution in any field of science for the benefit of the Navy or Marine Corps.

* The *Alfred Thayer Mahan Award* is awarded for literary achievement to a Navy or Marine Corps officer, enlisted person or civilian, who has made a notable literary contribution concerning the importance of sea power in the United States.

* The *Stephen Decatur Award* is awarded to a Navy officer or enlisted

person who has made an outstanding personal contribution in the course of actual naval operations.

Most recipients of the *Professional Excellence Awards* are selected by a specially appointed board, usually chaired by a former Secretary of the Navy, and typically includes a former Chief of Naval Operations, Commandant of the Marine Corps (or another retired Marine Corps general officer), and the chairperson of the National Awards Committee of the Navy League.

The League has created a broad spectrum of other awards for outstanding achievement in various professional specialties or fields of expertise. As of 2005, in addition to the original five, *Professional Excellence Awards* presented to Navy and Marine Corps selections include:

* *The Captain Winifred Quick Collins Awards for Inspirational Leadership,* awarded to an officer and an enlisted woman whose exceptional leadership and performance have resulted in outstanding contributions.

* *The Lieutenant General John A. Lejeune Award for Inspirational Leadership,* awarded to a Marine Corps officer who has made an outstanding contribution to the high standards of leadership traditional in the naval service.

* *The Honorable J. William Middendorf II Award for Engineering Excellence,* awarded to a Navy or Marine Corps officer or enlisted person who has demonstrated outstanding leadership and professional competence while attached to a deployed ship of the operating fleet.

* *The Admiral Ben Moreell Awards for Logistics Competence,* awarded to one Navy or Marine Corps officer and one Navy or Marine Corps enlisted person who have made outstanding personal contributions that have advanced the logistics readiness and competence of the naval service.

* *The Admiral Claude V. Ricketts Awards for Inspirational Leadership,* awarded to two Navy enlisted persons (one pay grade E-7 or above; the other pay grade E-6 or below) who have demonstrated outstanding leadership and professional competence.

* *The General Gerald C. Thomas Award for Inspirational Leadership,* awarded to a Marine enlisted person who, by his or her performance of duty, has made an outstanding contribution to the high standards of leadership traditional in the naval service.

* *The General Holland M. Smith Award for Operational Competence,* awarded to a Marine officer or enlisted person who has made an

outstanding personal contribution that has advanced the readiness and competence of the naval service.

Professional Excellence Awards selected by a committee appointed by the commandant of the U.S. Coast Guard are:

* The *Captain David H. Jarvis Award for Inspirational Leadership*, awarded to a Coast Guard officer who has made an outstanding contribution to the high standards of leadership traditional in the Coast Guard service.

* The *Douglas A. Munro Award for Inspirational Leadership*, awarded to a Coast Guard enlisted man or woman who has demonstrated outstanding leadership and professional competence.

Professional Excellence Awards selected by the commander of the U.S. Military Sealift Command are:

* The *Able Seaman Oscar Chappell Award for Outstanding Maritime Stewardship*, awarded to an outstanding Military Sealift Command civil service unlicensed crewmember who displays selfless dedication to shipmates.

* The *Captain Arthur L. Johnson Award for Inspirational Leadership*, awarded to a Military Sealift Command civil service licensed officer in the deck or engine departments, or staff officer in the supply department, who has made significant and innovative contributions to the American maritime-defense team.

In addition, the Navy League has established eight Special Awards to recognize key individuals in leadership roles in either the military or industrial components of the national security establishment.

* The *Vincent T. Hirsch Maritime Award*, awarded to an individual in public or private life who contributed substantially to an increased public awareness of the vital role played by the privately owned American flag merchant fleet, both to the U.S. defense establishment and to the nation's economic well-being.

* The *Fleet Admiral Chester W. Nimitz Award*, awarded to that person who, or organization that, has made an exemplary contribution to the enhancement of the nation's naval/maritime strength and national security.

* The *Admiral Arleigh Burke Leadership Award*, awarded to an outstanding leader from government (civilian or military), industry, or academia whose life is in keeping with the example set by Admiral Burke.

* The *Admiral Vern E. Clark and General James L. Jones Safety Award*, awarded to individuals, teams, or organizations who best exemplify and advance a culture of safety through ideas and programs to reduce avoidable injuries and fatalities.

* The *Albert A. Michelson Award*, awarded to a civilian scientist, technology innovator, or technical organization from the Navy League's corporate membership or from academia, for scientific or technical achievement resulting in a significant improvement in the strength of the U.S. maritime forces or to the enhancement of America's industrial technology base.

* The *Vice Admiral Robert F. Batchelder Award*, awarded for operational competence to a Supply Corps officer who has made the most significant personal contributions to the supply readiness of the operating forces.

* The *Nicholas Brango Award for Inspirational Leadership*, awarded to the Naval Sea Cadet Corps officer who has excelled in all phases of Cadet Corps training and whose outstanding leadership has made a significant contribution toward attainment of Navy League goals in the training and education of American youth during the preceding year.

* The *Naval Intelligence Foundation Award*, awarded to an officer of the sea services in grades 04-06 who has demonstrated exceptional leadership in providing excellence in operational intelligence support to the fleet.

Other awards that can be bestowed include the *Meritorious Citation*, awarded to government employees, uniformed or civilian, "who have made significant contributions to the maintenance and improvement of the national security of the United States and to the strengthening of its maritime forces"; individuals, companies, or corporations making similar contributions to national programs of the League at the national level; and/or any member of the Navy League who has made significant contribution to national programs at the national level.

The *Scroll of Honor* is the second highest Navy League award on the national level and the highest award that can be bestowed at the region, area, and council levels. It may be awarded to government employees, uniformed or civilian, Navy League members, or companies or corporations "who have contributed in an outstanding manner to the furtherance of Navy League programs."

For League members only, the *Distinguished Service Award* can be awarded "for outstanding contributions to the Navy League." Recommendations for this award can be made by any council president or member of the Board of Directors. Neither the national president, chairperson of the national advisory council, national vice presidents, national judge advocate, national corporate secretary, and national treasurer, nor any member of the national headquarters staff is eligible for this award while in office.

In 1988 the Navy League Hall of Fame was established by the Board of Directors, recognizing Navy Leaguers who have been members for 25 years or more, have served in a volunteer capacity, and have made significant contributions to the organization on a national level. Nominations for selection to the Hall of Fame can be submitted only by the national president or past national president. Selection is made by the National Awards Committee and approved by the national Executive Committee.

The national president of the Navy League can bestow an *Annual President's Award* to "that member of the Navy League who has given the president the most support during the past year." A *National President's Medal* can also be presented, at the discretion of the national president, "for special recognition to foreign dignitaries who exemplify the highest ideals of the Navy League through their significant contributions to world peace, national security, and/or outstanding service to his country and/or his fellow citizens." Members of the Navy League or other U.S. citizens are not eligible for this award.

Youth awards sponsored by the Navy League recognizing achievements over a broad spectrum of accomplishments are presented to Naval Academy, Coast Guard Academy, Merchant Marine Academy, and Naval Reserve Officer Training Corps students for outstanding academic and/or leadership achievement.

Other awards are presented to outstanding graduates of the Naval War College, the National War College, the Industrial College of the Armed Forces, and the Marine Corps Command and Staff College.

Additional awards honor outstanding achievement within the Naval Air Training Command, the Naval Air Reserve, the Marine Corps Reserve, the Marine Corps Air Reserve, and the Coast Guard Reserve.

Outstanding Recruit Awards are presented on a weekly basis to the outstanding recruit at the Naval Training Command, Great Lakes, Illinois; Coast Guard Training Center, Cape May, New Jersey; and Marine Corps Recruit Depots in San Diego, California, and Parris Island, South Carolina.

Many Navy League councils sponsor their own awards programs honoring, for example, the "Sailor of the Year" of a ship adopted by a council, or Marine Recruiter of the Year in the area, or Coast Guardsman of the Year assigned to a local Coast Guard facility or ship. Notable among the councils participating in these local awards programs is the Navy League's overseas Madrid, Spain, Council. Starting in 1983, each year the Madrid Council has awarded the Spanish Naval

Academy's top graduating cadet with a ceremonial sword and a trip to the United States. Upon arrival in America, the Spanish cadet is hosted by members of the Annapolis, Maryland, and Hampton Roads, Virginia, Councils; during the seven days, the awardee will visit both the Naval Academy at Annapolis and the world's largest naval base in Norfolk, Virginia.

Youth Program Awards established by the League include a *Youth Medal* awarded annually in recognition of the outstanding Sea Cadet and/or Naval Junior Reserve Officer Training Corps or Marine Corps Junior Reserve Officer Training Corps cadet in a unit or school sponsored by a Navy League council or other organization. Naval Sea Cadet headquarters defines the awards criteria for selection of Sea Cadets; Junior Reserve Officer Training Corps awards criteria are determined by the sponsoring council and unit leader, and are required to be sufficiently flexible to avoid duplication of any other available awards.

The eligibility and selection criteria for all awards are detailed in the Navy League's Operations Manual and on the Navy League website, *www.navyleague.org*

The Naval Sea Cadet Corps has established its own set of annual awards for the Sea Cadet and Navy League Cadet programs to recognize outstanding adults, units, and individual Sea Cadets. As delineated in the *2004 Annual Report*, there are eight major national awards bestowed on individuals and five on Sea Cadet units:

* *The Nicholas Brango Award, Officer of the Year* is given to an individual Sea Cadet officer for inspirational leadership.
* *The Judge R.T.S. Colby Award, Naval Sea Cadet Corps Instructor of the Year*, is awarded to a Sea Cadet instructor for inspirational service, dedication and devotion to duty.
* *The Willis E. Reed Award, Naval Sea Cadet of the Year*, is awarded to a Sea Cadet for excellence and achievement in all phases of the Naval Sea Cadet Corps training and academic achievement in high school studies.
* *The Keith T. Weaver Award, Navy League Cadet of the Year*, is awarded to a League Cadet for excellence and achievement in all phases of the Navy League Cadet Corps training and in academic achievements.
* *The Naval Sea Cadet Corps Hall of Fame Award* is awarded to a founder or volunteer who provided noteworthy national leadership and service for 15 years or more.
* *The Fred D. Carl Regional Director of Year Award* is awarded for superior performance as a Regional Director.
* *The Bruce B. Smith Regional Director of the Year Award* is awarded for superior recruiting and growth.
* *The Chairman's Medal* is awarded for sustained superior performance while serving in senior leadership roles in support of the Naval Sea Cadet Corps national program. This award can be given to multiple individuals.

* *The John J. Bergen Trophy* recognizes the most outstanding Naval Sea Cadet Corps unit in the nation.
* *The Morgan L. Fitch Trophy* recognizes the most outstanding Navy League Cadet Corps training ship in the nation.
* *The George S. Halas Trophy* is awarded to the outstanding combined Naval Sea Cadet Corps unit/Navy League Cadet Corps training ship in the nation.
* *The Navy League of Canada Challenge Trophy* is awarded to the most improved Naval Sea Cadet Corps unit in the nation.
* *The Anthony H. Murray, Sr., Seaman Award* is awarded to the Naval Sea Cadet Corps unit achieving the most advancements.

G. Navy League Foundation and Scholarships

Another significant aspect of the Navy League's awards programs involves awarding of academic scholarships. The Navy League Scholarship Program was formally established in 1989 under the initial leadership of Ernest G. Campbell. Complementing similar programs maintained by some League councils, the program is intended to provide financial assistance and personal guidance to as many eligible high school seniors and college students as resources permit. There is a special emphasis on increasing students' interest in science and engineering disciplines.

The Scholarship Program has become a fundamental element of the Navy League Foundation. High school seniors entering their freshman year of college are eligible to apply for one of 22 awards bestowed to assist in meeting tuition and academic expenses; amounts awarded are $2,500 ranging from one- to four-year grants. Each of the Navy League Foundation's scholarships is endowed through a named award. With contributions from individuals, foundations, corporations, and individual League members, the League was able to award more than $47,000 in scholarship money in 2004.

Recipients of scholarships are determined by the Scholarship Committee, and, besides financial needs, selection is based on academic records, achievements in leadership, character, and all-around ability. Commenting on the significance of the Navy League Scholarship Program and the Navy League Foundation, Jewell H. Bonner, chairwoman of the Scholarship Committee in 2004, observed in the August 2004 issue of *Seapower*:

> The scholarship program is such a rewarding way to honor our commitment to look after our sailors, Marines, mariners, Coast Guardsmen and their families. These service members have sacrificed so much in defense of our country, and the Navy League is pleased to help ease the financial burden of college for their outstanding sons and daughters.

The eligibility and selection criteria for all scholarships are detailed in the Navy League's Operations Manual and on the Navy League website, *www.navyleague.org*

Similar to the Navy League itself, there is a Naval Sea Cadet Corps Scholarship program, available to deserving Cadets who wish to further their education at the college level. As stated in the *U.S. Naval Sea Cadet Corps 2004 Annual Report*, since inception of the scholarship program in 1975, 188 scholarships have been awarded to 178 cadets, aggregating more than $208,000.

In 2004 a Naval Sea Cadet Corps Foundation was established to accept gifts provided from other foundations, memorials, individuals, and corporate contributors to benefit its youth programs.

NOTES
Chapter I

1. Internal Revenue Code Section 501(c)(3) considers tax exempt public charities or private foundations established for purposes that are religious, educational, charitable, scientific, literary, testing for public safety, fostering of national or international amateur sports, or prevention of cruelty to animals and children. Section 501(c)(3) organizations are proscribed from participating in political campaigns for or against persons running for public office and substantial engagement in legislative political activities.

In 1973 the Internal Revenue investigated the Navy League to determine its continued eligibility for Section 503(c)(3) status. The organization's Sea Cadet and other youth programs and its scholarship programs were substantial enough to satisfy the IRS's criteria for an "educational" non-profit corporation.

Navy League of the United States, *Maritime Policy 2005*. (Arlington, Virginia, 2005), 8. In the 13-page document, this is the only use of both italics and underlining to express the League's concern. The League's support and advocacy of Coast Guard issues was particularly noticeable in the years following the terrorist attacks of September 2001, as homeland defense and maritime domain awareness of the sea approaches to the United States became issues of national security.

The League's current *Operations Manual* specifies that the Executive Committee shall consist of "members of the Steering Committee, all past presidents who are willing and elect to serve, all region presidents, and 10 national directors appointed by the national president with the approval of the Board of Directors." The Executive Committee exercises the powers of the Board of Directors when it is not in session.

The Board of Directors is the highest governing body in the organization, and is charged with the "control and management of the property and affairs of the Navy League." The Board consists of "not less than 23 and not more than 210 national directors ... elected for a term of one year or until their successors are elected and qualified." In 2005, there are 253 national directors. Directors are nominated by members of the Nominating Committee, themselves "knowledgeable Navy Leaguers and, insofar as is feasible, geographically distributed and representative of various levels of the Navy League."

The ability of the Steering Committee to handle day-to-day operations rests in the fact that it "can exercise all the powers of the Executive Committee" (when neither the Executive Committee nor Board of Directors is in session), "provided that action by the Steering Committee shall require approval of two-thirds of all members of the Steering Committee, consultation with the chairperson of any affected committee, and affirmative opinion of the judge advocate that any such action is

not contrary to the bylaws. Meetings of the Steering Committee may be conducted by telephone conference call but not by individual polling." Navy League of the United States, *Operations Manual*, 5th ed. with chg 1. (Arlington, Virginia: 2004): 6, 12-13.
4. Calvin H. Cobb Jr., interview with John D. Stegman. November 2002.
5. John J. Spittler, interview with John D. Stegman. November 2002.
6. National committees for 2005-2006 were the following: Awards, Budget/Audit, Bylaws, Coast Guard Affairs, Communications, Corporate Affairs, Corporate Affairs Advisory Board, Development, Information Technology for Council Initiatives, Investment, Legislative Affairs, Legislative Affairs Advisory Board, Marine Corps Affairs, Maritime Policy and Resolutions, Membership and Marketing, Merchant Marine/Maritime Industry Affairs, National Meetings, Navy Affairs, Property Development, Public Education, Public Relations, Scholarship, Strategic Planning, Youth Programs. The Youth Programs Committee was composed of three subcommittees: Naval Sea and League Cadets, Naval Junior Reserve Officer Training Corps, and Youth.
7. Peter Atkinson, "Steering Committee Members Guide Navy League's Strategies, Priorities," *Seapower,* September 2005, 63.
8. Cobb, "Change and Continuity," *Sea Power,* June 1991, 8.
9. Patricia L. Howard, "Cincinnati Council Honors World War II Submarine Heroes," *Sea Power,* February 1993, 52.
10. Peter Atkinson, "Reagan Visit to Santa Barbara Demonstrates Power of Partnerships," *Seapower,* November 2005, 49.
11. Peter Atkinson, "Hampton Roads Council Showcases 'Admiral's Quarters' At 'Homearama,'" *Seapower/Navy League News* (December 2004).
12. Gerald Havens, e-mail message to Sasebo Navy League Council Members and Friends of the Navy League, October 16, 2005.
13. Doyle Hodges, e-mail message to Sasebo Navy League Council, October 16, 2005.
14. Sheila McNeill, e-mail message to Richard L. Wright, October 17, 2005.
15. Sheila McNeill, Public Address, Camden Kiwanis Club/ Rotary /Daughters of the American Revolution, Camden, Georgia, August 15, 2005.
16. Deborah Cozzone, e-mail to Sheila McNeill, November 1, 2005.
17. Personal experiences of author as Commander, Destroyer Squadron 28 and Sea Combat Commander, *Operation Allied Force*, March-July 1999. In 2005 Ms. Cozzone is President of the Northern Europe Area and a National Director of the Navy League.
18. William Thompson, "The Navy League of the United States — A Status of Forces." Research Paper. United States Naval War College, 1964, 31.
19. United States Naval Sea Cadet Corps, *U.S. Naval Sea Cadet Corps 2004 Annual*

Report. (Arlington, Virginia, 2005): 1.
20. Peter Atkinson, "Council Assistance is Critical for Cadet Corps Programs," *Seapower*, October 2005, 55.
21. United States Naval Sea Cadet Corps, 1.
22. "High Praise from MCPON for Sea Cadets," *Sea Power*, October 1991, 54.
23. Ibid. In the late 1960s/early 1970s, Sea Cadets reporting to the Naval Academy in Annapolis, Maryland, for admission in the beginning of the summer were immediately identified by upperclassmen for "special" treatment. Because of their initial personal appearance, knowledge of military/naval terminology and protocols, and the manual of arms, Sea Cadets, as "Plebe" midshipmen, were often given squad leader duties and other special responsibilities within hours of passing through the Naval Academy's main gate to begin the major passage in their lives to becoming officers in the United States Navy and Marine Corps.
24. "The Navy League: Programs, Activities, Leadership, and Organization," *The Almanac of Seapower, 1997*: 302. Leestma, as a Naval Academy senior in 1st Company in 1969, made it a personal matter to seek out former Sea Cadets, now "Plebes," and grant them permission to escape the normal "rituals" observed when eating meals on weekends in the mess hall.
25. United States Naval Sea Cadet Corps, 14.
26. Ibid., 8.
27. Ibid., 10.
28. Members of the International Sea Cadet Association in 2005 include the Royal Sea Cadet Corps Belgium, Bermuda Sea Cadet Corps, The Navy League of Canada, Deutsche Marine Jugend e.V. (Sea Cadet Corps of Germany), Junior Sea Friends' Federation of Japan, Zeekadetkorps Nederland (Sea Cadet Corps of the Netherlands), South African Sea Cadet Corps, Sjovarnskarernas Riksforbund (Swedish Sea Cadet Corps Association), Sea Cadet Corps of the United Kingdom, United States Naval Sea Cadet Corps, Australian Naval Reserve Cadets, Hong Kong Sea Cadet Corps, Sea Cadet Corps of India, Sea Explorers of Korea, Sea Cadet Association of New Zealand, Zimbabwe Sea Cadet Corps, Young Mariners League of Russia, and the Singapore National Cadet Corps (Sea). International Sea Cadets Association, *www.isca-seacadets.org*
29. John Keegan, *A History of Warfare* (New York: Vintage Books, 1994), 313, quoted in Deepak Lal, *In Praise of Empires, Globalization and Order* (New York: Palgrave Macmillan, 2004), 30.

Chapter II

1. Loretta Britten and Paul Mathless, eds., *Our American Century, Dawn of the Century 1900-1910* (Alexandria, Virginia: Bishop Books, Inc., 1998), 23.

2. John F. Lehman Jr., *On Seas of Glory, Heroic Men, Great Ships, and Epic Battles of the American Navy* (New York: The Free Press, 2001), 207.
3. Edmund Morris, *The Rise of Theodore Roosevelt* (New York: Coward, McCann & Geoghegan, Inc., 1979), 612. Five members of the extended Roosevelt family served as Assistant Secretary of the Navy: Theodore Roosevelt, 1897-1898, Franklin Delano Roosevelt, 1913-1920, Theodore Roosevelt, Jr., 1921-1924, Theodore Douglas Robinson (son of Corinne Roosevelt, Theodore Roosevelt's sister), 1924-1929, and Henry Latrobe Roosevelt, 1933-1936.
4. Another eager reader of Mahan was 15-year-old Franklin Delano Roosevelt. Given a copy of *The Influence of Sea Power, Upon History* for Christmas 1897, Roosevelt quickly read it cover to cover and quoted from it extensively when he returned to Groton School in 1898.
5. Of the influence of Mahan's seminal work, Warren Zimmerman writes, it was "unprecedented for the audacity of its scope and for the brilliance of its application of history to modern naval strategy. Even more important, it was a masterpiece of popularization and propaganda ... More than anybody else, Mahan now set the terms of the debate about the naval contribution to America's expansion." Zimmerman, *First Great Triumph, How Five Americans Made Their Country a World Power* (New York: Farrar, Straus and Giroux, 2002), 101.
6. Morris, *Theodore Rex* (New York: Random House, 2001), 180
7. Lehman, *On Seas of Glory, Heroic Men, Great Ships, and Epic Battles of the American Navy*, 211.
8. The Naval Order of the United States was founded in 1890 by descendants of New England seafarers who fought in the Revolutionary War. Originally termed the "Naval Commandery of the United States of America," in 1893 it entered into a provisional consolidation with the Naval Legion of the United States. The merger led to renaming the organization the Naval Order of the United States. As delineated in H.R. 5995, a bill to incorporate the Naval Order of the United States, submitted in the U.S. House of Representatives on February 26, 1894, "the particular business of said society is to encourage research and publication of data pertaining to naval art and science and the collection and preservation of documents, books, and relics relating to the Navy and its heroes at all times; also, as many of the principal battles and famous victories of the several wars in which the United States has been engaged were fought and achieved by the naval forces, to cultivate the spirit of patriotism, to honor and respect the illustrious deeds of the great naval commanders, and their companion officers in arms and their subordinates, and to transmit to posterity their glorious names and memories." See *http: //www. navalorder.org*
9. Armin Rappaport, *The Navy League of the United States* (Detroit: Wayne State University Press, 1962), 3. Dr. Rappaport 1916-1983, was author or editor of several books examining American diplomatic history and was founding editor of the

quarterly *Diplomatic History*. At the time of his authorship of the Navy League's history, he was associate professor of history at the University of California, Berkeley. A graduate of the University of Virginia, he earned a Master of Arts degree from Yale University, and received his doctorate at Stanford University. In addition to *The Navy League of the United States*, Rappaport wrote an unpublished manuscript that updated the League's story: *"The Decade of the Diamond Jubilee: 1953-1962."*

10. Morgan Fitch, national president 1965-1967, a lawyer by training, and an individual who has devoted more than a half century to League and Naval Sea Cadet matters, has noted that, 103 years after its founding, the Navy League of the United States remains a New York Corporation, "to be governed by a Board of Directors numbering some 250, which is responsible for the destiny of the Navy League." Morgan Fitch, e-mail message to Richard L. Wright, July 26, 2005.

11. Ronald Spector, "The Triumph of Professional Ideology: The U.S. Navy in the 1890s" *In Peace and War, Interpretations of American Naval History*, 1775-1984, 2nd ed., Kenneth J. Hagan, (Westport, Connecticut: Greenwood Press, 1984), 174-175.

12. Rappaport, 4.

13. William C. Kelley Jr., "A personal note to my fellow members of the Navy League," *The Almanac of Seapower, 1992*, 297.

14. Rappaport, 6.

15. Ibid., 6.

16. Ibid., 2.

17. Theodore Roosevelt was as good as his word. In her review of his presidency, Patricia O'Toole notes that "despite the bellicosity of his rhetoric" Roosevelt used his military buildup "in the interest of defense, not aggression. He received the Nobel Peace Prize for his work ending the war between Russia and Japan, he was the first head of state in the world to send a dispute to The Hague for arbitration, and not a shot was fired at a foreign enemy during his seven and one-half years in office." Patricia O'Toole, *When Trumpets Call, Theodore Roosevelt after The White House*. (New York: Simon and Schuster, 2005), 31-32. Marine Corps Assistant Commandant General Robert Magnus, speaking at the opening of the new Navy League headquarters building November 28, 2005, noted that Roosevelt was successful in negotiating the Treaty of Portsmouth with both antagonists because Japan and Russia "understood the power of the U.S. fleet ... and that the leadership of the United States knew how to broker power." Robert Magnus, (public address, Navy League of the United States 2300 Wilson Boulevard Building Opening Ceremony, November 28, 2005).

18. Henry J. Hendrix, II, "An Unlikely Location," *Naval History* August 2005, 37. More than a century after Roosevelt brokered the Treaty of Portsmouth that ended the Russo-Japanese War, Chief of Naval Operations Admiral Michael Mullen, in a

September 2001 speech before the 17th International Seapower Symposium in Newport, Rhode Island, cited both Roosevelt's advocacy of a strong Navy and strenuous diplomacy to achieve peace as examples of "naval engagement" still applicable in the 21st century.

19. Ibid., 11.

20. Morris, *Theodore Rex*, 455.

21. Although a Civil War veteran of considerable repute and seniority, Porter's principal claim to fame was his finding of the 113-year-old unmarked grave of John Paul Jones, America's first naval hero, in a destitute cemetery in Paris in 1905. (America's "first" sea captain had died there in 1792.) As U.S. ambassador to France, Porter had Jones's remains exhumed and returned with a formal naval escort to the United States. The hero's remains were brought to Annapolis, Maryland, where the crypt was placed beneath the chapel of the U.S. Naval Academy. In July 2005, celebrating the centennial of Jones's return to America, his crypt was rededicated following a $1,000,000 restoration funded by the Naval Academy Class of '55.

22. Morris, *Theodore Rex*, 501. Roosevelt's motives for dispatching the Great White Fleet were complex, and intimately linked with domestic California politics as well as concerns over Japanese designs in the Pacific, where America now had colonial interests in the Philippines, Guam, and several lesser island possessions. As early as July 1907, Admiral Dewey had recommended that "the battle fleet should be assembled and dispatched for the Orient as soon as practicable." Biographer Morris notes, however, the concept also appealed to the showman side of TR: "He had just 17 months left in office, and wanted to make a grand gesture of will, something that would loom as large historically in his second term as the Panama Canal coup had in his first. What could be grander, more inspirational to the Navy, and to all Americans, than sending 16 great white ships halfway around the world — maybe even farther?" Ibid., 493-494.

Roosevelt's ploy for recognition and publicity for his new Navy worked. "It had become a diplomatic phenomenon, attracting worldwide press attention." In February 1908 the President announced that the Great White Fleet's itinerary would expand to include Hawaii, New Zealand, Australia, the Philippines, Japan, China, Ceylon, the Suez Canal, Egypt, and Gibraltar. It would return to Hampton Roads February 22, 1909, 10 days before his presidency was concluded. Ibid., 509-510. While admonishing Congress that he would "tolerate no control by any individual senator or congressman of the movements of the fleet" this stricture did not apply to the President himself. Upon receipt of a letter from a Civil War veteran serving as a lay missionary to a leper settlement on the Hawaiian island of Molokai expressing hope that his patients might one day receive a visit from a Navy ship, Roosevelt dispatched orders from the White House to Rear Admiral Charles Sperry,

embarked in the battleship USS *Connecticut:* "Divert from course. Pass Molokai Island in battle formation. Show naval power ... Dip colors. Then continue Japan." See Michael F. Fitzpatrick, letter, *Naval History*, August 1005, 10.
23. Rappaport, *The Navy League of the United States*, 13.
24. Ibid., 14.
25. Morris, *Theodore Rex*, 549.
26. Rappaport, *The Navy League of the United States*, 19. The author adds, tellingly given the state of the Navy League at this time, "This exhortation was not so much a call to action as a plea to maintain the League's newly found animation, for it was apparent to all that, at last, the society had bestirred itself."
27. Ibid., 20.
28. Ibid., 21.
29. Andrew Carnegie, opposed to the Navy League and all such preparedness associations, was growing increasingly concerned that the arms race between Great Britain and Germany might lead to war. He had already spent $25 million of his own money toward establishing the world court at The Hague when he courted Theodore Roosevelt by partially funding the latter's post-Presidential African safari. Carnegie hoped the former President, on returning to America in 1910 via the capitals and crowned heads of Europe, would promote the cause of peace by advocating in public speeches and private meetings arbitration and disarmament, not the further building of fleets and armies. Patricia O'Toole, *When Trumpets Call, Theodore Roosevelt After The White House* (New York: Simon & Schuster, 2005), 54.

Chapter III

1. "Navy League to Meet," *New York Times*, January 7, 1912, E2.
2. Rappaport, *The Navy League of the United States*, 32.
3. Ibid., 40.
4. Ted Morgan, FDR, *A Biography* (New York: Simon and Schuster, 1985), 33. Personally, Wilson's thoughts regarding Germany were not quite so neutral. In his personal papers (see Seymour, I, 293), Colonel Edward M. House, the President's confidant and principal representative seeking to negotiate a peace amongst the warring European nations, wrote that the President "recognized that if Germany won, it would change the course of civilization and make the United States a military nation."
5. Ibid., 33. The relationship between Roosevelt and his administrative superior in the Department of the Navy, Josephus Daniels, are covered in detail by both Morgan in his biography of FDR and Lehman in *On Seas of Glory*. In summary, while Roosevelt was viewed by many (particularly the President) as disloyal to the Wilson Administration on matters affecting the Navy, and Daniels on more than

one occasion thought of firing him in the end they departed on amicable terms of mutual admiration and respect. When FDR became President he appointed Daniels ambassador to Mexico, and always called him "Chief" when their paths crossed during his White House years.

6. Thompson lived in the home from 1915 until 1921. Designed by the architecture firm of Carrere and Hastings, who also designed the Manhattan Bridge in New York City (1905), the Carnegie Institute, the Cannon House Office Building in Washington, D.C., and the Memorial Ampitheater in Arlington Cemetery, the mansion was sold to Prince Antoine Bibesco, Minister of the Legation of the Romanian Government, in 1921. Renowned for the sophisticated diplomatic receptions given within its walls, its status declined with the onset of the Cold War in 1947. In 1989, with the dissolution of the Soviet empire, relations between Romania and the United States improved dramatically, and today the Washington home of the Navy League's third National President, still located in the distinctive neighborhood of Sheridan-Kalorama, functions as the Embassy of Romania.

7. Rappaport, *The Navy League of the United States*, 53.

8. Ibid.

9. Ibid., 55.

10. Ibid., 59.

11. Ibid., 66.

12. The fear of an attack on the United States was not confined to the uninformed general public. Franklin Roosevelt was sufficiently concerned to write wife Eleanor that "if by any perfectly wild chance a German submarine" should begin to shell Eastport, Maine (near their summer home), "I want you to grab the children and beat it into the woods." Meirion and Susie Herries, *The Last Days of Innocence, America at War, 1917-1918*, 82.

13. The Coast Guard, while receiving feature treatment in several issues of *Sea Power,*, was not considered to be a sea service extensively involved in national defense, a conclusion that would change over the ensuing decades.

14. An original copy of *The U.S. Navy League* sheet music, personally inscribed by Alberta Johnston Denis, was found on e-bay in November 2005 by a Navy League staffer at national headquarters. This relatively unknown composer would subsequently author three books, *Questionings* (1920), *Spanish Alta California* (1927), and *Houseboating in Kashmir* (1934). The lyrics accurately captured the sentiments of the League, and American society at large, during the war years:

Don't parcel out your patriot's work for other folks to do,
Just do your little bit yourself — Begin and put it through.
By choice or by election, Join a 'Self-supporting Section'
And sing a 'Hallelujah!' With the U.S. Navy League.

With your pocketbook o'erflowing, And your larder good and full,
Just do without a dainty, And buy a hank o'wool,
After careful introspection Join a 'Self-supporting Section'
And sing a 'Hallelujah!' With the U.S. Navy League.

Suppose you can't give quite so much, Or something big and grand.
Just weave a little of yourself with every stitch and strand:
Things none can see, perhaps a sigh; A loving thought, a pray'r,
And send it to some sailor lad: It's more than jewel rare.

By choice or by election, Join a 'Self-supporting Section'
And sing a Hallelujah!' With the U.S. Navy League.

15. Rappaport, *The Navy League of the United States*, 78.
16. "Daniels Attacks Navy League Heads," *New York Times*, August 15, 1917, 3.
17. *New York Times*, August 15, 1917, 3.
18. Ibid.
19. "Navy League's 1918 Plans, " *New York Times*, January 3, 1918, 7.
20. "Thompson Resigns Navy League Office," *Washington Post*, 8.
21. Rappaport, *The Navy League of the United States*, 74.

Chapter IV

1. Margaret MacMillan, Paris 1919, *Six Months That Changed the World*. (New York: Random House, 2001), 178.
2. Rappaport, *The Navy League of the United States*, 76.
3. Kelley made similar contributions over the next several years, and Thompson also helped ease the continuing financial challenges the League faced. The exact amount of the latter's donations are not shown in the League's budget records for that era, but Thompson later established a $67,000 League trust fund, the interest from which is still used to help defray the League's operating expenses.
4. Rappaport, *The Navy League of the United States*, 81. The author notes that senior leadership, particularly National President Henry Breckenridge and financial contributors Thompson and Kelley, believed by the summer of 1921 that there was no alternative but to dissolve the Navy League.
5. Arthur Krock, "In the March of History," review of *A Front Row Seat*, by Nicholas Roosevelt, *New York Times*, September 6, 1953: B26.
6. James F. Cook, *Carl Vinson, Patriarch of the Armed Forces* (Macon, Georgia: Mercer University Press, 2004), 49-51. At the age of 30, Carl Vinson became a member of the House of Representatives in November 1914, the youngest congressman in U.S. history to date. By 1923, due to eight other Democrats on the House Naval Affairs

Committee being defeated, resigning, or dying, Vinson, at age 40, was the ranking party member. Vinson served in the House of Representatives for 26 consecutive terms, spanning the terms of nine U.S. Presidents from Woodrow Wilson to Lyndon Johnson. An unequivocal supporter of national defense and the U.S. Navy (his oft-voiced watchword was "The paramount duty of government is self-preservation"), Vinson rightly earned the title "Father of the Two Ocean Navy" in his partnership with Franklin Roosevelt throughout the 1930s and World War II. After the war, the House Naval Affairs Committee was merged with the Military Affairs Committee to become the House Armed Services Committee. Possessing, as did Franklin Roosevelt, an ability to be domineering without offending, Vinson became the new committee's first chair, and held that leadership position until his retirement from Congress in 1965. Biographer Cook notes that Vinson's response to those who questioned his choice to remain in the House of Representatives, rather than run for the Senate or become Secretary of the Navy, was "I'd rather run the Navy from here." The Navy named a Nimitz-class nuclear-powered aircraft carrier for him, the USS *Carl Vinson*; he became the first living American to have a U.S. Navy ship named after him. In March 1980, at age 96, he attended the ship's dedication ceremony; he died in June 1981. Former Georgia Senator Sam Nunn notes in the introduction to Cook's biography, "Carl Vinson's story is, in large part, the story of America's national security in the 20th century."

7. Rappaport, *The Navy League of the United States*, 81.

8. Ibid., 93.

9. Navy Day continues to be celebrated more than eight decades after it was first recognized in 1922. The original date of October 27 had been proposed by the Navy League for two reasons: It was Theodore Roosevelt's birthday and the Continental Congress had taken its first action to build a Navy on that date. However, subsequent research determined that on October 13, 1775, Congress first voted funds for two vessels "of ten carriage guns ... for a cruise of three months" against British supply ships. In 1972 the calendar date for observance was changed to October 13 to coincide with the historically determined date of the Navy's "founding." Navy League National President Thomas Morris discussed this with the Board of Directors at its semi-annual meeting in San Juan, Puerto Rico, in 1971, observing that "while he regretted the abandonment of the tradition" he felt it important that the League conform to the Navy Department's determination of October 13 as the birthday of the service. ("Navy Day Date is Changed," *Sea Power*, January 1972, 3)

10. United States Department of Defense. DefenseLINK: Armed Forces Day History, *http://www.defenselink.mil/afd/military/navy.html*> (April 16, 2004)

11. "Coolidge Endorses Navy Day, October 27; Commends Choice of Roosevelt Birthday," *New York Times*, September 10, 1923, 1.

12. "Navy Day and Roosevelt Day," *New York Times*, October 27, 1923, 12.
13. William M. Galvin, "How the Navy League Stands," *Washington Post*, January 15, 1925, 6.
14. Ibid., 6.
15. Rappaport, *The Navy League of the United States*, 105.
16. Douglas Waller, *A Question of Loyalty, Gen. Billy Mitchell and the Court-Martial That Gripped the Nation* (New York: HarperCollins Publishers Inc., 2004), 144-145.
17. Geoffrey Till, "Adopting the Aircraft Carrier, The British, American, and Japanese case studies," Williamson Murray and Allan R. Millett, eds. *Military Innovation in the Interwar Period*, 209-211. As will be seen, two decades later the Navy League would again fervently support naval aviation, in both public statements and congressional testimony, when its continued existence was threatened in another "time between the wars," this time bracketed by World War II and the Korean War.
18. Rappaport, *The Navy League of the United States*, 112.
19. Ibid., 121.
20. Ibid., 133.
21. Ibid., 144.
22. Ibid., 145.
23. "Navy League Should Act," *Washington Post*, November 2, 1931, 6. In fairness to Herbert Hoover, while enacting substantial cuts in shipbuilding and force structure, his firm and continued support of naval aviation throughout his tortured presidency should be acknowledged. On two separate occasions, he overrode recommendations from Chiefs of Naval Operations that Rear Admiral Moffett be retired. Hoover, an engineer long before becoming a politician, was appreciative of both the pioneer naval aviator's technical acumen in developing this nascent combat capability and his skilled advocacy of the service, and naval aviation in particular, on Capitol Hill.
24. Ibid. The majority of the nation's newspapers supported the Hoover Administration rather than the Navy League position. Rappaport notes, "There seemed to be an uneasy feeling among certain newspapers, hitherto stout League champions, that in assailing the President personally the society was challenging civilian control of military policy." (Ibid., 148).
25. Ibid., 146.
26. "Gridiron Club Runs Gamut of News; Hoover Sees Himself Defeat the Navy League in Skit Built on 'Pinafore,'" *New York Times*, December 13, 1931, N1. Other than creating the committee to investigate the League's allegations, Hoover never formally replied to his critics; he did not demand an apology from National President Gardiner. Of note, the dust jacket for Rappaport's 1962 book *The Navy League of the United States* contains on its back cover a reproduction of the *Louisville*

(Kentucky) Times cartoon of two sailors facing off, one named "Hoover" and the other "Navy League," with the caption "Sez You!"—"Sez I!"
27. "Sees Navy League Backed By Cupidity," *New York Times*, January 25, 1932, 15.
28. Ibid. Beard's book was not the only book of the era to be highly critical of the Navy League. National President Calvin Cobb, 1989-1991, in his overview of the Navy League written in 1991 for *Shipmate*, the magazine of the Naval Academy Alumni Association, would cite two additional books, *Iron, Blood, and Profits* by Gilbert Seldes, and *Merchants of Death* by H.C. Engelbrecht, as containing "stinging criticism of the Navy League" and alleging "an unholy alliance between the League and industry." (Calvin H. Cobb Jr., "To Enlighten the People on Naval Matters," *Shipmate,* April 1991, 16. Reprinted in *Sea Power,* May 1991. Citation is from *Sea Power* adaptation.)
29. Rappaport, *The Navy League of the United States*, 146. The aforementioned (Note 26) cartoon on the dust jacket of Rappaport's book has beneath it a "teaser" for the book that reads in part, "Perhaps the most significant contribution made by the League to American naval policy was in keeping alive the spark of navalism during the lean years of the twenties and early thirties."
30. Eric Larrabee, *Commander in Chief, Franklin Delano Roosevelt, His Lieutenants, and Their War* (New York: Harper & Row, Publishers, 1987), 24.
31. Robert H. Jackson, *That Man, An Insider's Portrait of Franklin D. Roosevelt* (New York: Oxford University Press, 2003; Oxford University Press, 2004, edited and introduced by John Q. Barrett with Foreword by William E. Leuchtenburg), 167-168. Citations are from 2004 edition.
32. "Reserve Fleet Plans Assailed by Navy League," *Chicago Daily Tribune*, May 10, 1933, 16.
33. Ibid.
34. Rappaport, *The Navy League of the United States*, 158.
35. Historical Documents and Speeches–National Industrial Recovery Act (1933), *http://www.historicaldocuments.com/National IndustrialRecoveryAct.htm*
36. Ernest J. King quoted in Rappaport, *The Navy League of the United States*, 158.
37. "Navy League Calls Fleet 'Third Rate,'" *New York Times,* April 28, 1934, 2. "Third rate" it may have been when the League made the accusation, but together the 1933 and 1934 acts began reviving the entire U.S. shipbuilding industry, and, most importantly in view of subsequent events, in enough time to have major impact before war broke out in Europe five years later. The President's signature on these bills, and the subsequent "Two-Ocean Navy" 1938 Vinson-Trammell Act essentially authorized for construction the fleet that won World War II.

Between 1934 and Hitler's invasion of Poland September 1, 1939, the Navy built 69 major combatants and submarines and 37 smaller craft. Subsequent shipbuilding acts and appropriations would only replace combat losses with ships that would arrive too late to affect the prosecution of the war. Using the authority granted the Department of the Navy under both Vinson-Trammell Acts, the Navy adopted a 10-year shipbuilding and expansion program that would produce 14 battleships, five aircraft carriers, 27 cruisers, 78 destroyers and 49 submarines through 1948. See Joel R. Davidson, *The Unsinkable Fleet, The Politics of U.S. Navy Expansion in World War II* (Annapolis, Maryland: Naval Institute Press, 1996), 10-11.

Reviewing the restoration of the Navy under the third Roosevelt Administration and with the initiative and support of Carl Vinson, former League National President Nelson Macy would write in a 1941 issue of *Sea Power*: "Congress at last awoke to the fact that possibly someday there might be another war, and shipbuilding was started again." Quoted in David Vergun's, "Sea Power Resurfaces After 14 Years in the Depths," *Sea Power*, May 2003, 61-62.

38. John R. Stobo, "Brooklyn Navy Yard in the Inter-War Era, The New Deal Yard, 1033-1937, Part 2," *http://www.columbia.edu/~jrs9/BNY-Hist-ND2.html*

39. Rappaport, *The Navy League of the United States*, 163.

40. "Roosevelt Saved Our Sea Power, Says Navy League," *New York Times*, July 30, 1934, 1.

41. Ibid., 1, 4.

42. Vergun, "*Sea Power*, Resurfaces After 14 Years in the Depths," *Sea Power*, May 2003, 61.

43. Ibid.

44. Ibid.

45. "Backs Roosevelt On Merchant Ships," *New York Times*, September 1, 1934, 5.

46. "Renaissance of U.S. Sea Power Keynote of Navy Day Observance," *New York Times*, October 24, 1937, 37. USS *North Carolina*, considered a "fast" battleship with a top speed of 28 knots, was the first capital ship built in the United States since the USS *West Virginia* (1923). Japan's announcement in March 1934 that it would not renew any naval treaties allowed the President Roosevelt to invoke the "escalator clause" of the 1930 London Naval Treaty. For *North Carolina*, that meant increasing the ship's armament from 14-inch to 16-inch guns.

Brooklyn Navy Yard was where the first United States ironclad, the USS *Monitor*, was commissioned in 1862, as well as the building yard for battleships USS *Arizona* (1917) and USS *Missouri* (1944). USS *North Carolina*, decommissioned in June 1947, was transferred to the state of North Carolina in 1961. Dedicated in April 1962 in Wilmington, North Carolina, the Navy's first modern, fast battleship serves today as a memorial to North Carolinians of all services killed in World War II. Chuck Hawks, *The Treaty Battleships. http://www.chuckhawks.com/treaty_ battleships.htm*

47. Rappaport, *The Navy League of the United States*, 176.

48. Loretta Britten and Paul Mathless, eds. *Our American Century, Decade of Triumph, The 40s* (Alexandria, Virginia: Bishop Books, Inc., 1998), 31.

49. Ibid., 33.
50. "Sham Battle Planned Here on Navy Day," *Washington Post*, October 24, 1941, 11. FDR was introduced at the Navy Day banquet by Colonel William B. Donovan, the Administration's "Defense Information Coordinator." "Wild Bill" Donovan would later gain fame as the World War II head of the Office of Strategic Services (OSS), forerunner to the post-war Central Intelligence Agency.
51. Franklin D. Roosevelt, "Total National Defense." Navy Day address to the nation, October 27, 1941. Congressional Record, Appendix, 77th Congress, 1st Session, A4877-A4878.
52. Ibid.

Chapter V

1. Franklin D. Roosevelt, "Request for a Declaration of War." Message to 77th Congress, December 8, 1941. Congressional Record, 77th Congress, 1st Session, 9519-9520.
2. Donald J. Young, "Was FDR planning to intervene on Great Britain's behalf before Pearl Harbor? Winston Churchill, for one, thought so." *Military Heritage,* October 2005, 25.
3. Loretta Britten and Paul Mathless, eds. *Our American Century, Decade of Triumph, The 40s* (Alexandria, Virginia: Bishop Books, Inc., 1998), 42.
4. Ibid., 46.
5. David Vergun, "Keeping the Home Fires Burning," *Sea Power,* September 2003, 50.
6. Ibid.
7. Rappaport, *The Navy League of the United States*, 182.
8. The position of Executive Secretary, established in 1940, was created to directly support the National President. Evelyn Collins would hold this position until her 1968 retirement. Jane Collins Grover became Executive Secretary, and would serve in that position until her own retirement in July 1986.
9. Chicago Council, Navy League of the United States. *Program, 25th Anniversary Dinner, October 27, 1967.* Chicago, Illinois,1967.
10. Joel R. Davidson, *The Unsinkable Fleet, The Politics of U.S. Navy Expansion in World War II.* (Annapolis, Maryland: Naval Institute Press, 1996), 36-37. The disparity between American and Japanese abilities to replace combat losses is telling. Following the battle of Midway, June 1942, Japan built a total of seven aircraft carriers before the war ended; the United States built more than 100. Between the summer of 1942 and August 1945, American industry produced 300,000 aircraft; Japan built about 12,000 a year during the same period. Geoffrey Till, "Midway, the Decisive Battle?" *Naval History* (October 2005), 35.

11. "300,000 Acclaim Navy Day Parade," *New York Times*, October 25, 1942, 1.
12. Rappaport, *The Navy League of the United States*, 182.
13. "Post-War Fleets Urged, Navy League Head Cites Need for Security, Prosperity," *New York Times*, December 9, 1944, 15.
14. Ibid.
15. James V. Forrestal, *Sea Power,* November 1945, 15, quoted in Rappaport, 184.
16. Rappaport, *The Navy League of the United States*, 185.

Chapter VI

1. John F. Lehman Jr., "Navy, U.S.: Since 1946," in John Whiteclay Chambers, II, ed. *The Oxford Companion to American Military History*. (New York: Oxford University Press, 1999), 490. Principal units, as reported in Fleet Admiral King's 1946 *U.S. Navy at War, 1941-1945, Official Reports to the Secretary of the Navy* included 40 fleet aircraft carriers, 24 battleships, 36 heavy cruisers, 57 light cruisers, and 450 destroyers. In addition there were 79 escort carriers, 263 submarines and 359 destroyer escorts. There were also hundreds of minesweepers, patrol boats, amphibious craft of all types and a massive fleet service force of tenders, repair ships, and medical evacuation ships.
2. "End of Atom Bomb Is Urged By Halsey," *New York Times*, October 27, 1946, 47.
3. Loretta Britten and Paul Mathless, eds. *Our American Century, Decade of Triumph, The 40s* (Arlington, Virginia: Bishop Books, 1999), 167. Baruch's comment, made in April 1947, marked one of the first times the phrase "Cold War" had been employed in discussing the relationship between the United States and the Soviet Union. Historian Norman Friedman dates the Cold War from February 9, 1946 when Stalin, "speaking during the Soviet election campaign abandoned the conciliatory tone he had adopted as a wartime ally. No peaceful international order could be constructed in a world with a capitalist economy." Friedman, *The Fifty-Year War, Conflict and Strategy in the Cold War* Annapolis, Maryland: Naval Institute Press), 57.

Writing in the September 1996 issue of *Sea Power*, First Deputy Commander in Chief of the Russian Federation Navy, Igor V. Kasatonov, provided the Russian naval historian view that the Cold War could be divided into five periods: 1945-1954, where the United States Navy was "supreme throughout the world"; 1955-1962, where America's "naval and military superiority continued throughout the world," culminating in the Cuban Missile Crisis; 1963-1975, an era where the "Soviet Navy expanded and evolved into a nuclear-powered, missile-armed, blue-water fleet, reached out into the open ocean and embarked on out-of-area deployments on a regular basis," with the period concluding in "a series of bilateral and multilateral treaties and arms agreements"; 1975-1980, where the American and

Soviet Navies' standoff "continued at an operational as well as a strategic level, but without actual conflict in the Middle East, Mediterranean, Indian Ocean, and numerous other areas, ending in the late 1970s with a dramatic escalation of tensions"; 1981-1989, where "radical changes in the Soviet Union led to dissolution of the Warsaw Pact and the end of the Soviet Union itself." Igor v. Kasatonov, "Facets of Cooperation," *Sea Power*, September 1996, 35.

4. Gilven Slonium, "Beyond Pearl Harbor: A SEA CHANGE!" (*Vital Speeches of the Day*, March 1992), 310.

5. David McCullough, *Truman* (New York: Simon & Schuster, 1992), 741. Biographer McCullough considers Louis Johnson "possibly the worst appointment Truman ever made" and notes that both Secretary of State Dean Acheson and Chairman of the Joint Chiefs of Staff Omar Bradley, respectively, considered the Secretary of Defense "unbalanced" and a "mental case." McCullough, 741-742.

6. As previously cited, the issue of which service should "own" aviation had been initially argued in the 1920s. At the conclusion of World War II, the arguments for a "national" Air Force would resurface, tantamount with service unification and creation of the Department of Defense. Naval aviators were adamant in arguing for the efficacy of sea-based air power, maintaining that the sea service's only error in the 1920s and 1930s was to underestimate the strategic significance of maritime air power. In 1945, what Navy leadership argued was not the irrelevance of battleships, cruisers, destroyers, and submarines, but rather the need for all of these elements, along with the aircraft carrier and embarked air wing, to comprise a balanced fleet. Fleet Admiral King, in his report to Secretary of the Navy Forrestal on World War II, was clear and unequivocal on the future role of naval aviation: "The outstanding development of the war in the field of naval strategy and tactics has been the convincing proof and general acceptance of the fact that, in accordance with the basic concept of the United States Navy, a concept established some 25 years ago, naval aviation is, and must always be, an integral and primary component of the fleet." (See *Ernest King, U.S. Navy at War, 1941-1945, Official Reports to the Secretary of the Navy*, 170.)

7. "Navy League Assails Services Unity 'Grab,'" *New York Times*, December 2, 1945, 19.

8. Rappaport, *The Navy League of the United States*, 189.

9. Ibid. 193.

10. Ibid., 195.

11. Richard L. Wright, "Forty Years Ago: *United States* vs. B-36." Memorandum submitted to Deputy Chief of Naval Operations (Naval Warfare, OP-07), August 22, 1989, 3.

12. Rappaport, *The Navy League of the United States*, 195, 260. The Secretary of Defense's directive, considered a "gag rule" by Hecht, was withdrawn in July 1949.

13. Ibid., 196.
14. "Navy League Defends Sea Force Air Arm As It Clashes Again With Aviation Group," *New York Times*, August 6, 1949, 6.
15. "Navy League Bows to Johnson, Drops Annual Navy Day," *Chicago Daily Tribune*, September 9, 1949, 1.
16. Michael A. Palmer, *Origins of the Maritime Strategy, American Naval Strategy in the First Postwar Decade* (Washington, Naval Historical Center: Government Printing Office, 1988), 50.
17. Wright, 4.
18. Ibid., 3.
19. Ibid., 5.
20. Ibid., 6.
21. Rappaport, *The Navy League of the United States*, 197.
22. Ibid., 196.
23. Ibid., 198. Matthews also maintained that Secretary Johnson was not playing favorites at the expense of the Navy, and that Admiral Denfeld "had not suffered from a retaliatory action."
24. Wright, 5.
25. Mark Perry, Four Stars: *The Inside Story of the Forty-Year Battle Between the Joint Chiefs of Staff and America's Civilian Leaders.* (New York: Houghton-Mifflin Company, 1989), 19.

Chapter VII

1. McCullough, 764.
2. Loretta Britten and Sara Brash, eds. *Our American Century, The American Dream, The 50s* (Arlington, Virginia: Bishop Books, Inc., 1998), 77.
3. Austen Stevens, "'Cold War' Is Laid By Truman to Lack of a Training Law," *New York Times*, May 20, 1950, 1.
4. McCullough notes that Johnson had been loyally carrying out the President's policy of slashing defense expenditures to balance the budget. But early setbacks in Korea revealed that, "along with defense budget fat, it was now painfully apparent, a great deal of bone and muscle had been cut. For all its vaunted nuclear supremacy, the nation was quite unprepared for war. ... " McCullough, 790. In Thomas Reed's opinion, Louis Johnson was "another in the long line of establishment elders on both sides of the Cold War who were unqualified for their jobs but who held them by virtue of political connections or coincidence." Thomas C. Reed, *At the Abyss, An Insider's History of the Cold War* (New York: Random House, 2004; Presidio Press Trade Paperback Edition, 2005), 106. Citations are from Presidio Press edition. On July 19, 1950, in response to events in Korea, President Truman

asked Congress for an emergency defense appropriation of $10 billion, nearly as much as the entire defense budget planned for that year. The President also increased the draft call and activated certain National Guard units. McCullough, 791-792.
5. "Navy League Chief Sees Patriotic Cleanup Need," *Los Angeles Times*, October 5, 1950, 8.
6. Frank A. Hecht, "The Proper Growth of Naval Aviation," *Vital Speeches of the Day*, May 1952, 476.
7. Ibid.
8. Ibid., 477.
9. "It's Still Navy Day," *New York Times*, October 27, 1952, 29.
10. Ibid.
11. New York Council, Navy League of the United States, *Program, Golden Anniversary Dinner*, 1902-52. New York, 1952.
12. Ibid.
13. Ibid.
14. Ibid.
15. John F. Lehman Jr., *On Seas of Glory, Heroic Men, Great Ships, and Epic Battles of the American Navy* (New York: The Free Press, 2001), 306.
16. Rappaport, 207.
17. Morgan Fitch, e-mail message to Richard L. Wright, July 26, 2005. Fitch would address several of these issues over the next decade, culminating in his key role in drafting new bylaws in the 1960s.
18. Ralph A. Bard, 2, December 6, 1946.
19. Frank A. Hecht, *Report of Meeting of the National Directors and Council Presidents April 29-May 1, 1953,* 1.
20. Ibid., 4.
21. E.V. Richards Jr., *Report of E.V. Richards Jr., President, Navy League of the United States, at the Annual Meeting of Members Held in Detroit, Michigan on Friday, December 3, 1954,* 1.
22. Carney's stormy relationship with President Eisenhower came to a head over the issue of China shelling the Tachen Islands, 200 miles northeast of Taiwan, in January 1955. Carney wanted to defend the islands; Eisenhower, unwilling to risk an armed confrontation with China, wanted the Navy's assistance in evacuating them. When the Chief of Naval Operations reiterated for the third time his objections to using the fleet to evacuate civilians, Eisenhower "ordered him to silence, saying that the decision had been made and he should begin working on evacuation plans." Perry, 61. In early February 29,000 Nationalist Chinese civilians and troops were evacuated by units of the Seventh Fleet; six months later, Carney was relieved as Chief of Naval Operations.

23. Burke was the fifth Chief of Naval Operations in six years since Denfeld had been fired in 1949 during the Revolt of the Admirals. In addition to the hapless victim of the Truman Administration's ire, Burke was preceded by Sherman, Fechteler, and Carney. Part of the challenge the Navy (and by extension, the Navy League) faced during this period was the turmoil occasioned by such turbulence in senior leadership. Between the end of World War II and 1953 the Army had only three Chiefs of Staff, and one of those, Eisenhower, had left to eventually become President; another, Omar Bradley, became the first chairman of the Joint Chiefs of Staff. During the same time period, the Air Force had only two Chiefs of Staff, Generals Carl Spaatz and Hoyt S. Vandenberg.
24. Ken Jones and Hubert Kelley Jr., *Admiral Arleigh (31-Knot) Burke, The Story of a Fighting Sailor*, 1962. (Annapolis, Maryland: Naval Institute Press, 2001), 187.
25. Ibid. Between July 31 and October 1, 1964, the Navy conducted *Operation Sea Orbit*, a 30,565-mile unreplenished circumnavigation of the world conducted by all-nuclear Task Force One, consisting of carrier *Enterprise*, cruiser *Long Beach*, and frigate *Bainbridge*. The most celebrated image of the cruise, an overhead view of *Enterprise*'s flight deck with the crew assembled to spell out "$E=MC^2$," invoked the displeasure of Rear Admiral John S. McCain, who maintained to his personal friend, Morgan Fitch, that "the crew should have been lined up to spell 'Seapower.'" McCain, Fitch asserted in a November 2002 interview, "was always promoting seapower." Fitch, interview by John D. Stegman. November 2002.
26. Eisenhower told Admiral Burke that he considered members of the Joint Chiefs of Staff no different than civilian members of his Cabinet. He reiterated on several occasions that while he was "always happy" to hear about disagreements with Administration policy or his views on issues of national security, once the decision was made, he expected all of the service chiefs to go along with, and aggressively support, his decision.
27. Richards, 4.
28. William Thompson, "The Navy League of the United States–A Status of Forces." Research Paper. United States Naval War College, 1964, 35-36.
29. Richards, 4.
30. Armin Rappaport, "The Decade of the Diamond Jubilee: 1953-1962" (working paper, photocopy, undated), 8.
31. The 252-foot-long Type IX-C German submarine (the only one of its type still existent, and the only German submarine of any type in the United States), was captured by a U.S. Navy hunter-killer group (escort carrier USS *Guadalcanal* and five accompanying destroyer escorts) commanded by Captain Daniel V. Gallery in June 1944 off the African Coast near Cape Verde. It was the first enemy ship boarded and captured on the open ocean by the U.S. Navy since the War of 1812.

In May 1961 the Navy League hosted a high-ranking delegation of twenty-two foreign officers from ten nations touring the Chicago area for three days of scientific, industrial, and naval briefings. Accompanied by National President Robert Crown, Ninth Region President Leo Porett, Illinois State President Randall Cooper, Lake County President Marshall Meyer, and Chicago Council President Gordon Rosberg, the delegation toured U-505 as part of the itinerary.

On June 4, 1974, in celebration of the 30th anniversary of the capture of the submarine, the Chicago Museum of Science and Industry hosted a large civic dinner attended by Admiral Gallery and many of his "boys." The event was jointly sponsored by the Museum, The Chicago Council of the Navy League, and the Illinois Naval Commandery.

The submarine remains one of the museum's most popular attractions, with over 20 million visitors taking a tour through the submarine in her 47 years on display. In April 2004 U-505 began a $35 million renovation that saw it moved from an outdoor exhibit to a specifically constructed underground hall along with 200 related artifacts. The "new" U-505 exhibit opened in June 2005.

32. Rappaport, "The Decade of the Diamond Jubilee: 1953-1962" (working paper, photocopy, undated), 11.

33. George C. Gilman, interview by Rosalind K. Ellis. (Undated).

34. The fiscal impact on League finances of the Sea-Air-Space Exposition is substantial, and, concomitant with the purchase of its own building for national headquarters, is the primary reason why every national president in the last two decades has not had to worry about making payroll or paying the rent as was true for much of the organization's first eight decades of existence. The Navy League, in conjunction with the National Capital Council, sponsors the Sea-Air-Space Exposition. Initially the council kept a large percentage of the profits generated: 60 percent in 1970; 50 percent in 1971. By the 1970s, it had succeeded the New York City Council as the League's "wealthiest," and it was the contribution of $50,000 to national accounts that allowed the League to buy its new headquarters building in the early 1980s. Allocations of profits from the event are currently divided, with 90 percent going to the Navy League itself and 10 percent going to the National Capital Council.

35. Rappaport, "The Decade of the Diamond Jubilee: 1953-1962" (working paper, photocopy, undated), 21.

36. Fitch, e-mail message to Richard L. Wright, July 28, 2005. Fitch notes that, even with development of a vibrant Sea Cadet program, the Shipmate program remains viable, broadening its focus to encompass the Naval Academy's "Blue and Gold Program" to assist high school students in preparing for and gaining admission to Annapolis, the Junior Naval Reserve Officer Training Corps units found in high schools nationwide, and other sea service youth undertakings.

37. Fitch, e-mail message to Richard L. Wright, July 28, 2005. Navy leadership was also concerned that private individuals were establishing local sea cadet programs,

neither officially affiliated with the Navy nor possessing any supervisory authority or regulations. Particular concern was expressed over these ad hoc groups establishing independent standards for uniforms and appearance and creating "ranks" for adult leaders up to and including "admiral."

38. Fitch's concern regarding the perceived intent was well-founded. Almost a decade after its founding, James M. Hannan, then in charge of the program, would have to remind Navy Leaguers, "We are not a recruiting program ..." Hannan, "The Sea Cadet Program Offers Rich Rewards," *Navy –The Magazine of Sea Power*, November 1965, 7.

39. Thompson, 35.

40. For Burke's opposition to the 1958 Department of Defense Reorganization Bill see E.B. Potter, *Admiral Arleigh Burke* (Annapolis, Maryland: Naval Institute Press, 1990), 424-425. Interestingly, when rumor spread that Admiral Burke, like the hapless Admiral Denfeld during the Revolt of the Admirals, would be fired for opposing Administration policy, Secretary of Defense Neil McElroy quickly called a press conference and stated, "Admiral Burke is a man. He has a right to make a decision. I wish he had supported the President's position, but nobody's going to tell Admiral Burke what to say if he doesn't believe it." Potter, 425. Eisenhower valued Burke's judgment on naval matters, personally liked him, and regarded him as a genuine hero of World War II; he kept his job. Ironically, as Congress passed legislation stripping the Chief of Naval Operations of control of operational forces, Admiral Burke was actually engaged in just such control, directing and overseeing 7th Fleet units off the Chinese Coast in the Formosa Strait crisis and 6th Fleet units conducting amphibious landings in Lebanon.

41. Fitch, e-mail message to Richard L. Wright, July 28, 2005.

42. *An Act to Incorporate the Naval Sea Cadet Corps*. Public Law No: 87-655 (September 10, 1962). The law specified that "John J. Bergen, William J. Catlett Jr., Morgan Fitch, George Halas, John S. Leahy Jr., and J. Paull Marshall, members of the Navy League Sea Cadet Committee and their associates and successors, are hereby created and declared to be a body corporate by the name of the Naval Sea Cadet Corps."

43. Frank Gard Jameson, interview by William Thompson. May 5, 1967, 102.

44. Robert Crown, interview by William Thompson. March 13, 1967, 67. When the federal charter was finally approved by Congress, Secretary of the Navy Fred Korth treated Crown and Fitch, along with their wives, to an evening cruise on the Potomac River aboard the Presidential yacht USS *Sequoia*. Fitch, e-mail to Richard L. Wright, July 28, 2005.

Following his national presidency, Robert Crown would return to the Naval Reserve, where he assumed command, as a captain (O-6), of the reserve unit at Great Lakes Naval Base. While there, he was asked by the Boy Scouts of America to chair their Sea Explorer Program at the national level, but had to turn it down because of his command responsibilities. But he recommended his trusted subaltern, Morgan Fitch, who was winding up his own League presidency term, as a suitable candidate. The Boy Scouts agreed, and Fitch joined the National Committee for Exploring and became Commodore of the Sea Explorer program, and later Vice Chairman in charge of Specialty Exploring. The Sea Exploring Program is now designated the Sea Scouts. Morgan Fitch, e-mail message to Richard L. Wright, October 30, 2005.

45. Robert Crown, *Annual Report of Robert Crown, National President Navy League of the United States, 61st Annual Convention, San Juan, Puerto Rico, April 29-May 4, 1963.*

46. Jack Raymond, "Pentagon Troubled by Rise in Industry Groups Asking for Help," *New York Times,* November 14, 1961, 7.

47. Ibid.

48. Thompson, 36-37.

49. David Vergun, "Navy League Confronts Cold War Challenges," *Sea Power,* August 2003, 52. Vergun's article, intended as a "heritage" piece referencing past August issues of League publications, makes no mention of the controversial aspects of *Project Alert* or the termination of any League connection with, or sponsorship of, the Advisory Council on Naval Affairs in the early 1960s.

50. Rappaport, "The Decade of the Diamond Jubilee: 1953-1962" (working paper, photocopy, undated) 41.

51. Crown, *Annual Report of Robert Crown, National President Navy League of the United States, 61st Annual Convention, San Juan, Puerto Rico, April 29-May 4, 1963.*

52. Robert Barnum, interview by William Thompson, December 28, 1963.

53. Crown interview by Thompson. Crown was concerned that an institution purporting to have education about, and support of, the sea services as its primary reason for existence, would be involved, in his words, with the "radical right." But in the same time frame, with his approval, the League would be involved in the production of a film entitled "Challenge to Americans," discussing American citizenship responsibilities and possessing a strong anti-communism message. The film won the *1961 Vigilant Patriot Award* and the *1962 George Washington Honor Medal.* Crown would report these accomplishments in his *1963 Annual Report* as League National President. Thompson, 40.

54. Crown interview by Thompson.

55. Ibid.

56. Ibid.

57. Frank Gard Jameson, interview by William Thompson, May 5, 1967.

58. Ibid.

59. Ibid.

60. Crown interview by Thompson.

61. Ibid.
62. Ibid.
63. Thompson, e-mail message to Richard L. Wright, August 1, 2005.
64. Linda Hoffman, e-mail message to Richard L. Wright, October 26, 2005. Hoffman noted that over the years provisions for the executive secretary and editor of the League's magazine were removed from the bylaws; those positions were placed under the executive director, vice the national president. Currently the only staff position addressed in the League's bylaws is that of executive director. In December 1982 a bylaws amendment was approved that changed the title of executive secretary to corporate secretary.
65. Crown, *Annual Report of Robert Crown, National President Navy League of the United States, 61st Annual Convention, San Juan, Puerto Rico, April 29-May 4, 1963.*
66. Thompson, *"The Navy League of the United States–A Status of Forces,"* 23.
67. Ibid., 28-29.
68. Ibid., 29-30.
69. Ibid.

Chapter VIII

1. Marquis Childs, "Air Force Lobby and Test Ban," *Washington Post*, September 18, 1963, quoted in William Thompson, "The Navy League of the United States–A Status of Forces." Research Paper. United States Naval War College, 1964, 55.
2. Uncertain as to latent congressional efforts to override Secretary McNamara's decision to make the ship conventionally powered, the Navy designed the engineering spaces of USS *John F. Kennedy* in many respects similar to nuclear-powered standards, with extensive use of stainless steel piping, etc.; the hybrid nature of *Kennedy*'s propulsion plant remains, almost four decades since its keel was laid. In 2005, it and the USS *Kitty Hawk*, remain the only two conventionally powered U.S. aircraft carriers still in commission. The disagreement over nuclear propulsion in Navy surface combatants would continue for the next two decades; most often the Navy League's stated position was that the government should "proceed with nuclearization of the surface fleet." The enthusiasm for nuclear power would continue throughout the 1970s, and wane only during the Reagan Administration when the most pro-defense administration since World War II opted to utilize gas turbine propulsion plants for AEGIS air dominance cruisers and destroyers.
3. William Anderson, "Urges Better Navy Balance in Ship Types," *Chicago Tribune,* April 24, 1965.
4. Following his tenure as National President, Robert Crown would remain active in both League affairs and the Navy. At his untimely passing in July 1969, he held

the rank of captain in the Naval Reserve, and was commanding officer of the reserve unit at Great Lakes Naval Base. Among his many legacies is the Robert Crown Sailing Center at the U.S. Naval Academy, Annapolis, Maryland, which opened in the spring of 1972, and the Crown Park at the Coast Guard Academy, New London, Connecticut. The Robert Crown Memorial Foundation, which subsequently merged into the Crown Family Foundation, still supports the Naval Reserve Officer Training Corps units at the University of Illinois, Northwestern University, and the Illinois Institute of Technology with a $2,500 grant per unit per annum. Crown also was an avid Holstein dairy farmer, and hosted on his farm, with his wife Joanne, foreign officers at the Naval War College, Newport, Rhode Island. Fitch, e-mail message to Richard L. Wright, October 30, 2005.
5. Robert H. Barnum, *Annual Report of Robert H. Barnum, National President Navy League of the United States, 62nd Annual Convention, Dallas, Texas, May 19-22, 1964.*
6. Ibid.
7. Robert H. Barnum, "Penny Wise Pay Policy," *Navy–The Magazine of Sea Power,* January 1965, 4.
8. Morgan L. Fitch Jr. Interview by Richard L. Wright, August 2, 2005.
9. Barnum, *Report of Robert H. Barnum, National President Navy League of the United States 1963-1965, 63rd Annual Convention, Washington, D.C., April 20-24, 1965.*
10. Hugh H. Mayberry, "A Salute to Industry," *Sea Power,* April 1996, 6.
11. Fitch. Annual Report of Morgan L. Fitch Jr., National President Navy League of the United States 1965-1966, 64th Annual Convention, Santa Monica, California. May 23-27, 1966.
12. "House Group Approves New Rivers Pay Bill," *From the Office of the President, Association of the United States Army* (Newsletter) July 1965: 3.
13. Frances Maxam, "Home Runs Infrequent For Navy League Head," *Jacksonville Journal,* May 2, 1967, 6.
14. Fitch. Meeting with Richard L. Wright April 26, 2005, and e-mail message to Richard L. Wright, July 23, 2005. Fitch's "shirt-sleeve" sessions would not continue many years beyond his term in office. Candidly, and reflective of his continued concern over League affairs, Fitch would assert that his open-ended sessions with the League's directors had been "largely avoided by later Presidents who appear regionally for receptions and speeches which do little to educate the directors as to their responsibilities." e-mail message to Richard L. Wright, July 23, 2005.

"The Whip" was not the only sobriquet Fitch earned during his more than half-century involvement in the Navy League. In 1962 he was placed in charge of organizing and executing the 60th Annual Convention; 53 years later, he would note with pride it was the first Navy League National Convention to stay on budget and not lose money. Commenting after the event, past National President Frank Gard Jameson, in a May 22, 1962 letter to Fitch, commented, "They say that

Stockmar sat in the background and pulled the strings on the thrones of Europe during Queen Victoria's time. It is quite evident that you are our Stockmar. I know of no one in the Navy League who has more respect and stature than you." Frank Gard Jameson, letter to Morgan Fitch, May 22, 1962. (Stockmar, Belgian diplomat and courtier, was an unofficial adviser to Queen Victoria and was instrumental in bringing about her marriage to Prince Albert.)

15. "Navy League Leader Notes Dual War Role," *San Diego Union,* March 7, 1965, B-1.

16. David L. McDonald, letter to Morgan Fitch, August 10, 1965.

17. Ibid.

18. Tom Wieder, "Navy League President Lays Viet Nam Protests To Ignorance, Fear," *Monterey Peninsula Herald* (Monterey, California), October 22, 1965.

19. "Navy League Official Protests Cuts in Military Budget," *Oregonian* (Portland, Oregon), December 7, 1965.

20. "Fitch Points Up Aid in Vietnam," *Times-Picayune* (New Orleans, Louisiana), August 26, 1966.

21. Charles F. Duchein, "With the Marines," *Navy–The Magazine of Sea Power,* November 1965, 41.

22. "Navy League President Links Adult Inaction, Youth Problems," *Evening Capital* (Annapolis, Maryland), April 8, 1967, 1, 3.

23. Dick Crouch and Bill Middleton, "Patriotism Is Not a Nasty Word," *Florida Times-Union* (Jacksonville, Florida), May 6, 1967, B-4.

24. Ibid.

25. "Philadelphia to Get Army-Navy Museum," *Washington Post,* October 10, 1965, B3. Joseph Pemberton, a Quaker sugar and Madeira wine merchant, bought the property on Chestnut Street between 3rd and 4th Streets, from the Carpenters' Company, and built his mansion shortly after the First Continental Congress finished its initial meeting in the adjoining Carpenters' Hall in the autumn of 1774. With the Second Continental Congress banning British imports after hostilities commenced, Pemberton eventually went bankrupt. In the 1840s, Benjamin Franklin's grandson, Richard Bache, used the house as a post office. The original structure was razed in 1862; a reproduction was built a century later. The Navy League and the Association of the United States Army assembled and supported several exhibits in Pemberton House, devoting some 4,000 square feet to a history of the Army and the Navy from 1775-1800, including panoramic and dioramic displays, pictures, arms, uniforms and other historic items. Highlights included a film of the military history of the Revolutionary War and, on the second floor, a model gun deck of a frigate, with instructions on maneuvering for naval battle. The Army-Navy Museum was dedicated September 27, 1968; Navy League National President Charles Duchein and Association of the United States Army National President

Frank Pace Jr., represented their respective organizations.

In the mid-1970s, in connection with the U.S. Bicentennial commemoration and ongoing efforts to restore the complex of historic structures in the old, colonial-era section of Philadelphia, the National Park Service shifted the museum's contents to New Hall, a modern copy of a hall built in 1791 (also by Carpenters' Company), which served as the first headquarters for the War Department headed by America's first Secretary of War, Henry Knox. The New Hall Military Museum, as it is now called, is also the repository of an extensive collection of Marine Corps memorabilia; the Corps was founded in nearby Tun Tavern; military exhibits from all three services from the American Revolution through the last decades of the 18th century now fill the building. Federally owned Pemberton House now serves as the bookstore and gift shop for an enlarged and expanded 22-acre Independence National Historical Park.

26. "Nitze Says the Navy Is Counting on the Sea Cadet Program," *Navy–The Magazine of Sea Power,*, November 1965, 6. In the context of the Cold War and Vietnam, Nitze's pronouncement reflected, perhaps, the unstated intent of the Navy, vís-â-vís the Sea Cadet Corps at the time. But the League would subsequently go to considerable lengths to stress the educational aspects of membership in the Sea Cadet program, as opposed to using it as a subtle recruiting tool for the armed services. In the September 2005 issue of *Sea Power*, James H. Erlinger, League Vice President for Youth Programs, would assert that the League needed to "do a better job of conveying the fact that military service is not a commitment after graduating from the Sea Cadets." This misperception persisted 40 years after James Hannan, then-President of the Naval Sea Cadets, had strongly asserted in the same issue focused on the League's youth programs that the Nitze comment was cited, that the Sea Cadets were "not a recruiting program." *Navy–The Magazine of Sea Power,* November 1965, 7.

27. Fitch, "Pass Up the Butter!" *Navy Times,* January 5, 1966, 2-3.

28. "'The Forgotten Men,'" *Jacksonville Journal,* April 20, 1966, 7.

29. *The Pentagon Papers*, Gravel Edition, Volume 4 (Boston: Beacon Press, 1971: 658-659.

30. Fitch. *Annual Report of Morgan L. Fitch, Jr.*

31. Ibid.

32. Four decades later, Fitch remains concerned that the League has lost focus, and is spread too thin for the assets, time, and fiscal resources available to execute its missions and goals: "Since then [1966] and today, the Navy League has expanded its programs and does not focus on what it can realistically do." Fitch, *Annual Report of Morgan L. Fitch, Jr.* and e-mail message to Richard L. Wright, July 23, 2005. Fitch expressed much the same concern in a November 2002 interview with John D. Stegman. Using the example of Kraft Foods (a client of his Chicago-based law

firm), and marketing decisions that went awry, Fitch pointed out that scarce capital must be used to focus on a limited number of challenges: "The League, like Kraft Foods, needs to spend its money where it can make an effective rate of return." Fitch, interview by John D. Stegman. November 2002.

33. Fitch. *Annual Report of Morgan L. Fitch, Jr.*

34. Fitch. *Annual Report of Morgan L. Fitch, Jr.* and e-mail message to Richard L. Wright, July 23, 2005.

35. Fitch, (public address, Annual Meeting, Navy League of the United States, Santa Monica, California, May 27, 1966.)

36. Ibid. Fitch also was insistent that the League's national directors each be a member of a committee. In the mid-1960s the League had around 250 national directors; each was a member of at least one League committee. Four decades later, less than half (146 of 253) of the organization's national directors are members of any League committee.

37. William Thompson, memorandum to Paul H. Nitze, Secretary of the Navy. June 10, 1966.

38. Thompson, memorandum to Paul H. Nitze, Secretary of the Navy. July 29, 1966. Fitch, like his predecessor Frank Hecht, also insisted on having positive control over official League communications with Johnson Administration officials or members of Congress. In a July 1965 letter, Fitch admonished a Navy League Jacksonville, Florida, council member for communicating with Secretary Nitze on the issue of legislation improving military pay for armed forces personnel utilizing Navy League stationery. Fitch reminded him that while as a private citizen he was free to communicate with the Secretary, "You should not use Navy League stationery to promote legislation." Fitch pointed out the "importance of not involving the Navy League directly in legislative matters in the Congress and in the Administration," because if it did "it [the League] becomes a lobby group which must play under a whole new set of rules." Then, reflecting his close ties with Secretary Nitze, Fitch added, "You should also know that the secretary's office has taken umbrage to your letter and does not believe that the Secretary needs coaching from a Navy League council on a subject to which he has devoted the majority of his time for the past nine months." Fitch, letter to James D. Holmes III. July 26, 1965.

39. Such meetings and adoption of joint positions on issues affecting the sea services had been first suggested by then-Secretary of the Navy James Forrestal to Evelyn Collins toward the end of World War II when the upcoming debate over issues such as service unification and naval aviation were apparent. Nothing had ever come of the suggestion. Fitch, with the support of Commander William Thompson (who was Secretary Nitze's executive assistant), proposed forming a council of such groups. While initially successful, over time the meetings waned in import; commented Fitch in 2005, "No policy decisions appeared to be reached. Parochial inter-

ests precluded joint policy positions." Morgan L. Fitch, Jr. *Annual Report of Morgan L. Fitch, Jr.* and e-mail message to Richard L. Wright, July 23, 2005.
40. Letter printed as "A Message From The Commandant of the Marine Corps" in Navy League of the United States, *A Day in Vietnam*. Program, Navy League of the United States, 64th Annual Convention, 1966.
41. Throughout the 1960s, Senator Jackson was a strong proponent of nuclear-powered ships, a belief that Admiral Hyman Rickover leveraged to become the most powerful Navy flag officer on Capitol Hill. Rickover survived several attempts by both the civilian and uniformed leadership of the Department of the Navy to have him retired. The most famous was Secretary of the Navy Paul Nitze's 1967 attempt, which saw him coming to Senator Jackson's office to explain why he was intending to ask for the admiral's retirement, only to find Rickover, appraised of Nitze's intent by "insiders" in the Secretary's office, sitting next to Jackson, smiling. Nitze felt his own job was at risk, and would later characterize Admiral Rickover as "flagrantly insubordinate." Fourteen years after Nitze's stillborn attempt, Secretary of the Navy John Lehman, with the backing of President Reagan, finally was able to gain Rickover's retirement. L. Edgar Prina, "The End of an Era—And Beginning of Another," *Sea Power,* December 1981, 15.
42. Henry M. Jackson, "Five Dangerous Myths," *Navy–The Magazine of Sea Power,,* May 1969, 27-28.
43. "Johnson Is Scored on Shipping Goals," *New York Times*, May 14, 1968, 93.
44. Perry, 240.
45. U.S. Grant Sharp, "The Story Behind the Bombing," *New York Times*, August 6, 1971, 31. More than two years later, with the United States disengaging from Vietnam, Chairman of the Joint Chiefs of Staff Admiral Thomas H. Moorer, asserted in a speech before naval aviators in Las Vegas, Nevada, that the December 1972 "Linebacker II" air campaign against the North Vietnamese "served as a catalyst for the negotiations which resulted in the ceasefire, the return of our prisoners of war, and the complete withdrawal of our forces from Vietnam." Reinforcing Sharp's points, Moorer concluded: "Air power, given its day in court after almost a decade of frustration, confirmed its effectiveness as an instrument of national power in just nine and one-half flying days." "Scoop & Scuttle," *Sea Power,* November 1973, 5.
46. "Admiral Warns of Soviet Fleet Gains," *New York Times*, September 28, 1969, 82.
47. "Nixon Doctrine and the Blue Water Strategy," *Navy–The Magazine of Sea Power,* January 1971, 8.
48. Alvin J, Cottrell, "Indian Ocean of Tomorrow," *Navy–The Magazine of Sea Power,* March 1971, 11.
49. "Nixon Doctrine and the Blue Water Strategy," 8.
50. "Nixon Doctrine and the Blue Water Strategy–Part II," *Navy–The Magazine of Sea Power,* February 1971, 6.

51. James M. Hannan, "Extend the Draft," *Navy–The Magazine of Sea Power,* April 1971, 6.
52. Ibid.
53. Hannan, "The President's Annual Report-Fiscal 1971," *Navy–The Magazine of Sea Power,* May 1971, 5.
54. Thomas E. Morris, "Our Greatest Challenge," *Navy–The Magazine of Sea Power,* June 1971, 4.
55. Morris, "Time to Turn To!" *Navy–The Magazine of Sea Power,* July-August 1971, 3.
56. Morris, "Sea Cadets–A Golden Opportunity Is Being Missed," *Sea Power,* September 1971, 7.
57. Morris, "We Need Vigorous Local Leadership," *Sea Power,* March 1972, 2.
58. Ibid.
59. "Navy League Signs on for Four-Year Tour," *Sea Power,* July-August 1972, 53.
60. Morris, "Yesterday and Tomorrow, National President's Annual Report," *Sea Power,* June 1972, 3.
61. Ibid.
62. Morris, "Recruiting: Numbers Up; Quality Still Short," *Sea Power,* November 1972, 4.
63. Morris, "Shipbuilding Budget Warrants Strong Support," *Sea Power,* February 1972, 4.
64. These reforms would also include moving away from nuclear propulsion in Navy ships with the exception of aircraft carriers and submarines. Both chiefs of naval operation viewed the expense of nuclear power in smaller surface combatants as too great for the minimal increase in combat effectiveness that resulted. This change in Navy policy was vehemently opposed by Admiral Hyman Rickover, and though he would win some victories in the future in building additional cruisers with nuclear power plants, the fervent advocacy of nuclear power in the 1960s was history. The Navy League remained a proponent of nuclear power for all significant ship classes for much of the 1970s, and would only slowly lose its enthusiasm after Secretary of the Navy John Lehman succeeded where Navy Secretaries from Lyndon Johnson's Administration forward had failed: Admiral Rickover was retired November 13, 1981.
65. Morris, "Lowest Level of Capability in Years," *Sea Power,* March 1973, 5. Morris, a Navy captain (O-6) in the Naval Reserve before becoming National President, would return to the reserves after his tour as League National President was concluded. Having held seven commands during his naval career, he was promoted to rear admiral August 1, 1974. Subsequent to his time as League National President, he would be a national director of the Surface Navy Association, founding director of the Naval War College Foundation and founding director of the USS *Constitution* Museum, among other leading positions in non-profit organizations. He was twice

awarded the Distinguished Public Service Award by the Secretary of the Navy, and similarly honored by the Secretary of Transportation for his support of the Coast Guard. In 2005 he continued to serve as a League director from Juno Beach, Florida, and was appointed to the 11-member American Battle Monuments Commission by President George W. Bush.

66. Arleigh Burke. Letter to the Editor. *Sea Power,* April 1973.

67. "Men Such as These." *Sea Power,* May 1973, 3.

68. Ernest M. Eller, "The Postwar Follies," *Sea Power,* May 1973: 34.

69. Ernest A. Carrere Jr., "Let's Make It work," *Sea Power,* June 1973, 5.

70. Ibid.

71. "Navy Leaguers View on Amnesty," *Sea Power,* June 1973, 19.

72. Stockdale was awarded the Medal of Honor in 1976 for his extraordinary leadership as the senior naval officer held in captivity during the Vietnam War. Upon his retirement from the Navy, the Secretary of the Navy established the "Vice Admiral Stockdale Award for Inspirational Leadership," presented annually in both the Atlantic and Pacific Fleets. Vice Admiral Stockdale died July 5, 2005, and was buried with honors at the United States Naval Academy July 23, 2005.

73. "Men Such as These." *Sea Power,* May 1973, 3.

74. "A Fresh Look and Unbiased Appraisal," *Sea Power,* February 1975, 6.

75. "Speeches and Symposia," *Sea Power,* June 1973, 45.

76. Eller, "Sea Power: The Anchor of Freedom," *Sea Power,* November 1973, 15-16.

77. Ibid., 16.

78. The March 1974 issue of *Sea Power,* noted that Admiral Maurice F. Weisner, Commander in Chief, Pacific Fleet, citing an "atmosphere of lawlessness, intimidation and defiance of established authority" among enlisted men in the fleet, had directed commanding officers to tighten discipline throughout the Pacific Fleet. "Scoop & Scuttle," *Sea Power,* March 1974, 5.

79. Hessman, "Farewell to a Surface Warrior," *Sea Power,* February 2000: 1.

80. Ibid. For a detailed evaluation, from the perspectives of both Navy admirals and naval historians, of Admiral Zumwalt's period as Chief of Naval Operations, see Edgar F. Puryear Jr., *American Admiralship, the Moral Imperatives of Naval Command.* (Annapolis, Maryland: Naval Institute Press, 2005), 450-480. Of particular value is Admiral Holloway's assessment, both as Zumwalt's successor and as his personal friend. Holloway opens his discussion by noting, "Admiral Zumwalt is too important a figure in modern naval history to be given a superficial assessment." Puryear, 452.

81. "Hail and Farewell," *Sea Power,* April 1974, 5.

82. John G. Norris, "CVX and the Nuclear Navy," *Sea Power,* May 1974: 16-22. Admiral Zumwalt had a much different view. When author Norman Polmar asked the admiral what he considered the greatest threats to the U.S. Navy during his

time as Chief of Naval Operations, he replied, "The Soviet Navy, Admiral Rickover, and the U.S. Air Force, in that order." Puryear, 469.
83. Thomas E. Morris, "The Case for a National Insurance Policy," *Sea Power,* April 1973, 2.
84. Walter A. Zitlau, "Energy Overview: Obstacles and Opportunities," *Sea Power,* February 1974, 6-12.
85. J. Kenney Matthew. Letter. *Sea Power,* April 1974, 2.
86. "Interview with Navy Secretary Middendorf," *Sea Power,* August 1974, 14.
87. J. William Middendorf, "A Smaller Fleet, and a Formidable Competitor," *Sea Power* January 1975, 16.
88. Accounts of Navy League involvement and support of the May 1975 visit to Boston, Massachusetts, are derived from Ivan Samuels's "After Action Report" to Navy League headquarters and a June 3, 2005, interview with Richard L. Wright.
89. James D. Hessman, "Okean, Leningrad/Boston, *Nimitz*, and the SES," *Sea Power,* June 1975, 20.
90. "Vice President Ford addressed Navy League of the United States in New Orleans," *Sea Power,* May 1975, 23
91. Ibid.
92. DeWitt James Griffin, "The Lessons of Vietnam," *Sea Power,* June 1975, 2-3.
93. Griffin, "Hard Decisions Become Harder," *Sea Power,* December 1975, 9.
94. Middendorf, "Unknown Events, Disturbing Trends, and a Rebuilding of Strength," *Sea Power,* January 1976, 10. Secretary Middendorf, departing as Secretary of the Navy with the outgoing Ford Administration in January 1977, would join the Navy League that same year. As a member, he has chaired the League's Awards Board for the past 28 years.
95. Ibid., 10, 11.
96. Griffin, "Why?" *Sea Power,* February 1976, 6.
97. "Scoop & Scuttle," *Sea Power,* June 1976, 4.
98. Griffin, "A Letter, and a Reply," *Sea Power,* November 1976, 29.
99. L. Edgar Prina, "Ford Cuts Carrier, *Long Beach* Conversion; Congressional Restoration Possible," *Sea Power,* January 1977, 26, 28.
100. Griffin, "The President's Annual Report," *Sea Power,* May 1977, 31.
101. Ibid., 33.
102. Ibid.
103. Ibid., 35.
104. Perry, 244. Regardless of Holloway's lack of budgetary success, John Lehman, no stranger to the political and fiscal realities of Washington, is unstinting in his praise of the admiral's leadership during this difficult time: "He was an inspiration to me, a role model of what a leader should be. The success of the 600-ship Navy in the Reagan years owes more to Holloway than to any other person." John F.

Lehman Jr., *On Seas of Glory, Heroic Men, Great Ships, and Epic Battles of the American Navy.* (New York: The Free Press, 2001), 349.
105. Vincent T. Hirsch, "A Dubious Decision, and a Disturbing Pattern," *Sea Power,* August 1977, 3.
106. Prina, "Brown Budget Cuts Threaten Navy/United States Marine corps Air, Five-Year Ship Program," *Sea Power,* September 1977, 17.
107. Hirsch, "The Canal Treaty: Too Far, and Too Fast," *Sea Power,* September 1977, 8.
108. Hirsch, "Treaty Reprise: Sincere and Honest Doubt," *Sea Power,* January 1978, 3.
109. Ibid., 4.
110. Ibid.
111. James D. Hessman and Vincent H. Thomas, "Interview with Navy Secretary Claytor," *Sea Power,* October 1977, 27-28.
112. Ibid., 26.
113. Hirsch, "It's Now Up to Congress," *Sea Power,* February 1978, 4.
114. Prina, "Claytor Fires Back; Disputes New Defense Strategy," *Sea Power,* April 1978, 31. William Graham Claytor had a distinguished career in both public and private sectors. Volunteering for naval service in 1940, he rose in rank from ensign to lieutenant commander and had command of three warships. As commanding officer of USS *Cecil J Doyle* in August 1945, Claytor left his radar picket station without orders and sped to the reported location of a large number of men in the water, clinging to life rings and wreckage in shark-infested waters. The men were the survivors of the heavy cruiser USS *Indianapolis,* and had been in the water five days before being sighted by a patrol aircraft. As Claytor approached the scene of the sinking, he turned searchlights on the water and straight up into the low hanging clouds to alert the survivors of his ship's presence and to assist in the rescue. As he would later recount to *Washington Post* reporter Don Phillips, turning on the lights violated Navy Regulations, but while "you tried not to thumb your nose at rules ... we didn't let it interfere with our judgment as to what was best." The sinking of the USS *Indianapolis* resulted in the deaths of 883 of its crew of 1,199; *Cecil J. Doyle* rescued 93, and administered final rites to 21 found dead in the water upon arrival. Captain Claytor's actions were cited by survivors as preventing additional loss of life.

After the war Claytor, a lawyer by training, worked for the Southern Railway, eventually becoming chairman of the board and chief executive officer. He was President Jimmy Carter's Secretary of the Navy 1977-1979 and Deputy Assistant Secretary of Defense 1979-1981. In 1982 President George H.W. Bush appointed him President and chairman of the board of the National Railway Passenger Corporation, (Amtrak). His retirement from government service in 1993 occasioned passage of public law 103-165, specifically citing his rescue of the *Indianapolis* sailors and thanked him "for a lifetime of dedication and superb service to the Nation." He died less than a year later. (Don Phillips, "W. Graham Claytor, Jr.", *Washington Post*, May 15, 1994 (Electronic data base); *To Express Appreciation to W. Graham Claytor, Jr., for a lifetime of dedicated and inspired service to the Nation*. Public Law No. 103-165 (December 2, 1993).

115. Ibid., 30-31. Writing three years later, in an article praising new Secretary of the Navy John Lehman's plan to rebuild the fleet and implement a new strategy, Prina still fondly recalled Claytor's "thundering denunciation" of the "consolidated guidance" emanating from the office of the Secretary of Defense, and considered Claytor's letter to Secretary Perry "one of the most devastating letters ever written by a service Secretary to a high-ranking official in the Office of the Secretary of Defense." Prina, "Budget Increases Reflect 'A Major Change in Naval Strategy,'" *Sea Power*, April 1981, 19.

116. Hirsch, "The President's Annual Report-fiscal 1978," *Sea Power*, June 1978, 27.

117. Hirsch, "The Real Losers," The Navy and the Nation," *Sea Power*, October 1978, 6.

118. John Culhane, "The Man Who Bought an Aircraft Carrier," Intrepid Sea, Air & Space Museum, *http://www.intrepidmuseum.org*

119. "Kelley Presents Resolution of Appreciation to Fishers," *Sea Power*, February 1993: 8. The Navy League was not alone in recognizing Zachary Fisher. In 1998 he received the Presidential Medal of Freedom from President William J. Clinton "in honor of his wide-ranging contributions on behalf of the young men and women in the U.S. Armed Forces." A Russian immigrant to America with a lifelong interest in the United States military, when interviewed shortly before his passing in June 1999, he commented, "It's a privilege to live in this great country of ours. They don't owe me a thing. I owe them." In December 1999, Congress conferred upon Fisher the title "Honorary Veteran of the United States," only the second American to receive such recognition (Bob Hope was the first). *www.intrepidmuseum. org/pages /FounderZacheryFisher*

120. Hirsch, "The President's Annual Report," *Sea Power*, May 1979, 7.

121. John J. Spittler, "An Open Letter to the President of the United States," *Sea Power*, October 1979, 5. Spittler, in a letter to Janet Mescus, senior director of communications for the League in 2005, recalled that when the letter was written with the help of Vince Thomas, before it was released publicly, "in fairness, an appointment was scheduled at the White House prior to distribution. When apprised of the material (two decades later Spittler characterized the open letter as 'accusing Carter, a Naval Academy graduate, of betraying his roots') President Carter dismissed it out of hand. The release was made and the lines drawn." Spittler, letter to Janet Mescus. October 16, 2005.

122. Spittler, "The President's Annual Report," *Sea Power,* May 1980, 6.
123. Spittler, "New Senior VP Will Need Lots of Help," *Sea Power,* January 1981, 22.
124. Spittler, letter to Janet Mescus, October 16, 2005. In a November 2002 interview, Spittler noted that the need to find a new location for League headquarters was largely due to the "overwhelming expense of rents" in the District of Columbia. Spittler, interview by John D. Stegman, November 2002.
125. Quoted in Spittler, "Courage, Not Caution," *Sea Power,* April 1980, 6.
126. Ibid. The author, as a lieutenant aboard the Spruance-class destroyer USS *Kinkaid* (DD-965) in 1980, frequently mustered working parties to remove anti-Carter graffiti from the white fence surrounding the perimeter of the San Diego Naval Station. The naval chain-of-command in Pacific Fleet was concerned about letters to the two local San Diego newspapers expressing the frustrations of men and women in uniform, for whom, from their President's perspective, "pay" should not be an issue.
127. Ann Hughey, "The age of aircraft carrier diplomacy," Forbes July 21, 1980, 57.
128. Spittler, Time to Get on with the Job," *Sea Power,* December 1980, 3.
129. *Sea Power,* cover, December 1980, caption on inside front cover.
130. Warren P. Baker, "A Sea Change in Congress?" *Sea Power,* December 1980, 47.

Chapter IX

1. *Sea Power,* cover, January 1981, caption on inside front cover.
2. Spittler, "Plans, Politics, and Practical Realities," *Sea Power,* January 1981, 3.
3. Hughey, 62.
4. Lehman, *On Seas of Glory, Heroic Men, Great Ships, and Epic Battles of the American Navy* (New York: The Free Press, 2001), 362. Ironically, Reagan was speaking at the December 1982 re-commissioning of the battleship USS *New Jersey*, whose return to active duty was funded in the last Carter Administration defense budget approved by Congress.
5. Floyd D. Kennedy, "From SLOC Protection to a National Maritime Strategy," in *In Peace and War, Interpretations of American Naval History, 1775-1984*, 2nd Edition, Kenneth J. Hagan (Westport, Connecticut: Greenwood Press, 1984), 354.
6. Hessman and Thomas, "Interview with the Secretary of the Navy," *Sea Power,* March 1981, 17, 24, 30.
7. Spittler, "We Must Go to General Quarters," *Sea Power,* April 1981, 3.
8. Prina, "Budget Increases Reflect 'A Major Change in Naval Strategy,'" *Sea Power,* April 1981, 13, 19-20.
9. Ibid., 13
10. Vincent C. Thomas Jr., "Sea Services: Navy on Course, Maritime on Shoals." In James D. Hessman, and Thomas B. Allen, Eds. *The Almanac of Sea Power 1983.*

(Arlington, Va.: 1983), 5. At the same time the *Almanac* was published, a March 1983 profile of John Lehman in *The Pennsylvania Gazette* quoted him on his relationships with Capitol Hill: "This town works like a Stradivarius if you know how to make it work, if you have the patience to understand the laws of its physics." Michael Levin, "U.S.S. Dauntless," *Pennsylvania Gazette* March 1983: 17.

11. The two additional carriers, CVN 72, USS *Abraham Lincoln*, and CVN 73, USS *George Washington*, were commissioned in November 1989 and July 1992, respectively. The ballistic-missile submarine USS *George Washington* (SSBN 598) was still in commission when CVN 73 was named. Secretary Lehman desired both carriers to be named before their start to preempt congressional sentiment to name one of the ships for Admiral Hyman Rickover. Subsequently, Rickover would be honored when SSN 709 a Los Angeles-class nuclear attack submarine, was named for the "Father of the Nuclear Navy."

12. Spittler, "The President's Annual Report," *Sea Power*, May 1981, 5.

13. Ibid., 6, 8. Beyond his tour as National President, John Spittler would again have the opportunity to display his acumen as a League recruiter. Moving to a suburb of Chattanooga, Tennessee, at the age of 85, he was disappointed to find the nearest League councils to be in Knoxville, Nashville, and Memphis. Not wanting to travel long distances for council meetings and events, Spittler decided to form a council in the local area. Obtaining the required 25 members, he petitioned then-League National President Tim Fanning for council status. At the 2002 Centennial Convention in New York City, the request was granted and Spittler became a council president for a second time. Not satisfied with 25, Spittler personally recruited over 100 additional members and at the 2004 San Diego National Convention was recognized as one of the "Navy League's Top Ten Sponsors for 2003." By 2005 the Chattanooga council boasted almost 200 members. Spittler, letter to Janet Mescus, October 16, 2005, and letter, Jim Hoffman, senior director of member services, to John Spittler, March 29, 2004.

14. John M. Rau, e-mail message to Richard L. Wright, August 1, 2005.

15. Accounts of his worldwide trips to Navy, Marine Corps, and Coast Guard units and installations are drawn from John M. Rau's interview by Richard L. Wright, tape recording, June 3, 2005, Navy League National Convention, Norfolk, Virginia, and his e-mail message to Richard L. Wright, August 1, 2005. Subsequent trips to sea service units during his national presidency included a 14-hour anti-submarine mission on a Navy patrol aircraft, a week spent with a Marine unit embarked in a Navy amphibious ship in the Mediterranean, a trip through Florida, Haiti and Guantanamo Bay, Cuba, with the vice commandant of the Coast Guard during Haitian refugee interdiction operations, and a four-day submerged cruise on a Los-Angeles Class nuclear attack submarine.

16. Rau, "Foreword," in James D. Hessman, and Thomas B. Allen, Eds. The

Almanac of Sea Power 1983. Arlington, Va.: 1983.
17. Accounts of the purchase and funding of the League's headquarters building are drawn from John M. Rau's interview by Richard L. Wright, tape recording, June 3, 2005, Navy League National Convention, Norfolk, Virginia, his e-mail message to Richard L. Wright, August 1, 2005, John Spittler's letter to Janet Mescus, October 16, 2005, and Morgan L. Fitch's e-mail message to Richard L. Wright of November 24, 2005. Fitch has in hand a copy of the April 1981 sales contract and the minutes of the Steering Committee meeting. The League's Howard B. Siegel, senior director of finance, provided Fitch with information on the contract that was finally executed.
18. Rau, e-mail message to Richard L. Wright, November 8, 2005.
19. Louis Kriser, Memorandum to Hugh Mayberry, President, Navy League of the United States, December 2, 1996.
20. Ibid.
21. Kriser, interview by Richard L. Wright, tape recording, June 3, 2005, Navy League National Convention, Norfolk, Virginia; interview by Richard L. Wright, tape recording, June 21, 2005, Army-Navy Country Club, Arlington, Virginia.
22. It was also at Kriser's suggestion that League stationery was changed to have the words "Navy-Marine Corps-Coast Guard-Merchant Marine" appear; he was concerned that, for too many people, the League was concerned only about issues affecting the Navy, to the exclusion of the other sea services. Kriser recommended publication of *The Navy Leaguer* to cover the broad spectrum of council activities beyond the purview of *Sea Power* magazine. Kriser also proposed formation of a Congressional Caucus to address sea service issues. Although the League's Legislative Advisory Board initially recommended waiting until the organization had a firmer legislative affairs program to ensure expectations could be met and the League could fulfill its obligations, the Navy-Marine Corps Caucus would come into existence in 2001 through the support and advocacy of the League National President Timothy O. Fanning and Vice President for Legislative Affairs Sheila McNeill.
23. Fitch, e-mail message to Richard L. Wright, July 26, 2005.
24. At the November 1985 Honolulu meeting, the issue of limiting the number of terms of the judge advocate was also considered. An exceptional speech from Calvin Cobb, the incumbent, citing the advantage of continuity in the personage of the judge advocate, as well as the limited pool of available talent to fill a key League leadership position, decided the issue in favor of leaving the term unlimited. (Cobb would subsequently become a senior League Vice President, and eventually National President, 1989-1991). In November 1991, the board reversed its position and voted to limit the position to no more than five consecutive terms. Seven years later, with another popular judge advocate, Ward Shanahan, occupying the position, the board again reversed its position, and removed any limitation on the

number of terms a judge advocate may serve; this remains the policy in 2005.
25. Navy League of the United States, *Resolution in Appreciation to Jane Collins Grover,*: July 2, 1986.
26. Ibid. Ms. Linda Hoffman assumed Jane Grover's position, but kept the title of Executive Secretary until 1988, when the Executive Director changed the title to Director of Executive Services. In January 2004 the Executive Director moved the position of Director of Meetings under that of the Director of Executive Services and changed the latter's title to Senior Director of Administration.
27. Norman Polmar, "The 600-Ship Fleet Enters Political Narrows," James D. Hessman and Thomas B. Allen, eds. *The Almanac of Sea Power 1983.* (Arlington, Va.: 1983), 15.
28. Norman Friedman, *The Fifty Year War, Conflict and Strategy in the Cold War* (Annapolis, Maryland: Naval Institute Press, 2000), 462. Dean C. Allard in his review of the U.S. Navy's strategy on Europe's northern flank during the Cold War has observed of the Forward Maritime Strategy, "Although widely viewed as a new policy, the strategy's stress on a close-in offensive, featuring attacks against key bases and oceanic choke points, were part of a long tradition in Anglo-American naval thinking. One major difference was the fact that the Maritime Strategy was highly publicized, whereas previous strategies typically were highly secret. The Maritime Strategy aroused considerable controversy in the United States and abroad. But the doctrine served as an essential intellectual underpinning for the naval build-up of the Reagan era."
http://www.luftfart.museum.no/Engelsk/Research/Dean C. Allard
29. Thomas C. Reed, *At the Abyss, An Insider's History of the Cold War* (New York: Random House, 2004; Presidio Press Trade Paperback Edition, 2005), 5. Citations are from Presidio Press edition.
30. Peter Robinson, "Echoes of the Gipper," *Wall Street Journal*, March 31, 2005.
31. Reed, 228.
32. Tarron Lively, "USS *Ronald Reagan* (CVN-76) commissioned; The former President's wife ordered the crew of the new aircraft carrier to 'bring her to life.'" *Washington Times*, July 13, 2003, A01.
33. Lehman, 396.
34. Hessman and Thomas, "Individual Human Beings and the Responsibilities of Leadership—A Valedictory Interview with Navy Secretary John F. Lehman Jr.," *Sea Power,* April 1987, 81.
35. Prina, "The Mathematics of Retrenchment," *Sea Power,* March 1987, 18.
36. Ibid., 19.
37. Hessman, "The Obligations of Military Leadership," *Sea Power,* March 1987, 29.
38. Bernard Bennett, "The Navy and the Nation," *Sea Power,* April 1987, 3.
39. Jack H. Morse, "A Scenario for Decline," *Sea Power,* May 1987, 3-4.

40. Prina, "The Possibility of Military Defeat," *Sea Power,* December 1987, 32.
41. Morse, "President's Message," *Sea Power,* January 1988, 1.
42. Norman Polmar, Letter to the Editor "Objections and Objectivity," *Sea Power,* February 1998, 5. John Lehman had anticipated such a development. He confided to the author in August 1983 that during the first two years of the Reagan Administration he had had to get his programs in place, fully funded, and get the Forward Maritime strategy "out there where everyone is talking about it, including the Soviets." According to Lehman, the remaining two years of Reagan's first term, and the entire second term, (of which he was confident there would be one), "would be spent fending off retrenchment efforts and 'raids' by the other services on his budget."

The high point of the Navy in ship count in the 1980s was 589; the "600-ship Navy" goal was never reached. Regardless, "15 carrier battle groups/600-ship Navy" was a remarkably successful mantra for the Reagan Administration's naval restoration program, and resonated in the United States, Europe, and the Soviet Union. It is still nostalgically remembered by the men and women of the Navy who served during the halcyon days when Ronald Reagan was President.
43. "Morse Comments on Webb Resignation and Reductions in Force Structure," *Sea Power,* April 1988, 36.
44. Calvin H. Cobb Jr., Letter to James D. Hessman, September 27, 2004. For his personal initiative and leadership, in August of 1990, Baltimore Council President Bruce Copeland received the Meritorious Public Service Award from Secretary of the Navy H. Lawrence Garrett III. Copeland later became Maryland State President of the Navy League and a member of the National Executive Committee. Alan Walden subsequently became President and chairman of the Baltimore Council.
45. Cobb, "To Enlighten the People on Naval Matters," *Shipmate,* April 1991, 16. Reprinted in *Sea Power,* May 1991. Citation is from *Sea Power* adaptation.
46. In July 1991, the Washington-based Heritage Foundation released a detailed report entitled "The Defense Budge Debate." In it, author Jay Kosminsky noted that "even in a changing strategic environment, the Navy will continue to be the service most responsible for influencing regional events wherever America's interests may be at state." Since 1945, he pointed out, "American forces have been involved in 240 crises, of which maritime forces were involved in 202; only 18 of these crises directly involved the Soviet Union." Kosminsky's report, along with similar findings by Senator John S. McCain, was cited in League National President William C. Kelley Jr.'s "Presidents Message" in the September 1991 issue of *Sea Power*.
47. Cobb, "On the Way, Sir!" *Sea Power,* October 1990, 5.
48. Michael A. Palmer, *On Course to Desert Storm: The United States Navy and the Persian Gulf*. (Washington: Naval Historical Center: Government Printing Office,

1992), xviii.
49. Cobb, interview by John D. Stegman, November 2002. Cobb also noted in the interview that he had started a Navy League council in Marseilles, France, tried and failed to establish a similar organization in Paris, and succeeded in obtaining the acquiescence of the Madrid, Spain, council in allowing two women (his wife and that of the local council President) to attend a dinner in his honor. Of note, the Madrid council now has female members, and a woman has served as the local council president.

Chapter X

1. Calvin Cobb Jr., "On The Scene, In Force," *Sea Power,* March 1991, 5-6.
2. Ibid., 6.
3. Mary I. Nolan, "SAS 1991: A 'Combat-Tested' Success." *Sea Power,* May 1991, 51.
4. Dudley Carlson, "Executive Director's Notes," *Sea Power,* May 1991, 52.
5. Frank B. Kelso II, "Charting a Course for the Future," *Sea Power,* April 1991, 14.
6. Ibid., 16.
7. Ibid., 18.
8. Cobb, "A Rationale For Reality," *Sea Power,* May 1991, 5.
9. Ibid., 6.
10. Navy League of the United States. *1991-92 Resolutions.* (Arlington, Virginia, August 1991).
11. William C. Kelly Jr., "Salute and Challenge," *Sea Power,* September 1991, 6.
12. Patricia L. Howard, "The Key Mission: Community Education," *Sea Power,* October 1991, 53.
13. Navy League of the United States. *1991-92 Resolutions.*
14. Charles E. Bennett, "The Navy League and Its Report on Desert Shield/Storm," *Congressional Record, http://Thomas.loc.gov/cgi-bin/query/z>* (July 16, 1991).
15. Ibid. The White Paper, entitled "The Sea Services's Role in Desert Shield/Storm" was reprinted in its entirety in the September 1991 issue of *Sea Power*, 27-33.
16. Robert W. Kesteloot, "Sealift After The Storm, A Plan to Revitalize the U.S.-Flag Fleet," *Sea Power,* June 1991, 37.
17. Herbert F. Hill, "The Navy League, Past, Present, and Future," *Sea Power,* December 1918.
18. The Cargo Preference Act of 1954, as amended, requires that at least 50 percent of the gross tonnage of all government-generated cargo be transported on privately owned, U.S.-flag commercial vessels "to the extent such vessels are available at fair and reasonable rates." In 1985, the Merchant Marine Act of 1936 was amended to require that the percentage of certain agricultural cargoes to be carried on U.S.-flag

vessels be increased from 50 to 75 percent. In the 21st century, an era of increasing deregulation in the transportation industry, efforts have focused on changing the Jones Act of 1920. These efforts, championed by such interests as the Steel Manufacturers Association, have been opposed by the Maritime Cabotage Task Force, a coalition of companies joined together to preserve the Jones Act.

The U.S. Maritime Administration is the government agency charged with "the development and maintenance of an adequate, well-balanced Merchant Marine, sufficient to carry the nation's domestic waterborne commerce and a substantial portion of its waterborne foreign commerce, and capable of serving as a naval and military auxiliary in time of war of national emergency." It maintains the National Defense Reserve Fleet as a ready source of ships for use during national emergencies and assists in fulfilling its traditional role in logistically supporting the military when and where needed. Its antecedents date from the Merchant Marine Act of 1936, which created the U.S. Maritime Commission. Abolished in May 1950, the Commission's functions were transferred to the Department of Commerce where they were assigned to the Federal Maritime Board and the Maritime Administration. The U.S. Maritime Administration now functions as an organization within the U.S. Department of Transportation.

The Navy League's *Maritime Policy 2005* states that "the problems facing the U.S.-flag Merchant Marine are severe and pervasive and require Presidential attention." It specifies League support of the Jones Act and "urges opposition to any legislative initiatives or trade agreements" that would weaken this vital support mechanism.

19. Kesteloot, 37.

20. Thomas C. Reed, *At the Abyss, An Insider's History of the Cold War* (New York: Random House, 2004; Presidio Press Trade Paperback Edition, 2005), 2. Citations are from Presidio Press edition.

21. Cheney's speech, given before the American Political Science Association, was quoted at length by League National President William C. Kelley Jr. in his "President's Message" in the October 1991 issue of *Sea Power*,.

22. Ibid.

23. Frank B. Kelso II. "Challenges on the Horizon." *Sea Power*, October 1991, 12.

24. Gilven Slonium, "Beyond Pearl Harbor: A SEA CHANGE!" *Vital Speeches of the Day*, March 1992, 311.

25. Ibid.

26. Ibid.

27. Vincent C. Thomas Jr., "The Restructuring of the Marine Corps," *Sea Power*, September 1991, 32.

28. Ibid., 38.

29. Evan Baker, interview by Richard L. Wright, tape recording, June 3, 2005, Navy

League National Convention, Norfolk, Virginia.
30. Baker, "Is the Navy Doomed To Becoming a Hollow Force?" White Paper, Spring 1994, 2.
31. Ibid.
32. Ibid., 3.
33. Ibid., 12.
34. Baker, "A year ago we asked: Is the Navy Doomed To Becoming a Hollow Force? Today, our assessment is: Yes, unless ... " White Paper, Spring 1995, 2.
35. Ibid., 5.
36. Ibid., 6. In a June 2005 discussion at the League's National Convention, Baker confided to Richard L. Wright that, in his opinion, the League "drinks its own bathwater" in believing it still influences major budgetary decisions regarding the sea services. He noted that, even with the effort expended on both White Papers, "it had no effect on what the Clinton Administration did to the Navy."
37. Navy League of the United States, *Annual Report 1994*, (Arlington, Virginia: 1994), 3. Baker also commented, on page 5 of the same report, on the League's support for the "Flag Protection Amendment" to the Constitution of the United States, the League's work, along with similar organizations, to successfully oppose the Smithsonian Institution's Air and Space Museum intention "to re-write history and portray the Enola Gay's mission at the end of World War II improperly, and in such a way that would have been revisionist and offensive to all patriotic Americans who are knowledgeable about World War II."
38. "Mayberry Announces Kickoff of New Highline Program, A New Opportunity for Pride, Service, Patriotism." *Sea Power,* March 1996, 52.
39. Jack M. Kennedy, "Much Ado About Very Little," *Sea Power,* February 1999: 5.
40. Hessman, "Our Navy Story," *Sea Power,* May 2000, 1.
41. Kennedy, "The Day of Reckoning," *Sea Power,* April 1999, 9.
42. Kennedy, "The Logistics Factor," *Sea Power,* May 1999, 5.
43. John R. Fisher, "A Call to Action," *Sea Power,* September 1999, 7.
44. John G. Kinney and Gordon I. Peterson, "The U.S. Engagement Strategy," *Sea Power,* September 1999, 42.
45. John R. Fisher, "A Tale of Two Centuries." *Almanac of Seapower 2000,* 1, 4.
46. "Warner Takes the Helm of Senate Armed Services Committee," *Sea Power,* February 1999, 17.
47. James H. Hessman and Gordon I. Peterson, "Interview with Secretary of Defense William S. Cohen," *Sea Power,* April 2000, 18.
48. Jack Dorsey, "*Cole* Survivors Think About, But Don't Dwell On, Bombing," *Norfolk Virginian-Pilot* October 12, 2005 (Electronic data base). Mullen added, "I can say with certainty that because of that attack the Navy is more aware of the threat, more prepared to thwart it and more ready, willing and able to take the fight to the

enemy than ever before."

Chapter XI

1. National Commission on Terrorist Attacks Upon the United States, *The 9/11 Commission Report* (New York: Barnes & Noble Books, 2004), 1.
2. Ibid., 311.
3. Ibid., xvi.
4. Vern Clark, (public address, Sea-Air-Space Exposition, Navy League of the United States. Washington, D.C., April 12, 2001).
5. Ibid.
6. Ibid.
7. "Navy League of the United States Kicks Off Centennial Celebration; 100 Years of 'Citizens in Support of the Sea Services,' " *U.S. Newswire*, Washington, D.C. June 21, 2001, 1.
8. James D. Hessman, "The First Century Is the Hardest," *Sea Power,* December 2002, 3.
9. "EPA Administrator Whitman to Break Ground on New Navy League Building; Structure Is First 'Green Building' in Arlington County," *U.S. Newswire*, Washington, April 8, 2003, 1. Reflecting the reality of real estate prices in Northern Virginia, former National President Fanning estimates that the Navy League's equity in the new building is now worth five times its initial investment. Timothy O. Fanning e-mail to Richard L. Wright, November 16, 2005.The national headquarters staff moved across the street to the new building in late August 2005. A "Welcome Aboard" reception was held in the new quarters during the League's Winter Meeting in early November 2005. A formal "2300 Wilson Boulevard Building Opening Ceremony" was held November 28, 2005, presided over by Fanning, now Chairman of the Property Development Committee. Both the Commandant of the Coast Guard and Assistant Commandant of the Marine Corps attended and gave short remarks saluting, in the words of Coast Guard Admiral Thomas J. Collins, the "complete and complementary relationship between the Navy League and the sea services." Admiral Collins also noted that Theodore Roosevelt, who in addition to being an ardent navalist, was an affirmed environmentalist, would have "been proud that the organization he helped found was now headquartered in a 'green building.'" Thomas J. Collins, (public address, Navy League of the United States 2300 Wilson Boulevard Building Opening Ceremony, Arlington, Virginia, November 28, 2005).
10. Scott C. Truver, "To Dissuade, Deter, and Defeat, U.S. Naval Power in the 21st Century," *Sea Power,* February 2003, 32.
11. Less than three years later, another Sea Cadet unit was involved in a similar

incident, this time in the Baltimore, Maryland, harbor. In the spring of 2004 a microburst of wind and an attendant rogue wave capsized a Baltimore Seaport Taxi near Fort McHenry and the Naval Reserve Center where the local Sea Cadet division was training. One of the Sea Cadet officers, Art Eisenstein, a retired Navy master diver, dove into the water and rescued a girl who had been trapped beneath the overturned vessel. After the survivors were brought ashore, the Sea Cadets provided blankets and refreshments for those individuals requiring them. The Sea Cadets and Naval Reserve Center personnel involved were subsequently awarded certificates of commendation and appropriate decorations by a representative of the Secretary of the Navy and members of the Maryland congressional delegation.

12. "Navy League Sends a Message and a Check To Family of WTC Hero Cop." *The Log, Official Publication of the Navy League of the United States, New York Council* 14, no. 3 (September-December 2001), 4.

13. Timothy O. Fanning, "Preemptive Action and Global Peace," *Almanac of Seapower 2003*, VII.

14. Peter Atkinson, "Council Support Efforts Can Help Military Families Cope," *Seapower,* June 2004, 48.

15. Atkinson, "Operation Homefront Offers Councils Chance to Build Mission, Membership," *Seapower,* February 2005, 48.

16. Department of the Navy, *Citation, Meritorious Public Service Award, Department of the Navy, to Connie O'Shaughnessy-Los,* May 29, 2002. Under Ms. Los's leadership, the Santa Barbara Council adopted USS *Ronald Reagan* (CVN-76), U.S. Coast Guard Cutter *Blackfin* (87317), and the local Coast Guard Marine Safety Detachment. She also spearheaded efforts to coordinate League ship visit activities with the Santa Barbara Boys and Girls Club of America, and worked to organize a new Naval Sea Cadet unit in Santa Barbara. In both 2000 and 2001, the Santa Barbara Council hosted more ships than any other League council in the Pacific Southwest Region.

17. Atkinson, "Clever Ideas, Luck Can Pay Off for Council Fundraisers," *Seapower,* February 2004, 48.

18. John W. Alexander and Stephen R. Pietropaoli, eds., *Our Navy Marine Corps Team Defending Freedom* (Hong Kong, PRC: Elegance Printing & Book Binding, Inc., 2005), 2.

19. James D. Hessman, "A Vision of Continuing Excellence," *Almanac of Seapower 2003*, 5.

20. Sheila M. McNeill, "Sea Power Ambassadors: Building Support for U.S. Fleets," *Sea Power,* December 2003, 3.

21. David A. Vergun, "Fanning asks Navy League members to support Navy/Marine Corps caucus, *Sea Power,*, July 2002, 55.

22. Ibid.

23. Fanning, "The Challenges Ahead," *Sea Power,* June 2003, 5.

24. McNeill, "Sea Power Ambassadors: Building Support for U.S. Fleets," 3. McNeil's reiteration of the League's mission of educating the American people on the need for strong sea services was correct, but also overlooked its founders' reluctance to get involved in particular aspects of fleet size and force structure. Certainly, this reluctance has not always been in evidence, from the time of Warren G. Harding and Herbert Hoover, to Jimmy Carter and George H. Bush. Still, writing in the May 1991 issue of *Sea Power*, then-National President Calvin Cobb noted, "As stated in the first edition of *The Navy League Journal* ... it was the League's resolve never to formulate specific needs for the Navy in such matters as ship types and force levels but, rather, to educate the American people on the importance of seapower. That mission continues to be fundamental today." Calvin H. Cobb Jr., "To Enlighten the People on Naval Matters," *Sea Power,* May 1991: 16. Cobb is correct in the League's education mission remaining fundamental, but in the eyes of many Navy Leaguers, the issue of fleet size and combat capability is an equally important issue for League consideration, deliberation, and publication as an issue of policy.
25. Hunter Keeter, "Navy Strives for Eight Carrier Battle Groups Ready to Roll," *Sea Power,* December 2003, 7.
26. "Navy League Looks Ahead to 2005," *Seapower Almanac 2005* January 2005, 184.
27. Ibid.
28. McNeill, "Shipbuilding Strategies for Success," *Seapower Almanac 2005*, January 2005, VII.
29. Jim Mottern, "Ask Tough Questions On Shipbuilding," *Seapower*, February 2005, 5.
30. Richard C. Macke, "Navy League concerned about the consequence of shrinkage," *Fore 'n Aft Magazine* (Honolulu Council Navy League), March 2005, 6.
31. Navy League of the United States, *Maritime Policy 2005* (Arlington, Va., 2005), 4-5. Part of the League's challenge on the issue of the size of the Navy is the disparity in both the number of ships and their combat capability in the early years of the 21st century. As Carl Vinson warned after World War II, the Navy is largely a victim of its own success. A monograph and briefing prepared by the faculty and staff of the Naval War College in mid-2005, entitled "Is the United States Navy Relevant in an Age of Global War on Terror?" notes that "for the first time in a century the Navy has no global challenger." While admitting that "the Navy has fewer than 300 ships for the first time since World War II," it notes that the "current U.S. Battle Force comprises 2.86 million tons while the entire rest of the world's navies amass a combined total of 3.04 million tons." The U.S. Navy has 80 percent of all aircraft carriers in the world. In surface combatants and submarines, the Navy can put 6,827 missile cells to sea; the rest of the world can put but 1,208 cells to sea and every one of these ships are in allied, not potential adversary, navies. The Naval

War College quotes A.D. Baker III, editor of *Combat Fleets of the World*: "The U.S. Navy's fleet is essentially unchallengeable ... from the standpoint of military technology, there is simply no other nation with the same naval capabilities, and it appears that no challenger will be likely to appear for two to three decades in the future." Ron Ratcliff, Rand LeBouvier, Susan Fink, and Alan Boyer, "Is the United States Navy Relevant in an Age of Global War on Terror?" Monograph and Briefing, United States Naval War College, 2005.

On the subject of numbers of fleet units, the Senate Appropriations Committee's fiscal year 2006 defense spending bill commented, "The committee remains focused on the warfighting prowess each ship and submarine provides the fleet rather than on the total number of vessels in the Navy's inventory." *Inside the Navy, www.InsideDefense.com*, October 10, 2005.

32. The capabilities of the U.S. Navy in the 21st century are certainly understood by America's most likely global challenger in the years ahead, China. After interviewing several government officials and academics in Beijing and Shanghai following China's bid for Union Oil of California in June 2005, Peter Goodman wrote, "Officials in Beijing envision being cut off from energy supplies by the U.S. Navy in the event of a war (over Taiwan). Owning oil fields does not ensure access, because getting oil where it is needed depends largely on shipping lanes policed by the U.S. Navy." Peter Goodman, "Big Shift on China's Oil Policy," *Washington Post*, July 13, 2005, D12.

33. Michael G. Mullen, (public address, National Defense University. Washington, D.C., August 16, 2005).

34. Mullen, FlagSES Web Mail, 131236Z Oct 05, "Subj: CNO Guidance 2006."

35. "Shipbuilding Discussed Repeatedly at Hearing for Young, Etter," *Inside the Navy*, October 31, 2005 (Electronic data base).

36. Patricia Kime, "Admiral Keating Says Coast Guard Was 'Pivotal' Force," *Sea Power,* October 2003, 6. The Coast Guard's official colors carry battle streamers from the French Naval War of the late 18th century to the Persian Gulf War of the 21st. Admiral Keating awarded Bronze Stars to four Coast Guard patrol boat commanders serving in the conflict.

37. Patrick M. Stillman, "Need for *Deepwater* Rises as CG Workload Expands," *Sea Power,* August 2003, 23.

38. Thomas J. Collins, "Collins Strikes Balance Between Present, Future Resources," *Sea Power,* August 2004, 42.

39. Collins, "Transforming the United States Coast Guard," (public address, National Convention, Navy League of the United States, Norfolk, Virginia, June 3, 2005). Symbolic of the increasingly close relationship between the Navy League and the Coast Guard, in October 2004 National President Sheila McNeill was given the "2004 U.S. Armed Forces Spirit of Hope Award" (named for the renowned

entertainer of American forces overseas from World War II to the Persian Gulf, Bob Hope) during the Coast Guard Ball in Arlington, Virginia. In his presentation of the award, Coast Guard Commandant Collins cited the Navy League President's role in advancing the Coast Guard's legislative agenda and supporting the sea service as it transitioned to the new Department of Homeland Security. "Sheila McNeill has been one of the Coast Guard's most consistent supporters," Collins noted, adding that "her influence is felt throughout the Coast Guard at all levels, from adopting local units and taking on quality-of-life issues for our sailors, to providing trusted counsel to our senior leaders." Peter Atkinson, "Hampton roads Council Showcases 'Admirals Quarters' at 'Homerama,'" *Seapower/Navy League News*, December 2004.

40. Michael Bruno, "Maritime strategy, Katrina seen buttressing *Deepwater* prospects," *Aerospace Daily & Defense Report*, September 22, 2005. Two weeks later, Navy Admiral John B. Nathman would cite the National Strategy for Maritime Security as having "strong implications for the Navy." Nathman asserted, "If you want to stop a terrorist in Iraq, you have to be there. If you want to stop a threat on the high seas, you have to be there. Would you want to stop a container ship with a weapon of mass destruction aboard, in Yemen, or would you rather stop a container ship at the entrance to the harbor at Long Beach? We want the war on terrorism to be an away game." Jim Hodges, "Admiral defends role of Navy in combating terrorism," *Newport News Daily Press*, October 6, 2005 (Electronic database).

41. McNeill, "Port Security Funds: A Framework for Failure," *Sea Power*, September 2003, 3.

42. McNeill, "Memo to Congress: Streamline Homeland Security Oversight," *Seapower*, August 2004, 3. Ironically, McNeill went on to praise the Truman Administration's Legislative Reorganization Act of 1946 which merged both congressional houses' Naval Affairs and Military Affairs Committees into Armed Services Committees for each deliberating body, an initiative specifically opposed and vainly fought against by the Navy League in the years immediately following the Second World War.

43. "Experts Fault Paltry Funding, Lack of Port Security Strategy," *Seapower*, October 2004, 6.

44. Robert S. Branham, (public address, 2005 Winter Meeting, Navy League of the United States, Arlington, Virginia. November 3, 2005).

45. Michael Bruno, "Congress to appropriate $933 million for Coast Guard's *Deepwater*," *Aerospace Daily & Defense Report*, September 30, 2005.

46. Vern Clark, "Sea-Air-Space Exposition, Navy League of the United States," (public address, Washington, D.C., March 23, 2005).

47. Ibid.

48. Mullen, Message to All Navy Admin, 231853Z JUL 05, "Subj: All Ahead Full."

49. John A. Panneton, "A Navy League Agenda: Duty, Honor and Country." *Seapower,* July 2005, 3.
50. Thom Shanker, "All Quiet On The Home Front, And Some Are Asking Why." *New York Times,* July 24, 2005, 17. Reflecting the "joint" approach to defense issues prevalent in the 21st century, the author identified the Navy League as a "private organization that supports the individual armed services" and one "urging greater contributions from members now in the civilian world."
51. Mullen, (public address, 17th International Seapower Symposium, Naval War College, Newport, Rhode Island, September 21, 2005). The admiral's focus on military, vice emergency response, duties for the uniformed military was reflected in Marine General Peter Pace's first interview as the new Chairman of the Joint Chiefs of Staff. While admitting that Americans "are right to expect our military will act during a disaster," he cautioned that the military had to "respect their civil rights at the same time," and opined that "we must now absorb those lessons from Katrina." James Brady, "In Step With Gen. Peter Pace," *Parade,* October 2, 2005, 15.

Admiral Timothy Keating, now four-star commander of U.S. Northern Command, echoed the new chairman, and the Secretary of Defense, in assessing the military's role in disaster response. While lauding the effort which at its peak saw more than 70,000 U.S. active duty and guard personnel deployed to the Gulf Coast region, Keating noted that only in extreme cases, when first responders were overwhelmed, as they were in the immediate aftermath of Hurricane Katrina, is there "a role to be considered for the active-duty forces." Ann Scot Tyson, "Military Forces Stretched by Hurricanes," *Washington Post,* October 2, 2005, A20.
52. Ibid.

REFERENCES
Primary Sources

Diaries, Memorandums, Letters and Papers

Adams, Charles Francis. Letter to Mr. Walter Bruce Howe, Navy League of the United States, July 20, 1931.

Baker, Evan S. "A year ago we asked: Is the Navy Doomed To Becoming a Hollow Force? Today, our assessment is: Yes, unless ..." White Paper, Spring 1995.

—-. "Is the Navy Doomed To Becoming a Hollow Force?" White Paper, Spring 1994.

—-. Letter to Richard L. Wright, June 28, 2005.

Bard, Ralph A. *The Navy League of the United States Report to Members, December 6, 1946.*

Barnum, Robert H. *Annual Report of Robert H. Barnum, National President Navy League of the United States, 62nd Annual Convention, Dallas, Texas, May 19-22, 1964.*

—-. *Report of Robert H. Barnum, National President Navy League of the United States 1963-1965, 63rd Annual Convention, Washington, D.C., April 20-24, 1965.*

Bonnet, Emile R. "Happy Anniversary! Navy League Incorporated in New York 2 January 1903." Working paper, Historian General Emeritus, Naval Order of the United States, 1978.

Chicago Council, Navy League of the United States. *Program, 25th Anniversary Dinner*, October 27, 1967. Chicago, Illinois 1967.

—-. *The Bullhorn* June 2005.

Church, A.T., III, memorandum "Implementation of Chief of Naval Operations (CNO) Guidance Global War on Terrorism (GWOT) Capabilities," to Staff, Office of Chief of Naval Operations, July 6, 2005.

Cobb, Calvin H., Jr. Letter to James D. Hessman, September 27, 2004.

Collins, Winifred Quick with Herbert M. Levine. *More Than a Uniform–A Navy Woman in a Navy Man's World*. Denton, Texas: University of North Texas Press, 1997.

Crawford, J.H. Letter to H.L. Miller, Chief of Information (U.S. Navy). August 19, 1965.

Crown, Robert. *Annual Report of Robert Crown, National President Navy League of the United States, 61st Annual Convention, San Juan, Puerto Rico, April 29-May 4, 1963.*

Department of the Navy. *Citation, Distinguished Service Award, Department of the Navy, to Evelyn Mary Collins*, April 23, 1959.

—-. Citation, *Meritorious Public Service Award, Department of the Navy, to Connie O'Shaughnessy-Los*, May 29, 2002.

Fitch, Morgan L., Jr. *Annual Report of Morgan L. Fitch Jr., National President Navy League of the United States 1965-1966, 64th Annual Convention, Santa Monica, California May 23-27, 1966.*
—-. Letter to James D. Holmes III. July 26, 1965.
Flint, Sanford C. Letter to National Officers and Directors, Navy League of the United States. March 15, 1965.
Hecht, Frank A. *Report by Committee on Council Development, April 23-25, 1952. Forwarded to Navy League Officers, Directors and Council Presidents, June 30, 1952.*
—-. *Report of Meeting of the National Directors and Council Presidents April 29-May 1, 1953.*
Hoffman, Jim. Letter to John J. Spittler, March 29, 2004.
Hubbard, Nathaniel Mead, Jr. "Our Merchant Marine–Shall It Sink or Swim?" Press Release, Navy League of the United States, August 22, 1935.
Jameson, Frank Gard. Letter to Morgan L. Fitch Jr. May 22, 1962.
Kelley, Robert W. Letter to Robert M. Thompson, March 10, 1922.
Kennedy, Jack M. Letter to Louis Kriser, February 23, 2000.
King, Ernest. *U.S. Navy at War, 1941-1945, Official Reports to the Secretary of the Navy.* Washington: United States Navy Department, 1946.
Kriser, Louis. Letter to Jack Morse, President, Navy League of the United States, December 1, 1987.
—-. Memorandum to Hugh Mayberry, President, Navy League of the United States, December 2, 1996.
McDonald, David L. Letter to Morgan L. Fitch Jr., President, Navy League of the United States, August 10, 1965.
—-. Letter to Morgan L. Fitch Jr., President, Navy League of the United States. April 4, 1967.
McNeill, Sheila M. Camden Kings Bay Council History memorandum to Richard L. Wright, October 2005.
—-. Letter to Richard L. Wright, October 3, 2005.
Miller, H.L. Letter to Morgan L. Fitch Jr., President, Navy League of the United States. April 12, 1967.
—-. Letter to David L. McDonald, Chief of Naval Operations. August 2, 1966.
Navy League of the United States. *1996-1997 Resolutions*. Arlington, Virginia: June 1996.
—-. *1991-92 Resolutions*. Arlington, Virginia: August 1991.
—-. *A Day in Vietnam*. Program, Navy League of the United States, 64th Annual Convention, 1966.
—-. *Annual Report 1994*. Arlington, Virginia: 1994.
—-. *Centennial Council Kit*. Arlington, Virginia: 2001.

—-. *Maritime Policy 2005*. Arlington, Virginia: 2005.
—-. Minutes, National Advisory Council. Arlington, Virginia: March 26, 2002.
—-. *Operations Manual*. Arlington, Virginia: April 1981.
—-. *Operations Manual*. 5th ed. with chg 1. Arlington, Virginia.: 2004.
—-. *Resolution in Appreciation to Evelyn Mary Collins*: April 26, 1968.
—-. *Resolution in Appreciation to Jane Collins Grover*: July 2, 1986.
—-. *Resolution–Panama Canal Treaties*. December 3, 1977.
Navy League of the United States and Association of the United States Army, *Dedication Program, Army-Navy Museum, Pemberton House, Independence Square, Philadelphia, Pennsylvania:* September 27, 1968.
Navy Office of Information. "Katrina: Navy Relief Efforts." *Rhumb Lines, Straight Lines to Navigate By, Special Supplement,* September 1, 2005.
New York Council, Navy League of the United States. *Program, Golden Anniversary Dinner*, 1902-52. New York 1952.
Nitze, Paul H. Letter to Morgan L. Fitch Jr., President, Navy League of the Untied States. April 12, 1967.
Porett, Leo I. Letter to the National Nominating Committee, Navy League of the United States. March 3, 1965.
Rau, John M. *Report of and Recommendations from the Property Redevelopment Sub-Committee of the Building Committee* to National Directors, Navy League of the United States, November 20, 1987.
Richards, E.V., Jr. *Report of E.V. Richards Jr., President, Navy League of the United States, at the Annual Meeting of Members Held in Detroit, Michigan on Friday, December 3, 1954.*
Seymour, Charles. *The Intimate Papers of Colonel House*, I. Boston: Houghton Mifflin, 1926.
Spittler, John J. Letter to Janet Mescus. October 16, 2005.
Swanson, Claude A. Letter to Mr. Nelson Macy, President, Navy League of the United States, July 5, 1935.
Thompson, William. Letter to Morgan L. Fitch Jr., President, Navy League of the United States. April 6, 1967.
—-. Memorandum for the Record. March 8, 1965.
—-. Memorandum to Paul H. Nitze, Secretary of the Navy. June 10, 1966.
—-. Memorandum to Paul H. Nitze, Secretary of the Navy. July 29, 1966.
United States Naval Sea Cadet Corps, *U.S. Naval Sea Cadet Corps 2004 Annual Report*. Arlington, Virginia: 2005.
Wright, Richard L. "Forty Years Ago: *United States* vs. B-36." Memorandum submitted to Deputy Chief of Naval Operations (Naval Warfare, OP-07), August 1989.

Interviews, Public Addresses and Oral Histories

Baker, Evan. Interview by Richard L. Wright. Tape recording. June 3, 2005, Navy League National Convention, Norfolk, Virginia.

Balisle, Philip M. "Navy Ball and Birthday Celebration." Keynote address, Navy League and Oklahoma City Chamber of Commerce Navy Ball, Oklahoma City, Oklahoma, September 27, 2003.

Barnum, Robert. Interview by William Thompson. December 28, 1963.

Bergen, John J. Public address, 57th Annual Banquet, Navy League of the United States. Philadelphia, Pennsylvania. May 8, 1959.

Branham, Robert S. Public address, 2005 Winter Meeting, Navy League of the United States, Arlington, Virginia. November 3, 2005.

Cheney, Richard B. Public address, Commissioning of USS *Arleigh Burke* (DDG-51), Norfolk, Virginia. July 4, 1991.

Clark, Vern. Public address, Sea-Air-Space Exposition, Navy League of the United States. Washington D.C. April 12, 2001.

—-. Public address, Sea-Air-Space Exposition, Navy League of the United States. Washington D.C. March 23, 2005.

Cobb, Calvin H., Jr. Interview by John D. Stegman. November 2002.

Collins, Thomas J. Public address, "Transforming the United States Coast Guard." National Convention, Navy League of the United States, Norfolk, Virginia, June 3, 2005.

—-. Public address. Navy League of the United States 2300 Wilson Boulevard Building Opening Ceremony, Arlington, Virginia. November 28, 2005.

Crown, Joanne. Interview by Rosalind K. Ellis. January 8, 1989.

Crown, Robert. Interview by William Thompson. March 13, 1967.

Fanning, Timothy O. Public address. Navy League of the United States 2300 Wilson Boulevard Building Opening Ceremony, Arlington, Virginia. November 28, 2005.

Fargo, Thomas B. Public address, National Convention, Navy League of the United States, Honolulu, Hawaii. June 21, 2003.

Fitch, Morgan. "Commissioning of the USS *Fox*." Public address, Long Beach, California. May 28, 1966.

—-. Interview by William Thompson. March 12-13, 1967.

—-. Interview by John D. Stegman. November 2002.

—-. Interview by Richard L. Wright. August 2, 2005.

—-. Public address, Annual Meeting, Navy League of the United States, Santa Monica, California. May 27, 1966.

Gilman, George C. Interview by Rosalind K. Ellis. (Undated).

Grover, Jane Collins. Interview by Richard L. Wright. Tape recording. June 3, 2005, Navy League National Convention, Norfolk, Virginia.

—-. Phone conversation with Richard L. Wright. October 22, 2005.

Hoffman, Linda. Interview by Richard L. Wright. October 19, 2005. National Headquarters, Navy League of the United States.
Jameson, Frank Gard. Interview by Rosalind K. Ellis. December 22, 1988.
—-. Interview by William Thompson. May 5, 1967.
Johnson, Lyndon B. Public address, "Our Objective in Vietnam." Navy League of the United States, Manchester, New Hampshire, September 12, 1966.
Keating, Timothy J. "Beyond Borders." *Seapower* April 2005: 32-34.
Kelso, Frank B., II. "Challenges on the Horizon." *Sea Power* October 1991: 11-19.
Kriser, Louis. Interview by Richard L. Wright. Tape recording. June 3, 2005, Navy League National Convention, Norfolk, Virginia.
—-. Interview by Richard L. Wright. Tape recording. June 21, 2005, Army-Navy Country Club, Arlington, Virginia.
McNeill, Sheila M. Public address, Camden Kiwanis Club/Rotary/ Daughters of the American Revolution, Camden, Georgia, August 15, 2005.
Magnus, Robert. Public address, Navy League of the United States 2300 Wilson Boulevard Building Opening Ceremony. November 28, 2005.
Mullen, Michael G. Public address, 17th International Seapower Symposium, Naval War College, Newport, Rhode Island. September 21, 2005.
—-. Public address, National Defense University. Washington, D.C. August 16, 2005.
Myers, Richard B. Public address, Sea-Air-Space Exposition, Navy League of the United States. Washington, D.C. March 23, 2005.
Rau, John M. Interview by Richard L. Wright. Tape recording. June 3, 2005, Navy League National Convention, Norfolk, Virginia.
Ravitz, Robert A. Interview by Richard L. Wright. Tape recording. June 3, 2005, Navy League National Convention, Norfolk, Virginia.
Renehan, Edward J. Public address, "TR and the Navy." 80th Annual Dinner of the Theodore Roosevelt Association, Norfolk, Virginia, October 29, 1999.
Roosevelt, Franklin D. "Request for a Declaration of War." Message to 77th Congress, December 8, 1941. Congressional Record, 77th Congress, 1st Session, 9519-9520.
—-. "Total National Defense." Navy Day address to the nation, October 27, 1941. Congressional Record, Appendix, 77th Congress, 1st Session, A4877-A4878.
Samuels, Ivan R. Interview by Richard L. Wright. Tape recording. June 3, 2005, Navy League National Convention, Norfolk, Virginia.
Spittler, John J. Interview by John D. Stegman. November 2002.
Stockholm, Carl G. Interview by Rosalind K. Ellis. January 7, 1989.

Congressional and Executive Documents

An Act to Incorporate the Naval Sea Cadet Corps. Public Law No: 87-655 (September 10, 1962)

National Commission on Terrorist Attacks Upon the United States. *The 9/11 Commission Report*. New York: Barnes & Noble Books, 2004.

National Strategy for Maritime Security. September 2005.

Mullen, Michael G. *CNO Guidance for 2006: Meeting the Challenge of a New Era.* October 13, 2005.

Pace, Peter. *The 16th Chairman's Guidance to the Joint Staff*. October 1, 2005.

To Express Appreciation to W. Graham Claytor Jr., for a lifetime of dedicated and inspired service to the Nation. Public Law No: 103-165 (December 2, 1993)

Electronic Sources

Allard, Dean C. "The U.S. Navy, SACLANT, and the Northern Flank during the Cold War," *http://www. luftfart.museum .no/Engelsk/ Research/Dean C. Allard*

Bennett, Charles E. "The Navy League and Its Report on Desert Shield/Storm," *Congressional Record,http://Thomas.loc.gov/cgi-bin/query/z>* (July 16, 1991).

Chung, Paul T. e-mail message to Sheila M. McNeill, October 18, 2005.

—-. e-mail message to Sheila M. McNeill, October 19, 2005.

Coates, Dan and Dee. e-mail message to Janet Mescus, October 17, 2005.

Cozzone, Deborah. e-mail message to Sheila M. McNeill, November 1, 2005

Culhane, John. "The Man Who Bought an Aircraft Carrier." Intrepid Sea, Air & Space Museum, *http://www.intrepidmuseum.org*

Denegre, Tom. e-mail message to Sheila M. McNeill, October 21, 2005.

Fanning, Timothy O. e-mail message to Richard L. Wright, November 16, 2005.

Federal Maritime Administration at Lawdog. *http://www.lawdog. com/ transport /sea2.htm*

Fitch, Morgan. e-mail message to Richard L. Wright, July 23, 2005.

—-. e-mail message to Richard L. Wright, July 26, 2005.

—-. e-mail message to Richard L. Wright, July 28, 2005.

—-. e-mail message to Richard L. Wright, August 11, 2005.

—-. e-mail message to Richard L. Wright, October 30, 2005.

—-. e-mail message to Richard L. Wright, November 24, 2005.

Hackley, Carol Ann. e-mail message to Sheila M. McNeill, November 1, 2005.

Hawks, Chuck. The Treaty Battleships. *http://www. chuckhawks.com/ treaty_ battle ships.htm.*

Havens, Gerald. e-mail message to Sasebo Navy League Council Members and Friends of the Navy League, October 16, 2005.

Historical Documents and Speeches–National Industrial Recovery Act (1933), *http://www.historicaldocuments.com/National IndustrialRecoveryAct.htm*

Hodges, Doyle. e-mail message to Sasebo Navy League Council, October 16, 2005.

Hoffman, Linda. e-mail message to Richard L. Wright, October 26, 2005.

Inside the Navy, *www.InsideDefense.com*, October 10, 2005.

—-. October 17, 2005.

—-. October 24, 2005.

—-. October 31, 2005.

International Sea Cadets Association. *www.isca-seacadets.org*

Intrepid Sea, Air & Space Museum, *www.intrepidmuseum.org*

Kriser, Louis. "NL Executive Director role revised." e-mail message to John A. Panneton, February 3, 2000.

McNeill, Sheila M. e-mail message to Richard L. Wright, October 17, 2005.

Miller, Hank L. Message to Secretary of the Navy and Chief of Naval Operations, et al., 020133Z JAN 66, "Subj: Nuclear Task Group in Combat."

Miller, Jack. e-mail message to Sheila M. McNeill, October 17, 2005.

Morris, Thomas E. e-mail message to Richard L. Wright, October 30, 2005.

Mullen, Michael G. FlagSES Web Mail, 131236Z Oct 05, "Subj: CNO Guidance 2006."

—-. Message to All Navy Admin, 231853Z JUL 05, "Subj: All Ahead Full."

Museum of Science and Industry, U-505 Submarine, The First Exhibit, Chicagoans Save the U-505, *http://www. msichicago.org/exhibit /U505/history.firstexhibition/b_at_the_museum.html*

National Park Service of the United States, Independence National Historic Park, Survey of Historic Sites and Buildings, *http://www.cr.nps.gov/history/online_books/constitution/site231.htm*

Navy League of the United States. *www.navyleague.org*

Palmer, Michael A. "The Navy: The Transoceanic Period, 1945-1992." *http://www.history.navy.mil/history/history4.htm*

Parson, W.H. e-mail message to Kathryn Hobbs, Captain, United States Navy, July 30, 2005.

Rau, John M. e-mail message to Richard L. Wright, August 1, 2005.

—-. e-mail message to Richard L. Wright, November 8, 2005.

Ravitz, Robert A. e-mail message to Richard L. Wright, August 3, 2005.

Romania, Embassy of. "The Embassy of Romania." *http://www.roembus.org/ english/contact/descriere_ambasada.htm*> (July 18, 2005)

Rositzke, Robert. e-mail message to Richard L. Wright, November 16, 2005.

Stobo, John R. Brooklyn Navy Yard in the Inter-War Era, The New Deal Yard, 1933-1937, Part 2, *http://www.columbia.edu/~jrs9/BNY-Hist-ND2.html*

Thompson, William. e-mail message to Morgan L. Fitch Jr., August 1, 2005.

—-. e-mail message to Richard L. Wright, November 2, 2005.

United States Department of Defense. DefenseLINK: Armed Forces Day History, *http://www.defenselink.mil/afd/military/navy.html*> (April 16, 2004)

United States Department of Defense. DODNEWS-L@DTIC.MIL: "Department of the Navy Announces the Death of Retired Vice Admiral James B. Stockdale" news release, July 5, 2005.

United States Maritime Administration. *http://www.marad.dot.gov*

Wilson, Ralph. e-mail message to Richard L. Wright, November 1, 2005.

Musical Score

Denis, Alberta Johnston. *The U.S. Navy League* (March), 1917

Secondary Sources

Books

Alexander, John W., and Stephen R. Pietropaoli, eds. *Our Navy Marine Corps Team Defending Freedom*. Hong Kong, PRC: Elegance Printing & Book Binding, Inc., 2005.

Allard, Dean C. "An Era of Transition, 1945-1953." Hagan. 290-303.

Britten, Loretta, and Paul Mathless, eds. *Our American Century, Dawn of the Century 1900-1910*. Alexandria, Virginia: Bishop Books, Inc., 1998.

—-. Our American Century. Decade of Triumph, the '40s. Alexandria, Virginia: Bishop Books, Inc., 1999.

Britten, Loretta, and Sara Brash, eds. *Our American Century, The American Dream, The '50s*. Alexandria, Virginia: Bishop Books, Inc., 1998.

Bacevich, Andrew J. *The New American Militarism, How Americans Are Seduced By War.* New York: Oxford University Press, 2005.

Bellamy, Christopher. "Cold War." Holmes 211.

Brugioni, Dino A. *Eyeball to Eyeball, The Inside Story of the Cuban Missile Crisis*. ed. Robert F. McCort. New York: Random House, 1990.

Chambers, John Whiteclay, II, Ed. *The Oxford Companion to American Military History*. New York: Oxford University Press, 1999.

Chambers, John Whiteclay, II, and Brian Adkins. "McNamara, Robert S." Chambers 424-425.

Clements, Kendrick A. "Wilson, Woodrow." Chambers 807-808.

Clifford, J. Garry. "Roosevelt, Franklin D." Chambers 623-624.

Cook, James F. *Carl Vinson, Patriarch of the Armed Forces*. Macon, Georgia: Mercer University Press, 2004.

Davidson, Joel R. *The Unsinkable Fleet, The Politics of U.S. Navy Expansion in World War II*. Annapolis, Maryland: Naval Institute Press, 1996.

Friedman, Norman. *The Fifty-Year War, Conflict and Strategy in the Cold War.*

Annapolis, Maryland: Naval Institute Press, 2000.
Hagan, Kenneth J., ed. *In Peace and War, Interpretations of American Naval History, 1775-1984*. 2nd ed. Westport, Connecticut: Greenwood Press, 1984.
Harries, Meirion and Susie. *The Last Days of Innocence, America at War, 1917-1918*. New York: Random House, 1997.
Hessman, James D. and Thomas B. Allen, eds. *The Almanac of Sea Power–1983*. Arlington, Virginia: 1983.
Holmes, Richard, ed. *The Oxford Companion to Military History*. New York: Oxford University Press, 2001.
Hoopes, Townsend. "Forrestal, James V." Chambers 274-275.
Jackson, Robert H. *That Man, An Insider's Portrait of Franklin D. Roosevelt*. New York: Oxford University Press, 2003. Reprinted, edited and introduced by John Q. Barrett with Foreword by William E. Leuchtenburg. New York: Oxford University Press, 2004.
Jones, Ken and Hubert Kelley Jr. *Admiral Arleigh (31-Knot) Burke, The Story of a Fighting Sailor.* 1962. Annapolis, Maryland: Naval Institute Press, 2001.
Keegan, John. *A History of Warfare*. New York: Vintage Books, 1994.
Kennedy, Floyd D. "The Creation of the Cold War Navy, 1953-1962." Hagan 304-326.
—-. "From SLOC Protection to a National Maritime Strategy: The U.S. Navy Under Carter and Reagan, 1977-1984." Hagan 347-370.
Korb, Lawrence J. "The Erosion of American Naval Preeminence, 1962-1978." Hagan 327-346.
Lal, Deepak. *In Praise of Empires, Globalization and Order*. New York: Palgrave Macmillan, 2004.
Larrabee, Eric. *Commander in Chief, Franklin Delano Roosevelt, His Lieutenants & Their War*. New York: Harper & Row, 1987.
Lehman, John F., Jr. Command of the Seas. New York: Charles Scribner's Sons, 1988.
—-. *On Seas of Glory, Heroic Men, Great Ships, and Epic Battles of the American Navy.* New York: The Free Press, 2001.
—-. "Navy, U.S.: Since 1946." Chambers 490-491.
Love, Robert William, Jr. "Fighting a Global War, 1941-1945." Hagan 263-289.
MacMillan, Margaret. Paris 1919, *Six Months That Changed the World*. New York: Random House, 2001.
Major, John. "The Navy Plans for War, 1937-1941." Hagan. 237-262.
Massie, Robert K. *Castles of Steel, Britain, Germany, and the Winning of the Great War at Sea*. New York: Random House, 2003.
McCullough, David. *Truman*. New York: Simon & Schuster, 1992.
Morgan, Ted. *FDR, A Biography*. New York: Simon and Schuster, 1985.

Morris, Edmund. *Theodore Rex*. New York: Random House, 2001.
—-. *The Rise of Theodore Roosevelt*. New York: Coward, McCann & Geoghegan, Inc.
Muir, Malcolm, Jr. "Navy, U.S.: 1866-1898." Chambers 488-489.
—-. "Navy, U.S.: 1899-1945." Chambers 489-490.
Murray, Williamson and Allan R. Millett, eds. *Military Innovation in the Interwar Period.* New York: Cambridge University Press, 1996.
Nashel, Jonathan. "Cold War (1945-91)." Chambers 147-155.
O'Toole, Patricia. *When Trumpets Call, Theodore Roosevelt after The White House*. New York: Simon and Schuster, 2005.
Oyos, Matthew. "Roosevelt, Theodore." Chambers 624.
Palmer, Michael A. *Origins of the Maritime Strategy, American Naval Strategy in the First Postwar Decade*. Washington, D.C., Naval Historical Center: Government Printing Office, 1988.
—-. *On Course to Desert Storm: The United States Navy and the Persian Gulf.* Washington, D.C., Naval Historical Center: Government Printing Office, 1992.
Perry, Mark. Four Stars: *The Inside Story of the Forty-Year Battle Between the Joint Chiefs of Staff and America's Civilian Leaders*. New York: Houghton-Mifflin Company, 1989.
Polmar, Norman. "The 600-Ship Fleet Enters Political Narrows." In James D. Hessman and Thomas B. Allen, eds. *The Almanac of Sea Power 1983*. Arlington, Virginia: 1983.
Potter, E. B. *Admiral Arleigh Burke*. Annapolis, Maryland: Naval Institute Press, 1990.
Puryear, Edgar F., Jr. American Admiralship, The Moral Imperatives of Naval Command. Annapolis, Maryland: Naval Institute Press, 2005.
Rappaport, Armin. *The Navy League of the United States*. Detroit: Wayne State University Press, 1962.
Rau, John M. "Foreword." In James D. Hessman and Thomas B. Allen, eds. *The Almanac of Sea Power–1983*. Arlington, Virginia: 1983.
Reed, Thomas. *At the Abyss, An Insider's History of the Cold War*. New York: Random House, 2004.
Rosen, Philip T. "The Treaty Navy, 1919-1937." Hagan 221-236.
Rosenberg, David Alan. "Burke, Arleigh." Chambers 96-97.
Schaller, Michael. "Reagan, Ronald." Chambers 592.
Spector, Ronald. "The Triumph of Professional Ideology: The U.S. Navy in the 1890s." Hagan 174-185.
Sweetman, Jack. *American Naval History, An Illustrated Chronology of the U.S. Navy and Marine Corps 1775-Present.* Annapolis, Maryland: Naval Institute Press, 1984.
Thomas, Vincent C., Jr. "Sea Services: Navy on Course, Maritime on Shoals." In

James D. Hessman and Thomas B. Allen, eds. *The Almanac of Sea Power 1983.* Arlington, Virginia: 1983.
Till, Geoffrey. "Adopting the Aircraft Carrier, The British, American, and Japanese case studies." Murray 191-226.
—-. "Naval Power." Holmes 632-639.
Trask, David F. "The American Navy in a World at War, 1914-1919." Hagan 205-220.
Turk, Richard W. "Defending the New Empire, 1900-1914." Hagan 186-204.
United States Naval Sea Cadet Corps. *2004 Annual Report*. Arlington, Virginia, 2005.
Waller, Douglas. *A Question of Loyalty, Gen. Billy Mitchell and the Court-Martial That Gripped a Nation*. New York: HarperCollins Publishers Inc., 2004.
Zimmerman, Warren. First Great Triumph, How Five Americans Made Their Country a World Power. New York: Farrar, Straus and Giroux, 2002.

Articles

"63rd Annual Convention." *Navy–The Magazine of Sea Power* June 1965: 44-51.
"300,000 Acclaim Navy Day Parade." *New York Times,* October 25,1942: 1.
"Admiral McCain Cites 4-Ocean Challenge." *1964 Navy League Convention Booster* May 21, 1964: 2.
"Admiral Warns of Soviet Fleet Gains," *New York Times,* September 28, 1969: 82.
Ahern, Dave. "Navy Nominee Seeks More Fixed-Price Contracts; Etter: Keeping Two Shipbuilders Open Must Be Cost Effective." *Defense Today* October 26, 2005 (Electronic database).
"A Fresh Look and Unbiased Appraisal." *Sea Power* February 1975: 6.
"A Letter and a Reply." *Sea Power* November 1976: 27-32.
Alwyn-Schmidt, L.W. "Keeping Our Grip Upon Ocean Trade." *Sea Power* August 1919: 82-85.
Anderson, William R. "The National Dividends From a Nuclear Navy." *Navy–The Magazine of Sea Power* January 1965: 13-15.
—-. "Urges Better Navy Balance in Ship Types." *Chicago Tribune*, April 24, 1965.
Ashworth, George W. "The $50 Billion Navy Building Program." *Sea Power* October 1971: 24-27.
Atkinson, Peter. "Clever Ideas, Luck Can Pay Off for Council Fundraisers." *Sea Power* February 2004: 48-49.
—-. "Council Assistance is Critical for Cadet Corps Programs." *Seapower* October 2005: 55-56.
—-. "Council Support Efforts Can Help Military Families Cope." *Sea Power* June 2004: 48-49.

—-. "Councils Lend Support to Recruiters." *Seapower* June 2005: 72-73.
—-. "Halsey Ceremony Highlights Busy Navy League Commissioning Schedule." *Seapower* October 2005: 57-59.
—-. "Hampton Roads Council Showcases 'Admiral's Quarters' At 'Homearama,'" *Seapower/Navy League News* (December 2004)
—-. "MassBay Council Symposium Promotes Education Mission." *Seapower* April 2004: 70-72.
—-. "Navy League, Councils, Face Challenge of Recruiting Younger Members." *Seapower* March 2005: 68-70.
—-. "Operation Homefront Offers Councils Chance to Build Mission, Membership." *Seapower* February 2005: 47-48.
—-. "Panneton Named Navy League Senior VP at 2004 Winter Meeting." *Seapower* December 2004: 48-49.
—-. "*Reagan* Visit to Santa Barbara Demonstrates Power of Partnerships." *Seapower* November 2005: 48-49.
—-. "Steering Committee Members Guide Navy League's Strategies, Priorities." *Seapower* September 2005, 62-64.
"A Visionary Naval Chief Prepares to Depart." *Seapower* March 2005: 7.
"Backs Roosevelt on Merchant Ships." *New York Times,* September 1, 1934: 5.
Baker, Evan S. "The 'Contract' With America." *Sea Power* February 1995: 5.
Baker, Warren P. "A Sea Change in Congress?" *Sea Power* December 1980: 47.
Balisle, Philip M. "NAVSEA's Balisle: Architect of Change in a Violent World." *Sea Power* September 2003: 17-20.
Barnard, Richard C. "A SEAPOWER Makeover." *Seapower* December 2004: 4.
—-. "England Charts a Careful Course Through Political Fire." *Seapower* November 2004: 12.
—-. "New Missions." *Seapower* November 2005: 1.
—-. "Sea Basing Concept Promises a Revolution in Power Projection." *Seapower* June 2004: 10-12.
—-. "To the Rescue." *Seapower* October 2005: 37-42.
"Barnard to Succeed Hessman as Editor in Chief." *Sea Power* March 2003: 1.
Barnum, Robert H. "Penny Wise Pay Policy." *Navy–The Magazine of Sea Power* January 1965: 4.
Beach, Edward L. "The U.S. Navy's Remarkable Transformation." *Almanac of Seapower* 2000: 5-14.
Beecher, William. "Gorshkov Papers Signify New Russian Naval Doctrine." *Sea Power* May 1973: 14-17.
Bennett, Bernard. "The Navy and the Nation." *Sea Power* April 1987: 3-4.
Boschert, Terence. "Navy Unit Asked To Help Build Image." *LaCrosse (Wisconsin) Tribune*, February 22, 1966: 9.

Brady, James. "In Step with Gen. Peter Pace." *Parade,* October 2, 2005: 14-15.
Brandon, Veronica. "The Navy League Starts a 'Green' Trend." *Sea Power* April 2003: 31.
Brice-O'Hara, Sally. "In My Own Words." *Seapower* Dec. 2004: 56.
Brill, Arthur P., Jr. "Krulak Is Painstakingly Preparing Marines to Win 'Dirty Little Battles' of 21st Century." *The Almanac of Seapower 1997*: 14-22.
—-. "The Jungle of the 21st Century." *The Almanac of Seapower 1999:* 13-20.
—-. "Warriors for the 21st Century." *The Almanac of Seapower 1998:* 15-24.
"Brooklyn Navy Yard Rediscovers Its Past." *Naval History* August 2005: 63-65.
Bruno, Michael. "Congress to appropriate $933 million for Coast Guard's *Deepwater.*" *Aerospace Daily & Defense Report* September 30, 2005.
—-. "Maritime strategy, Katrina seen buttressing *Deepwater* prospects." *Aerospace Daily & Defense Report,* September 22, 2005.
Burgess, Richard R. "Admiral Fallon: 'We Are on Our Way to a New Navy.'" *Seapower* November 2004: 26.
—-. "Navy Cracking Glass Wall Between Reserve, Active Forces." *Seapower* July 2004.
Carlson, Dudley L. "Executive Director's Notes." *Sea Power* May 1991: 52.
Carrere, Ernest A., Jr. "Let's Make It Work." *Sea Power* June 1973: 5.
—-. "The President's Annual Report." *Sea Power* September 1974: 4-6.
—-. "Words Worth Listening To." *Sea Power* May 1974: 4-5.
Cativo, Fulvio. "John Paul Jones's Birth, Arrival in Annapolis Marked." *Washington Post,* July 10, 2005: C3.
Clark, Vern. "The Revolutionary." *Seapower* June 2005.
Cobb, Calvin H., Jr. "A Rationale For Reality." *Sea Power* May 1991: 5-6.
—-. "Change and Continuity." *Sea Power* June 1991: 7-8.
—-. "On The Scene, In Force." *Sea Power* March 1991: 5-6.
—-. "'On the Way, Sir!'" *Sea Power* October 1990: 5-6.
—-. "The Mantle of Leadership." *Sea Power* April 1991: 10.
—-. "To Enlighten The People On Naval Matters." *Sea Power* May 1991: 16-18.
Collins, Thomas H. "Added Capacity, New Capabilities, and 'More in the Pipeline.'" *Sea Power* August 2003: 22.
—-. "Collins Strikes Balance Between Present, Future Resources." *Seapower* August 2004: 40-43.
—-. "The Coast Guard's Closest Point of Approach to Maritime Homeland Security." *Sea Power* April 2003: 51-58.
"Comments on Commentary." *Sea Power* October 1978: 7.
"Coolidge Endorses Navy Day, October 27; Commends Choice of Roosevelt Birthday." *New York Times,* September 10, 1923: 1.
Cottrell, Alvin J. "Indian Ocean of Tomorrow." *Navy–The Magazine of Sea Power*

March 1971: 10-16.

Crea, Vivien. "Sentinel of the Atlantic." *Seapower* September 2005: 46-50.

Crick, Rolla J. "Defense Cuts Rapped By Navy League Chief." *Oregon Journal,* December 6, 1965.

Crouch, Dick and Bill Middleton. "'Patriotism Is Not a Nasty Word,' California Publisher Addresses Navy League." *Florida Times-Union,* May 6, 1967: B-1, B-4.

"Daniels Attacks Navy League Heads." *New York Times,* August 15, 1917: 3.

David, Heather. "An In-Depth Interview with Secretary Warner." *Sea Power* July-August 1972: 27-31.

"Declaration of Objectives." *Sea Power* June 1973: 46-48.

Dodge, Homer Joseph. "Around the World With the American Dollar." *Sea Power* August 1919: 90-95.

Dorsey, Jack. "*Cole* Survivors Think About, But Don't Dwell On, Bombing." *Norfolk Virginian-Pilot,* October 12, 2005 (Electronic database)

Dowdy, Earl B. "Navy Vets Urge Battleship's 'KO Punch' in Vietnam." *The Detroit News,* March 24, 1966: 7-F.

Duchein, Charles F. "With the Marines." *Navy–The Magazine of Sea Power* November 1965: 41.

Eisman, Dale. "Admiral Clark: Unconventional Officer Led With a Unique Vision." *Norfolk Virginian-Pilot*. (Electronic database)

Eller, Ernest M."*Sea Power*: The Anchor of Freedom." *Sea Power* November 1973: 5.

—-. "The Postwar Follies." *Sea Power* May 1973: 31-35.

"End of Atom Bomb Is Urged by Halsey." *New York Times,* October 24, 1946: 47.

"EPA Administrator Whitman to Break Ground on New Navy League Building; Structure is First 'Green Building' in Arlington County," *U.S. Newswire,* Washington, April 8, 2003: 1.

"Experts Fault Paltry Funding, Lack of Port Security Strategy." *Seapower* Oct. 2004: 6-7.

Fallon, Susan K. "Honor Wall Pays Tribute to Those Who Help the Sea Services." *Seapower* July 2004: 40.

—-. "Navy League Foundation Scholarship Program and 2004 Awards." *Seapower* August 2004: 44.

Fanning, Timothy O. "The Challenges Ahead." *Sea Power* June 2003: 5.

—-. "Persistence." *Sea Power* May 2003: 5.

—-. "Preemptive Action and Global Peace." *Almanac of Seapower 2003*: VII-IX.

Ferguson, Stuart. "Historic America." *Wall Street Journal* August 5, 2005: W2.

Fisher, John R. "A Call to Action." *Sea Power* September 1999: 7.

—-. "A Tale of Two Centuries." *Almanac of Seapower 2000*: 1-4.

Fitch, Morgan L., Jr. "No Second Best for U.S. Navy." *Congressional Record* (Extension of Remarks of Congressman E.C. Gathings) January 19, 1966: A205-A206.

—-. "Pass Up the Butter!" *Navy Times* January 5, 1966: 2-3.

—-. "The President's Message." *Navy Magazine* June 1965: 2.

—-. "Will We Lose Sea Control?" *San Francisco DAILY PILOT/News Press*, January 21, 1967:16.

"Fitch Points Up Aid In Viet Nam." *The Times-Picayune, New Orleans, Louisiana* August 26, 1966.

Fitzgerald, Mark P. "Fitzgerald: Re-capitalization Poses Challenge for Naval Air." *Seapower* March 2004: 28-30.

Fitzpatrick, Michael F. Letter. *Naval History* August 2005, 10.

"Fleet Week '91, Zachary Fisher, Chairman, Honored Navy/Gulf Heroes 6 June-10 June." *The Log, Official Publication of the Navy League of the United States, New York Council* 5, No. 2 (Summer 1991): 1-2.

Forrestal, James V. *Sea Power* November 1945: 15.

"40,000 View First Navy Day Parade Here." *Washington Post,* October 28, 1944. 1.

"From Russia With Love." *The Log, Official Publication of the Navy League of the United States, New York Council* 14, No. 3 (September-December 2001): 1.

Galvin, William M. Letter. "How the Navy League Stands." *Washington Post,* January 15, 1925: 6.

Gangle, Randy. "Gangle: New Threats Demand Thinking Outside the Box." *Seapower* December 2004: 36-39.

Goldstein, Lyle J. and Yuri M. Zhukov. "Superpower Showdown in the Mediterranean, 1973." *Sea Power* October 2003: 32-35.

Goodman, Peter S. "Big Shift in China's Oil Policy," *Washington Post*, July 13, 2005, D1, D12.

"Gridiron Club Runs Gamut of the News; Hoover Sees Himself Defeat the Navy League in Skit Built on 'Pinafore.'" *New York Times,* December 13, 1931: N1.

"Great Lakes Honors Navy League." *Great Lakes Bulletin,* April 21, 1967: 1,6.

Griffin, DeWitt James. "A Backslide on Recruiting." *Navy–The Magazine of Sea Power* November 1976: 7-8.

—-. "Doubts About Détente." *Sea Power* March 1976: 4-5.

—-. "'Fringe Benefits' and Unfair Competition." *Sea Power* July 1975: 5-6.

—-. "Hard Decisions Become Harder." *Sea Power* December 1975: 8-9.

—-. "The Lessons of Vietnam." *Sea Power* June 1975: 2-3.

—-. "The President's Annual Report." *Sea Power* May 1977: 31-35.

—-. "The Triad and the B-1." *Sea Power* May 1976: 5.

—-. "Why?" *Sea Power* February 1976: 6-7.

Griswold, Lawrence. "Strait is the Way." *Sea Power* October 1971: 11-17.

—-. "The Dwindling Presence: U.S. Overseas Bases Cut Precipitously." *Sea Power* July 1974: 22-28.
—-. "The Eagle and the Dragon." *Sea Power* April 1972: 28-32.
—-. "The Russo-Cuban Pincers Thrust in Caribbean-Panama Canal is Target." *Sea Power* December 1971: 18-24.
Haffa, Robert P., Jr. and Robert E. Mullins. "Trends in America's Post-Cold War Military Conflicts: The Implications for Sea Power." *Sea Power* July 2003: 13-16.
"Hail and Farewell." *Sea Power* April 1974: 5.
Hannan, James M. "The Soviets-First at Sea-First in R&D??" *Navy–The Magazine of Sea Power* January 1971: 6.
—-. "Drug Abuse is Our Problem, Too!" *Navy–The Magazine of Sea Power* March 1971: 5.
—-. "Extend the Draft." *Navy–The Magazine of Sea Power* April 1971: 6.
—-. "The Sea Cadet Program Offers Rich Rewards." *Navy–The Magazine of Sea Power* November 1965: 7-9.
"Headlines, Omissions, and Media Responsibility." *Sea Power* August 1976: 5-6.
Hecht, Frank A. "The Proper Growth of Naval Aviation." *Vital Speeches of the Day* May 1952: 476-477.
Heine, Irwin A. "The Coming Energy Crisis." *Sea Power* September 1972: 27-32.
Hendrix, Henry J., III. "An Unlikely Location." *Naval History* August 2005: 37-41.
Hessman, James D. "A Navy League Building 'For the Next 100 Years." *Sea Power* May 2003: 1.
—-. "A Vision of Continuing Excellence." *Almanac of Seapower 2003*: 2-8.
—-. "An Unfunny Thing Happened on the Way to the 600-Ship Fleet." *Sea Power* April 1988: 78-96.
—-. "Clinton Proposes $243.4 billion FY 1997 Defense Budget, Congress Says Total 'Insufficient,' Promises Increase." *Sea Power* April 1996: 25-32.
—-. "Congress, President Face a Year of Decision In National Security and Homeland Defense." *Sea Power* February 2003: 9-12.
—-. "Farewell to a Surface Warrior." *Sea Power* February 2000: 1.
—-. "Okean, Leningrad/Boston, Nimitz, and the SES." *Sea Power* June 1975: 20-26.
—-. "Our Navy Story." *Sea Power* May 2000: 1.
—-. "The First Century Is the Hardest." *Sea Power* December 2002: 3.
—-. "The Obligations of Military Leadership." *Sea Power* March 1987: 25-29.
Hessman, James D. and Patricia L. Howard. "Seapower for the 21st Century." *Sea Power* February 1995: 51-53.
Hessman, James D. and Gordon I. Peterson. "Interview with Secretary of Defense Cohen." *Sea Power* April 2000: 15-26.
Hessman, James D. and Jean A. Scheel. "The Platform War." *Sea Power* July 1974:

17-21.
Hessman, James D. and Vincent C. Thomas. "A Long, Strong Bravo Zulu, Interview With [Then] Secretary of the Navy James H. Webb, Jr." *Sea Power* April 1988: 15-36.
—-. "Debriefing: A Citizen's Trip to the Indian Ocean." *Sea Power* July 1981: 27-42.
—-. "Disasters by the Year 2000." *Sea Power* May 1988: 7-14.
—-. "Individual Human Beings–and the Responsibilities of Leadership–A Valedictory Interview with Navy Secretary John F. Lehman Jr." *Sea Power* April 1987: 81-96.
—-. "Interview with Navy Secretary Claytor." *Sea Power* October 1977: 22-28.
—-. "Interview with the Secretary of the Navy." *Sea Power* March 1981: 17-30.
Hicks, William L. Letter. *Sea Power* September 1996: 7.
"High Praise From MCPON for Sea Cadets." *Sea Power* October 1991: 54.
Hill, Herbert F. "The Navy League, Past, Present, and Future," *Sea Power* December 1918.
Hirsch, Vincent T. "A Dubious Decision and a Disturbing Pattern." *Sea Power* August 1977: 3-4.
—-. "It's Now Up to Congress." *Sea Power* February 1978: 3-4.
—-. "The Canal Treaty: Too Far, and Too Fast." *Sea Power* September 1977: 4-8.
—-. "The President's Annual Report–Fiscal 1978." *Sea Power* June 1978: 27-31.
—-. "The President's Annual Report–Fiscal 1979." *Sea Power* May 1979: 7-10.
—-. "The Real Losers: The Navy and the Nation." *Sea Power* October 1978: 5-6.
—-. "Treaty Reprise: Sincere and Honest Doubt." *Sea Power* January 1978: 3-4.
Hodges, Jim. "Admiral defends Role of Navy in Combating Terrorism." *Daily Press,* Newport News, Virginia: October 6, 2005. (Electronic data base)
Hoffman, Paul. Letter. *Seapower* July 2005: 5.
Horowitz, Robert S. "Evelyn Collins, Navy League 'Den Mother,' to Retire." *Navy Times,* August 16, 1967: 25.
"House Group Approves New Rivers Pay Bill." *From the Office of the President, Association of the United States Army* (Newsletter) July 1965: 3.
Howard, Patricia L. "Cincinnati Council Honors World War II Submarine Heroes." *Sea Power* February 1993: 51-52.
—-. "The Key Mission: Community Education." *Sea Power* October 1991: 53-54.
Hughey, Ann. "The age of Aircraft Carrier Diplomacy." *Forbes,* July 21, 1980: 57-62.
Huhn, S. Peter and Roberta McCorkle. "House Reviews Sealift Shortfall." *Sea Power* October 1990: 4.
—-. "How to Further Navy League Goals." *Sea Power* October 1990: 4.
"It's Still Navy Day." *New York Times,* October 27, 1952: 29.
Jackson, Henry M. "Five Dangerous Myths." *Navy–The Magazine of Sea Power* May

1969: 26-29.
—-. "The Suez Canal and International Stability." *Sea Power* May 1974: 8-9.
Johnson, Ben. "Need For Sea Power Told Navy Leaguers." *Imperial Valley (California) Press,* March 7, 1967: 2.
"Johnson is Scored on Shipping Goals." *New York Times,* May 14, 1968: 93.
Jones, James L. "Jones: Transforming NATO Into 21st-Century Alliance." *Seapower* November 2004: 28-33.
Kasatonov, Igor V. "Facets of Cooperation." *Sea Power* September 1996: 35-40.
Keeter, Hunter. "Coast Guard Mulls Major Changes to Deepwater Program Requirements." *Seapower* April 2004: 24-26.
—-. "Congress, DOD Balance Industrial Base Support, Acquisition Priorities." *Seapower* August 2004: 12-14.
—-. "Navy Strives for Eight Carrier Battle Groups Ready to Roll." *Sea Power* December 2003: 7-8.
—-. "U.S. Navy's 'Fleet Response Plan' Charts Course." *Sea Power* October 2003: 18-22.
Keeter, Hunter C. and Richard R. Burgess. "Sea Change: NAVSEA Charts Course for Navy of 21st Century." *Seapower* February 2004: 10-17.
Kelley, William C., Jr., "America–A Maritime Nation." *Sea Power* December 1991: 5-6.
—-. "A personal note to my fellow members of the Navy League." *The Almanac of Seapower* 1992: 297.
—-. "Salute and Challenge." *Sea Power* September 1991: 5-6.
—-. "Symbols and Commitments." *Sea Power* August 1991: 5-6.
—-. "The Course is Clear." *Sea Power* October 1991: 5-6.
Kelly, Edward V. Letter. *Sea Power* October 1990: 10.
Kelly, John M. "Kelly: Sea Basing Presents 'Infinite Number of Problems' for the Enemy." *Seapower* June 2004: 22-24.
"Kelley Presents Resolution of Appreciation to Fishers." *Sea Power* February 1993: 8.
Kelso, Frank B., II. "Charting a Course for the Future, Navy's Goal: To Maintain Maritime Superiority." *Sea Power* April 1991: 13-20.
Kennedy, Jack M. "Much Ado About Very Little." *Sea Power* February 1999: 5.
—-. "Rhetoric, Reality and Unanswered Questions." *Almanac of Sea Power 1998*: 1-4.
—-. "The Day of Reckoning." *Sea Power* April 1999: 9.
—-. "The End of the American Century?" *Almanac of Sea Power 1999:* 1-4.
—-. "The Logistics Factor." *Sea Power* May 1999: 5.
"Kennedy Succeeds Mayberry as NLUS President; Navy League Sets Sail for 21st Century."*Almanac of Sea Power 1998:* 297-304.
Kenney, J. Matthew. Letter. *Sea Power* April 1974: 2.

Kesteloot, Robert W. "A Helping Hand for the Withered Arm." *Sea Power* May 1987: 19-26.

—-. "Sealift After the Storm, A Plan to Revitalize the U.S.-Flag Fleet." *Sea Power* June 1991: 37-41.

Kime, Patricia. "$933.1 million earmarked for Coast Guard modernization." *Navy Times,* September 29, 2005.

—-. "Admiral Keating Says Coast Guard Was 'Pivotal' Force." *Sea Power* October 2003: 6-8.

—-. "Coast Guard is Seeking Broader Authority to Make Arrests on Land."
Seapower April 2004: 20-21.

—-. "Collins Shakes Up Command Chain With Six New Sectors in 2004." *Seapower*
April 2004: 22.

—-. "Integrated Warfare Systems Office Consolidates Programs, Cuts Costs." *Seapower* February 2004: 20-21.

—-. "Maritime 'Fusion' Centers Expand Coast Guard Intelligence Capabilities." *Seapower* May 2004: 16-18.

—-. "MSC Transformation Strategies Serve as Model for Sea Power 21." *Seapower* October 2004: 20-22.

Kinney, John G. and Gordon I. Peterson. "The U.S. Engagement Strategy." *Sea Power* September 1999: 42-48.

Klamper, Amy. "Snowe, Collins Point to Katrina as Rationale for Two Major Shipyards." *Seapower* October 2005: 6-9.

Krock, Arthur. "In the March of History." Review of *A Front Row Seat*, by Nicholas Roosevelt. *New York Times,* September 6, 1953: B26.

"League's Oversea Councils: Outposts of America." *Sea Power* November 1996: 45.

"Let's Face It, 'The U.S. Navy–What Is Its Role in the Nuclear Age'" *Television and
Radio News & Programs, Sunday Oregonian*, December 12, 1965: 1.

Levin, Michael. "U.S.S. Dauntless." *Pennsylvania Gazette,* March 1983: 16-23.

"Liberty Celebration Opsail and The International Naval Review." *The Log, Official Publication of the Navy League of the United States, New York Council* 1, no. 9 (Summer 1986): 1-2.

Linsky, Martin. "Threading the Shoals of the Media in Pursuit of a 600-Ship Navy." *Government Executive* May 1998: 34.

Lively, Tarron. "USS *Ronald Reagan* (CVN-76) commissioned; The former President's
wife ordered the crew of the new aircraft carrier to 'bring her to life.'" *Washington
Times,* July 13, 2003: A01.

MacBain, Merle. "Will Terrorism Go to Sea." *Sea Power* January 1980: 15-24.

"Mayberry Announces Kickoff of New Highline Program." *Sea Power* March 1996: 52.

Mayberry, Hugh H. "A New Look in Communications." *Sea Power* March 1996.
—-. "A Salute to Industry." *Sea Power* April 1996: 6.
—-. "A Salute to the Coast Guard." *Sea Power* August 1996: 3.
—-. "Preface." *The Almanac of Seapower 1997*: 1.
McNeill, Sheila M. "Admiral Thomas J. Collins: A Leader for Our Times." *Seapower* March 2005: 3.
—-. "Admiral Vern Clark: A Visionary Naval Chief." *Sea Power* October 2003: 3.
—-. "A Legislative Agenda For Transformational Times." *Seapower* May 2005: 3.
—-. "A Second Century of Service." *Sea Power* July 2003: 5.
—-. "Congress: Maintain Balance With MMPA." *Seapower* Feb. 2004: 3.
—-. "Europe Visit Highlights Foreign Councils' Unique Challenges." *Seapower* August 2004: 58-59.
—-. "Fleet Size Must Be in Balance With Security, Mission Needs." *Seapower* November 2004: 3.
—-. "Memo to Congress: Streamline Homeland Security Oversight." *Seapower* August 2004: 3.
—-. "Military Is Top-Rated Institution, But Education Still Vital." *Seapower* July 2004: 3.
—-. "Navy League Approach to BRAC Makes Everyone a Winner." *Seapower* June 2004: 3.
—-. "Navy League Needs 'Grass Roots' to Flourish in Years Ahead." *Seapower* October 2004: 3.
—-. "Navy League, Sea Services Rise to Tough Challenges Ahead." *Seapower Almanac 2004*, VII.
—-. "Note to Congress: Be Careful What You Ask For." *Seapower* March 2004: 3.
—-. "Port Security Funds: A Framework for Failure." *Sea Power* September 2003: 3.
—-. "Reassess Ready Reserve Force." *Seapower* December 2004: 3.
—-. "Rebalance Security and Environmental Needs." *Sea Power* August 2003: 3.
—-. "Sea Power Ambassadors: Building Support for U.S. Fleets." *Sea Power* December 2003: 3.
—-. "Shipbuilding Strategies for Success."*Seapower Almanac 2005* January 2005: 3.
—-. "Support of Coast Guard Is Vital." *Seapower* June 2005: 3.
—-. "Tour of Asia, Pacific Councils Reveals Strong Sea Service Support." *Seapower* August 2005: 56-59.
Macke, Richard C. "Navy League concerned about the consequence of shrinkage." *Fore 'n Aft Magazine* (Honolulu Council Navy League), March 2005: 6.
Maxam, Frances. "Home Runs Infrequent For Navy League Head, But Wife Is Fan." *Jacksonville Journal,* May 2, 1967: 6.

Medina, Vic. Letter. *Seapower* July 2005: 5.
"Men Such as These." *Sea Power* May 1973: 3.
"Merchant Marine Held Inadequate." *New York Times,* February 23, 1936: N12.
Middendorf, J. William. "A Smaller Fleet, and a Formidable Competitor." *Sea Power* January 1975: 10-16.
—-. "Interview with Navy Secretary Middendorf." *Sea Power* August 1974: 8-15.
—-. "Unknown Events, Disturbing Trends, and a Rebuilding of Strength." *Sea Power* January 1976: 7-13.
Miller, George H. "Blueprint for Bluewater." *Sea Power* February 1972: 8-12.
—-. "The Low Profile Approach." *Sea Power* February 1973: 26-29.
Miller, Jeremy. "Schrock, Davis Receive Award." *The Navy Leaguer* September 2004: 1.
—-. "The 2005 Legislative Initiative." *The Navy Leaguer* February 2005: 1.
Moorer, Thomas H. "Naval Aviation: Ready For Battle, Both Overseas and on Capitol Hill." *Sea Power* June 1991: 25-28.
Morris, Thomas E. "An Emergency of Long Duration." *Sea Power* May 1972: 6.
—-. "Lowest Level of Capability in Years." *Sea Power* March 1973; 4-5.
—-. "Our Greatest Challenge." *Navy–The Magazine of Sea Power* June 1971: 4.
—-. "Recruiting: Numbers Up; Quality Still Short." *Sea Power* November 1972: 4.
—-. "Sea Cadets-A Golden Opportunity Is Being Missed." *Sea Power* September 1971: 7.
—-. "The Case for a National Insurance Policy." *Sea Power* April 1973: 2.
—-. "The President's Annual Report–Fiscal 1973." *Sea Power* May 1973: 4-6.
—-. "Time to Turn To." *Navy–The Magazine of Sea Power* July-August 1971: 3.
—-. "We Need Vigorous Local Leadership." *Sea Power* March 1972: 2.
—-. "Yesterday and Tomorrow, National President's Annual Report." *Sea Power* June 1972: 2-4.
Morse, Jack H. "A Scenario for Decline." *Sea Power* May 1987: 3-4.
—-. "In Defense of Our National Interests." *Sea Power* March 1988: 3.
—-. "President's Message." *Sea Power* January 1988: 1.
"Morse Comments on Webb Resignation and Reductions in Force Structure." *Sea Power* April 1988: 36.
Mottern, Jim. Letter. *Seapower* February 2005: 5.
Munns, David W. "Rise in Murders, Kidnappings at Sea Makes Piracy a Top Naval Priority Worldwide." *Seapowe*r October 2004: 10-10-14.
—-. "Ship's Library." Review of *At the Abyss: An Insider's History of the Cold War,* by Thomas C. Reed. *Seapower* April 2004: 66.
"Navy Day and Roosevelt Day." Editorial. *New York Times,* October 27, 1923: 12.
"Navy Day Date is Changed." *Sea Power* January 1972: 3.
"Navy Day Rallies Urge Strong U.S." *New York Times,* October 28, 1947: 21.

"Navy League Assails Services Unity 'Grab.'" *New York Times,* December 2, 1945: 19.
"Navy League Attacks Hoover." *Wall Street Journal,* November 28, 1931: 5.
"Navy League Bows to Johnson, Drops Annual Navy Day." *Chicago Daily Tribune,* September 9,1949: 1.
"Navy League Calls Fleet 'Third Rate.'" *New York Times,* April 28, 1934: 2.
"Navy League Chief Sees Patriotic Cleanup Need." *Los Angeles Times,* October 5, 1950: 8.
"Navy League Defends Sea Force Air Arm As It Clashes Again With Aviation Group." *New York Times* August 6, 1949: 6.
"Navy League Ends Support of Sea Power Ambassador Program." *Seapower* November 2004: 9.
"Navy League Leader Notes Dual War Role." *San Diego Union,* March 7, 1965: B-1.
"Navy League Looks Ahead to 2005."*Seapower Almanac 2005*: January 2005: 184-191.
"Navy League Official Protests Cuts in Military Budget." *The Oregonian,* December 7, 1965: 24.
"Navy League President Links Adult Inaction, Youth Problems." *Evening Capital* (Annapolis, Maryland), April 8, 1967: 1, 3.
"Navy League of the United States Kicks Off Centennial Celebration; 100 Years of 'Citizens in Support of the Sea Services'," *U.S. Newswire*, Washington, June 21, 2001: 1.
"Navy League Sends a Message and a Check to Family of WTC Hero Cop." The Log, *Official Publication of the Navy League of the United States, New York Council* 14, No. 3 (September -December 2001): 4.
"Navy League Set to Fete 67 Today." *New York Times*, May 2, 1957: 33.
"Navy League Should Act." Editorial. *Washington Post,* November 2, 1931: 6.
"Navy League Signs on for Four-Year Tour." *Sea Power* July-August 1972: 53.
"Navy League to Meet." *Washington Post*, January 7, 1912: E2.
"Navy League's 1918 Plans." *New York Times*, January 8, 1918: 7.
"Navy League's View on Amnesty." *Sea Power* June 1973: 19.
"Navy to Use Lake Yachts to Train Cadet Classes." *Chicago Daily Tribune*, April 8, 1942: 24.
"New York Council Honors Admiral Joseph J. 'Jocko' Clark." *The Log, Official Publication of the Navy League of the United States, New York Council* 1, No. 13 (Fall 1987): 1-2.
"New York Welcomes Centennial National Convention." *The Log, Official Publication of the Navy League of the United States, New York Council* 15, No. 1 (January-June 2002): 1.
Niblack, A.P. "Naval Stations and Naval Bases." *Sea Power* January 1917: 24-27.

"Nitze Says the Navy Is Counting on the Sea Cadet Program." *Navy–The Magazine of Sea Power* November 1965: 6.
"Nixon Doctrine and the Blue Water Strategy." *Navy–The Magazine of Sea Power* January 1971: 8.
"Nixon Doctrine and the Blue Water Strategy–Part II." *Navy–The Magazine of Sea Power* February 1971: 6.
Nolan, Mary I. "Community Affiliate Program=Grassroots Support." *Sea Power* December 1991: 53-54.
—-. "Perot Wins Burke Leadership Award." *Sea Power* March 1991: 55-57.
—-. "SAS 1991: A 'Combat-Tested' Success." *Sea Power* May 1991: 51-54.
Norris, John G. "CVX and the Nuclear Navy." *Sea Power* May 1974: 16-22.
"Numbers, Technology & Courage." *Sea Power* February 1979: 10.
"NYC Hosts 1992 Navy League Convention; 500 Members Attend; 'Well Done' to All Hands." *The Log, Official Publication of the Navy League of the United States, New York Council* 6, No. 3 (Summer 1992): 1.
Ousley, Clarence. "New Battleship Designs." *Sea Power* January 1917: 9.
—-. "Our Politico-Economic Situation." *Sea Power* January 1917: 7.
—-. "The League with Reservations." *Sea Power* August 1919: 57-59.
—-. "The Naval Fuel-Oil Reserves." *Sea Power* January 1917: 8.
Panneton, John A. "A Navy League Agenda: Duty, Honor, and Country." *Seapower* July 2005: 3.
—-. "A Warfighting Concept for Tomorrow's Forces." *Seapower* October 2005: 3.
—-. "The Sea Services After Katrina: Dedication, Courage and Inspiration." *Seapower* November 2005: 3.
Peterson, Gordon I. "Military Spending Bill Signed; Clinton 'Putting People First.'" *Sea Power* November 1999: 17-20.
—-. "USS *Theodore Roosevelt* Diverted to Adriatic. Operation Allied Force: Cruise Missiles Strike First From Sea and Air." *Sea Power* May 1999: 13-15.
"Philadelphia to Get Army-Navy Museum." *Washington Post*, October 10, 1965: B3.
Phillips, Don. "W. Graham Claytor." *Washington Post*, May 15, 1994 (Electronic database).
Philpott, Tom. "A Shrinking Navy Is Still Making Significant Contributions Around the World." *The Almanac of Seapower 1997*: 5-13.
—-. "Rising Technology, a Declining Fleet." *Almanac of Seapower 1998*: 5-14.
—-. "The Year Of Declining Readiness." *Almanac of Seapower 1999*: 5-12.
Polmar, Norman. Letter "Objections and Objectivity." *Sea Power* February 1998: 5.
"Post-War Fleets Urged." *New York Times*, December 9, 1944: 15.
"President Ford addressed U.S. Navy League in New Orleans." *Sea Power* May 1975: 23-25.

Prina, L. Edgar. "Brown Budget Cuts Threaten Navy/USMC Air, Five-Year Ship Program." *Sea Power* September 1977: 17.

—-. "Budget Increases Reflect 'A Major Change in Naval Strategy.'" *Sea Power* April 1981: 13-22.

—-. "Claytor Fires Back; Disputes New Defense Strategy." *Sea Power* April 1978: 30-32.

—-. "Ford Cuts Carrier, Long Beach Conversion; Congressional Restoration Possible." *Sea Power* January 1977: 26-31.

—-. "Jones Committee Focuses on Sealift Deficiencies." *Sea Power* November 1990: 46-50.

—-. "New Defense Guidelines Postulate Sideline Status for Navy." *Sea Power* February 1978: 35-36.

—-. "Reorganization and Reality, The Goldwater-Nichols Act." *Sea Power* January 1987: 19-23.

—-. "The End of an Era–And Beginning of Another." *Sea Power* December 1981: 13-27.

—-. "The Mathematics of Retrenchment." *Sea Power* March 1987: 18-24.

—-. "The New Secretary of Defense: Donald H. Rumsfeld." *Sea Power* December 1975: 17-18.

—-. "The Possibility of Military Defeat." *Sea Power* December 1987: 23-24.

"Questions for Mac the Knife." *Honolulu Star-Bulletin* December 31, 1965: A-4.

Rau, John M. "Debriefing: A Citizen's Trip to the IO." *Sea Power* July 1981: 27-42.

—-. "Debriefing II: On Maneuvers With the Marines *Sea Power* June 1982: 39-54.

"Ray Kerrison of the New York Post Eloquent Article on the Intrepid and Zachary Fisher." *The Log, Official Publication of the Navy League of the United States, New York Council* 3, no. 3 (Winter 1989): 6-7.

Raymond, Jack. "Pentagon Troubled by Rise in Industry Groups Asking for Help." *New York Times*, November 14, 1961: 7.

"Reception to Honor Navy League." *Washington Post*, January 8, 1908: 14.

"Renaissance of U.S. Sea Power Keynote of Navy Day Observance." *New York Times*, October 24, 1937: 37.

"Reserve Fleet Plans Assailed by Navy League." *Chicago Daily Tribune*, May 10, 1933: 16.

Reynolds, Jean B. "Kennedy Cites SAS, Education and Awards Programs; Middendorf Selected for Burke Award; Fisher Elected Senior VP." *1999 Almanac of Sea Power 1999*: 297-304.

Rivera, Ray. "Stockdale Recalled as One Who Led and Inspired." *Washington Post*, July 24, 2005: C1, C7.

Robinson, Peter. "Echoes of the Gipper." *Wall Street Journal*, March 31, 2005: A24.

"Roosevelt May Head Navy League." *Washington Post*, December 13, 1917: 2.

"Roosevelt Naval History Award to Ronald H. Spector." *The Log, Official Publication of the Navy League of the United States, New York Council* 1, no. 9 (Summer 1986): 16.

"Roosevelt Prize for Navy History Awarded to Naval Historical Center Historians." *The Log, Official Publication of the Navy League of the United States, New York Council* 13, no. 2 (July-September 2000): 5.

"Roosevelt Saved Our Sea Power, Says Navy League." *New York Times,* July 30, 1934: 1.

Roth, Margaret. "LPD 17 Leads to Dramatic Changes in Design, Systems Integration." *Seapower* February 2004: 18-19.

—-. "New Technologies, Changing Priorities Foretell Need for Fewer Naval Personnel." *Seapower* June 2004: 25-26.

—-. "Only Highly Trained Need Apply in Navy's 'New World' of Optimal Manning." *Seapower* December 2004: 14-15.

Schwartz, Stephan A. "Navy Must Change to Survive in Coming All Volunteer Age." *Navy–The Magazine of Sea Power* January 1971: 15-19.

"Scoop and Scuttle." *Sea Power* November 1973: 5.

—-. *Sea Power* March 1974: 5.

—-. *Sea Power* June 1976: 4.

"Sea-Air-Space 2003: 'America's Best' Expo," *Sea Power*, May 2003: 56.

"Sea-Air-Space Exposition Sets Stage For an Increasingly Active Year for NLUS." *The Almanac of Seapower* 1997: 297-303.

"Sea Cadets on L.I. to Train on Boat Capone Gang Used." *New York Times,* November 12, 1968: 49.

"Sea Power Stressed." *New York Times*, November 16, 1958: 46.

"Sees Navy League Backed By Cupidity." *New York Times*, January 25, 1932: 15.

"Seventh Annual Roosevelt Naval History Award to Edward S. Miller." *The Log, Official Publication of the Navy League of the United States, New York Council* 6, no. 3 (Summer 1992): 11.

"Sham Battle Planned Here on Navy Day." *Washington Post*, October 24, 1941: 11.

Shanker, Thom. "All Quiet On The Home Front, And Some Are Asking Why." *New York Times*, July 24, 2005: 17.

Shanker, Thom and Eric Schmitt. "Critics and Fans Alike as Navy Chief Steps Down." *New York Times*, July 17, 2005. (Electronic database, *New York Times* website)

Sharp, U.S. Grant. "The Story Behind The Bombing." *New York Times,* August 6, 1971: 31.

Sherman, Jason. "Changing Vision." *Seapower* March 2005: 10-14.

—-. "Getting It Right." *Seapower* June 2005: 14-16.

—-. "Doing More." *Seapower* October 2005: 24-26.

—-. "White House Issues New Strategy to Block Sea-Based Terrorist Attacks." *Inside the Navy,* October 17, 2005 (Electronic database)

"Shipbuilding: An Uncertain Future." Forum of Michael Petters, Northrop Grumman Newport News; Michael W. Toner, General Dynamics Marine Systems Group; and Ronald O'Rourke, Congressional Research Service, Richard C. Barnard, moderator. *Seapower* February 2005 (Reprinted): 1-4.

Sigler, Joe. "Television Tarnishes Tar, League Leader Laments." *The Florida Times-Union,* April 20, 1966.

Siler, Owen W. and James H. Thatch, III. "A Global Maritime Service, The U.S. Coast Guard Today." *1998 Almanac of Seapower 1998*: 25-30.

Slonium, Gilven. "Beyond Pearl Harbor: A SEA CHANGE!" *Vital Speeches of the Day* March 1992: 308-313.

"Speeches and Symposia." *Sea Power* June 1973: 42-45.

Spittler, John J. "An Open Letter to the President of the United States." *Sea Power* October 1979: 3-5.

—-. "Courage, Not Caution." *Sea Power* April 1980: 5-6.

—-. "New Senior VP Will Need Lots of Help." *Sea Power* January 1981: 22g.

—-. "Plans, Politics, and Practical Realities." *Sea Power* January 1981: 3-4.

—-. "The President's Annual Report." *Sea Power* May 1980: 3-6.

—-. "The President's Annual Report." *Sea Power* May 1981: 5-9.

—-. "We Must Go to General Quarters!" *Sea Power* April 1981: 3-6.

Stevens, Austin. "'Cold War' Is Laid By Truman to Lack of a Training Law." *New York Times,* May 20, 1950: 1.

Stillman, Patrick M. "Need for Deepwater Rises as CG Workload Expands." *Sea Power* August 2003: 23-24.

—-. "Stillman: 'Ruthless Execution' Is Key To Keeping Deepwater On Course." *Sea Power* April 2004: 28-31.

Stoffregen, Elliott, III. Letter. *Naval History* August 2005, 11.

Sullivan, Paul F. "Sub Director Foresees 'Revolutionary' Power of SSGNs." *Seapower* July 2003: 21-23.

Thatch, James H., III. "Prepared for Any Eventuality at Sea." *Almanac of Seapower 1999*: 21-26.

"The Forgotten Men." *Jacksonville Journal*, April 20, 1966: 7.

"The Navy League: Programs, Activities, Leadership, and Organization." *The Almanac of Seapower 1997:* 297-303.

"Theodore & Franklin D. Roosevelt Naval History Book Award Expanded." *The Log, Official Publication of the Navy League of the United States, New York Council* 15, no. 1 (January-June 2002): 2.

Thomas, Vincent C. Jr. "The Restructuring of the Marine Corps." *Sea Power* September 1992: 31-38.

—-. "The Sea Services' Role in Desert Shield/Storm." *Sea Power* September 1991: 27-33.

Thompson, Robert M. "Colonel Thompson Discusses Universal Training." *Sea Power* January 1917: 30.

—-. "Colonel Thompson Makes a Suggestion." *Sea Power* August 1919: 81.

"Thompson Resigns Navy League Office." *Washington Post,* January 9, 1918: 8.

Till, Geoffrey. "Midway, the Decisive Battle?" *Naval History* October 2005: 32-36.

"Time to Get on With the Job." *Sea Power* December 1980: 3-4.

"Tributes Continue for Evelyn Collins McKee–Navy League's First Hall of Fame Member." *Sea Power* March 2000: 59.

Truver, Scott C. "To Dissuade, Deter and Defeat, U.S. Naval Power in the 21st Century." *Sea Power* February 2003: 31-34.

Tyson, Ann Scott. "Military Forces Stretched by Hurricanes." *Washington Post,* October 2, 2005: A20.

"USS *Theodore Roosevelt* (CVN 71) Commissioned October 25, 1986 at Newport News, Virginia." *The Log, Official Publication of the Navy League of the United States, New York Council1,* no. 10 (Fall 1986): 5.

Vergun, David A. "Centennial Salute: Rebuilding the U.S. Military; A Cry For More Ships; Navy League's Readiness Warnings Go Unheeded. *Sea Power* (Reprint) March 2002: 6-7.

—-. "Cold War Challenges–and 'The Hour of Decision.'" *Sea Power* (Reprint) July 2002: 13-15.

—-. "Dreadnoughts and Dollars: Navy League Sounds the Alarm Over Naval Disarmament." *Sea Power* (Reprint) February 2002: 3-5.

—-. "Fanning asks Navy League Members to Support Navy/Marine Corps Caucus." *Sea Power* (Reprint) July 2002: 55.

—-. "Keeping the Home Fires Burning." *Sea Power* September 2003: 50.

—-. "Navy League Confronts Cold War Challenges." *Sea Power* (Reprint) August 2003: 52.

—-. "Navy League Fights Complacency–Before, During, and After World War II." *Sea Power* (Reprint) April 2002: 8-10.

—-. "Navy League Supports Sea Services During the 1960s." *Sea Power* (Reprint) July 2002: 15-17.

—-. "Navy League Vanguard of Sea-Service Support." *Sea Power* (Reprint) October 2002: 22-24.

—-. "NLUS Councils Provide Funds and Fun for Sea Services." *Sea Power* October 2003: 54-57.

—-. "NLUS Remains a Reliable Partner From Knitting to Knot-Tying." *Sea Power* (Reprint) April 2003: 28-30.

—-. "Sea Cadets and the Shipmate Program." *Sea Power* July 2003: 50-51.

—-. "Seapower–and Sea Power–in the 1970s." *Sea Power* (Reprint) October 2002: 20-21.

—-. "Secretary of the Navy Lauds NLUS Contributions; Seapower Resurfaces After 14 Years in the Depths." *Sea Power* (Reprint) May 2003: 30-32.

—-. "The Best Military Minds are Sometimes Wrong." *Sea Power* (Reprint) May 2002: 11-13.

—-. "Two Exciting Youth Programs: Sea Cadets and the Shipmate Program." *Sea Power* (Reprint) July 2003: 35-37.

"Warner Takes the Helm of Senate Armed Services Committee." *Sea Power* February 1999: 17.

Weaver, Janet. "She Sets Sails On Seeing Sea." *Florida Times-Union*, May 3, 1967: C-1.

"White House Issues New Strategy to Block Terrorist Attacks From the Sea." *InsideDefense.com* Defense Alert. October 11, 2005. (Electronic database)

"White House Set to Issue New Maritime Security Strategy." *InsideDefense.com* Defense Alert. June 30, 2005 (Electronic database)

Wieder, Tom. "Navy League President Lays Viet Nam Protests To Ignorance, Fear." *Monterey Peninsula Herald*, October 22, 1965: 5.

Winkler, David F. "Vinson-Trammell and the Nuclear Carrier." *Sea Power* April 2002 (Electronic data base, Navy League of the United States website)

"Women Aboard Ship: The Quigley Commentary." August 1978: 7.

Young, Donald J. "Was FDR planning to intervene on Great Britain's behalf before Pearl Harbor? Winston Churchill, for one, thought so." *Military Heritage* October 2005: 20-25.

Young, John J. "Young Creates More 'Tools' for Navy Program Managers." *Sea Power* October 2002: 13-16.

Zimmerman, Stan. "The 'Navy After Next' Looms Out of the Fog of Peace." *The Almanac of Seapower 1997:* 59-66.

Zitlau, Walter A. "Energy Overview: Obstacles and Opportunities." *Sea Power* February 1974: 6-12.

Dissertations, Monographs and Research Papers

Rappaport, Armin. "The Decade of the Diamond Jubilee: 1953-1962" (working paper, photocopy, undated).

Ratcliff, Ron, and Rand LeBouvier, Susan Fink, and Alan Boyer. "Is the United States Navy Relevant in an Age of Global War on Terror?" Monograph and Briefing, United States Naval War College, 2005.

Thompson, William. "The Navy League of the United States–A Status of Forces." Research Paper. United States Naval War College, 1964.

ACKNOWLEDGMENTS

This book was not a solo project. I am indebted to all of those who have helped make it a reality.

To date, only one comprehensive historical survey of the Navy League of the United States has been undertaken, that by Armin Rappaport, entitled *The Navy League of the United States*. Published in 1962, long out of print and now difficult to obtain, it detailed the first half-century of the organization's existence, 1902-1952. Rappaport had access to six bound volumes of *Minutes and Records of the Board of Directors and Executive Committee of the Navy League* as well as reports by Navy League presidents, executive secretaries, treasurers, auditors, and various regular and ad hoc committees. The end result, *The Navy League of the United States*, has provided a wellspring from which I have drawn.

The Navy League of the United States, Our First 100 Years ... and Beyond brings up to date the narrative that Armin Rappaport began. Contributors have been many, including earlier draft manuscripts authored by Kit Bonner and James D. Hessman. Research and interviews conducted in the 1960s by Commander, later Rear Admiral, William Thompson were invaluable, as were subsequent research efforts conducted by Paul Dickson in the Library of Congress. Archival photographs were important in telling the Navy League's story and John Alexander of the Navy-Marine Corps Relief Society proved essential in making available the photographic resources of the Naval Historical Foundation and the Theodore Roosevelt Association. My colleague at *Strategic Insight Ltd*, Jim Warren, Professor of Joint Maritime Operations, College of Distance Education, Naval War College, provided able assistance in locating several historical references, and procured for me an affordable copy of Armin Rappaport's work from a used book store in the United Kingdom.

To help keep this story focused and accurate, several Navy League veterans, including several past national presidents and senior leaders, read it in its several draft forms and provided their comments and suggestions. This group included John W. Alexander, Evan S. Baker, Calvin H. Cobb Jr., Morgan L. Fitch Jr., Jane Collins Grover, James D. Hessman, Linda Hoffman, William C. Kelley Jr., Sheila M. McNeill, Stephen R. Pietropaoli, Jerry Rapkin, John M. Rau, Robert A. Ravitz, Ivan R. Samuels, and William Thompson. Calvin Cobb's keen sense of naval history was particularly helpful in carefully reading and editing each draft in its entirety. Anna Gardner, another *Strategic Insight Ltd* colleague, free of the language and experiences of a sailor, provided dispassionate review, editorial and indexing assistance, and was never hesitant to insist on plain "non-Navy" phrasing and sentence construction. Jean Reynolds did yeoman's work, tirelessly proofreading every page multiple times to ensure consistency in punctuation, capitalization, spelling syntax, and much, much more. Each of these individuals made important contributions to this project.

Finally, a special note of appreciation is owed to Morgan Fitch, whose more than five years of leadership and devotion to this project, through good times and bad, have finally borne the results he so earnestly desired when the subject of a book telling the story of the Navy League of the United States was first discussed at the turn of the century. There is no doubt that without Morgan's foresight, firmness of purpose, and generosity, the book you are holding would not have come into being.

INDEX

D

E

F

G

H

I

J

K

L

M

N

O

P

R

S

T

U

V

W

Z

Book Committee Acknowledgments

This book was made possible by the selfless contributions and unflagging support of our Navy League Councils and Members around the world. We wish to acknowledge and salute the following Councils and individuals for answering the call ... and for their generous support of this historical keepsake book:

Altoona Council
Atlanta Metropolitan Council
Channel Islands Council
Charleston Council
Contra Costa Council
Corpus Christi Council
Dallas Council
Elko Council
Golden Isles Council, Inc.
Helena Montana Council
Honolulu Council
Lake County Council
Marin County Council
Massachusetts Bay Council
Mayport Florida Council
Monterey Peninsula Council
National Capital Council
New York Council
Phoenix Council
Pittsburgh PA Council
Puerto Vallarta Council
Reno Council
Salt Lake City Council
San Juan Council
Seattle Council
St. Maarten/St. Martin Council
Utah Navy League
Vieques Council

Mr. and Mrs. James T. Bonner, Jr.
Mrs. Rose Burnett
Mr. and Mrs. Edwin L. Carter
Mrs. Olive W. Cobb
Mr. Carter B. Conlin
LCDR W. L. Crouch, USN (Ret.)
Mr. Philip L. Dunmire
Mrs. Rosalind K. Ellis
Mr. and Mrs. Morgan L. Fitch, Jr.
Mr. T. C. Hackley
VADM A. J. Herberger, USN (Ret.)
CAPT Shirley A. Hill, USN (Ret.)
RADM and Mrs. John B. Holmes, USN (Ret.)
Mr. and Mrs. William C. Kelley, Jr.
Mr. and Mrs. Louis Kriser
Mr. Jerome S. Lafferty
Mr. Keith R. Larson
Mr. Harold W. Learson
ADM Richard C. Macke, USN (Ret.)
Mr. and Mrs. Arlie M. McNeill
Mr. Bradley W. Nemeth
Mr. and Mrs. John A. Panneton
Mr. John M. Rau
RADM Robert A. Ravitz, USNR (Ret.)
LCDR Ward A. Shanahan, USNR (Ret.)
CDR and Mrs. W. R. Sharkey, III USNR (Ret.)
LCDR Samuel A. Sorenson, USN (Ret.)